*Breakthrough
International
Negotiation*

# Breakthrough International Negotiation

*How Great Negotiators
Transformed the World's Toughest
Post-Cold War Conflicts*

Michael Watkins
Susan Rosegrant

Foreword by Shimon Peres

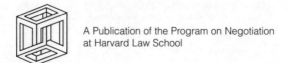

A Publication of the Program on Negotiation
at Harvard Law School

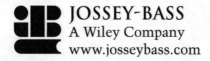

JOSSEY-BASS
A Wiley Company
www.josseybass.com

Published by

**JOSSEY-BASS**
A Wiley Company
989 Market Street
San Francisco, CA 94103-1741

www.josseybass.com

Jossey-Bass is a registered trademark of John Wiley & Sons, Inc.
Jossey-Bass books and products are available through most bookstores.
To contact Jossey-Bass directly, call (888) 378-2537,
fax to (800) 605-2665, or visit our website at www.josseybass.com.
Substantial discounts on bulk quantities of Jossey-Bass books are avail-
able to corporations, professional associations, and other organizations.
For details and discount information, contact the special sales
department at Jossey-Bass.

We at Jossey-Bass strive to use the most environmentally sensitive paper stocks
available to us. Our publications are printed on acid-free recycled stock whenever possible, and our paper always meets or exceeds minimum GPO and EPA
requirements.

**Library of Congress Cataloging-in-Publication Data**

Watkins, Michael, date.
Breakthrough international negotiation: how great negotiators transformed
the world's toughest post-Cold War conflicts/Michael Watkins, Susan Rosegrant;
foreword by Shimon Peres.
p. cm.
Includes biographical references and index.
ISBN 0-7879-5743-7 (alk. paper)
1. Diplomatic negotiations in international disputes. 2. Mediation, International.
3. Conflict management. 4. Complexity (Philosophy) I. Rosegrant, Susan, date.
II. Title.

JZ6045.W38 2001
327.1'7—dc21                                                    2001038577

FIRST EDITION
*HB printing*   10 9 8 6 7 8 5 4 3 2 1

# CONTENTS

Foreword   ix
*Shimon Peres*

Preface   xi

Introduction: Seven Principles of Breakthrough Negotiation   xvii


PART ONE: FOUNDATIONS OF THE BREAKTHROUGH APPROACH   1

1   The United States Engages a Cold War Orphan   3

2   Diagnosing the Structure   17

3   Tensions Escalate on the Korean Peninsula   38

4   Identifying Barriers to Agreement   56

5   Carter Achieves a Breakthrough   81

6   Managing Conflict   87

7   The United States and North Korea Reach Agreement   101

8   Building Momentum   109

## PART TWO: BUILDING THE BREAKTHROUGH TOOLBOX    131

 9  Getting to the Table in Oslo    133

10  Transforming the Balance of Forces    164

11  Assembling the Persian Gulf Coalition    178

12  Building Coalitions    211

13  Ending the War in Bosnia    228

14  Leading Negotiations    266

Conclusion: Becoming a Breakthrough Negotiator    279

Suggested Readings    281

Update of the Cases    285

Notes    307

The Authors    333

Index    335

# FOREWORD

## Shimon Peres

Michael Watkins and Susan Rosegrant present a unique combination of practical politics and academic theorization. Their book not only elucidates the process of negotiation, it also provides valuable tools to enhance its management. Watkins and Rosegrant rightly state that *complexity is the rule in real-world negotiation.* Such situations indeed call for breakthrough thinking, and Watkins and Rosegrant succeed in shedding light on the crucial link between the process of negotiation and the dynamics of a reality that continues to move forward in parallel. Moreover, they highlight the vast margin of political creativity that this link puts at the disposal of the negotiating parties.

It seems that some of the qualities that make a person a great negotiator are inbred; the missing elements must be acquired by means of never-ending study. Watkins and Rosegrant's book therefore constitutes compulsory reading for all those who seek to develop and upgrade their skills in the complex art of negotiation.

March 19, 2001

Shimon Peres

*To Shawna, Aidan, and Maeve*
M.W.

*To David, Joanna, and Luisa*
S.R.

# PREFACE

Our purpose in writing this book is both to inspire and to instruct. The inspiration comes in the form of illuminating behind-the-scenes accounts of momentous international negotiations. The four case histories presented in this book are based on frank in-depth interviews with the key participants, supported by other sources. The stakes in every case were high, affecting not only the economic stability of entire regions of the world, but also the lives of millions of people. Because all of these negotiations took place in a context of deep-rooted ethnic and ideological conflicts that had resisted earlier efforts to craft settlements, the barriers to agreement were formidable.

Together, these cases offer unique insight into the actions of leading diplomatic negotiators whose efforts shaped the post–Cold War international order. These skilled negotiators—Robert Gallucci in Korea, Terje Larsen in the Middle East, James Baker during the Persian Gulf crisis, and Richard Holbrooke in Bosnia—drew on their skills and experience to change the game and achieved breakthroughs in situations that had long been locked in bitter acrimony. It is to these breakthrough negotiators that we dedicate this book.

*Breakthrough International Negotiation* offers more than an opportunity to admire the skill of professional negotiators. It also offers specific, actionable frameworks and guidelines that readers can use immediately to negotiate more effectively. In the course of our research, we asked skilled diplomats and expert observers about what differentiates great negotiators from those who are merely good. Their views differ, of course, but on one point they almost uniformly agree: the notion that great negotiators are born, not made, is just plain wrong. Certainly charisma, persuasiveness, and a high tolerance for ambiguity are helpful, but these personality traits are by no means sufficient. Not even the best negotiators are endowed with inborn abilities to assess complex situations and craft breakthrough strategies. Skills, by their nature, must be learned, and negotiation is a skill—or, more accurately, a set of skills.

Another persistent fallacy that our interview subjects punctured was the notion that expert negotiators' repertoires consist of a grab bag of tactical tricks and ploys, bluffs, and psych-outs. It is noteworthy that this myth glamorizes the at-the-table phase of negotiation, certainly the most highly visible aspect of the process but arguably not the most influential. Although tactical skill is important, our interview subjects emphasized that skilled negotiators also work away from the table to involve new players, define the agenda, develop creative options, and manage the pace. Accordingly, we focus not just on tactics but on broader strategies for achieving breakthroughs—strategies that may get activated well before the first face-to-face meeting is even scheduled.

Our examples are drawn from the world of diplomatic negotiation, but the ideas and approaches we extract from them can be applied to any negotiation in government, business, and even private life. The factors that complicate diplomatic negotiations—many influential parties, complex sets of issues, preexisting animosities, contentious internal decision making—often arise in business negotiations. In fact, it is useful to think of the high-stakes negotiations that top business executives conduct as corporate diplomacy. Serious business negotiators will find considerable help in this book.

The central theme of this book is the need to craft breakthrough strategies in order to overcome the significant barriers to agreement that inevitably arise in negotiations. In complex negotiations like those this book describes, agreement does not come easily. The barriers to agreement are formidable and often multiple. It is precisely because these situations seem so intractable that breakthroughs are necessary. Breakthrough negotiators reconfigure the landscape in ways that lead to agreements that were not possible before. They also harness the power of process to build momentum in promising directions.

There are plenty of how-to books on negotiating, but few of them provide guidance on how to manage complex negotiations. The models of the negotiation process presented in most books for practitioners are misleading in their simplicity. They offer advice on conducting two-party negotiations, but there is little guidance on how to build coalitions in multiparty negotiations, or manage internal decision making in negotiations between organizations, or deal with linkages among sets of negotiations, or prevent disputes from escalating into violence. It is also unrealistic—and potentially dangerous—to pretend that negotiators' interests and alternatives will remain static as the process unfolds. As we will see, opportunities flow from the ability to shape others' perceptions of their interests and alternatives in a dynamic negotiating game.

Complexity is the rule in negotiation. And it is because of the complexity and uniqueness of each situation that a negotiator needs to be equipped with more than a few generic tactics and a talent for persuasiveness. Our approach, which is grounded in systems analysis, provides a powerful framework for managing the fluid and intricate situations that characterize most negotiations. Individual negotiations are analyzed in terms of the structure of basic components—the parties and the issues—and the processes through which they interact. More complex negotiating situations are made up of linked sets of individual negotiations that interact in predictable ways. Key dynamics, both within and among negotiations, can be described in terms of feedback loops: virtuous cycles that build momentum toward agreement and vicious cycles that contribute to impasse and breakdown. A negotiator who grasps the basic structure of a situation possesses a strong antidote to confusion and manipulation, and is in a powerful position to shape the negotiating system in a consistently clear-eyed and productive way.

The ultimate goal of learning to conduct breakthrough negotiations is therefore to be an architect of structure and process rather than a passive participant in situations that others have defined. Readers hoping for maxims and techniques that apply to all types of negotiations should revise their expectations now. Breakthrough negotiation strategy cannot be summed up in three or four rules of thumb because negotiators need to be able to play many different games. In fact, the process of negotiation is largely devoted to defining the game—or, to put it another way, to shaping the structure in which the at-the-table deliberations will proceed.

Because strategy is contingent on situation, there is no single best way to negotiate. But the limitations of rules of thumb do not mean that breakthrough strategies need to be constructed anew with each negotiation. Great negotiators, like great chess players, do not waste time by exhaustively evaluating every single possibility. Through years of experience, they develop an intuitive sense for the state of play and for combinations of moves that will and will not work. They draw on their own mental libraries of openings, gambits, and counters— combinations of moves that have worked well in similar situations—and construct customized strategies out of familiar materials.

So how does anyone learn to be a breakthrough negotiator? The right training helps. There is a compelling reason that more and more schools of public policy, business, and law teach negotiating skills. Negotiation is a first-year requirement at the Harvard Business School, and more than half of our students take advanced negotiation electives. But how can you acquire and hone your negotiating abilities if you are already out in the trenches? Experience can be a superb teacher, but only if it produces a systematic set of effective mental models for the wide array of situations you can expect to face. Moreover, learning by experience alone can be time-consuming and haphazard, and it carries significant risk of failure.

This book offers, in an accessible and practical format, a set of tools for sizing up difficult negotiations and achieving breakthroughs. You will learn to negotiate more skillfully by tracing the decisions and actions of expert negotiators who faced challenges that demanded breakthrough thinking, and you will gain insight into the general principles and lessons that flow from these examples. In the process, you will acquire a powerful framework for approaching any complex negotiation.

# RESEARCH NOTES

This book originated in Michael's efforts to develop material on negotiation for executive programs offered to national security professionals at the Kennedy School of Government. There was ample material on policy questions, but few cases explored the complexity of negotiation processes or highlighted the impact of process on outcomes. As a result, he began working with Susan on a series of case histories of breakthrough negotiations in the Middle East, the Balkans, and the Korean Peninsula. We jointly defined the scope of the cases, and Susan researched and wrote the narratives. Meanwhile, Michael worked with a colleague of Susan, Kirsten Lundberg, on a similar case about the Oslo negotiations.

The cases are not intended to be definitive histories. Each of these negotiations merits multiple book-length manuscripts. Instead they are *thick descriptions*—that is, carefully researched accounts of negotiation processes as seen through the eyes of the negotiators and knowledgeable observers, which are intended to reveal dynamics that commonly arise in complex negotiations.[1]

In parallel with the work on the cases, Michael developed the conceptual framework and analysis. His approach to analyzing negotiations as complex systems grew directly out of his early training as an engineer. Systems analysis provides a powerful framework for diagnosing and managing the fluid and intricate situations that characterize most negotiations. The properties of complex, nonlinear systems—irreversibility, sensitivity to initial conditions, discontinuous change, and feedback loops—are all present in negotiations. Success in understanding and shaping negotiation dynamics flows from breaking these complex situations into their component parts and understanding their interactions.

# ACKNOWLEDGMENTS

Many people's contributions are reflected in this book. Foremost were the skilled negotiators and experts on international affairs who generously shared their experiences and insights: James Baker III, John Bolton, Robert Carlin, Richard Cheney, Richard Christenson, Wesley Clark, William Clark, Richard Clarke, Ivo Daalder, Peter Galbraith, Robert Gallucci, Avi Gil, Richard Haass, Marshall Harris, Christopher Hill, Richard Holbrooke, Allen Holmes, Thomas Hubbard, Arnold Kanter, Robert Kimmitt, Robert Manning, Robert Oakley, Roberts Owen, Shimon Peres, Thomas Pickering, Daniel Poneman, Ron Pundik, Dennis Ross, Gary Samore, Uri Savir, Brent Scowcroft, Walter Slocomb, Gordon Smith, Richard Solomon, Robert Suettinger, Alexander Vershbow, Kent Wiedemann, Norman Wulf, and Philip Zelikow, as well as others who asked to remain anonymous.

The intellectual foundation on which we constructed our conceptual framework owes a great deal to the work of Max Bazerman, Roger Fisher, David Lax, Robert McKersie, Bob Mnookin, Howard Raiffa, Robert Robinson, Jim Sebenius, William Ury, and Richard Walton. We are grateful for their insight and support. Our thinking about breakthrough negotiation has also been strongly influenced by our work with Joel Cutcher-Gershenfeld, Sam Passow, Sydney Rosen, and Kim Winters. Howard Husock, director of case programs at the Kennedy School, provided invaluable guidance on the writing of case studies. Terry Scott, former director of the National Security Program at the Kennedy School, has been a constant source of encouragement. Thanks too to colleagues at the Kennedy School and Harvard Business School, especially Nancy Beaulieu, Guhan Subramanian, Kathleen Valley, and Michael Wheeler.

We were fortunate to work with an outstanding research assistant, Usha Thakrar, on this project. Many thanks to our editor, Ann Goodsell, for her support and efforts to make this book more accessible.

The research for this book was supported by the Program on Negotiation (PON) at Harvard Law School and the Division of Research (DOR) at the Harvard Business School. We very much appreciate the support of PON executive directors Marjorie Aaron and Sara Cobb and DOR research directors Teresa Amabile, Dwight Crane, and Mike Yoshino.

*August 2001*                                                                 Michael Watkins
*Cambridge, Massachusetts*                                          Susan Rosegrant

# INTRODUCTION

*Seven Principles of
Breakthrough Negotiation*

We begin with a handful of overarching ideas about breakthrough negotiation. The seven principles that follow represent an overview of how breakthrough negotiators operate. Keep them in mind as you make your way through the cases, concepts, and analysis that follow.

## PRINCIPLE 1:
## BREAKTHROUGH NEGOTIATORS SHAPE THE STRUCTURE OF THEIR SITUATIONS

Breakthrough negotiators never view their negotiating situations as preordained or fixed. They understand that they cannot afford to get mired down in reacting to counterparts' moves; they must shape their situations. So they work to mold the basic structure of the negotiation by involving the right people, controlling the issue agenda, creating linkages that bolster their bargaining power, and channeling the flow of the process through time. They understand that actions taken away from the negotiating table can be as important as what goes on at the table, if not more so.[1]

Specifically, skilled negotiators recognize that much of what influences outcomes takes place *before* the parties sit down across the table from each other. Even after negotiations begin, they continue to shape the structure by molding the agenda, introducing action-forcing events, and linking or delinking negotiations. When based on clear-eyed analysis, adept efforts to shape the structure of the game can have a powerful impact on outcomes.

# PRINCIPLE 2:
## BREAKTHROUGH NEGOTIATORS ORGANIZE TO LEARN

Skilled negotiators learn by doing the necessary preparation to negotiate: they diagnose the essential features of the situation, familiarize themselves with its history and context and with the record of prior negotiations, and probe the backgrounds and reputations of their counterparts. At the same time, they recognize that conventional preparation has limitations. Even the best-equipped negotiating team must cope with constraints on time, expertise, money, data, and access to documents. Skilled negotiators therefore focus on continuing to learn at the negotiation table as they carefully gauge reactions and responses while testing hypotheses by asking questions and putting offers on the table.

The best negotiators also work to foster organizational learning, both during and after a negotiation. They pay careful attention to managing the team learning process, establishing clear roles and responsibilities for observation and analysis, and devoting substantial time between at-the-table sessions to integration and distillation of insights.

# PRINCIPLE 3:
## BREAKTHROUGH NEGOTIATORS ARE
## MASTERS OF PROCESS DESIGN

Control of the process yields control over outcomes. Skilled negotiators think hard about the impact of process on perceptions of interests and alternatives, on the part of their counterparts and those they represent, and on their own side. Then they work to fashion—often to negotiate—processes likely to lead in favorable directions.

Skilled negotiators know, for example, that one-on-one negotiations are suited to some issues and group negotiations to others. They are cognizant of the potential benefits and costs of setting up a secret channel. They understand that details as small as the timing of a meeting or the size and shape of the negotiating table can make a difference. Above all, they are reflective about the process design choices they make; they know that a bad process—one perceived as unfair, illegitimate, or simply confusing—can create unnecessary barriers to agreement and that good process design can promote breakthroughs.

# PRINCIPLE 4:
# BREAKTHROUGH NEGOTIATORS FOSTER AGREEMENT WHEN POSSIBLE BUT EMPLOY FORCE WHEN NECESSARY

Breakthrough negotiators understand the delicate interplay between negotiation and coercive power. Speaking of the U.S. failure in Vietnam, Henry Kissinger said, "Treating force and diplomacy as discrete phenomena caused our power to lack purpose and our negotiations to lack force."[2] This observation was echoed by Kofi Annan in his description of dealing with Iraq: "You can do a lot with diplomacy, but with diplomacy backed up by force you can get a lot more done."[3]

Great negotiators make skilled use of explicit and implicit threats. They also recognize the need for threats to be credible, because the cost of using force can be very high. The Gulf War, for example, cost the U.S.-led coalition $61 billion; allied casualties were low, but tens of thousands of Iraqis lost their lives. Experienced negotiators recognize too that their counterparts will probably view any agreement achieved by means of coercive power as illegitimate and will feel free to violate its terms unless power is applied on an ongoing basis to enforce it. They also understand that backing weak players into a corner triggers resistance and escalation.

# PRINCIPLE 5:
# BREAKTHROUGH NEGOTIATORS ANTICIPATE AND MANAGE CONFLICT

Negotiators' efforts to advance their sides' interests almost always go hand in hand with management of conflict, both between the sides and within them. Often, negotiators or those they represent are already locked in adversarial relationships when negotiations begin, and the experience of past conflict is likely to have distorted their perceptions. Even if the parties are not already "at war," every effort at deal making is a dispute waiting to happen.

To paraphrase Roger Fisher, breakthrough negotiators mediate their own disputes.[4] They are skilled at diagnosing potential sources of conflict. They recognize the potential for escalation in zero-sum thinking, mutual perceptions of vulnerability, a history of distrust or injury that has transformed perceptions, and cultural misunderstandings. They are also equipped to craft strategies to overcome these barriers, such as by reframing issues or setting up confidence-building mechanisms.

The ability to foster productive working relationships is another key to managing conflict. Such relationships act as a kind of psychological buffer during difficult times. As one negotiator put it:

> You have to have the ability to interact on human terms with the other party. Don't get me wrong. It's not that you have to play the nice guy. Not at all. It's the ability to sense the other party, to understand him. You don't have to fall in love with the other party in order to understand. You don't even have to sympathize with the other party in order to understand what's going on with him. But you have to be able to understand and you have to be able to develop trust. But also to project a kind of seriousness and, if necessary, also toughness with regard to principles and positions that you believe you have to protect.

At the same time, skilled negotiators are careful not to let agreement or avoidance of conflict become ends in themselves. No agreement is preferable to a bad agreement. The best negotiators never get so caught up in the process that they lose sight of the end they are trying to achieve. Said one negotiator, "Getting to yes is easy: all you have to do is roll over. It's getting what you want that's hard."

# PRINCIPLE 6:
## BREAKTHROUGH NEGOTIATORS BUILD MOMENTUM TOWARD AGREEMENT

Negotiations do not proceed smoothly from initiation to agreement. They ebb and flow, with periods of deadlock or inaction punctuated by bursts of progress until an agreement is reached or breakdown occurs. Decision makers make hard choices (such as to make an unfavorable concession) only when they lack more attractive alternatives and doing nothing is not an option. As long as counterparts believe that the costs of action outweigh the potential benefits of inaction, they cannot be expected to act.

Breakthrough negotiators thus work to channel the flow and pace of the process. Sometimes developing an attractive vision of a desirable future pulls the other side forward toward agreement. Sometimes a logjam can be broken by proposing a formula or framework or face-saving compromise. Movement can also be created by erecting barriers to backsliding that impel the process forward—taking advantage of the irreversibilities characteristic of complex negotiation systems. By securing early agreement on basic principles or a framework for detailed bargaining, a negotiator can make reversal more costly.

# PRINCIPLE 7:
# BREAKTHROUGH NEGOTIATORS LEAD FROM THE MIDDLE

Great leaders are often great negotiators, but the reverse is also true. The actions of skilled negotiators have a big impact on the outcomes of complex negotiations. In negotiations between groups, external negotiations and internal decision making within the groups invariably interact. How they do so can enhance or undermine the potential for agreement. Representatives must work internally to shape their mandates and negotiating instructions, and to sell the resulting agreements to constituents. At the same time, they must build credibility and productive working relationships externally while advancing the interests of their sides. But good external moves may have adverse consequences for selling agreements inside, and vice versa. A negotiator explained:

> You can do things that help you to progress in relationship to your external partner . . . but they would have created problems for you on the home front. The gap between those who are leading the negotiations and all those people who have to come afterward would grow, beyond the point where it could be bridged. But if you walked too slowly, you might stay close to your constituents, but you would have been very far away from the other side.

Managing internal decision making, which often consists of shaping internal negotiating processes, is frequently more challenging than negotiating with the other side. Breakthrough negotiators also pay close attention to how the other side makes decisions, and they use their insights to tailor their own moves and sometimes even to help their counterparts sell agreements.

Because skilled negotiators have substantial control over the flow of information between inside and outside, they are seldom mere passive messengers carrying out the instructions of their principals. According to this negotiator:

> The traditional model [of the process] is that the leadership sets the goals, and then from those goals [the lead negotiator] can make decisions regarding strategy, tactics, and then produce instructions for the team. But that scenario doesn't represent real life, as far as I understand it or experience it, because the goal and the strategy is changing constantly. There is a dynamic throughout the process. And the leadership is not fully in control of it because that dynamic is the product of the interaction between you and the other party, and sometimes more than one party. . . . And since things are changing, then you can have an impact whatever your position in the loop. You can have a big impact if you handle it cleverly and effectively.

Acting as a bridge between internal decision making and external negotiating and reconciling the divergent interests of fractious constituencies demands leadership grounded in credibility and skill rather than authority. Negotiators who participate in shaping their mandates, have a clear and unwavering vision

of what they want to achieve, and work to shape internal and external perceptions to maximize their ability to advance their sides' interests—and their own.

## PLAN OF THE BOOK

Part One of this book outlines the foundations of the breakthrough negotiation
framework: diagnosing negotiating situations, identifying barriers to agreement,
managing conflict, and building momentum.[5] Key concepts are illustrated by
examining a case history of high-stakes U.S. efforts to contain North Korea's
nuclear program and avoid a war. Successive chapters juxtapose a narrative of
the negotiation with commentary and analysis.

Part Two builds the breakthrough toolbox by presenting and analyzing three
more case studies: the Bush administration's extraordinary efforts to build a
coalition to oust Iraq from Kuwait, international efforts to end the Arab-Israeli
conflict in the Middle East, and Richard Holbrooke's dramatic success in ending the war in Bosnia. The accompanying conceptual chapters explore
approaches to transforming the dynamics of conflicts, building coalitions, and
leading negotiations.

# PART ONE

# FOUNDATIONS OF THE BREAKTHROUGH APPROACH

In the first eight chapters of the book, we use the high-stakes negotiation between the United States and North Korea over the latter's nuclear weapons program to illustrate the core concepts in the breakthrough negotiation framework. Specifically, we examine four core tasks that are fundamental to achieving breakthroughs:

1. *Diagnosing the structure:* Systematically assessing the architecture of the situation and identifying the parties to the negotiation, the issue agenda, linkages among negotiations, and action-forcing events

2. *Identifying barriers to agreement:* Pinpointing structural, strategic, psychological, and institutional barriers that could prevent you from achieving your negotiating goals

3. *Managing conflict:* Avoiding escalation, defusing tensions, and involving third parties to help move the process forward

4. *Building momentum:* Formulating strategies for learning, shaping the structure, and crafting creative deals in order to build momentum toward favorable agreements

Chapter One introduces the North Korea case, tracing early efforts by the Bush and Clinton administrations to engage the North Koreans in dialogue over their nuclear program. Chapter Two uses the North Korean case illustratively to explore how to diagnose the structure of complex negotiations. Chapter Three returns to the North Korean case, describing the enormous difficulty of getting to the table for serious negotiations. Chapter Four in turn examines how to identify structural, strategic, psychological, institutional, and cultural barriers to agreement. Chapter Five continues the story of the U.S.–North Korean negotiations, describing the intervention by former president Jimmy Carter that broke the deadlock and got the parties back to the negotiating table. Chapter Six examines strategies for managing conflict, focusing on the roles that negotiators and third parties can play in managing disputes. Chapter Seven completes our account of the U.S.–North Korean negotiations, tracing the path that eventually resulted in a 1994 agreement that ended the crisis. Chapter Eight focuses on building momentum toward favorable agreements.

As you read Chapter One, think about the structure of the U.S.–North Korea negotiation. Who are the parties, and what are their interests? What are the issues? Who is controlling the pace of the negotiation?

# CHAPTER ONE

# The United States Engages
# a Cold War Orphan

In June 1994, the administration of President Bill Clinton faced what many officials considered its most delicate and potentially explosive foreign-policy crisis yet. The United States had been negotiating with the North Korean government of Kim Il Sung for almost a year, intent on discovering whether the isolated Communist regime already had nuclear weapons, and on halting any efforts on its part to build atomic bombs.

The on-again, off-again negotiations had broken down in alarming fashion a month earlier. Thumbing its nose at U.S. negotiators and the international nonproliferation community, North Korea unloaded the core of its 5-megawatt (5-MW) nuclear reactor, removing enough plutonium-rich fuel rods to provide the raw material for as many as five nuclear bombs. "In many ways, Korea poses the greatest security threat to the United States and the world today," Defense Secretary William Perry declared after the unloading. "We have to regard the situation as very dangerous."[1]

The provocative defuelling had other implications besides the obvious threat that North Korea could amass a small arsenal of nuclear bombs by year's end. If

---

This is an abridged version of "Carrots, Sticks, and Question Marks: Negotiating the North Korean Nuclear Crisis," a case written by Susan Rosegrant in collaboration with Michael D. Watkins, assistant professor of public policy, for use by the National Security Program, at the John F. Kennedy School of Government, Harvard University. Copyright © 1995 by the President and Fellows of Harvard College. Reprinted with permission of the Kennedy School of Government Case Program, Harvard University.

the hermitic state continued to flout international nuclear regulations, it could discredit U.S.-supported efforts to control the worldwide spread of atomic weapons. Moreover, if North Korea were known to have produced an atomic bomb, it might well spark a nuclear arms race in Asia. To make matters worse, many believed a nuclear North Korea would export weapons to other rogue nations like Iran and Libya.

Most chilling of all was the threat that the spiraling tensions surrounding the nuclear standoff could pull the United States into immediate war with an unpredictable, and perhaps desperate, adversary. Military leaders had already warned the president that if the North invaded America's South Korean ally, more than one million people could be killed, including as many as fifty thousand Americans. Military strategists believed that allied U.S. and South Korean troops would ultimately repel a North Korean attack, but the South's capital city of Seoul, just 25 miles south of the demilitarized zone (DMZ) between the two Koreas, would almost certainly be devastated. (For a map of the Korean Peninsula, see Figure 1.1.) "If North Korea attacked the South, they would lose," declared General Robert Riscassi, a former commander of U.S. forces in Korea. "The problem is: at what price?"[2]

The United States was determined not to let the nuclear dispute escalate. But finding a way to influence North Korea's behavior without worsening the conflict proved increasingly elusive. No common ground existed on which to base a new round of negotiations. China, one of North Korea's few remaining allies, appeared either unwilling or unable to broker a resolution. And a Clinton administration drive to pressure the North with the threat of United Nations economic sanctions seemed only to provoke Kim Il Sung, who declared repeatedly that sanctions would constitute an act of war.

Many viewed Kim's threat as bluster, but the administration could not afford to be unprepared. By mid-June, officials were making secret plans to send ten thousand more troops to South Korea and laying out the first steps the United States should take to prepare for war. In Seoul, skeptical South Koreans participated in air-raid drills and stocked up on food and emergency supplies. In the North Korean capital of Pyongyang, meanwhile, the rhetoric grew ever more bellicose. To most observers, a second Korean war still appeared unlikely. But for the U.S. officials who had managed the long, and now paralyzed, negotiations, the likelihood of resolving the dispute without military conflict appeared slimmer every day.

# A HISTORY OF SUBJUGATION

The 1994 nuclear dispute occurred against a backdrop of centuries of regional hostilities. For most of its history, a unified Korea had struggled to repel invasions by its more powerful neighbors, in particular China and Japan. These

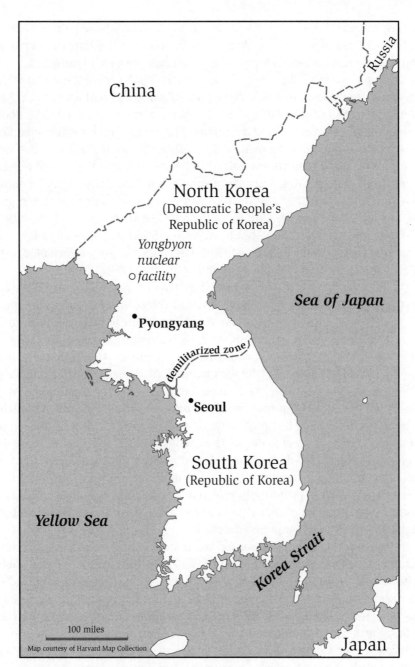

**Figure 1.1**. The Korean Peninsula.

recurring aggressions—including a repressive 35-year Japanese occupation that ended with Japan's defeat in World War II—had left the Korean people with both a profound nationalism and a deep residual mistrust of outsiders.

Korea's sense of being a pawn in an international game did not end with its liberation from Japan in 1945. Victorious Allied forces had agreed that Korea should revert to self-rule, but the small nation's destiny continued to be defined by other nations' interests and ambitions. The Soviet Union had invaded Korea in its final assault against Japan, and a hasty postwar deal allowed the Soviet Union to occupy the northern half of the Peninsula and the United States to occupy the South. An Allied trusteeship and a joint U.S.-Soviet commission were to help transfer power to a unified Korean provisional government, but growing tensions between the United States and the Soviet Union soon blocked reunification. In 1948, the Republic of Korea (ROK) was formed in the South under right-wing leadership. One month later Kim Il Sung was installed as Premier of the Democratic People's Republic of Korea (DPRK) in the North.

**What key events shaped each side's perceptions of the other?**

Less than two years later Kim's Communist regime invaded the South, launching the bloody Korean War.[3] The Chinese-backed DPRK battled the ROK and a U.S.-led United Nations alliance up and down the length of the Peninsula; Seoul changed hands four times. Armistice talks began early in the conflict—after the Communist leaders concluded they could not rout the UN forces, and the UN Command decided it could not retake North Korea without a full-scale assault on China—but it took more than two years to negotiate a cease-fire.[4] By the end of the war, more than one million people had been killed, including 250,000 civilians and more than fifty-four thousand Americans. Subsequent Western views of the Kim Il Sung regime were profoundly affected by Communist tactics, such as the North's brainwashing of many prisoners of war. North Korea had established itself as a sinister and cunning adversary.

In the decades following the cease-fire, both Koreas seized on eventual reunification of the Peninsula as a rallying cry and a justification for extreme political behavior. In the South, rebuilding a nation with formidable economic and military strengths became a consuming goal, and only U.S. pressure discouraged the ROK from developing its own nuclear weapons. A series of authoritarian military leaders made frequent use of martial law and torture in the cause of eradicating Communism and resisting the North. Nevertheless the United States supported the South Korean government staunchly, helping to fuel a long-standing student-led protest movement that blamed the United States for the totalitarian regime.

Kim Il Sung, meanwhile, built his autocratic rule around an almost religious devotion to the concept of *juche,* or political and economic self-reliance. The

"Great Leader," whose image loomed on statues dotted across the North Korean countryside, also masterminded terrorist activities aimed at undermining the South, including bombing a South Korean airliner, killing all 115 aboard, in an apparent attempt to disrupt the 1988 Seoul Olympics. Kim's renegade status in the international community was solidified by the North's export of missiles to other terrorist nations, and its pursuit of a nuclear program—to unclear ends.

The United States viewed Kim as the dangerous and unpredictable leader of one of the world's most repressive and authoritarian regimes, and maintained a tough stance toward the DPRK. In addition to tens of thousands of troops, the United States had installed nuclear weapons in South Korea, a capability decried by the North as a flagrant threat.[5] Annual U.S.-ROK war games, known as Team Spirit, served as a regular reminder to the North of the forces—including nuclear—allied against it. The United States wanted to avoid military conflict on the Korean Peninsula, but its longstanding goal was the nonviolent overthrow or collapse of the government in the North and reunification of Korea under the rule of the ROK.

Almost four decades after the Korean War ended, hostilities continued to simmer. Even at the end of the Cold War in the early 1990s, nearly one million troops still faced off on either side of the 150-mile-long DMZ, the most heavily armed border in the world. In fact, North Korea, the most militarized country anywhere, maintained the world's fifth largest army. Since no peace treaty was ever signed, the two Koreas were still technically at war.

## THE BUSH ADMINISTRATION TAKES ON
## THE NORTH'S NUCLEAR PROGRAM

North Korea had had a nuclear program since the mid-1950s, and in 1980 it had begun building a small 5-MW reactor—merely, Pyongyang insisted, to power its electrical grid. But the intelligence and nonproliferation agencies that monitored the North's nuclear activities were expressing growing alarm. The DPRK had begun building two more powerful reactors, which would eventually be able to produce enough plutonium for forty-five bombs a year. Covert construction of a large plutonium-reprocessing facility had reportedly begun. Moreover, North Korea had quietly closed down the 5-MW reactor for almost 100 days in 1989. Although officials in Pyongyang claimed the shutdown was for routine maintenance, international intelligence agencies weren't so sure: the duration of the shutdown would have allowed North Korea to completely refuel the reactor, generating material that could be processed into enough weapons-grade plutonium for one or two nuclear weapons.

No mechanism was in place to inspect or verify the activities of the reclusive Communist state, but by September 1991 Bush administration officials felt conditions might finally be right for a shift in U.S. policy toward North Korea. Their goal was to open up the North's hitherto-opaque nuclear program and to put a stop to its increasingly aggressive program of nuclear-weapons construction.

Several factors contributed to the Bush administration's assessment. By the 1980s, North Korea's isolation, unwise agricultural practices, and heavy investment in the military at the expense of other ventures had contributed to a serious economic decline. With few trading partners and little to trade, the North's estimated GNP was a mere $23.3 billion by 1991—less than a tenth of the South's $273 billion. "Self-reliance may have looked like a good policy in 1945 when Kim Il Sung came of age," says Bruce Cumings, an historian and Korea expert, "but it doesn't look very good in a world without borders today."[6] North Korea was also losing the few major allies and trading partners it had had to the economically booming ROK. The Soviet Union recognized South Korea in 1990 and ended its aid and trade concessions to the DPRK the next year. China did $2 billion worth of trade with South Korea in 1991, about five times its estimated trade with North Korea. Moreover, South Korea was admitted to the United Nations in 1991 with Chinese and Soviet support, despite North Korea's wish to be the Peninsula's sole representative.

> What confluence of factors led the parties to the negotiating table?

Fears about its bomb program were also hurting North Korea's tentative attempts to reach out. In 1991 Japan cut off normalization talks, the South suspended the modest trade initiatives between the two countries, and the United States cancelled troop withdrawals from South Korea begun the previous year.[7] Kim and the North's elite must also have been shaken by the failures of other longstanding Communist regimes: the breaching of the Berlin Wall in 1989, the overthrow the same year of Romania's dictator Nicolae Ceaucescu, with whom Kim reportedly identified closely, and the coup in the Soviet Union that preceded its 1991 collapse.

In the wake of these radical realignments, Pyongyang began to make overtures to the United States. In fact, some Korea watchers believe the isolated regime had been trying to engage the United States since the early 1970s. Selig Harrison, senior associate at the Carnegie Endowment for International Peace, met with Kim Il Sung in 1972 as one of the first American journalists to enter the country after the Korean War, and later pressed the United States to relax restrictions on North Korea. With modest exceptions, though, the United States continued to prohibit direct contact between representatives of the two governments. "North Korea was viewed as the most repugnant totalitarian regime in the world, and we didn't want to have anything to do with them," Harrison explains. "South Korea has also done its best to make sure that we didn't have any improvement of relations with North Korea."[8]

# A THAWING RELATIONSHIP

In this period of global change, however, the Bush administration began to consider modifying its policy, particularly if it might induce the DPRK to come clean on its nuclear program. Both the United States and South Korea may have been influenced by Germany's painful reunification following the fall of the Berlin Wall. Korea experts agreed that assimilation problems in the event of a sudden failure of the DPRK regime would dwarf those experienced in Germany, leading many policymakers to stress the merits of a gradual reconciliation over sudden short-term reunification.

Two avenues for engaging the North showed promise. First was the nuclear Non-Proliferation Treaty (NPT), an international agreement designed to check the spread of nuclear weapons.[9] North Korea had signed the NPT in 1985 at the Soviet Union's urging, but had never negotiated the safeguards agreement required within 18 months of entry. If it finally complied, Pyongyang's nuclear program would become more transparent: not only would North Korea have to provide a list of nuclear facilities to the International Atomic Energy Agency (IAEA), an arm of the United Nations, it would also have to open its facilities to IAEA inspectors. International pressure on North Korea to fulfill its safeguards obligations had been growing, but Pyongyang refused to comply until the United States removed its nuclear weapons from South Korea and pledged not to use nuclear weapons against the regime.

Even more promising, in the eyes of many in the Bush administration, was a regional denuclearization agreement. Despite tensions between North and South, the two Koreas had begun drafting a plan requiring both to remain nuclear-weapons-free. Such a "two-sided" strategy was doubly appealing to the United States, one official confides, since it would also deter the South, which had shelved its own nuclear ambitions only in response to U.S. admonitions. Some in government described the North-South approach as "parallel" to the NPT. Others—chastened by the discovery that Iraq had come close to developing nuclear weapons despite IAEA inspections—saw it as a reinforcement, or even replacement. Indeed, the belated discovery of Iraq's nuclear-bomb program had severely undermined the Vienna-based agency's credibility as an effective monitor. "In the Gulf War, we saw the limits of the IAEA in terms of undeclared nuclear activities," says Robert Manning, then adviser to the assistant secretary for East Asian and Pacific Affairs. "We all wanted to have a mechanism where, if something was detected, there could be some kind of short-term challenge-inspection capability [that would give the U.S. the ability to demand inspections of specified North Korean facilities on short notice]."[10]

In September 1991, the United States gave a nudge to the nuclear logjam when President Bush announced the unilateral withdrawal of all U.S. ground- and sea-launched tactical nuclear weapons employed abroad.[11] Two months later, ROK President Roh Tae Woo declared that there were no nuclear weapons in the South. Bush's decree was intended to elicit a response in kind from the soon-to-topple Soviet Union, but it did double duty by stripping North Korea of its main excuse for not cooperating with the IAEA.

The weapons withdrawal, coupled with hints that the United States might reward North Korean cooperation with direct dialogue, helped initiate a string of auspicious events. On December 13, 1991, North and South completed an agreement pledging eventual reconciliation and nonaggression. On December 31, the two Koreas signed the North-South Declaration on a Non-Nuclear Korean Peninsula, the most sweeping arms control accord ever. Under the pact, neither country could "test, manufacture, produce, accept, possess, store, deploy or use nuclear weapons." Nor could either possess a reprocessing facility, a restriction ignored in the NPT. Although implementation still had to be negotiated, the agreement was to go into effect by February 21, 1992. North and South privately agreed that on January 7 there would be two simultaneous announcements. The ROK, with Bush administration backing, would suspend its annual Team Spirit military exercise with the United States for the first time since the war maneuvers began in 1976.[12] And the DPRK would announce its willingness to sign its long-overdue NPT safeguards agreement.

U.S. officials greeted the North-South denuclearization agreement with enthusiasm tinged with skepticism. Some believed the North had its own reasons for backing the agreement, such as gaining access to U.S. military facilities in the South to confirm withdrawal of U.S. nuclear weapons. Others believed the North only signed to win a meeting with the United States. In any event, the Bush administration informed North Korea in January that it was ready to hold a high-level meeting for the first time since the Korean War.

The extent of North Korea's nuclear program remained to be revealed, but 1992 began on a high note. The unprecedented series of breakthroughs—dual UN entry, withdrawal of U.S. nuclear weapons, joint North-South agreements, suspension of Team Spirit, North Korea's promise to sign the safeguards agreement, and upcoming U.S.-DPRK dialogue—led one magazine to declare, "The Korean Peninsula looked a little safer this week."[13] Adds General Brent Scowcroft, Bush's national security adviser, "There was some hope that the North

was finally emerging from its isolation and was prepared to become a more normal member of international society."[14]

# A FIRST MEETING

The U.S. decision to hold high-level talks was not made lightly. According to
Arnold Kanter, the undersecretary for Political Affairs chosen to meet with the
DPRK, "It was politically significant that someone at my level was meeting with
the North Koreans after almost forty years."[15] But the Kanter meeting repre-
sented a compromise between those who favored a positive gesture toward the
North and those who considered any meeting inappropriate.

Kanter believes the North Koreans hoped for a joint communiqué and the
promise of a second meeting, but they got neither. The administration's mixed
feelings were reconciled, Kanter says, by holding
the meeting but delivering a tough message. "If
they lived up to their obligations, and if they followed through on what they'd agreed to do, both
in a bilateral context and in the NPT context, then
that would open the door to them partaking of the
economic miracle that was going on in East Asia,"
he explains in summarizing the U.S. position. "If
they chose the other path, they would continue to be isolated politically, undermined economically, their people would suffer, and their regime didn't have a
future." The DPRK was also to stop missile exports, adhere to international rules
on chemical and biological weapons, return the remains of MIAs, renounce terrorism, and improve human rights.[16]

> **Why did Kanter
> end up with so
> little flexibility
> to negotiate?**

What the United States would do in response was stated in more general
terms. "We did not even talk about normalizing relations," recalls Richard
Solomon, assistant secretary for East Asian and Pacific Affairs. "We talked about
improving relations, but we were under pretty strict instructions not to seem to
take that dialogue very far."[17] The United States, after all, had removed its tactical nuclear weapons and suspended Team Spirit. Now it was time for North
Korea to deliver.

The DPRK delegation may have left disappointed, but one U.S. participant
who applauds Kanter for treating the North Koreans "like people from planet
Earth" describes the meeting as "the catalyzing diplomatic effort" that convinced the DPRK to comply with the NPT and accept IAEA inspections. North
Korea signed the safeguards agreement and submitted a report describing its
nuclear materials and seven nuclear sites. In May, Hans Blix, the IAEA's director general, visited the declared facilities.

The Bush administration had cause to celebrate. But the appearance of unanimity and cooperation turned out to be an illusion. Within a few months, both IAEA inspections and North-South talks began to unravel.

## DEADLOCK AND DETERIORATION

By mid-1992 the North and South had met repeatedly but remained deadlocked over the de-nuclearization agreement. Partly at the urging of U.S. experts, South Korea was pushing an intrusive inspection regimen that would include challenge inspections of declared and suspected nuclear sites. North Korea maintained that this was a ruse to get access to its military sites, and insisted that each inspection be mutually approved in advance.

As the process inched forward, Robert Carlin, chief of the State Department Intelligence and Research Bureau's Northeast Asia Division, claims that South Korean hard-liners decided to sabotage the talks. First, South Korean intelligence agents publicized the discovery of a North Korean spy ring, a move he believes was meant to irritate the North. In October the South Koreans warned that the Team Spirit war games would be reinstated in 1993 unless the North-South talks progressed. "It was guaranteed to stop the process because it's holding a gun to North Korea's head," Carlin explains. "Normally the announcement for Team Spirit came in December or January. Announcing it in October was either an ill-conceived move—which it was—or it was part provocation."[18] DPRK representatives said they would suspend the North-South talks unless Team Spirit was canceled. Washington and Seoul, however, continued to predicate the decision about Team Spirit on progress in North-South talks.

What were the key barriers to reaching agreement?

Meanwhile, the IAEA inspections were going bad. North Korea had admitted producing mere "laboratory" amounts of plutonium in 1990. But by late 1992 IAEA inspectors had discovered inconsistencies, raising the suspicion that North Korea had reprocessed more than it had reported. The IAEA eventually concluded that the DPRK had separated plutonium at three different times. In January 1993, citing evidence of unreported fuel diversion, the IAEA demanded to inspect two undeclared sites suspected of harboring nuclear waste.

Some Korea experts attribute the simultaneous deterioration of the North-South talks and the IAEA inspections to the North digging in its heels because it had not reaped the rewards it expected for compliance. But the United States had never contemplated rewarding the DPRK simply for fulfilling its international obligations. Kanter says he would have liked to make some tangible offer, but just getting the single meeting "was swimming upstream as it was." Moreover, both the United States and South Korea had other priorities in late 1992. "Two of the three governments involved, Seoul and Washington, were not able to pay close attention because they were in the midst of elections and then transitions," explains Carlin of the State Department. "So in a very crucial period . . . there was no capacity for either government to respond to anything the North Koreans put out."

# HARDENED POSTURES

As two new presidents—Bill Clinton and Seoul's Kim Young Sam—took office in early 1993, the North-South talks remained frozen and tensions spiraled higher between North Korea and the IAEA. North Korea had refused the IAEA's request to examine the two suspect waste sites, insisting that they were military facilities. In February the IAEA requested "special inspections" of the two sites, citing U.S. intelligence photos of clumsily concealed underground storage tanks.[19] The IAEA's Board of Governors gave North Korea one month to allow special inspections, after which it would refer the matter to the UN Security Council.

The IAEA ruling, and in particular its use of U.S. intelligence, enraged the North Koreans, who claimed the United States was manipulating the IAEA. Many observers speculate that DPRK leaders were angry at having been caught in a clumsy lie. "When they signed up with the IAEA, they were looking at the old IAEA and they got the post-Iraq IAEA," explains William Clark, Richard Solomon's successor as assistant secretary for East Asian and Pacific Affairs. "The IAEA came in like gangbusters, and the North said, 'Whoa! Wait a minute. That's not what we signed on for. You guys are supposed to come and dust lightly and go away.'"[20] Some Korea experts assert that the IAEA, anxious to prove itself after its failure in Iraq, was overzealous about unmasking the DPRK nuclear program. There was also a matter of "face," since Kim Il Sung had denied the existence of a bomb program for years.

In any event, most officials in the new Clinton administration applauded the IAEA's aggressive stance and considered it essential not to interfere in the agency's affairs. The NPT would come up for renewal in 1995, and North Korean defiance of the IAEA could set a dangerous precedent and endanger the treaty's renewal prospects. "We were getting pressured by other countries," explains Kent Wiedemann, then National Security Council senior director for Asia, "especially our European friends and allies, who tended to see this thing almost exclusively as an issue of maintaining the integrity of the global non-proliferation regime."[21]

On March 8 the annual Team Spirit military exercise began. Four days later, North Korea announced its intention to withdraw from the NPT—the first member ever to threaten to do so. The IAEA demand for special inspections was, the North declared, "an undisguised strong-arm act designed to disarm the DPRK and strangle our socialist system." North Korea's withdrawal would begin in ninety days, and would last "until the U.S. nuclear threats and the unjust conduct of the IAEA against the DPRK will be recognized to have been removed."

**What was the DPRK trying to achieve?**

## AN UNPREPARED RESPONSE TEAM

North Korea's announcement gave new urgency to debate within the United States and the IAEA about the status of the DPRK's nuclear program. It also brought North Korea to sudden prominence in the consciousness of the American public. But figuring out how to respond was not easy. The Clinton administration was new on the job, and according to some State Department insiders North Korea's intransigence did not immediately capture the White House's attention. Within the State Department, it was unclear who would manage the nuclear conflict. Turf battles muddied the process. So many bureaus claimed a stake in the issue that the first press releases had to be cleared through twelve offices. Moreover, most political appointees were still subject to confirmation hearings.

Confronted with this confusion, the East Asian and Pacific Bureau's Korea Desk became a de-facto clearinghouse for ideas and initiatives, and a senior-level interagency working group formed to coordinate the administration's response. Initially, key members from State included Thomas Hubbard, deputy assistant secretary for East Asian and Pacific Affairs; Gary Samore, deputy director of the Political Military Bureau's Office of Regional Nonproliferation; Robert Carlin of Intelligence and Research; and Kenneth Quinones, an officer on the Korea Desk. Representatives from other agencies included Daniel Poneman, the NSC's senior director for Nonproliferation and Export Controls; Kent Wiedemann, deputy assistant secretary of defense for Asia and the Pacific; Captain Thomas Flanagan, chief of the Joint Staff's Asia/Pacific Division; and Norman Wulf, deputy assistant director of the U.S. Arms Control and Disarmament Agency.

**Did the United States do a good job of organizing to meet this challenge? If not, why not?**

The State Department, drawing on Gulf War lessons about the value of multilateral coalitions, was already working international forums. Pressed by the U.S. to take a position, the IAEA found North Korea in "noncompliance" with its safeguards agreement in April 1994. The matter was referred to the UN Security Council, which issued a mildly worded statement calling for the inspection controversy to be resolved.

Meanwhile, the interagency group furiously debated how to answer North Korea's challenge. The DPRK had called for high-level talks with the United States as a way to resolve its disputes with the IAEA, and some officials at State saw such direct contact as the most promising option. A Department of Defense task force had recommended that the United States shift its focus from getting "special inspections" to eliminating Pyongyang's entire nuclear program. A few in the administration were even ready to let North Korea drop out of the NPT. The precedent of withdrawal would be damaging but, in the words of Norman Wulf of the interagency group, "If they're going to be flagrantly violating it, I'd just as soon have them outside the treaty than staying inside and destroying it from within."[22]

# RISKS AND OPTIONS

As the conflict simmered, the State Department prepared for a second round at the Security Council. "The question was: what do we do to punish North Korea for taking this step? And that set off a fairly serious debate within the U.S. government," recalls Robert Suettinger, then a deputy national intelligence officer at the National Intelligence Council. "Do you impose sanctions? What kind of sanctions? How effective will they be? How do you enforce them? Do you enforce them militarily? Do you try to insist on the Chinese abiding by it? The whole range of questions."[23]

It quickly became clear to those working the UN process that the first step would have to be something far short of full economic sanctions. There were serious questions about the effectiveness of further isolating an already isolated regime: North Korea's only significant economic interactions were the oil and other goods it received from China, and cash remittances from Koreans living in Japan. Moreover, neither Japan's nor China's cooperation could be assumed. China had already indicated its reluctance to pressure its long-time ally, and, as a permanent member of the Security Council, it could veto any sanctions resolution.

Even were a resolution passed, analysts feared, it might only spur the North to redouble its bomb-building efforts, with potentially catastrophic consequences. If North Korea went nuclear, its near neighbors, including South Korea and Japan, might feel compelled to amass nuclear arsenals.[24] Furthermore, Pyongyang already exported ballistic missiles to such countries as Libya and Iran for cash, and most analysts believed it would gladly sell nuclear bombs if it had them.

Finally, there was the threat of armed conflict. As pressure built for international censure, North Korea warned that UN sanctions would constitute a declaration of war—a threat many in the U.S. government took seriously. "There was all along a realization that we were dealing with a very difficult and unpredictable country," says Robert Suettinger, "and that it was extremely difficult to discern what their trip wires were."

# CHAPTER TWO

# Diagnosing the Structure

Breakthroughs of the kind sought by the Bush and Clinton administrations in North Korea begin with diagnosing the structure of negotiations. Without a thorough diagnosis, negotiators would have to develop strategies from scratch for every negotiation, even those with underlying structural similarities. The following seven diagnostic questions provide a starting point for assessing a negotiation's structure.[1] Answering them will give you a comprehensive view of the terrain and equip you to identify barriers to agreement and formulate strategies for managing conflict and building momentum:

- *Parties:* Who will participate in the negotiation?
- *Issues:* What agenda of issues will be, or could be, negotiated?
- *Interests:* What goals are you and others pursuing?
- *Alternatives:* What will you do if you do not reach agreement?
- *Agreements:* Are there potential agreements that would be acceptable to all sides?
- *Linkages:* Are your current negotiations linked to other negotiations?
- *Action-forcing events:* Will time-related costs or events force action?

## PARTIES: WHO WILL PARTICIPATE IN THE NEGOTIATION?

It may seem obvious who the key parties to a negotiation are, and sometimes they are exactly as they appear. Often, however, particularly in nominally two-party negotiations, other players are already involved. Sometimes other parties unexpectedly enter the negotiation and change it in unforeseen ways, and sometimes you would gain by pulling in other parties yourself. It is essential to take the time to identify the active and potential parties to the negotiation and ask yourself whether you would benefit or suffer from the participation of others.

## Map the Parties

A *party map* of the key participants and linked sets of negotiations is a first step in diagnosing structure. Figure 2.1 is a party map of the U.S.–North Korean negotiation. On the face of it, the parties to this negotiation are the United States and North Korea. But others, such as South Korea, Japan, and the IAEA, are already involved.

In mapping the parties, it is important to identify not just already-involved participants but also those who could intervene. Negotiators may decide, for example, to invite mediators or other intermediaries to facilitate the process. And outside parties like China in this example may intervene unilaterally if they decide they have a stake in the process.

## Assess the Negotiating Representatives

Negotiating representatives serve as bridges between external negotiation and internal decision making. They simultaneously face outward to advance the interests of their institutions and inward to obtain mandates, craft consensus positions, and sell agreements. It is therefore crucially important to understand who they are, what their status and experience consist of, and what internal constituencies they represent. In negotiations between teams, this kind of analysis should be performed for every member of the other teams; different individuals are likely to represent different internal constituencies. As you continue to read the North Korea case, keep this in mind, because it becomes important.

## Analyze Internal Decision Making

In negotiations between organizations or nations, analysis of the parties should aim at understanding and trying to influence your counterparts' internal decision-making processes. Start with some basic questions about the other parties: How do they establish negotiating positions and ratify agreements? Do your counterparts have to contend with internal differences, or are their constituents unified? How long does it take them to make decisions? How likely is it that agreements will be implemented?

Instead of treating counterparts as unified monoliths, good negotiators seek to understand and influence the internal decision-making processes that shape their actions. On the U.S. side, for example, key players in 1993 included the National Security Council and Departments of Defense and State, as well as congressional leaders, former Bush administration officials, and the media—a large number of players with potentially divergent interests. Were there similar inter-

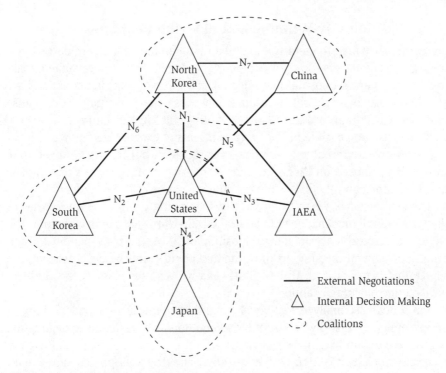

**Figure 2.1.**  Linked System of Negotiations.

nal differences within the DPRK? It was difficult to tell. But it was also danger-ous to assume that the North Koreans acted as a monolith. There were hints, for example, of differences between hawks in the North Korean military and doves in the foreign ministry.

In analyzing other parties' internal decision making, you should also assess speed, quality, and follow-through. Are decisions made quickly, or does each cycle of proposal and response take a lot of time? Do the resulting decisions appear to be well thought through, or are they lowest-common-denominator compromises? Once decisions are made, is follow-through assured or not? Gen-erally, there tend to be trade-offs among these dimensions. The DPRK's cen-tralized authority structure, for example, permitted it to move quickly. But such systems can isolate those at the top from external realities, and top-level deci-sions may be subtly resisted at lower levels. The U.S. decision-making system tends to be slower and more cumbersome, but it encourages wide-ranging debate. The process required to ratify decisions in the United States may appear fractious, but follow-through is generally assured—at least for a while.

## Identify Winning and Blocking Coalitions

Study the party map to identify existing and potential coalitions of parties. Are there groups of players—known as *winning coalitions*—that are capable of making decisions and imposing outcomes on the others?[2] Winning coalitions are able to impose their will either because they possess coercive power or because of decision-making procedures (such as voting rules in legislatures).

It may also be possible for *blocking coalitions* to exercise veto power. Blocking coalitions are not able to impose an agreement, but they can prevent one from being imposed on them. In other words, winning coalitions can impose new conditions on others; blocking coalitions can protect the status quo.

The key to success is to build your own winning coalitions and to prevent the formation of blocking coalitions. In the U.S.–North Korean negotiations, the DPRK would be able to block the imposition of UN economic sanctions only so long as it retained the support of China and could count on a Chinese veto in the United Nations. The United States, as we will see, therefore sought to weaken this blocking coalition.

You should also analyze coalitional dynamics *within* the other sides. To reach an agreement, you and your like-minded counterparts on the other negotiating teams have to build supportive coalitions within your own sides. A sufficiently powerful blocking coalition within any side can effectively prevent agreement. Significant disagreements within the United States, for example, made it very difficult for the administration to negotiate.

It is sometimes possible for the weaker party in a negotiation to build cross-cutting coalitions with interest groups on the other side who will exert influence over the negotiations. This strategy was successfully employed by the Canadians in negotiations with the United States over cross-border pollution. The Canadians reached out to environmental groups, affected states in the Northeast, and others in the United States who stood to gain from an agreement. Therefore, a thorough analysis of internal parties and their interests helps to shed light on whether and how to reach into the other sides. There are risks to doing an end run around negotiating representatives in this way, but the effects of a cross-cutting coalition on the balance of power can be dramatic.

# ISSUES: WHAT AGENDA OF ISSUES WILL BE NEGOTIATED?

Treating the issue agenda as fixed is easy but dangerous. To do so is to fail to take actions to shape it in favorable ways. The agenda—the set of issues the parties decide to negotiate—is itself subject to negotiation. The United States has its preferred agenda, but the DPRK will probably add or subtract issues. To make sure their issues are addressed, the sides usually seek to introduce them early on and perhaps even press for a prenegotiation about the agenda.

## Identify the Full Set of Issues

Start by identifying mutually acknowledged and latent issues and the interests they evoke (or could evoke) in the various parties—what we call the *issue architecture* of the negotiation. The issues may seem obvious, but it is important to probe beneath the surface. How has the agenda for this negotiation been defined, and who defined it? Is the agenda too narrow or too broad? What sources of conflict could become blocking issues? Are there toxic issues that could be deferred to another day? Do the parties frame the issues and the stakes in the same way?

In its negotiation with North Korea, the United States sought to frame the issues narrowly. Both the Bush and Clinton administrations wanted to focus on whether the DPRK would comply with the provisions of the NPT and permit special inspections of suspected waste sites. For several reasons, U.S. policymakers did not want the agenda to include broader political issues like the future of relationships on the Korean Peninsula. As we will see, their efforts to restrict the agenda ultimately proved unproductive.

## Think About Issue Sequencing

Will the process proceed issue by issue, or will multiple issues be dealt with in parallel? Decisions about whether to proceed sequentially or to work on package deals can have a decisive impact on the evolution and outcome of the process. One approach to building momentum is to break down a complex negotiation into a series of subnegotiations, tackling the easier issues first and deferring the harder issues for later. As Fred Iklé noted in *How Nations Negotiate:*

> The order in which issues are dealt with has several implications. To increase the chances for agreement, negotiators tend to take up the less controversial issues first in the hope that the parties will become increasingly desirous of an agreement and therefore willing to make greater sacrifices in solving the hard issues. . . . More important than the ordering of issues is the linkage of separable issues into package deals and tie-ins. In a package deal a party proposes to settle several issues that are considered part of the agreement under negotiation. In a tie-in a party includes an issue considered extraneous by the opponent and offers to accept a certain settlement provided this extraneous issue will also be settled to its satisfaction.[3]

As we will see in the U.S.–North Korea negotiations, the sequence in which negotiators address issues, and the way they are parsed into subsets, has a powerful impact on the negotiators' ability to find their way to agreement.

Identifying subsets of issues with substantial potential for cross-issue trades can open up new possibilities. But the order and grouping of issues are not neutral. How issues are arrayed can powerfully influence the ability of the negotiators to claim value. For instance, negotiators may attempt to lock in early gains by securing concessions from their counterparts on issues that are of high value to them.

In multiparty situations, sequencing can influence the formation of coalitions. Opening negotiations with an issue that divides potential opponents can forestall formation of a blocking coalition; beginning with an issue on which you and potential allies agree can help to seal a winning coalition.

# INTERESTS:
# WHAT GOALS ARE YOU AND OTHERS PURSUING?

Once you have mapped the parties and issues, you should assess how each party is likely to conceptualize its objectives and scope for action. How do they perceive their interests? What are they trying to achieve?

## Look Beyond Positions

Early on, often in parallel with hammering out the agenda, negotiators typically begin to stake out positions. *Positions* are essentially demands, often backed up by some mix of rationales, principles, commitments, and threats. The U.S. position, for example, was that the DPRK needed to submit to special inspections or face a campaign for sanctions in the UN Security Council. The DPRK position was diametrically opposed to this, and so the negotiations stalled.

As a rule, though, taking a hard position early is rarely a good idea. As Roger Fisher and William Ury stress in *Getting to Yes,* negotiators are likely to benefit more in the long run by concentrating first on assessing interests—the underlying goals and desires they and their counterparts are pursuing.[4] Even if the parties' positions are irreconcilable, their underlying interests may not be. They may well have some combination of the following kinds of interests:[5]

- *Conflicting interests* ("I want X to happen and you don't," or "I want more of a valuable resource, and so do you") are the reason that negotiation is necessary.

- *Shared interests* ("I want X to happen, and so do you") offer opportunities for pure joint gain.

- *Complementary interests* ("I want X a lot but don't care much about Y, and you want Y a lot but don't care much about X") represent an opportunity for mutually beneficial trades: "I get more of X in return for giving you more of Y."

The United States and the DPRK had a complicated mix of conflicting, shared, and complementary interests. The conflict over the North's acquisition of nuclear weapons is obvious. Less obvious is the parties' shared interest in avoiding war and their potentially complementary interests in trading the North's nuclear program for diplomatic recognition and economic support.

## Factor in Process Interests

Alongside their interests in substance, negotiators also have *process-related interests*—interests in how the process unfolds, and consequently how they appear to others and to themselves—that could powerfully influence their behavior.[6] Key types of process interests include these:

- *Enhancing relationships:* preserving or improving relationships with other parties, especially when the negotiations are not a one-time transaction but are part of a congenial long-term relationship

- *Preserving reputation:* maintaining or enhancing one's reputation as an effective (perhaps firm or even tough) negotiator

- *Demonstrating competence:* experiencing a sense of competence and skill as a negotiator or, more fundamentally, not feeling incompetent

- *Remaining consistent:* maintaining at least the appearance of consistency with prior commitments or statements of principle, as well as avoiding setting undesirable precedents[7]

- *Minimizing transaction costs:* minimizing the direct costs (time and resources) of negotiation, as well as the opportunity costs of not pursuing other initiatives

- *Achieving side effects:* achieving objectives external to the process, such as improved relationships with powerful third parties, access to new resources, or delay[8]

Process interests can either impede or promote a good substantive agreement. If one negotiator makes another feel incompetent, the result may be defensiveness and inflexibility. On the other hand, negotiators may be willing to concede a bit on substance to preserve relationships or achieve important side effects.

An analysis of U.S. and North Korean substance and process interests appears in Table 2.1. You might find it helpful to try your hand at a similar analysis of the interests of China, Japan, South Korea, and the IAEA.

## Assess Representatives' Interests

Assessment of negotiating representatives' personal stakes is an important part of a comprehensive analysis of interests. Representatives can subtly avoid pursuing options that would be acceptable to their principals or use their knowledge

Table 2.1. Analysis of Interests.

| Interests | United States | North Korea |
|---|---|---|
| Substance | Preventing proliferation of nuclear weapons<br><br>Preventing an arms race in Asia<br><br>Undermining the DPRK | Ensuring security by acquiring nuclear weapons<br><br>Bolstering a failing economy<br><br>Winning international recognition |
| Relationships | Retaining a close relationship with South Korea<br><br>Weakening relations between North Korea and China<br><br>Preserving the alliance with Japan | Weakening the relationship between the United States and South Korea<br><br>Preserving relations with China |
| Reputation | Preserving a reputation for toughness | Preserving a reputation for toughness and potential irrationality |
| Competence | Being perceived as competent at managing international crises | Remaining self-sufficient<br><br>Gaining international recognition |
| Consistency | Remaining consistent with previous commitments to South Korea | Remaining faithful to a longstanding political philosophy |
| Transaction costs | Substantial direct costs of managing a diplomatic effort<br><br>Opportunity costs of not paying attention to other things | |
| Side effects | Preserving the integrity of the NPT in advance of renewal negotiations<br><br>Achieving a delay that will further weaken the DPRK | Enhancing opportunities to sell missile and other technology to other rogue states |

of the process and control over information to advance their own interests or disrupt proceedings. Keep this in mind as you continue to assess the actions of negotiators in the U.S.–North Korea case.

## Predict Coalitional Alignments

You can also predict coalitional alignments by analyzing interests. Predicting how parties will line up on particular issues tells you whom to approach to build coalitions preemptively. By approaching parties in a particular order, you can powerfully influence coalition formation. A simple graphic matrix can be a helpful aid for spotting potential alignments. You can construct one by listing parties in the rows and issues in the columns and pinpointing interests in the cells.

A thorough interest analysis identifies conflicting interests, shared interests, and complementary interests among the parties. Shared interests provide self-evident opportunities for building coalitions. Both the United States and China, for example, wanted to avoid an arms race in Asia, and neither wanted the North Koreans to get nuclear weapons. At the same time, the Chinese were unwilling to desert a long-time ally or to give the United States free rein to operate in their sphere of influence. The South Koreans and the Japanese shared an interest in containing North Korea.

Although shared interests are necessary for a coalition to form, they are not sufficient. For one thing, barriers to open information sharing can prevent the parties from recognizing their common interests; this is one reason that negotiators often attempt to control who interacts with whom in multiparty situations.[9] Poor prior relationships can also prevent coalitions from forming. The long history of antagonism between Korea and Japan, for example, undermined their potential to form a coalition.

Also shared interests are not the only basis for building coalitions. Coalitions of convenience can be constructed by entering into short-term trades with others. Suppose, for example, that two parties in a large multiparty negotiation are too weak individually to influence the process but jointly constitute a blocking coalition. Suppose further that each is indifferent to the issues the other cares about. These two special interest groups can form a blocking coalition by agreeing to support each other in pursuing their respective interests—the classic "you scratch my back and I'll scratch yours" situation. Multiparty negotiations can make for strange bedfellows.

The most robust coalitions are founded on a combination of shared substantive interests and longstanding relationships of mutual support. The weakest coalitions are marriages of convenience—opportunistic trades without a substantial relationship buffer. They are the most vulnerable to classic divide-and-conquer tactics.

# ALTERNATIVES: WHAT WILL YOU DO IF YOU DO NOT REACH AGREEMENT?

It sounds self-evident that you should enter into an agreement only if doing so will yield more value than not doing so. But negotiators contemplating a potential agreement often fail to ask themselves the obvious question: Compared to what? Unless you have worked out what you will do if you cannot reach agreement, you will not know how to answer this question. Roger Fisher and William Ury called this alternate scenario the *best alternative to a negotiated agreement*, and its acronym, BATNA, has entered the standard vocabulary of negotiation.[10] Figure 2.2 illustrates the decisions that the United States and North Korea faced between agreement and their respective BATNAs.

## Build Your BATNA

A BATNA is a course of action; it is what you will do if there is no agreement. Depending on what is at issue, it could be to go to court, strike, seek a divorce, or let a deadline expire. Taking time to work out your BATNA rigorously will clarify your thinking. A good BATNA is one source of power in negotiation: the better your BATNA is, the better your agreements are likely to be.

The alternatives to agreement for the United States in its negotiations with North Korea do not seem particularly attractive. The principal no-agreement options are (1) military action, which could be very costly even if limited to a surgical strike; (2) economic sanctions, difficult to pull off and likely to be ineffective; and (3) doing nothing, which could allow weapons of mass destruction to proliferate and vastly complicate the security situation in Asia. As we will see, U.S. negotiators had to engage in some hardheaded cost-benefit analysis to identify which of these potential alternatives was the best.

At the same time, it sometimes is possible to change the game in ways that improve alternatives to agreement. BATNAs are not static, nor are they given; they have to be built. You can take actions away from the table to build your BATNAs and weaken those of your counterparts. As you continue to read the case, consider the following question: What could the United States have done to strengthen its BATNA? To weaken the DPRK's BATNA?

## Assess Your Counterparts' BATNAs

It is easy to forget that the other side also has to be convinced that a deal is beneficial—that it yields more value than their own independent BATNA. To craft an advantageous deal, U.S. negotiators needed to understand how the North Koreans perceived their alternatives (as distinct from how they themselves thought the DPRK *should* perceive their alternatives, a very common mistake).

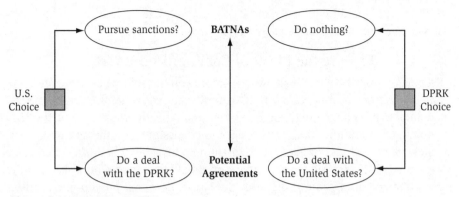

**Figure 2.2.** Assessing BATNAs.

Was "do nothing" a viable option for the North Koreans? If so, the United States was in a weak position.

But the DPRK's BATNA does not seem attractive either. Continued international isolation could accelerate collapse of the North Korean economy, degrade its military capabilities, and bring about the eventual fall of the regime. For both sides, a deal looks attractive.

## Define Your Walkaway Position

The next step is to define your walkaway position: What minimum value do you need to get to enter into an agreement? Establishing this value as a benchmark and keeping it in the forefront of your mind helps protect against the pitfalls of getting so committed to your demands that you refuse deals that are better than your walkaway. You should not allow yourself to be pushed below your walkaway in the heat of the process.

Translating a BATNA (a course of action) into your walkaway position (the minimum value you would accept in an agreement) is not always straightforward.[11] You have to work it out for the particular negotiation you are engaged in. For instance, suppose you are buying a new car and debating whether to sell your old one or trade it in. Is your walkaway price in a private sale identical to your walkaway in a trade-in? It may be higher, to compensate for the effort of privately advertising and selling your car.

Assessing walkaways is necessarily harder when you are negotiating multiple issues. The key is to look at possible trade-offs across the issues and then to develop an approach—even a spreadsheet model—that enables you to compare the values of different package deals. This means assessing the (subjective) value of different potential outcomes and trying to qualify the relative costs and benefits of different potential package deals.

### Explore the Effect of Coalitions on BATNAs

Establishing BATNAs and walkaways is more complicated when there are more than two parties to a negotiation. If your alternatives to submitting to others' demands look unappealing, you can often dramatically improve your BATNAs by joining a coalition. Similarly, changes in coalitional alignments can dramatically change BATNAs or even cause coalitional BATNAs to vanish. As we have seen, the DPRK was highly dependent on its alliance with China. Weakening that alliance could profoundly alter the North Koreans' perceptions of their alternatives. A key lesson therefore is not to become dependent on a coalition. It is often preferable to hang together rather than hang separately, but it is essential to think through what will happen if the coalition breaks down: you could end up twisting in the wind. This possibility calls for developing your own BATNA, as well as collective options.

# AGREEMENTS: ARE THERE POTENTIAL AGREEMENTS THAT WOULD BE ACCEPTABLE TO ALL SIDES?

If potential agreements exist that would benefit both you and your counterpart more than your respective walkaway values, a *zone of possible agreement* (ZOPA) exists.[12] Ordinarily, you will not know whether such a zone exists until you begin to explore interests and options at the table. Even so, you should do your best to discern the rough outlines of the ZOPA early on.

### Assess Who Knows What

When negotiators know a lot about each other's interests and walkaways, they can speak openly with little risk. Usually, however, there are substantial *informational asymmetries*—that is, each side knows a lot about its own interests, BATNAs, walkaways, and resources but much less about its counterparts'. When this is the case, negotiators can selectively withhold and dole out information in order to shape each other's perceptions. For example, the United States was uncertain whether the DPRK had already acquired nuclear weapons or had the capability to do so in the near future. Naturally, the North Koreans were eager to keep the United States in the dark. For its part, the United States tried to deflate the DPRK's expectations about what normalization of relations would entail.

When informational asymmetries are extreme, negotiators' perceptions of the ZOPA are susceptible to manipulation. The greater the asymmetries of information are, the more that negotiators will try to shape each other's perceptions of interests, BATNAs, and walkaways.[13] Because negotiators have to act on the basis of their perceptions, having better information is a clear advantage. But informational asymmetries, and the mutual efforts at manipulation they encourage, can prevent the parties from finding a ZOPA even when it exists—a strategic barrier to agreement that we discuss in Chapter Four.

Negotiations can also be complicated by *shared uncertainties*. Are there future events about which all the negotiators are uncertain? If so, both sides may make overly optimistic and self-serving predictions and reach very different conclusions about what the future holds. As a result, the parties may conclude erroneously that no agreement is preferable to agreement. As we will see, divergent beliefs about future events can either enhance or undermine the potential for negotiated agreement.

## Assess the Type of Negotiation

The nature of the ZOPA depends on whether a negotiation is, or its participants believe it to be, purely about *claiming value* (dividing the pie) or whether it offers opportunities to *create value* by enlarging the pie.[14] Negotiations that appear on their face to be highly distributive often have some integrative potential. Negotiators frequently assume that negotiations are more distributive than they actually are, an understandable defensive posture. But defensiveness can be a self-fulfilling prophecy, because value cannot be created unilaterally. For better or worse, perception is reality, particularly when negotiators view the same negotiation differently.

**Distributive Negotiations.**  Sometimes there is a fixed pie to be divided among the parties: anything one side gains, the other loses. A situation of this kind is a *distributive negotiation*. The objective of both sides in distributive negotiations is to claim value—to get as big a wedge of the pie as possible.[15]

Single-issue negotiations tend to be zero sum. Suppose hypothetically that the United States and the DPRK are negotiating over just one issue: the timing of special inspections of suspected North Korean nuclear waste sites. The United States wants faster inspections, and the DPRK wants to delay them as long as possible. The ZOPA for this distributive negotiation is illustrated in Figure 2.3a. The two axes represent the subjective value of an agreement to the United States and North Korea, respectively. The range of potential agreements is a straight line because any agreement that awards more value to one gives less value to the other. Because the line representing potential agreements falls outside the ZOPA, no agreement is possible. In other words, there are no feasible agreements in this case because of the incompatibility of the parties' aspirations.

If the United States and the DPRK take actions away from the table that worsen each other's alternatives to agreement, both could become willing to accept agreements that were previously unacceptable, as shown by the position

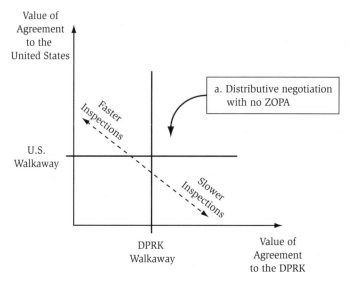

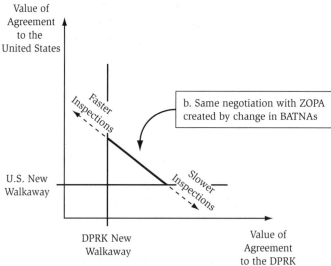

**Figure 2.3.** Distributive Negotiations.

of the line representing potential agreements in Figure 2.3b. The ZOPA is still a line, but any point along the line that falls on the right side of both parties' walkaways represents a potential agreement.

**Integrative Negotiations.**  When the parties' have some shared interests or opportunities to realize mutual gains through trades across multiple issues, negotiations can be *integrative* instead of distributive.[16] *Integrative* refers to the potential for the parties' interests to be integrated in ways that create joint value or enlarge the pie. The trick is to figure out how to do this without giving away the store.

One immediate implication is that negotiators who decide to simplify multi-issue negotiations by proceeding issue by issue may drive out the potential for integration and creation of joint value. To create value, negotiators must be able to deal with sets of issues and to assemble attractive packages. Negotiators may also have to find ways to prime the pump of value creation, perhaps by linking issues to create the potential for joint gain through trades. In this way, distributive negotiations sometimes can be transformed into integrative ones.

Suppose, for example, that the United States and North Korea decided to negotiate a trade whereby the DPRK would comply with the NPT in return for U.S. diplomatic recognition and investment by U.S. companies. Suppose too that such investment offered opportunities for pure joint gain, because U.S. industry would benefit and so would the North Koreans. The issues to be negotiated were (1) how quickly and comprehensively the DPRK would permit inspections to take place, (2) what level of recognition the United States would give, and (3) how much corporate investment the United States would permit.

The ZOPA for this negotiation is illustrated in Figure 2.4. Again, the axes represent the value to the parties of various package deals. Note that the ZOPA in an integrative negotiation is an area, not a line. This is because the existence of shared interests and opportunities for trades allows joint value to be created and expands the pie. At the same time, the resulting value can be divided or claimed in a multitude of ways. Creating value is not an end in itself. It does not do you much good to help your counterpart create a large pie, only to see it grab the lion's share.

## Seek More Efficient Agreements

Clearly, integrative negotiations are desirable for both parties, but it is still possible for them to produce agreements that are mediocre or worse. Specifically, integrative negotiations can result in agreements that are inefficient in the sense that other feasible agreements existed that would have made everyone better off. Suppose, for example, that the United States and the DPRK failed (for whatever reason) to reach agreement on the issue of corporate investment, but did agree to trade modest U.S. diplomatic recognition for partial inspections.

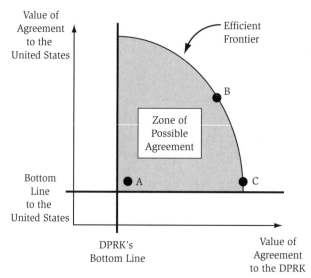

**Figure 2.4.** Integrative Negotiations.

Because the agreement is unambitious in terms of value creation but even-handed in terms of value capture, it is positioned at point A in Figure 2.4.

Now suppose instead that the parties agreed on rapid and comprehensive inspections in return for diplomatic normalization *and* substantial investment. This agreement, represented by point B, results in much more joint value and is thus more efficient than agreement A.

There are always limits on how much joint value the parties can create by making trades. These limits are represented by what is known as the *efficient frontier.*[17] Agreements on the frontier are efficient in the sense that one party cannot be made better off without making the other party worse off. The position of agreement B on the efficient frontier signifies that it is not possible to conceive of agreements that would create even more joint value for both the United States and North Korea.

When value is created in negotiations, it gets claimed. Suppose the United States traded substantial diplomatic recognition and investment for North Korean promises of future inspections. This agreement is represented by point C. Because they are positioned on the efficient frontier (and no further joint gains are possible), the agreements at points B and C are both efficient. But the DPRK claims much more of the resulting value at C than at B.

A, B, and C therefore represent different types of agreements that can be reached in integrative negotiations. Point A is an inefficient agreement because other potential agreements, such as B and C, could have made both negotiators better off if they had been able to find ways to create value. Point B is a balanced agreement in which a lot of value got created and divided relatively evenly. Point C is an unbalanced agreement: a lot of value got created, but one side claimed the lion's share of it. Because such agreements raise questions of equity and sustainability, assessments of outcomes in integrative negotiations are about equity as well as efficiency. Perceptions of equity (or lack thereof) often have a powerful impact on negotiators' behavior.

# LINKAGES: ARE YOUR CURRENT NEGOTIATIONS LINKED TO OTHER NEGOTIATIONS?

Stand-alone negotiations are surprisingly rare. Even as simple a negotiation as buying a house involves competition with other purchasers, dealings with mortgage lenders, and sometimes interactions with several sellers. Negotiators' BATNAs tend to be strongly influenced by such linkages. If the prospective seller gets another offer or the prospective buyer finds another attractive house, the dynamics of the negotiation shift dramatically.

This is why it is crucial, when diagnosing a negotiating situation and working to shape others' perceptions, to look beyond the immediate negotiation to the broader linked system in which it is embedded.[18] As James Baker put it in *The Politics of Diplomacy,* "I was taught that any . . . negotiation was actually a series of discrete problems that required solutions. How you worked the other side in developing the solution to the first problem had ramifications far beyond that single issue. Indeed, its resolution could set not just the logical precedents for subsequent issues, but the very tone of the relationship between negotiators."[19] The main types of linkages—sequential, competitive, and reciprocal—are illustrated in Figure 2.5.

## Identify Sequential Linkages

One way that negotiations get linked is sequentially in time. Relationships established in prior negotiations can influence current ones, and current negotiations can be affected by the prospect of future ones. The negotiations between the United States and North Korea took place in the context of prior negotiations that had constrained the actions of the parties. The United States was committed to the defense of South Korea and to forestalling proliferation of weapons of mass destruction, China was committed to protecting its traditional allies, and the IAEA was committed to upholding the integrity of the NPT. For its part, the DPRK had signed the NPT treaty and had to negotiate in the shadow of that prior agreement.

The Clinton administration was also unwilling to set adverse precedents for future negotiations. North Korean acquisition of nuclear weapons capability

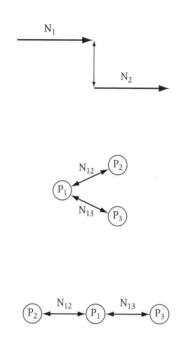

**Sequential Linkage**
- Negotiations $N_1$ and $N_2$ are linked in time.
- They may or may not involve the same parties.
- Current negotiations may influence future ones, or anticipated future ones may influence current ones.

**Competitive Linkage**
- Party $P_1$ engages in competitively linked negotiations $N_{12}$ with Party $P_2$ and $N_{13}$ with Party $P_3$.
- Only one set of negotiations can reach fruition ($P_2$ and $P_3$ are competitors).

**Reciprocal Linkage**
- Party $P_1$ engages in reciprocally linked negotiations $N_{12}$ with Party $P_2$ and $N_{13}$ with Party $P_3$.
- Both sets have to reach fruition in order for either to reach fruition ($P_2$ and $P_3$ are codependent).

**Figure 2.5.** Types of Linked Negotiations.

would be a severe blow to the global nonproliferation regime, especially in the upcoming negotiations over renewal of the NPT. North Korean possession of nuclear arms would also be likely to set off a regional arms race, complicating efforts to negotiate collective security agreements in Northeast Asia.

## Identify Concurrent Linkages

Simultaneous sets of negotiations can also affect each other's outcomes. Two negotiations are competitively linked if agreement in one precludes agreement in the other. The creation of a competitive linkage can powerfully affect other parties' perceptions of their BATNAs. North Korea and the United States competed, to a degree, for the support of China. Both sides engaged in talks with the Chinese, seeking to bolster their BATNAs and to weaken the other side's. The effect was to strengthen China's influence in this situation.

Concurrent negotiations are reciprocally linked if agreement must be reached in all in order for agreement to be reached in any. The United States' negotiations with the DPRK were reciprocally linked to its negotiations with South Korea, because it could not enter into unilateral agreements with the North without offending the South. This reciprocal linkage emerged as a key barrier to agreement.

### Reengineer the Linked System

Skilled negotiators advance their interests by creating favorable linkages and neutralizing unfavorable linkages. They also think carefully about how to sequence their moves in linked negotiations to build momentum and strengthen their alternatives. Adept use of linkage rests in part on having thoroughly mapped the structure of the linked system. A good map of the terrain facilitates shaping the structure in favorable ways.

## ACTION-FORCING EVENTS: WILL TIME-RELATED COSTS OR EVENTS FORCE ACTION?

What events will (or could) compel action on the part of the players? Some parties may be more sensitive to the passage of time than others. They may, for example, be experiencing high cumulating costs, either directly out of pocket or in the form of forgone opportunities. In general, more patient negotiators have an advantage over their less patient counterparts.

*Action-forcing events,* such as deadlines, can also force some or all of the parties to make hard choices, such as whether to accept a deal or break off negotiations.[20] In international negotiations, political events such as elections can drive or restrain action. In business, the planning and decision-making cycles of companies play a similar role. In the U.S.–North Korean negotiations, upcoming negotiations over renewal of the NPT and most-favored-nation trading status for China were both driving the United States to act. As the negotiations proceeded, other action-forcing events became salient.

### Consider the Impact of Time

In negotiation, it often is an option to do nothing, and, as we have noted, patient negotiators have an advantage over their less patient counterparts. Ask yourself whether there is a good reason to act now. Will your alternatives improve or worsen as time passes? What about your counterparts'? Will options that are currently unavailable open up?

In analyzing the potential impact of action-forcing events, negotiators should ask themselves two questions: What would eliminate delay as an option for the other side and how might the other side be induced to make the hard choices necessary to reach agreement? Negotiators often use deadlines and other forms of time pressure to raise tension and create movement toward agreement. The more patient party can sometimes claim value by delaying until the other side faces a hard deadline, and then extracting large concessions to close the deal.

The DPRK's threat to withdraw from the NPT in ninety days served as an action-forcing event. This deadline was neither so remote that action could be deferred nor so immediate that the United States had no chance to respond. The time limit also drew media attention, which helped to build pressure.

## Build Momentum

Negotiators build momentum by shaping their counterparts' perceptions of time-related costs and by setting up action-forcing events. In a typical negotiation, early discussions generate real progress toward agreement, until a point is reached when some or all parties face difficult choices, such as whether to make concessions that will disappoint key internal constituencies. Progress stalls and tensions rise. The negotiations remain at a stalemate until accumulating time-related costs become too great or an action-forcing event causes some or all participants to make concessions or break off negotiations. If the parties decide to make concessions, then accumulated tensions get released, and the process flows toward agreement. This process is illustrated in Figure 2.6.

Hydraulic metaphors can be useful in thinking about momentum-building efforts. The flow toward agreement can be dammed, for example, by purposefully engineering impasses. Tension can then be released and channeled in a desirable direction by proposing a new formula or face-saving compromise. In the process, the more patient and creative team may be able to create and claim substantial value. It is important, of course, not to let tensions build to the point that negotiation breaks down. Managing the flow in negotiation involves walking the knife's edge between promoting movement toward agreement and triggering breakdown.

## Use Linkages to Force Action

Linkages among negotiations can also be used strategically to force action. Legislative leaders may call a preliminary nonbinding vote as a way of forcing members to go on the record for or against a particular bill. The outcome of this vote shapes the starting point for subsequent negotiations over binding votes—an example of strategic use of sequential linkage. The need to complete one set of negotiations before beginning another can also be used to stimulate action or justify delay.

# PUTTING IT ALL TOGETHER

These seven diagnostic questions equip negotiators to do a first-cut assessment and identify salient structural features of negotiation situations. It is imperative to revisit these questions periodically, because the structure evolves during the course of the negotiation.

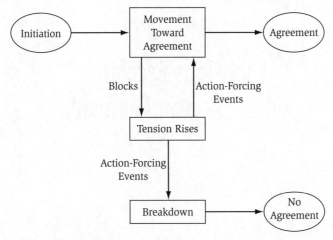

**Figure 2.6.** Channeling the Flow.

You might consider pausing at this point to use the diagnostic questions to analyze the structure of a negotiation of your choice—one in which you were directly involved or one you have read about. What are its essential structural features? How does its structure influence the behavior of the participants?

Having analyzed the structure of the North Korea negotiations, we move on to the next installment in Chapter Three and then to a discussion of barriers to agreement in Chapter Four. As you read Chapter Three, keep in mind two questions:

• Why are the parties having so much difficulty negotiating?
• What are the biggest barriers to a sustainable agreement?

# CHAPTER THREE

# Tensions Escalate
# on the Korean Peninsula

On May 11, 1993, the UN Security Council passed a U.S.-backed resolution urging North Korea—in terms mild enough not to offend the Chinese—to stay in the NPT. China abstained; Russia supported it, to the DPRK's chagrin. Although some critics called the resolution useless, it signaled to the North Koreans that they risked Security Council sanctions. It also urged member states to engage in dialogue with Pyongyang, giving the United States a basis to pursue high-level talks.

**Notice how many parties played a role in these negotiations.**

Indeed, pressure on the United States to negotiate with North Korea was growing. The IAEA board of governors, particularly France, Russia, and Britain, was pushing for talks. China too was urging bilateral talks and was unlikely to support further UN action unless the United States had exhausted all other possibilities. "Tactically," says the State Department's Gary Samore, "you had to try negotiations in order to make it possible to get further Security Council action."[1]

## IDENTIFYING BARRIERS TO AGREEMENT

Nevertheless, one official describes the debate over talks as "an agonizing process within the U.S. government." Those opposed to dialogue feared appearing to reward North Korea's bad behavior. What finally proved decisive, the official says, was the lack of alternatives. "The only other option," he says, "was punishment—what is now called counter-proliferation." Strikes against North Korea's reactors were discussed, but the Defense Department opposed any such move. "It was briefly considered, put to bed, and we developed a consensus: it is best to engage in dialogue."

The U.S. decision, most observers agree, realized a long-held DPRK goal: it gave the North the legitimacy of negotiating with the world's remaining super-power. South Korea, which the North was anxious to marginalize, would not be a party to the negotiation. Nor would the IAEA, potentially allowing Pyongyang to extend the dialogue beyond the nuclear issue to economic and diplomatic concerns.

The U.S. decision remained controversial. "What the North was doing was establishing the notion of direct negotiations between the United States and North Korea, which Democratic and Republican administrations for 40 years had refused to do," says Brent Scowcroft, President Bush's national security adviser. "We just charged into it without so much as a by-your-leave." He and others considered the offer to hold talks before the DPRK fulfilled any of its obligations too conciliatory. But Robert Manning rejects what he calls the "toughness fallacy." Given U.S. military and political toughness toward the North, he says, further threats had become gratuitous and counterproductive. Moreover, Manning notes that it was after Bush's unilateral removal of tactical nuclear weapons that North Korea signed the two North-South agreements and the IAEA safeguards. The United States has made progress with the DPRK, he says, "not when we've grabbed them by the neck and smashed them into a cor-ner and kept smashing them. I can guarantee, when you do that, they will not do what you want them to."

> Was the U.S. decision to engage in talks a sound one? Did the administration have any alternative?

Robert Gallucci, assistant secretary for political military affairs, was chosen to lead the high-level talks. Gallucci had two decades of nonproliferation experience, and he was also at a suitable level to lead the negotiation—neither too high in the administration nor too low. Winston Lord, assis-tant secretary for East Asian and Pacific affairs, was ruled out as a candidate, Gallucci guesses, because his greater name recognition in Korea and his regional orientation would have "put much more of an overall political spin on this, and that's not what we were engaged to do. Initially we defined this as a narrow nuclear issue."[2] To help coordinate agencies and give Gallucci access to regional expertise, Thomas Hubbard, Winston Lord's deputy and a member of the interagency group, was named deputy negotiator. Hubbard would also be responsible for keeping Japan and South Korea informed and involved. "We agreed from the outset that this would be a trilateral venture," Hubbard says.

"We would be the only ones dealing with the North Koreans, but we would be backstopped by this trilateral group."[3]

# U.S. GOALS

Gallucci began to attend the principals' meetings devoted to North Korea. Chaired by national security adviser Anthony Lake, these meetings brought together Clinton's top national security team of Defense Secretary Les Aspin, Secretary of State Warren Christopher, Chairman of the Joint Chiefs of Staff General Colin Powell, CIA Director James Woolsey, and Deputy National Security Adviser Samuel "Sandy" Berger, as well as U.S. Ambassador to the UN Madeleine Albright and several others.

**Why did the United States define the issue agenda in this way? What are the implications?**

Fundamentally, the United States had two goals: a nonnuclear Korean Peninsula and the creation of a strong, verifiable agreement limiting proliferation of weapons of mass destruction. The principals agreed not to address questions like North Korea's regional role or the eventual reunification of the peninsula. "People wanted to treat this as an arms control nonproliferation issue," says Samore, "because we did not want to be dragged into a discussion with the North Koreans on political questions."

Views diverged on why the DPRK had threatened to withdraw from the NPT and on what North Korea hoped to get from negotiations. Gallucci believed the North Koreans were "still winging it" and reacting to unexpected international pressure. The intelligence community insisted that North Korea was stalling while it covered up or speeded up its covert nuclear weapons program. Others claimed that Pyongyang had more complex motivations. "After they saw how upset the world became, and how hard we were trying to get them back in the NPT," Wiedemann of the interagency group notes, "it perhaps occurred to them that they could use this as a bargaining chip."

Lack of solid information made it impossible to reach consensus on which view was closest to the truth. What the United States wanted North Korea to do, however, was unambiguous: a full return to NPT membership; full implementation of IAEA safeguards, including special inspections; full implementation of the North-South denuclearization agreement; and resumption of North-South dialogue. Robert Carlin says the Clinton administration accepted inclusion of North-South dialogue—a hand-me-down from previous administrations—as "part of our prehistoric policy memory. You don't even have to think about it. You get it with mother's policy milk as you're growing up."

## THE FIRST MEETING: A JOINT DECLARATION

Gallucci and his negotiating team, composed of Hubbard and the rest of the interagency working group, first met North Korea's chief negotiator, Vice Foreign Minister Kang Sok Ju, on June 2, 1993, at the U.S. mission to the UN. One participant describes the interaction as "a disaster," replete with posturing, bruised egos, and cross-cultural clashes. "Gallucci didn't like the North Koreans and they knew it," he claims. "When he talked to them, the body language was amazing. Then Kang would look at him like a Cheshire Cat just about to claw you in the face, and we'd say, 'Oh no, here it comes.' He'd light a cigarette, turn to his interpreter and say, 'What the hell kind of noise is this guy telling you?' Then our interpreter would say, 'Mr. Kang is puzzled by your remarks.'"

> Is there a ZOPA? How does each side perceive its BATNA?

Gallucci acknowledges that the initial contact was "fairly hostile" but insists that it was largely unavoidable given the history of noncommunication between the two countries and that both sides were "applying a discount factor" to the blustering.[4] "We're not dealing with Canadians here," Gallucci says. "We've got troops on the border. This is a potentially volatile situation. You want to convey a readiness to negotiate, but neither side—I'll speak for Kang too—wanted to convey any weakness, so anybody who says anything that sounds like a threat, the other one is going to jump on it with both feet."

Given the hostility and time pressure—North Korea's NPT withdrawal would become effective ten days later—tension remained high.[5] It quickly became clear that two of the three U.S. demands—IAEA special inspections and North-South talks—could not be immediately resolved. Even keeping North Korea in the NPT would be a challenge. The DPRK appeared determined not to leave the table without concessions, and the United States was equally resistant to offering anything concrete in exchange for North Korean compliance. Gallucci admits that what the United States was putting on the table was not realistic: "I knew that it wasn't a great negotiating package: If they do everything we want, we send them a box of oranges. We knew it was pretty thin and it was going to work only if these guys wanted to avoid sanctions very much."

> Note the impact of the action-forcing event.

After a marathon session ending the night before the deadline, the two sides agreed to a Joint Declaration, and North Korea suspended its withdrawal from the NPT. "We went right up to the last minute," says Samore, "but that's the way the North Koreans negotiate." The declaration, which carefully avoided any direct reference to special inspections, affirmed support for the North-South denuclearization agreement and laid out three principles: (1) assurances against the threat and use of force, including nuclear weapons; (2) peace and security in a nuclear-free Korean Peninsula, including mutual respect for each other's sovereignty and noninterference in each other's internal affairs; and (3) support for the peaceful reunification of Korea. The two sides agreed to pursue unresolved issues the following month.

Although North Korea won no substantive concessions, many observers believed that it was pleased to have issued a joint statement with the United States. The document provided a road map for how North Korea could eventually engage the United States on other issues. Carlin, who calls the joint statement "incredibly important," explains that "both sides had something to refer back to. Whenever there were difficulties—problems resolving something—each side could go back to the language of the declaration and the other side would accept it, and you could bridge some problems that way."

According to Carlin, DPRK behavior changed immediately following the signing. On the anniversary of the outbreak of the Korean War, the usual anti-American rally in Pyongyang was canceled, and editorials, previously venomous toward the United States, spoke of making peace with the past.

South Korea's behavior also changed. President Kim Young Sam complained to U.S. reporters that Gallucci's team had given away too much. The charge surprised U.S. negotiators, who had been careful to get South Korean support for all proposals put to the North.

# THE SECOND MEETING:
## WRANGLING OVER SPECIAL INSPECTIONS

Now Gallucci began pursuing special inspections of the two suspected nuclear waste sites and resumption of regular IAEA inspections.[6] "The first meeting just bought time," says Samore. "The second meeting was an effort to find a solution to the problem of how can we get the North Koreans to accept access to these sites." Increasingly, the U.S. government and the IAEA were focusing on special inspections as the key to unlocking North Korea's nuclear past. Technical experts disagreed on what could be learned from the two suspect sites, but no one questioned the political significance of the inspections. If North Korea defied the IAEA request, it would belittle the agency's authority. And if Pyongyang were caught in a lie, explains Captain Thomas Flanagan, the Joint Staff's representative to the interagency group, the job of mustering international sanctions would be much easier. "To get multilateral support," Flanagan says, "you really needed to have positive proof that they were building nuclear weapons."[7]

When the two negotiating teams convened in Geneva on July 14, the North Koreans were as unyielding on the two sites as ever.[8] "We immediately collided," recalls one U.S. team member. "Gallucci came right out and said, 'We're going to have to have special inspections,' and immediately Kang said, '*No way.*'" The key problem, according to one outside observer, was that the U.S. government had not made the hard decisions necessary to negotiate. "The Clinton administration did not have a clear idea of what it wanted to accomplish in the July meeting," he declares. "The whole thing was special inspections. Now what are we prepared to give, if anything, in order for the North Koreans to do it? We had no idea."

> How would the North Koreans have perceived their choices about whether to allow special inspections?

Before the six-day session ended, however, Kang put a surprise offer on the table. The DPRK, he said, wanted to relieve the world's concerns. Therefore, it would give up its graphite-moderated nuclear reactors if the United States would provide it with light-water reactors (LWRs), a more proliferation-resistant nuclear technology. The offer, one team member recalls, was "a total shock."[9] Carlin says the proposal signaled a major breakthrough. "As soon as Kang said it, I wrote a note saying, 'They want out of this issue,'" he says. "They were framing it in a way that allowed them to back away from the program without any blame, and without a continuation of the confrontational situation with the United States."

Other team members were not impressed. Nor were senior officials who were advising Gallucci from Washington. Critics denounced the offer as a stalling tactic. Gallucci, who counted himself among the skeptics, says, "Not many people believed the North Koreans were ready to give up their program. Also, they couldn't figure out who was going to provide light-water reactors. So while I was allowed to say . . . that we would work to help form an international effort, it was really seven times removed from any commitment to give them light-water reactors."

The July session produced only separate press releases in which, as one participant puts it, "we agreed to list each side's demands—not agree to them, but just agree to list them." North Korea had not budged on special inspections, but indicated its willingness to resume consultations with the IAEA and the South. The United States pledged to explore the introduction of LWRs. The two sides agreed to meet again in September.

> Was this an effort to create value? A trick? Why did the United States respond as it did?

Gallucci and his team left Geneva frustrated by their inability to pry open North Korea's nuclear program. Ever-present in the minds of Gallucci and the other nonproliferationists was the stinging discovery of Iraq's unexpectedly advanced nuclear bomb program. "We were all surprised by how far along Iraq was," states Norman Wulf. "Now we had a country that's at least as bad, if not worse, in terms of erratic behavior."

The U.S. team pondered how to get North Korea to surrender access to the two suspected nuclear sites. Meanwhile, many observers speculate, North Korea pondered how to use the sites to win concessions from the United States. "My guess is that North Korea finally realized . . . that this is all they had," reasons Jon Wolfsthal, senior research analyst at the Arms Control Association. "This is the only thing the United States wanted, and therefore they had better get something good for it."[10]

## THE CONTINUITY-OF-SAFEGUARDS IMPASSE

Special inspections remained an issue, but on August 3 North Korea allowed three IAEA inspectors in for the first time since May to conduct limited "continuity-of-safeguards" inspections. It quickly became apparent that the two sides did not agree on what that meant. Hans Blix, the IAEA's director-general, had coined the phrase *continuity of safeguards* to describe inspections to guarantee that North Korea was not diverting or reprocessing any new plutonium during talks—to make sure, as Gallucci puts it, that the United States was not "losing ground." The IAEA had performed such inspections in May, but North Korea and the IAEA immediately clashed in August. "Nobody defined what was meant by continuity of safeguards, and nobody defined what was required in the inspections," declares a State Department official. "And problems began over the definition of those things." According to North Korea, continuity-of-safeguards inspections did not allow the IAEA to delve into the past, which it claimed the agency was trying to do. Pyongyang had developed what Gary Samore calls a "completely idiosyncratic legal theory" that its suspension of withdrawal from the NPT gave it a "special status" that exempted it from routine inspections.

> Note the linkages. How did the IAEA's history and institutional interests affect these negotiations?

This already contentious situation deteriorated, according to one State Department insider, after the IAEA inspectors, who complained that North Korea obstructed their investigations and forced them to work by flashlight, said they had found broken seals—placed by earlier inspectors—at the nuclear sites they visited. The entire episode, the State Department official insists, was misunderstood and exaggerated: only one seal was broken, quite likely by accident, and the flashlights were made necessary by power failures. The incident got major play in the press, he says, because it fit the agendas of the IAEA and the intelligence community. "There was a conviction, located primarily out at CIA," he says, "that the State Department had gone soft in its head and was beginning to trust the North Koreans."

Because North Korea had not made progress with either the IAEA or South Korea, Hubbard, Samore, and Quinones began meeting weekly with a North Korean ambassador to the UN to find a way to get the two sides back to the negotiating table.

Over the next few months, the continuity-of-safeguards debate degenerated in ways Gallucci calls "intellectually as well as politically sloppy." The IAEA and North Korea continued to disagree over what continuity-of-safeguards inspections should entail. The United States and the agency set deadlines for North Korea to allow inspections or face further UN Security Council action, but they failed to drum up a firm UN response. In what became a kind of IAEA mantra, Blix began to warn that continuity of safeguards was in imminent danger of being broken.

Blix's warnings alarmed the United States on two counts. As time passed and the safeguards never actually "broke," some observers questioned the legitimacy of the warning and claimed that the U.S. government was pressuring Blix to back down.[11] Worse, from the U.S. standpoint, was the danger that Blix actually *would* declare continuity broken, sending the matter back to the Security Council and calling a halt to talks. Blix received a clear message that this would be undesirable when he visited Asia in October. "What Blix hears out in the region from the South Koreans and the Japanese is basically 'be quiet,'" one observer recounts. "'We don't give a fig about whether safeguards are about to be broken. We're concerned about having a war, and we don't want to push the North Koreans over the edge.'"

Senior administration officials regularly briefed Congress. But with no new negotiation in sight, Gallucci was spending only about 20 percent of his time on North Korea. "As the assistant secretary of political military, he was stretched very thin," notes one State Department insider. Moreover, the Korean conflict paled next to other foreign entanglements. Disagreement over how to respond to North Korea's intransigence, and confusion over what its regime really wanted, continued to complicate formulation of U.S. policy. Uncertainty over whether any U.S. offer could entice North Korea back under the NPT umbrella lent a sense of futility to the interagency group's deliberations.

## THE "BROAD AND THOROUGH" APPROACH

North Korea's motives and desires remained opaque, but Gallucci continued to mull over Kang's offer to trade gas graphite reactors for light-water technology. In October, a U.S. congressman returned from Pyongyang with a North Korean proposal repeating the desire to switch to LWRs. Faced with the possibility that this was a serious offer, the interagency group began considering shifting U.S. goals to complete dismantlement of North Korea's existing nuclear program. "We began to explore a package that was larger and more comprehensive," says Gallucci, "where they would have to do more and we were willing to do more."

By late November, anxious for a breakthrough before Blix declared the continuity of safeguards broken, the Clinton administration agreed on a new effort to engage North Korea. The so-called comprehensive package approach, announced just prior to a Washington visit by South Korean president Kim Young Sam, was a process realignment designed to help lure North Korea back to the table. Instead of negotiating a step at a time, both sides would lay all their demands and offers on the table at once—a method that could give North Korea more incentive to cooperate.

President Kim was to spend fifteen minutes with Clinton giving his approval to the new negotiating approach. But Kim, facing political difficulties in Seoul, had had a change of heart. The meeting ran well over an hour, during which a "clearly agitated" Kim berated Clinton over the new policy. "Some of the press in his country had interpreted the term 'comprehensive approach' as a decision on the part of the United States to cut a bilateral deal with North Korea, totally excluding the ROK and normalizing relations with North Korea," explains Kent Wiedemann of the NSC, who was present. "For Kim Young Sam, it was seen as a challenge to the dignity of South Korea, a derogation from our alliance commitments, and a slap at him personally."

> This is an example of a pernicious reciprocal linkage between U.S.-DPRK and U.S.-ROK negotiations. Why did Kim behave this way?

National security adviser Lake, also present at the Oval Office meeting, quickly proposed a new name—the *broad and thorough approach*—although the fundamental concept stayed the same. The United States also redoubled its efforts to "keep the ROK's comfort level high," according to Wiedemann, and promised to continue to insist on North-South talks as a precondition for further U.S. negotiation. Senior officials briefed the press on the new broad and thorough approach, but their vague responses to reporters' questions made it clear that they did not know what they would be willing to put on the table. "The exact content of the broad and thorough approach—what precisely we'd do on what time scale and so forth—was not agreed," admits Wiedemann.

According to government insiders, the biggest sticking point was Team Spirit. The State Department wanted to use the annual U.S.-ROK war games again as a bargaining tool. The military exercise was abhorrent to North Korea, asserts Robert Carlin, and Kang would view its cancellation as an important concession. Moreover, the growing technological sophistication of the military had reduced Team Spirit's utility. But the Joint Chiefs of Staff and General Gary

Luck, the commander in chief of U.S. forces in South Korea, adamantly opposed sacrificing Team Spirit to the nuclear negotiations.[12]

# CONFLICT WITHIN THE U.S. TEAM

The U.S. government was divided over fundamental objectives. Thomas Hubbard recalls that the interagency debate had hardened into distinct schools of thought: one considered the integrity of the IAEA paramount; a second was intent on shutting down the nuclear effort in North Korea; a third asserted that the focus should be peace and security on the Korean Peninsula. A fourth school of thought, prevalent in the intelligence community, held that, in Hubbard's words, "it doesn't matter what you do—all negotiation is futile because you can't trust the bastards."

Even the intelligence agencies were divided on North Korea. The Central Intelligence Agency (CIA) and the Defense Intelligence Agency (DIA), the Joint Staff's intelligence agency, argued the most pessimistic assessment, and the State Department's Intelligence and Research Bureau promoted a more moderate view. "There was a range of views across the intelligence community that made it difficult to find a middle ground," recalls Robert Suettinger of the National Intelligence Council. "The absence of hard data—other than what we could see from satellite photographs—made it quite difficult to assess exactly what we were dealing with in terms of capabilities, and certainly gave us no idea whatever of what we were dealing with by way of intentions."

> Internal differences within the U.S. team complicated efforts to negotiate externally.

The intelligence community debate boiled over at the end of the year. President Clinton had declared in early November that "North Korea cannot be allowed to develop a nuclear bomb." But in December, the CIA, criticized after the Gulf War for failing to discern Iraq's true nuclear capabilities, asserted that North Korea already had a "better than even" chance of possessing one or two nuclear bombs. It was an assessment Gallucci had dreaded, giving hard-liners additional evidence of the need for prompt and decisive action. Although many Korea experts were skeptical, the CIA's assertion became part of the conventional wisdom parroted by politicians, reporters, and critics alike. "The CIA felt compelled to stand up about every other month and say, 'We think they might have a bomb,'" laughs Robert Manning, who believes the claim was made without sufficient evidence. "Intelligence is often used against policy. These guys are paid to give their worst-case assessment, and they gave it."

On December 2, Hans Blix told the IAEA board of governors that North Korea's safeguard system "cannot be said at present to provide any meaningful assurance of peaceful use of the DPRK's declared nuclear installations and materials." Blix's statement, the closest he had come to declaring safeguards broken, fueled suspicions that Clinton and his team were mishandling the North Korean conflict.

# ESCALATION

The new year, 1994, began inauspiciously. An agreement announced in early January, designed to get international inspectors back into North Korea, got the U.S. government in trouble for appearing to allow a one-time-only inspection of DPRK nuclear facilities and then quickly fell

**What factors contributed to escalation of the conflict?**

apart. Thomas Hubbard had held numerous meetings to convince North Korea to resume North-South talks and allow IAEA inspections. But as the standoff lengthened, pressure on the United States was building in several quarters. Against administration wishes, the Senate adopted a resolution demanding preparations for reintroducing nuclear weapons into South Korea. General Luck had already quietly requested Patriot air defense missiles to increase U.S.-ROK readiness. China, perhaps alarmed by these preparations, was reportedly urging DPRK compliance from behind the scenes.[13] And there was speculation that the IAEA was about to refer the conflict again to the Security Council.

Perhaps unnerved by these moves, the DPRK proposed a way to end the deadlock. "In retrospect," Hubbard says, "it was an agreement that probably had too many moving parts to succeed," but the February 25 deal was the biggest breakthrough since the previous summer. On March 1, a date Hubbard's team laughingly referred to as "Super Tuesday," four steps were to occur simultaneously: (1) IAEA inspectors were to reenter North Korea and begin inspections, (2) North and South were to meet to set a date for an exchange of envoys, (3) the ROK was to cancel Team Spirit '94, and (4) the United States and North Korea were to announce a date for the third round of high-level negotiations.[14] "Super Tuesday was a way of doing everything simultaneously and getting away from the step-by-step way we had used up until then," explains Hubbard. According to Robert Carlin of the State Department, it also gave North Korea for the first time in the negotiations the international diplomatic status it had long sought.

Super Tuesday appeared workable at first. The United States and the DPRK scheduled their next round of negotiations for March 21, and the IAEA reinstated inspections. But one piece of the package was still out of alignment. "While the IAEA wheel was spinning," Carlin explains, "you had the North-South wheel spinning at a different rate." Alarmed by the apparently improving U.S.–North Korean relationship, Seoul hardened its position again. If the U.S.-DPRK negotiations were to continue, the ROK insisted, North Korea's envoy would have to come to Seoul first, in essence bowing before Kim Young Sam's government. In response, North Korea dug in its heels and "did the worst possible thing," Carlin says: it disrupted the IAEA's final inspections.

Carlin believes that North Korea intended the suspension of inspections to be temporary. But on March 15, Hans Blix called his inspectors home. The impasse worsened four days later when the DPRK delegate to the North-South talks stormed out of a deadlocked meeting declaring that Seoul would be "a sea of fire." Even more alarming were North Korea's increasingly frequent threats that, for "technical" reasons, it would soon dump the core from its 5-MW reactor. The spent fuel would give the DPRK enough material to build four or five nuclear bombs.

On March 21, events took an ominous turn for Pyongyang. The IAEA board of governors declared North Korea in "further noncompliance" with its safeguards agreement and sent the matter to the UN Security Council. The United States canceled the third round of talks, and President Clinton publicly announced a decision many had been expecting: deployment of Patriot missiles to South Korea and the planned resumption of Team Spirit later that year. "The United States has responded to every broken promise, every lie, every threat, with the groundless optimism that tomorrow will be a better day," Senator John McCain, a frequent critic of Clinton's foreign policy, told the *New York Times.* "It is time for North Korea to overcome our concerns or live with the consequences—consequences that will hasten the collapse of that despicable regime."[15]

# REAPPRAISAL OF U.S. NEGOTIATING STRATEGIES AND POLICY

Against this backdrop, administration officials continued to hammer out and refine various negotiating strategies. Meanwhile, Robert Gallucci, who watched the heightening tension with real concern, looked for a wedge to reopen talks. "I've worked a lot of funny issues, and this is the one that not only did, but still does, have the largest potential to go bad in the worst sort of way," he says. "If the North Koreans didn't deal, and thumbed their nose at the IAEA, and dumped the reactor core, reprocessed, separated plutonium, I had a hard time seeing us walking away."

An administration official had recently testified before the Senate Subcommittee on East Asian and Pacific Affairs that special inspections of the

> Analysis of North Korean interests and BATNAs led to shifts in the U.S. position and removal of a toxic issue.

suspected waste sites would remain "the highest priority" in a third round of negotiations. But in hopes of reengaging North Korea, the administration began to redefine this fundamental tactical stance. "We finally came to recognize that, from the North Korean perspective, it's in their interest to maintain an ambiguity about the whole thing," explains Kent Wiedemann. Captain Thomas Flanagan, who was drafting a paper to convince the Joint Staff to drop special inspections as a precondition, argues that inspections were a "no-win situation" for the North. If the IAEA learned that the DPRK had diverted plutonium, the United States would rally the international community to impose sanctions. But if the IAEA discovered no diversion and no bomb program, the likely U.S. response would be to "take North Korea off the screen" and turn to more pressing concerns.

On March 28 Secretary of Defense William Perry, newly appointed to replace Aspin, acknowledged the evolving U.S. position by declaring that the emphasis of U.S. efforts should be on preventing North Korea's acquisition of new nuclear weapons rather than stripping it of any it already had. But this olive branch was not enough to reverse the downward spiral. Three days later, the UN Security Council urged North Korea to honor its NPT commitments and allow inspections. The following day, North Korea shut down its 5-MW reactor and informed the IAEA that it planned to pull the core beginning May 4. Two days later, Secretary Perry countered by refusing to rule out a preemptive military strike against the North if its nuclear program advanced.

This deterioration of relations was too much for South Korea. On April 15, the ROK dropped the exchange of envoys with North Korea as a precondition for continuation of U.S.-DPRK talks. "The South Koreans recognized that they were turning out to be, in a sense, the bad guys here by insisting on a political step that the North take before the United States would settle this nuclear issue," Gallucci says. "That was not a position the South Korean government wanted to be in." Adds Hubbard: "The direct linkage between our willingness to talk to North Korea and the willingness of the two Koreas to talk to each other was a deadly formula."

**Delinking negotiations changed the structure in favorable ways.**

In fact, Carlin says, it had become evident that the policy's architecture was fundamentally flawed. "It was a policy composed of three equal parts—that is, our negotiations with North Korea, the IAEA's negotiations with North Korea, and South Korea's negotiations with North Korea," he explains. "The idea was that all three of these had to be working and moving ahead more or less equally. Conceptually, movement on any one would help lift the other two. The problem was, it worked the other way around. When one of them didn't work, the other two couldn't move. And if you think about it, it's inevitable that one of them wouldn't be working at a given moment in time because each one of them was so complex."

The lifting of the South Korean condition was "an enormous shift" for the United States, Gallucci recalls; it cut one of the strands that had repeatedly entangled the process. But the sudden change did not help the Clinton administration, already struggling to portray its negotiating stance as reasoned, consistent, and strong. "We wanted to drop it properly, because we had been making it very clear there will be no talks unless there's an exchange of envoys," Gallucci says. "We had been saying that publicly over and over. All of a sudden, the South Koreans were saying, 'Well, that's okay.'" The reversal left Gallucci facing reporters' demands to know why a formerly essential condition had suddenly become dispensable. He adds, "What the press gets you on—and the press is important, because that's the public support for policy—is lack of consistency."

The Patriot missiles arrived in South Korea on April 18, and three days later Perry announced that the Team Spirit exercises had been rescheduled yet again, for November.

## ACHIEVING UNITY OF PURPOSE

Since early spring, there had been calls for the Clinton administration to appoint a senior coordinator dedicated exclusively to the Korean conflict. "The question was being asked, 'Who's in charge of North Korea?'" recalls Gallucci. "Well, the most senior person devoted full time to it was the deputy office director, and that's not good enough." Now Secretary of State Warren Christopher asked Gallucci to be senior coordinator. Gallucci retained his title as assistant secretary for political military but concentrated on North Korea full time.

> This effort to bring more focus to the situation helped move the United States out of its reactive posture.

Gallucci immediately requested past memos outlining the structure of special authorities. His favorite was one by Winston Lord setting up a senior steering group on China. It made Lord chair of an under-secretary-level interagency group, which was unusual for an assistant secretary. Gallucci successfully pressed for the same thing. He also asked for and got responsibility for coordinating with the press and Congress. Gallucci was thus, as he put it, "able to exert substantial control over policy formulation, negotiation and retailing."

On April 28, Hubbard and his negotiating team made an abortive attempt to reengage the North Koreans, reportedly offering a deal similar to that of Super

Why did the DPRK make this decision? How did it influence the United States' perceptions of its interests?

Tuesday, with the added provision that the IAEA monitor removal of the fuel core. But North Korea refused to accept IAEA terms for monitoring the defueling, claiming once again that the agency was trying to pry into the past instead of simply maintaining safeguards. On May 12, North Korea announced that it would begin removing the spent fuel rods shortly, and it did so two days later. The IAEA, for its part, continued to press North Korea to put aside a portion of the rods from certain locations in the reactor for future inspection.

## THE SITUATION DETERIORATES

For Gallucci, the fuel rod removal was deeply discouraging. The North Korean move defied and belittled recent U.S. efforts to soften its position and find a negotiating stance both sides could accept. The unloading also threatened to destroy the last opportunity to learn the truth about the regime's past nuclear activities. International sanctions now appeared unavoidable, threatening regional stability. And such a confrontational step on the North's part raised the possibility that the intelligence community had been right all along: the DPRK had been toying with U.S. negotiators and would never give up its bomb program without a fight.

Although the IAEA had not gotten DPRK consent to take samples during the defueling, inspectors had arrived in mid-May to watch the process from a distance. But on May 27, Hans Blix, noting that North Korea had begun unloading the spent rods at an alarming and unprecedented rate, warned that within days, the IAEA would not be able to account for all the nuclear material. The next day, the agency pulled all but two of its inspectors and declared that its efforts to monitor the program had failed.

With the IAEA essentially out of North Korea, few options remained to the United States and the international community. Again, the Defense Department briefly debated the pros and cons of a strike against North Korea's nuclear reactor. But the consequences of a military action against the North, including the likely devastation of Seoul, quickly led Defense Secretary Perry to reject any such move. Secretary of State Christopher asked the Chinese foreign minister to use whatever influence he could with Pyongyang. On May 30, the five permanent members of the Security Council, including Russia and China, made a final appeal to North Korea not to destroy all evidence of its nuclear program.

On June 2, Blix reported to the UN secretary-general that the IAEA could no longer conduct meaningful measurements and that its "ability to ascertain, with sufficient confidence, whether nuclear material from the reactor had been diverted in the past has . . . been lost." The same day, the Clinton administration finally called for international economic sanctions against North Korea, declaring that no grounds existed for a third round of meetings. The U.S. ambassador to the UN, Madeleine Albright, met with the permanent five members of the Security Council to discuss a sanctions resolution. The DPRK, for its part, retorted that "sanctions mean outright war."

## THE PUSH FOR SANCTIONS

The long-avoided move to sanctions posed daunting challenges for the United States. The first was to craft a resolution that would send North Korea a powerful message without further alienating or provoking the regime. "We weren't going to sanctions to bring these guys to their knees, because sanctions can't do that," Gallucci observes. "We were going to sanctions to drive them back to the negotiating table." The resolution would also have to win the approval of China, which had opposed sanctions throughout the conflict, or risk its veto. Relations between Washington and Beijing had recently improved when Clinton renewed China's most-favored-nation (MFN) status without attaching human rights conditions. After awarding the MFN status, in fact, the president had noted China's potential usefulness in mediating the North Korean conflict.[16] Nevertheless, the administration knew it would take a careful touch to keep China on board.

> Note the U.S. effort to shape the DPRK's perception of its BATNA. Was this a good idea?

Constrained by these pressures, Ambassador Albright began negotiating a resolution that Wiedemann describes as "mostly symbolic." The first phase, to begin in September, would suspend scientific and cultural exchanges, halt UN technical assistance (worth about $15 million over five years), and, most significant, impose a mandatory arms embargo and UN inspection of cargo flights to and from North Korea. If the North did not respond, the United States envisioned a second phase with more teeth, probably including a cutoff of remittances from Japan and an oil embargo that would depend on Chinese cooperation.

Albright warned that it could be weeks before a resolution was put to a vote. The United States had numerous hurdles to overcome besides China's reluctance to participate. Administration officials remained convinced that they could win a sanctions resolution, but critics pointed out the lack of international enthusiasm for the U.S.-led approach. Russia, grumbling that it had not been sufficiently consulted, called for an international conference to mediate the standoff. South Korea continued to run hot and cold, condemning the North's actions but fearing the consequences of a hard stand. And Japan was also vacillating in its support for a regional embargo, particularly after North Korea threatened direct retribution if it took part. "The whole interaction in the UN . . . would have persuaded Pyongyang that the international community's heart—to say nothing of its stomach—was not in tough sanctions, much less stronger measures," asserts one former Bush administration official.

As the "sanctions machine," as Gallucci called it, rolled forward, the Department of Defense prepared for the North Korean assault that some observers thought a resolution might precipitate. The United States took seriously North Korea's threat to consider sanctions an act of war, and most analysts believed the North capable of launching a large-scale offensive within forty-eight hours of deciding to do so. Although it tried not to draw undue attention to the military buildup, the Clinton administration began to position U.S. forces for a possible attack, replacing Cobra helicopters with superior Apache attack helicopters and moving in more Bradley Fighting Vehicles.[17]

## DOMESTIC COMPLICATIONS

In Washington, meanwhile, the sanctions effort, the military buildup, and the growing threat of war had finally made North Korea front-page news. Critics interpreted the disturbing turn of events as proof that the Clinton administration had clung too long to an accommodating stance. Commentator George Will noted caustically that "the Clinton Administration, with a learning curve as flat as Kansas, cannot wrap its mind around the thought that Kim Il Sung does not aspire to domesticity within the 'community of nations.' He has different dreams and aspirations."[18]

Far more attention-getting was a June 15 op-ed piece by Brent Scowcroft and Arnold Kanter advocating a military strike against the North's reprocessing facilities if it did not allow full IAEA monitoring. "Pyongyang must be made to understand that if war is unavoidable, we would rather fight it sooner than later, when North Korea might have a sizable nuclear arsenal," the piece concluded. "Likewise, it must understand that if war comes, it will result in the total defeat of North Korea and the demise of the Kim Il Sung regime. The stakes could hardly be higher. The time for temporizing is over."[19]

Did Scowcroft and Kanter's article help or hurt Gallucci's efforts to negotiate an agreement? Why would they publicly advocate for a military strike at this time?

Within the Department of Defense, war remained a grim last-ditch alternative. "The military understands the consequences of going into a conflict: lots of people get killed," Captain Flanagan states bluntly. "The American public does not have a full understanding of that, and Desert Storm has created a great delusion in the minds of Americans that we can have these sanitized wars where we don't lose anybody." Adds Gallucci, "This was not going to be the Gulf War redone. General Luck used to say, 'I can win this for you, but not right away.'"

To make sure that President Clinton understood both the human and the monetary costs of a war, the Joint Staff had summoned all regional commanders and four-star generals to Washington in late May to brief the president. Flanagan recalls the session as extremely sobering. According to General Luck's estimates, as many as 100,000 American soldiers would die in a new Korean war, and Korean troop casualties could reach the hundreds of thousands. If the North struck Seoul, according to Flanagan, "the number of civilian casualties would be staggering." The cost of such a war could top $1 trillion, Luck predicted, far higher than the almost $60 billion spent on Desert Storm.

Meanwhile, the anxiety in Seoul was palpable. "The Korean stock market went down 25 percent in two days," recalls Ambassador to Korea Gregg. "We had shipped Patriot missiles in. We were moving other weaponry in, and we were activating our infrastructure so that we could move troops. There were some people in the military structure who really felt we were headed for war."

At a White House meeting of Clinton, Gore, Christopher, and Gallucci on June 16, Defense Secretary Perry and General Luck laid out a plan to send more than ten thousand new troops to South Korea. Perry hoped that reinforcements would pressure the North and strengthen the U.S. position if military action became inevitable. The risk, Gallucci and others realized, was that the arrival of so many new U.S. troops could push the DPRK over the brink. But a better alternative for avoiding war did not appear to exist.

CHAPTER FOUR

# Identifying Barriers to Agreement

The next diagnostic task is to identify barriers to agreement.[1] The kinds of negotiations we are exploring are extraordinary difficult; that is why break-throughs are necessary. So it is essential to understand clearly what you are up against.

Sometimes negotiations fail for good reasons: there simply is not a zone of possible agreement, and the negotiators are better off going with their best alternatives. Often, however, negotiations fail when mutually beneficial agreements were possible. The consequences of failure may be mild: a deal is not consummated that could have been done. In other cases, lives are lost, valuable resources are irretrievably destroyed, or relationships are damaged beyond repair, all because the negotiators were not able to overcome barriers to agreement.

This chapter offers guidelines for diagnosing five key types of barriers to negotiated agreement:[2]

- *Structural barriers*—impediments that arise because of the way the negotiation is structured, that is, who participates, what the issues are, and what linkages exist with other negotiations. The wrong people (or too many people) may be negotiating, or the agenda may be too narrow or too broad, or communication channels may be nonexistent.

- *Strategic barriers*—pernicious interactions among negotiators' rational strategies for advancing their interests. For example, negotiators' mutual fears of vulnerability if they reveal their true interests may lead to break-downs or mediocre deals.

- *Psychological barriers*—biases in negotiators' perceptions and judgments. For example, negotiators faced with an uncertain outcome if they do not reach agreement (such as litigating a personal injury lawsuit) may be overly confident about their chances of winning, or those enmeshed in bitter conflicts may vilify and depersonalize "the enemy."

- *Institutional barriers*—internal political and organizational dynamics within institutions that complicate negotiations between them. For example, a negotiating representative may be constrained by internal political differences to offer only lowest-common-denominator positions, or one side may be so disorganized that it cannot negotiate effectively.

- *Cultural barriers*—differences in communication styles, norms, and worldviews, as well as ethnocentrism. For example, negotiations may be complicated by differing beliefs about what will create value or who should legitimately make decisions.

Barriers of these types arise in a wide array of negotiations. By carefully diagnosing them, you can develop strategies to overcome them—or to avoid creating them in the first place.

Distinctions among these five categories of barriers are not completely clear-cut, and the various types of barriers interact and reinforce each other. Poor channels of communication (a structural barrier) can increase the perceived riskiness of revealing information to counterparts (a strategic barrier), which can contribute to suspicion and stereotyping of the other side (a psychological barrier). We will trace the mutually reinforcing nature of barriers to agreement throughout this chapter.

## STRUCTURAL BARRIERS

The structure of your negotiations can prevent you from advancing your interests. Have blocking coalitions formed to oppose agreement? Are poor communication channels contributing to misunderstandings? Any of the dimensions of negotiation structure discussed in Chapter Two—the parties, agenda of issues, interests, BATNAs, agreements, linkages, and action-forcing events—can give rise to barriers to agreement.[3] As Table 4.1 illustrates, it is often possible to overcome structural barriers by reshaping the structure.

The most serious structural impediments to productive negotiations between the United States and North Korea were linked negotiations. The triangular linked negotiations among North Korea, South Korea, and the United States

Table 4.1. Structural Barriers.

| Structural Barriers | Approaches to Overcoming |
| --- | --- |
| The wrong parties are at the table. | Invite in allies and attempt to exclude adversaries. |
| Too many parties are at the table. | Reduce the number of parties by convincing some to be represented by others. |
| Blocking coalitions have formed. | Seek to co-opt the weakest links. |
| The parties lack good channels of communication. | Develop new channels for communication, perhaps by using third-party mediators or facilitators. |
| The agenda is too narrow or too broad. | Broaden or narrow the issue agenda. |
| The sequence in which issues get negotiated is disadvantageous. | Alter the sequence in which issues get negotiated. |
| Parties are locked into incompatible positions. | Focus on interests, and identify opportunities to enlarge the pie. |
| No zone of potential agreement seems to exist. | Take action away from the table to transform alternatives to agreement. |
| Linkages with other negotiations—past, present, or future—cause binding constraints. | Seek to delink negotiations to create more flexibility, or create new linkages of your own to tap into latent sources of power. |
| Action-forcing events such as deadlines limit flexibility. | Explore ways to relax action-forcing events. |
| There is no time pressure to reach agreement. | Set up action-forcing events. |

($T_1$ in Figure 4.1) were particularly problematic. South Korean factions that opposed accommodation with the North disrupted the negotiations by conveniently "discovering" a spy ring and threatening resumption of the Team Spirit war games if North-South dialogue were not resumed. South Korea also pressed the United States to insist on progress in North-South dialogue as a precondition for talks. The resulting linkage between U.S. willingness to talk to North Korea and the willingness of the two Koreas to negotiate was a serious impediment to progress.

A second set of linked negotiations among the United States, the International Atomic Energy Agency (IAEA), and North Korea ($T_2$ in Figure 4.1) also created dif-

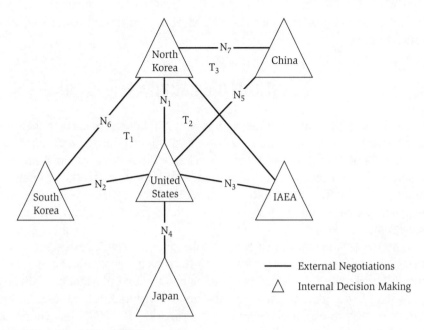

**Figure 4.1.** Linked Negotiations.

ficulties. Contention between North Korea and the IAEA tended to spill over and undermine U.S. efforts to engage the North Koreans. The United States and the IAEA were nominal allies, but they had substantially different interests. The IAEA focused on the nonproliferation treaty and was less concerned about overall regional security. It wanted to bolster its institutional credibility in the aftermath of its failure to restrain Iraq from building nuclear weapons. The IAEA was also responding to pressures from European nations anxious to protect the integrity of the NPT. Meanwhile, the North Koreans suspected that the IAEA was functioning as a puppet of the United States, suspicions fueled by the agency's use of U.S. satellite intelligence.

In a third set of linked negotiations ($T_3$ in Figure 4.1), the United States competed with North Korea for the support of China. China occupied a pivotal position as the sole remaining international influence on North Korea and as a permanent member of the UN Security Council; the Chinese could prevent imposition of UN economic sanctions. Successfully wooing the Chinese away from their traditional ally would have given the United States, in combination with its alliances with South Korea, Japan, and the IAEA, a winning coalition for imposing sanctions. But U.S. efforts to gain Chinese support were complicated by another linkage: U.S.-Chinese relations had been severely strained by the 1989 crackdown on prodemocracy protesters in Tiananmen Square and by U.S. efforts to link renewal of China's MFN trading status to improvements in human rights.

# STRATEGIC BARRIERS

Strategic barriers arise when negotiators' rational efforts to advance their interests interact in pernicious ways.[4] Barriers of this type flourish when uncertainty prevails about the size (or even the existence) of the zone of possible agreement, when the parties feel vulnerable and uncertain about each other's intentions, and when communication between the sides is poor. In such circumstances, negotiators make rational strategic choices that nevertheless lead to impasse or suboptimal agreements.

Consider U.S. demands that North Korea submit to special inspections of suspected waste sites. How might the North Koreans have perceived their alternatives? If they had said yes and inspections had turned up evidence of diversion of nuclear materials, the United States would have had the smoking gun necessary to rally international support for sanctions. But if the inspections had turned up nothing, U.S. alarm about North Korean nuclear weapons would have declined and North Korea would have lost bargaining leverage. Neither outcome was desirable from the North Korean point of view.

By refusing to permit inspections, North Korea preserved strategic ambiguity about its weapons program and denied the United States the evidence it needed to pursue sanctions. The North Koreans could even use U.S. threats as a tool to bolster internal cohesion and discipline. Only toward the end of the negotiations did the Clinton administration really, as Ury put it, "step to the other side" and look at the problem from the North Korean point of view. This kind of assessment, which Roger Fisher calls "currently-perceived-choice analysis," is illustrated in the form of a decision tree in Figure 4.2.[5]

## The Negotiator's Dilemma

As Lax and Sebenius have noted, negotiators confront the *negotiator's dilemma* whenever their efforts to create joint value are vulnerable to individual actions to claim value.[6] Each side faces a choice: Do I reveal what I really care about to my counterpart? If both negotiators do so, they can make a mutually beneficial trade that enlarges the pie. If one is candid and the other misleads, the trade gets made, but on terms that strongly favor the untruthful negotiator. If neither is candid, the trade may not get made at all. Asymmetries in information and mutual vulnerability once again drive out the potential for beneficial cooperation. The negotiator's dilemma is illustrated in Table 4.2.

The negotiator's dilemma is a variation on a more general social tension between cooperation and conflict known as the *prisoner's dilemma.*[7] In the clas-

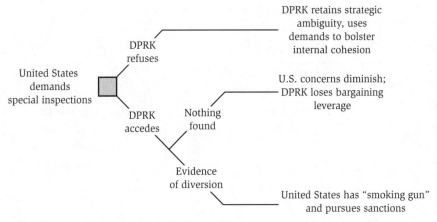

**Figure 4.2.** Currently Perceived Choice Analysis.

sic formulation, two felons jointly commit a crime and are captured. After capture, they are separated, and each is offered a deal: "If you confess and your partner doesn't, you will get two years in prison and your partner will get seven. If you both confess, you both get five years." If both refuse to confess, they will probably end up with three years each. But each fears the other will confess, so both confess and both get five years: a lose-lose outcome.

The prisoner's dilemma is illustrated in Table 4.3. If both parties cooperate with each other (they do not confess), then modest gains can be achieved (or, in this case, losses prevented). But the risks inherent in cooperating when the other side may not do so are very high. Paradoxically, whatever the other side does in this situation, you are better off if you choose to defect and confess. The problem, of course, is that the other player has the same options. So both defect and both do worse than they could have by cooperating.

Prisoner's dilemma–like situations arise frequently in conflicts. Even if all parties believe it to be in their best interests to negotiate a settlement, they may

Table 4.2. The Negotiator's Dilemma.

| | | Them | |
|---|---|---|---|
| | | *Be truthful about interests* | *Seek to mislead* |
| Us | *Be truthful about interests* | We make modest gains, and so do they. | We gain a little, and they gain a lot. |
| | *Seek to mislead* | We gain a lot, and they gain a little. | We get nothing, and so do they. |

Table 4.3. The Prisoner's Dilemma.

|  |  | Them | |
| --- | --- | --- | --- |
|  |  | *Cooperate* | *Defect* |
| Us | *Cooperate* | We make modest gains, and so do they. | We gain nothing, and they gain a lot. |
|  | *Defect* | We gain a lot, and they gain nothing. | Both sides fare worse than if both had cooperated, but better than if they had cooperated while the other side had not. |

be unable to do so. Negotiators for contending parties such as the United States and the DPRK often face a core choice: Should we risk making ourselves vulnerable or not? Suppose two countries are on the brink of war and are negotiating to avoid it. Each fears the other will launch a devastating first strike. Because each is uncertain about the other's intentions and both are vulnerable, the incentives to attack preemptively are very high.

Prisoner's dilemmas also arise in situations that are not overt conflicts, ranging from organizational incentive systems that promote internal competition to efforts by the Organization of Petroleum Exporting Countries to prevent its members from overproducing and undermining the oil cartel. If the players are engaged in an ongoing game, the threat of future contention and the desire to maintain relationships may promote a cooperative outcome.[8] But if the game is of limited duration, players may begin to defect as the end approaches, a phenomenon known as the *end-game effect*. Anticipating that their relationship will end, parties seek to claim value from others, and cooperation breaks down.

## Insecure Agreements

Some agreements are inherently more sustainable or secure than others.[9] Leaving the fox in charge of the hen house is inadvisable, even if you have an agreement that he will care for the chickens. When negotiators believe that others have incentives to abrogate or renegotiate agreements, this belief can create a strategic barrier to agreement. Suspicions about the sustainability of agreements are even more difficult to manage when there are ambiguities or uncertainties about what the future holds. This was the case in the negotiations between the United States and the North Koreans.

Worry about sustainability effectively shrinks the pie, because the parties try to hedge against risk by being conservative and even defensive. If negotiators trust each other, it may be possible to rely on goodwill to resolve ambiguities or address future contingencies. But what if you do not fully trust your counterparts?

## The Impact of Structure on Strategic Barriers

The structure of a negotiating situation can increase the likelihood that negotiators will face strategic barriers. Prisoner's dilemmas are particularly likely to cause problems in the following situations:

- *Agreements cannot easily be enforced.* If the negotiators can make binding agreements, which are enforced by law or by powerful outsiders, vulnerability is reduced.

- *The ability to verify compliance with agreements is low.* If the parties cannot perfectly observe each other's actions, lack of transparency and inability to verify compliance make them feel more vulnerable.

- *Communication channels are weak.* Inability to communicate and build relationships foments misunderstandings and perceived vulnerability.

- *Reaction time is short.* Narrow windows in which to respond to aggressive actions without suffering serious damage increase the likelihood of preemptive defensive actions, which can trigger an escalatory spiral.

- *Many parties have to cooperate.* If creating value requires the cooperation of many parties, the likelihood that one party will contend rather than cooperate rises with the number of parties.

- *There are no future interactions.* Future negotiations cannot be held hostage to cooperation in current negotiations.

Take a minute to think about which of these factors complicated negotiations between the United States and the North Koreans.

## Overcoming Strategic Barriers

How can contending parties negotiate with confidence when they are mutually vulnerable and do not trust each other? Useful techniques for fostering cooperation—or at least compliance—in the absence of trust include the following:

- *Verification regimes*—arranging to observe each other's actions as a way of reducing mutual uncertainty and increasing transparency

- *Mutual deterrence*—making credible mutual commitments to devastating retaliation in the event of noncompliance

- *Incrementalism*—proceeding in a series of small and mutually verifiable steps, making future gains contingent on meeting current obligations, and embedding current negotiations in a larger context to avoid endgame effects

- *Hostage taking*—having each side deposit resources (such as a large sum of money) into an escrow account supervised by an independent party, with the understanding that the proceeds will be forfeited for non-compliance

- *Outside guarantors*—involving powerful external parties as guarantors of the agreement with the understanding that they will punish non-compliance

# PSYCHOLOGICAL BARRIERS

Strategic barriers are often exacerbated by biases of perception and interpretation that shrink the potential for agreement.[10] Common psychological barriers include rigid mental models, overconfidence, loss aversion, partisan perceptions, and groupthink.

## Rigid Mental Models

In novel and complex situations, people orient themselves by using preexisting interpretive frameworks, or *mental models,* to decide where to direct their attention.[11] Mental models link observation to interpretation, allowing us to make sense of what we experience. They embody our beliefs about relationships between cause and effect, the intentions of others, and the lessons of history. Think of union leaders negotiating with corporate managers, or husbands negotiating with wives, or the United States negotiating with North Korea. How might these parties' mental models differ, and what implications could their differences have for their negotiations?

Without mental models, we would have to figure out every new situation from scratch. But established mental models can also promote rigidity and block learning in new situations. What happens, for example, if people consistently enter negotiations with a zero-sum mindset? The frameworks that negotiators use to interpret reality are typically so deeply embedded in their psyches that they are unaware of their biases. As a result, people block out information that is inconsistent with accepted "truths," a process known as *selective perception.* People also tend to seek evidence that confirms their assumptions.[12]

The way the United States initially defined the basic problem, and the well-established mental models that U.S. negotiators drew on in dealing with the North Koreans, clearly acted as barriers to agreement. U.S. decision makers, for example, continued to include North-South dialogue in their negotiating positions because, as one put it, it was "part of our prehistoric policy memory" and "mother's policy milk." Robert Gallucci's preoccupation with nonproliferation had been formed by many years of work on the issue and heightened by his involvement in the discovery of Iraq's unexpectedly advanced nuclear program. Their mental models enabled U.S. decision makers to make sense of a complex situation, but also led them to commit themselves to untenable positions.

## Overconfidence

Negotiators are often overly confident that future uncertainties will be resolved in their favor.[13] When both sides in a lawsuit believe they will prevail in court, for example, someone (perhaps everyone) is falling prey to overconfidence that may preclude an out-of-court settlement. Overconfidence is a manifestation of a deeper desire on the part of negotiators to feel competent and secure. Max Bazerman and Margaret Neale characterize this tendency in *Negotiating Rationally* as "need-based illusions" and "self-serving biases" that can contribute to irrational behavior. They further identify three kinds of need-based illusions: illusion of superiority, illusion of optimism, and illusion of control.[14]

## Loss Aversion

Research in cognitive psychology has revealed that people tend to be *loss averse,* or more sensitive to potential losses than to equivalent gains.[15] This built-in conservatism can magnify the impact of strategic barriers to agreement. Suppose you are asked to play the two prisoner's dilemma games shown in Table 4.4. In both games, you and your counterpart must submit simultaneous decisions about whether to cooperate or contend. You will not know what your counterpart has decided until after you make your own decision, and you cannot make binding commitments up-front. You will never see each other again. In which game would you be more likely to cooperate if the other player promised to cooperate?

The only difference between the two games is that the second involves gains and the first involves losses. But people are more likely to cooperate in the second situation. The implication is that situations that require people to allocate losses—whether they have to do with power and status or land or money—are much more difficult to manage than those in which the issue is how to divide up gains.

In conflicts, loss aversion can result in what Lee Ross and Andrew Ward call the *problem of intermediate steps.*[16] Even if the contending parties want to settle, the path to settlement may require them to accept painful short-term losses in return for larger long-term gains. In the early stages of the Oslo peace process, for example, the Israelis had to accept Arafat's return to Gaza and a handover of territory in the West Bank to the Palestinians. In the short run, this development increased the potential for terrorist attacks launched from Palestinian-controlled territory. But it was a necessary first step in moving toward a broader resolution. Because of loss aversion, the short-term downside tends to loom larger than the long-term benefits.

Table 4.4. Loss Aversion.

|  |  | Them | |
|---|---|---|---|
|  |  | *Cooperate* | *Contend* |
| You | *Cooperate* | You lose $1,000. They lose $1,000. | You lose $2,500. They lose nothing. |
|  | *Contend* | You lose nothing. They lose $2,500. | You lose $1,500. They lose $1,500. |

|  |  | Them | |
|---|---|---|---|
|  |  | *Cooperate* | *Contend* |
| You | *Cooperate* | You gain $1,500. They gain $1,500. | You get nothing. They gain $2,500. |
|  | *Contend* | You gain $2,500. They get nothing. | You gain $1,000. They gain $1,000. |

## Partisan Perceptions

The experience of conflict changes disputants' perceptions in ways that can make the conflict self-sustaining.[17] The combatants accumulate psychological residues—emotional associations and expectations that irreversibly alter their attitudes toward each other.[18] Their perceptions of the situation and of the actions of the other side are subsequently shaped by partisanship.

Given the long history of bitter conflict on the Korean Peninsula, it is not surprising that partisan perceptions acted as a powerful restraint on productive negotiations. Decision makers on each side viewed the actions of the other parties with profound suspicion. The negotiating tactics of the North Koreans had been characterized by Western observers as interminable stalling, deception, and grudging concession, a reputation that encouraged U.S. negotiators to adopt defensive tactics.[19] The North Koreans undoubtedly had corresponding negative beliefs about the United States. As a result, both sides adopted a punishment mentality, preferring sticks to carrots in ways that reinforced the vicious cycle.

The U.S. government's restrictions on communications also reinforced partisan perceptions. Since the Korean War, the United States had explicitly restricted its diplomats from engaging in direct interactions with North Korea. Many U.S. diplomats thus viewed any communication with the North Koreans as a concession, granting the North standing that it did not deserve.

Goal transformation, naive realism, and reactive devaluation are common perceptual distortions that arise in such situations.

**Goal Transformation.** Contending parties progress from simply wanting to protect themselves to wanting to hurt each other.[20] Feelings of victimization and desire for retribution and revenge sustain conflicts long after the causal factors have ceased to be important. Siblings continue to fight for parents' attention long after they are adults, and nations argue over scraps of land that no longer have strategic importance. In the case of the United States and the DPRK, the parties had become committed to destroying each other and were willing to expend a great deal of effort and incur very high costs to accomplish that goal.

**Naive Realism.** When conflicts become bitter, the contending parties begin to gather and interpret information about each other in ways that are profoundly biased, a phenomenon that Robert Robinson and his colleagues term *naive realism*.[21] According to these authors, contending parties' perceptions get distorted in three main ways. First, partisans assume that they themselves see things objectively, while their opponents' views are extreme and distorted. Second, they tend to misjudge the other side's motivations, overestimating the importance of ideology and underestimating the situational pressures their counterparts face. Third, as illustrated in Figure 4.3, partisans consistently overestimate the extent of the differences between themselves and the other side. At the same time, individual partisans tend to see themselves as more moderate than typical members of their own group—the *lone moderate* phenomenon.[22] The result is exaggeration of the actual differences between the sides, which are exacerbated by the communications breakdown that occurs when conflicts become more polarized. As a consequence, the parties experience *selective perception*— they interpret each other's actions in ways that confirm their preexisting beliefs and attitudes. They unconsciously overlook evidence that challenges their stereotypes and may also adopt a zero-sum mentality that prompts them to cast the negotiation in purely distributive terms. Finally, their behavior may contribute to *self-fulfilling prophecies*.

**Reactive Devaluation.** An especially unfortunate consequence of partisan perceptions occurs when gestures intended to be conciliatory are dismissed or ignored by the other side—a phenomenon known as *reactive devaluation*.[23] If one side believes that the other is intent on destruction, any conciliatory gesture tends to be treated as either a trick or a sign of weakness. Any other conclusion would require a fundamental reassessment of the other side. If the conciliatory overture is interpreted as a deception, the response is often counterdeception or rejection. If it is interpreted as a sign of weakness, the response may be to press forward aggressively.

The North Koreans' attempts to propose a formula for solving the conflict were met with a classic example of reactive devaluation: the tendency to treat conciliatory gestures as tricks or traps. At the first round of negotiations

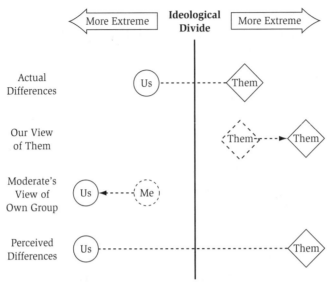

**Figure 4.3.** Naive Realism.

*Source:* Adapted from R. J. Robinson, D. Keltner, A. Ward, and L. Ross, "Actual Versus Assumed Differences in Construal: 'Naive Realism' in Inter-group Perception and Conflict," *Journal of Personality and Social Psychology* 68(1995): 404–417.

in Geneva in mid-1993, the North Koreans offered to give up their graphite-moderated reactors if the United States would provide more proliferation-resistant LWRs as replacements. This offer was denounced by U.S. critics as an elaborate stalling tactic designed to give North Korea time to pursue its nuclear weapons program.[24]

## Groupthink

When overt conflict breaks out between groups, further psychological transformations occur within both sides. Internal cohesion increases. A two-sided worldview develops in which "we" represent truth and justice, desire only security and self-respect, and respond reasonably to provocations, while "they" are dehumanized and vilified, their aggressive conduct seen as the result of flawed and even evil dispositions.

These attitudes discourage contact, and any communication is treated as a concession. The perceived need for solidarity in the face of external threats suppresses internal dissent, partly through pressure to conform but more perniciously through self-censorship. Moderate leaders get pushed aside by more radical ones. Individual inclinations toward overconfidence get magnified, and the illusion of invulnerability takes hold.

In his studies of the group decision making that led President Kennedy to approve the disastrous Bay of Pigs invasion of Cuba, Irving Janus labeled this

Table 4.5. Symptoms of Groupthink.

**Overestimation of the group**

An illusion of invulnerability, shared by most or all members, that creates excessive optimism and encourages risk taking

Unquestioned belief in the group's inherent morality, inclining members to ignore the ethical or moral consequences of their decisions

**Closed-Mindedness**

Collective rationalization to discount information that might lead members to reconsider their assumptions

Stereotyped views of the enemy as too evil to warrant genuine attempts to negotiate, or too weak and stupid to counter risky moves to defeat its purposes

**Pressures toward uniformity**

Self-censorship of deviations from the apparent group consensus

A shared illusion of unanimity

Direct pressure on members who dispute any of the group's stereotypes, illusions, or commitments

The emergence of self-appointed "mindguards"—members who protect the group from information that might disturb its complacency about the effectiveness and morality of its decisions

*Source:* Adapted from I. Janus, *Groupthink: Psychological Studies of Policy Decisions and Fiascoes* (Boston: Houghton Mifflin, 1982).

phenomenon *groupthink*.[25] Whether in disputes between pro- and antiabortion partisans, environmentalists and developers, Catholics and Protestants in Northern Ireland, or managers and union members, the effects of groupthink are everywhere to see. Its symptoms are summarized in Table 4.5.

## Overcoming Psychological Barriers

Mediation can play a useful role in overcoming psychological barriers, in part because the mediator can deal with the parties separately. Mechanisms that establish a common basis of "facts" can also help temper overconfidence. In legal disputes, for example, fact finding and mock trials provide the contending parties independent assessments of the likely outcome if the case goes to trial.

Partisan perceptions are sometimes tempered by bringing together representatives of the contending sides for extended negotiations. As we will see in Chapter Nine, this approach was employed successfully in the early stages of the Oslo peace process. It can also be productive to bring together respected people (but not official representatives) to engage in facilitated joint brainstorming exercises, as occurred in a border dispute between Ecuador and Peru in March 1995.[26]

The likelihood of groupthink in collective decision making can be reduced in the following ways:[27]

- *Legitimizing dissent*—explicitly authorizing and encouraging dissenting points of view, perhaps by appointing a devil's advocate
- *Involving outsiders*—inviting independent, relatively unbiased experts to render their opinions
- *Setting up parallel evaluation processes*—appointing competing groups to evaluate the same situation—the so-called red-team/blue-team approach
- *Establishing clear break points*—setting aside time for the group to step back and look at the big picture
- *Reality testing*—eliciting reflective evaluation of the weaknesses of one's own case, and perhaps using role plays[28]

# INSTITUTIONAL BARRIERS

In negotiations between institutions (groups, organizations, or nations), internal political and organizational factors can function as barriers to agreement.

## Internal Politics

Agreement at the negotiating table calls for a critical mass of support—a winning coalition—for the agreement within each side.[29] But as in the case of the United States and North Korea, political factions on either side may prefer no agreement. This two-level game is illustrated in Figure 4.4.

In bitter conflicts, moderates' moves toward negotiated agreement are fiercely resisted by hard-liners within both sides. Opponents of settlement allege that those in favor of negotiating are selling out. They also foment internal political turmoil that impedes compromise. Leaders thus have to work hard internally to build support for agreement while they are negotiating externally. Internal political dynamics of this kind often complicate international diplomatic negotiations. They also arise in negotiations between businesses seeking to merge, labor-management disputes, and a host of other situations.

Internal politics within the United States complicated efforts to negotiate with the DPRK. When the Bush administration first decided to talk to North Korea, for example, Arnold Kanter met with its representatives. But the administration was unable to reach an internal consensus on what to offer the North Koreans. Some saw the mere decision to talk as too conciliatory. The resulting lack of a coherent mandate made it virtually impossible for Kanter to conduct productive negotiations.

When the Clinton administration took over, internal disagreements with Congress also created barriers to agreement. Republican senators highly critical of

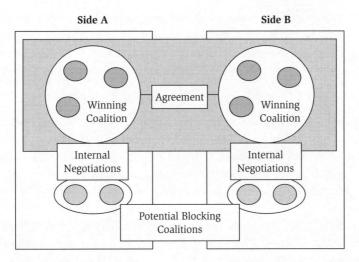

**Figure 4.4.** Two-Level Negotiations.

the administration's foreign policy record pushed through a resolution demanding preparations for the reintroduction of nuclear weapons into South Korea. The Clinton administration also opened itself to domestic criticism by committing itself early on to special inspections of suspected North Korean nuclear waste sites. When it later became evident that the North Koreans would never agree to such inspections, the administration appeared inconsistent and had difficulty justifying a change in the negotiating agenda. In dealing with North Korea, the administration was also laboring under the cloud of President Clinton's lack of military service, poor relationships with the Department of Defense, and policy setbacks in Bosnia, Haiti, and Somalia. As a result, the administration experienced pressure to engage in compensatory toughness.

Bureaucratic politics involving the intelligence agencies and the Departments of State and Defense further complicated internal decision making. By making worst-case assessments of North Korea's nuclear capabilities, for example, the intelligence agencies protected their own interests (it was better to be criticized for being overly pessimistic than too optimistic) at the cost of leaving the administration vulnerable to criticism that it was being too soft.

Paradoxically, spoilers on both sides reinforce each other's efforts to undermine negotiations.[30] Suppose, for example, that extremists on one side in a regional conflict launch a terrorist attack on the other side. The attack provokes pressure on the attacked side's moderate leaders by their internal opponents to respond aggressively. To avoid political damage, these moderate leaders demand that their counterparts on the other side crack down on the extremists who launched the attack. This demand places the other side's leaders in a terrible position: if they accede, they are seen as lackeys and lose credibility internally. If they refuse, the forces opposed to settlement are strengthened. Similarly, public calls for aggressive action by hard-liners on one side may provoke responses from hard-liners on the other side. This vicious cycle is illustrated in Figure 4.5.

## Organizational Weaknesses

An effective negotiating team must be internally organized and authorized to devote sufficient resources to the process. Representatives must come to the table ready for the hard work of hammering out an agreement, and they must have the authority to make commitments on behalf of their sides. Lack of focused attention, competing priorities, and internal disorganization all impede agreement.

Organizationally, the early responses of the Clinton administration were fragmented and reactive. The Korean situation was only one of several foreign policy issues competing for the attention of U.S. policymakers. The new administration was also facing crises in Somalia and Bosnia and seeking to fulfill its stated goal of focusing on domestic affairs. High-level attention thus quickly veered away from the Korean Peninsula during periods of relative calm, setting the stage for a vicious cycle of inattention and crisis response.

Clear lines of authority and accountability were also lacking. No single individual was responsible for coordinating the U.S. response. Too many departments, groups, and individuals were involved in signing off on responses, which slowed reaction times. In contrast, the leadership of the DPRK was highly focused and had few competing priorities. North Korea was thus able to exert disproportionate control over the pace of events by, for example, announcing its decision to withdraw from the NPT.

More fundamentally, the Clinton administration's key foreign policy people lacked the collective learning necessary to function effectively as a team. The Bush administration had managed the Gulf War and operations in Panama and Granada, resulting in solid working relationships and well-oiled decision-making routines. The Clinton administration had good people, but they had not yet had time to move up the learning curve.

## Principal-Agent Problems

Differences in interests between principals and agents are another common type of institutional barrier.[31] When agents represent principals, they may have expertise and access to information that is unavailable to those they represent, and this allows them to see the outlines of a deal more clearly and to shape perceptions. But agents may have their own interests that are not perfectly aligned with those of their principals. As a result, they may be able to use their superior expertise and access to information to advance their own interests. In situations where principals on both sides actually have substantial shared interests, principal-agent interest misalignments may act as a barrier to agreement.

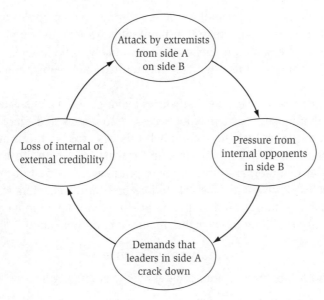

**Figure 4.5.** A Vicious Cycle.

As you read the next installment of the case, think about the role that Former President Jimmy Carter played. Was he an agent of the U.S. administration? If so, was he a good one?

### Overcoming Institutional Barriers

Aside from strong leadership and coalition-building skills, several tools are useful for overcoming political barriers. Secret diplomacy can short-circuit internal politics until an agreement can be presented as a fait accompli, with the attendant risks of further inflaming internal opposition. Multi-phase negotiation processes, typically beginning with principles and proceeding to details, can allow the internal political process to advance at a pace that can be sustained.

## CULTURAL BARRIERS

The members of a given culture tend to be ethnocentric—to see their own group's values as universal and superior to those of other groups. Ethnocentrism in turn reinforces partisan perceptions.[32] According to the anthropologist W. G. Sumner, ethnocentrism is "the view of things in which one's own group is the center of everything, and all others are scaled and rated with reference to it. Each group nourishes its own pride and vanity, boasts itself superior, exalts its own divinities, and looks with contempt on outsiders."[33] Different cultures also have distinctive patterns of communication and decision making. It is therefore important to understand the cultural filters through which one's counterparts view the world and to recognize that national culture is just one layer of the onion. Individual negotiators' behavior is also likely to be influenced by their professional training and its attendant subculture, and organizations have distinct cultures as well.

The ultimate goal is to ensure that you and your counterparts create a process of dialogue that makes sense. It is not necessary to understand every nuance of your counterparts' culture to accomplish this. As cross-cultural negotiation expert Stephen Weiss put it, you need to "at least recognize those ideas and behaviors that [counterparts] intentionally put forward as part of the negotiation process. Parties must also be able to interpret these behaviors well enough to distinguish common from conflicting positions, to detect movement from positions, and to respond in ways that maintain communication."[34]

## Analyzing Culture

A culture can be analyzed at four progressively penetrating levels:[35]

- *Artifacts,* which are the visible signs and symbols that differentiate one culture from another, including ceremonies and styles of dress.
- *Communication styles,* which include preferences for directness or indirectness, use of eye contact, and use of nonverbal communication.
- *Social norms,* which are shared rules that guide behavior, such as what constitutes an agreement (formal versus informal, relationships versus contracts) and attitudes toward time and timeliness.
- *Assumptions,* which are the deeper, often unspoken beliefs that infuse and underpin social systems. These beliefs are the air that everyone breathes but never sees. Examples include beliefs about what creates value and how decisions should be made.

Much of what shapes the behavior of members of a culture is neither explicit nor visible to outsiders, as the cultural iceberg in Figure 4.6 illustrates.

## Probing Underlying Assumptions

Understanding a culture requires getting below the surface to the underlying assumptions that its members take for granted. For negotiators, the most germane cultural assumptions are those involving power and value. In the U.S.–North Korean negotiations, the two sides embodied vastly different cultural assumptions. Politically, the conflict was a confrontation between pluralistic democracy and centralized authoritarianism. Economically, it was a clash between global free-market economics and socialist self-reliance.

The key question about power is who legitimately exercises authority and makes decisions. In some cultures, deference is paid to strength, age, or expe-

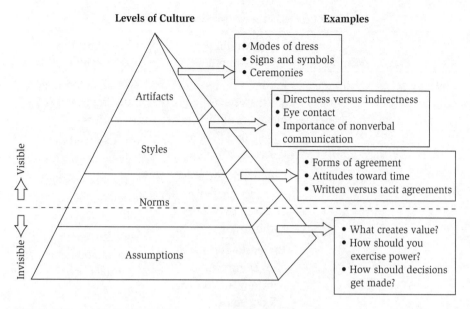

**Figure 4.6.** Analyzing Culture.

rience; in others, power is acquired through election to office or accumulation of expertise. In some cultures, negotiating representatives are given substantial flexibility and authority; in others, they are mere messengers.

Regarding value, it is useful to ask, To what does each side attribute social value? Sociologists assign cultures to two broad categories: collectivist and individualist.[36] Collectivist cultures stress group harmony and consensus more than do individualist cultures. Members of collectivist cultures exhibit greater readiness to sacrifice personal gain for the good of the whole than their more individualistic counterparts. The conflicting assumptions of North Korea and the United States about value, summarized in Table 4.6, can impede efforts to communicate and find bases for agreement.

When the two sides' assumptions about power and value differ sharply, their internal decision-making processes are likely to diverge. This difference can lead to mismatches and misunderstandings at the negotiation table. The sides may select their representatives according to very different criteria, one selecting for expertise and experience while the other stresses high social standing and connections. Some groups debate ratification of tentative agreements, while others empower a few decision makers.

Another window on cultural differences is their impact on the substance of what is negotiated and on the process through which negotiating takes place. Views may differ on what is negotiable and on the extent to which agreements

Table 4.6. Collectivist and Individualistic Cultures.

| | Example | Guiding Assumptions | Implications for Negotiation |
|---|---|---|---|
| Collectivist cultures | North Korea | Products of the culture see themselves more as members of their reference group than as individuals. | Negotiators focus more on the implications for their groups. |
| | | | Decisions tend to be made by consensus. |
| | | Legitimate power is exercised by those with seniority or positional authority. | Representatives are chosen on the basis of seniority or position. |
| | | Value is associated with communal harmony and ordered relationships. | Negotiators are more assertive and direct about their own interests. |
| Individualist cultures | United States | Products of the culture see themselves more as individuals than as members of a reference group. | Representatives are given more authority to reach agreements. |
| | | Legitimate power is acquired and exercised through democratic means. The rights of individuals are strongly defended. | Negotiators are chosen on the basis of expertise and experience. |
| | | Value is associated with individual achievement and independence. | |

are binding.[37] One culture may focus more on the issues, another on establishing relationships. In terms of process, different attitudes toward time and modes of expression (such as degree of directness) can make it difficult to communicate effectively.[38]

## Diagnosing Cultural Barriers

Negotiators should seek to predict how cultural differences are likely to affect the negotiation. The following diagnostic questions will help you probe cultural assumptions:

*Power*

- What sorts of people will be chosen to represent the other side? Will they be chosen on the basis of expertise and experience or personal connections and status?
- Will internal decisions get made by consensus or the exercise of authority?
- How important is "face"?

*Value*

- Is the culture more collectivist or more individualistic?
- How much weight is placed on relationships as opposed to formal contracts?
- What is it that persuades people to implement agreed terms? Reputation? Fear of reprisal?
- What causes offense, and what does not?

*Substance*

- What is negotiable, and what is nonnegotiable?
- What kinds of agreements are treated as binding?
- Are agreements put in writing or kept more informal?

*Process*

- What are acceptable moves in the game?
- How important are protocol and other formalities?
- Is communication direct or indirect?
- What does *yes* mean? What does *no* mean?
- How important are nonverbal cues?
- What are the norms concerning truth telling?
- How are disputes about implementation handled?

## Cautions on Culture

Awareness of cultural differences is very valuable, but making allowances for those differences can be fraught with peril. Cultural assessment can equip negotiators with insight into the behavior of their counterparts, but generalizations also contribute to biased perceptions and strategic disadvantages. Consider this anecdote. Following the death of Kim Il Sung (discussed in Chapter Five), Robert Gallucci sought advice from his cultural experts on how to express his condolences:

> I got my team together, and I asked my Korean folks, "What do I do?" They said you probably have to write something in a condolence book. There is a standard phrase that you use when you express condolences, which translates roughly into, "Words cannot express the depth of my sympathy for your situation." I said, "I got it. I can handle that." So I went to the North Korean mission, and I'm alone. I'm supposed to go in, bow before the picture of Kim Il Sung, and then walk over to the condolence book and sign it. They said, "You don't speak to anybody. You just bow and sign." So I walked in. I saw the cameras, and an image came to me of David Niven in *55 Days at Peking* when he walked in and kicked the emperor's pillow aside when he went to see him. I walked in and I stared at the picture and I did not bow. I didn't flinch; I just stared and walked away. Then I wrote in the book, "Words fail me," et cetera. I was careful. I wrote for the pain of the North Korean people expressing my sympathy.
>
> The next day, the South Koreans were very upset because the North Koreans quoted what I put in the book and highlighted that "words failed me." They were in an upheaval about this. So I got my cultural people together. I said, "What did you do to me?" And they said, "Well, it's what you say when you go to express sorrow." What I didn't do was put it through another filter about the politics of what I was dealing with, which was principally the South Korean reaction. I would have been much better off by saying "my sincerest sympathies" than trying to find out what was culturally right. It helped me in North Korea, but that isn't where the political problem was, because South Korean hawks were very nervous about the United States doing a deal with the North.[39]

This is a cautionary tale about not losing sight of negotiating objectives in the name of cultural sensitivity.

In addition to keeping an eye on political factors in dealing with culture, you should watch out for the following:

- *Stereotyping.* The generalizations that flow from cultural analysis are hypotheses to be tested, not guiding assumptions. It is easy to drift into self-fulfilling prophecies, whereby beliefs result in selective perception, which in turn confirms prior beliefs.

- *Subcultures.* National culture is merely one layer of cultural influence on negotiators' behavior. Negotiating representatives also belong to specific subcultures defined by clan, social class, religion, profession, or organization. It is worthwhile to explore the totality of cultural influences on counterparts' behavior.

- *Sophistication.* The individuals who represent their sides in complex negotiations are often quite sophisticated and experienced in dealing with other cultures. As a result, they may be strategic in their use of others' cultural expectations. They may, for example, play up the importance of relationships if they know their counterparts believe relationships to be culturally valued. Note that the same is true of gender role expectations.

- *Standards.* Cultural standards applied to insiders are not necessarily applied to outsiders. It may even be considered appropriate to deal with "civilized people" in one way and "barbarians" in another. Assessments of the ways in which cultures characteristically deal with outsiders are therefore a key component of an overall cultural evaluation.

- *Self-awareness.* It is difficult to anticipate potential cultural stumbling blocks if one is not self-aware about one's own culture. Pursuing cultural self-awareness can be a first step toward appreciating the impact of cultural differences. One way to do this is to read books written by people from other cultures about your own culture. Another is to solicit views from outside observers about your culture.

### Overcoming Cultural Barriers

The best way to shrink cultural barriers is to learn about your counterparts' culture, keeping the caveats in mind. One good way to do so is to live in the country for some time and, especially, to learn the language. Language shapes thought, and understanding a language makes a big contribution to understanding a cultural group's basic worldview. When this is impossible, the next best approach is to familiarize yourself with the culture by learning about its history, geography, and politics and by reading commentaries on the culture (cautiously, because they can be superficial). Translations of the culture's best fiction will offer deeper insight into its norms and basic assumptions.

It is often useful to engage the services of a cultural interpreter—someone you trust to act as a bridge. As one accomplished international diplomat put it, "You need somebody who really knows the cultural context, because it's easy to make mistakes."

## THE MUTUALLY REINFORCING NATURE OF BARRIERS

The various types of barriers to agreement—structural, strategic, psychological, institutional, and cultural—reinforce each other, contributing to vicious cycles. Structural barriers like poor communication channels exacerbate strategic barriers like the prisoner's dilemma. Defensive reactions to the prisoner's dilemma can feed the misperceptions that create psychological barriers. Such barriers can reinforce structural barriers by creating still greater impediments to communication. Cultural barriers too may give rise to misunderstandings that lead to escalation. Escalation in turn creates psychological barriers, and so on.

This is why it is crucially important to anticipate barriers and to avoid initiating vicious cycles. Careful attention to shaping the structure can mitigate the impact of prisoner's dilemmas. In intercultural negotiations, awareness of one's own cultural assumptions and insight into the other side's helps to prevent misperceptions from poisoning relationships.

Chapter Five picks up our story where we left off, with the conflict between the United States and North Korea in a dangerous phase of escalation. The next installment describes the breakthrough intervention by former president Jimmy Carter.

# Carter Achieves a Breakthrough

In mid-1994, as officials huddled in Washington to debate yet again why North Korea had unloaded the fuel core from its nuclear reactor and what the United States could do about it, former president Jimmy Carter arrived in Seoul. His trip garnered little attention. News accounts of the possible buildup to war made only passing mention of Carter's upcoming trip to North Korea in an effort to resolve the nuclear conflict.

When Carter had called President Clinton to say that North Korea had invited him to Pyongyang to help mediate the dispute, the reactions of administration officials had ranged from vague hope to alarm verging on horror. Captain Thomas Flanagan says he had already circulated a paper in the Joint Staff proposing that a senior envoy visit Pyongyang in a last-ditch attempt to avert war.

> How did Carter come to be the mediator? Was he a good choice from the U.S. perspective? The North Korean perspective?

Although Carter proposed to go not as a government representative but as head of the Atlanta-based Carter Center, known for addressing such global issues as public health, human rights, and conflict resolution, the offer seemed fortuitous to Flanagan.

But many others viewed Carter's proposal to insert himself into the conflict as a threat. Carter prized his independent status and had publicly challenged Clinton's policy in the past. Moreover, he had a reputation among critics for pursuing peace at any cost, an approach Former National Security Adviser Brent Scowcroft calls a "value-free process" designed "just to solve it so it goes away." If the North made Carter some new offer, however contrived or disingenuous, it could well derail all the careful preparations for a sanctions vote in the UN Security Council. There were also very real dangers that Carter might change the U.S. negotiating position and that North Korea might view the former president as an official envoy despite administration claims.

"It would have been unnatural for there not to have been thoughts that this was risky business," says Robert Gallucci. "The advantage of him 'going on his own hook,' . . . but not as an envoy, is that he's not an official representative. The disadvantage is he's not under instructions." Adds the Defense Department's Kent Wiedemann, "Anybody at that point, whether it was a congressman or Jimmy Carter or Billy Graham, would not be particularly welcome, because we felt it was important to ensure any message to the North Koreans was consistent."[1] Nevertheless, Clinton's national security team decided that Gallucci should at least brief Carter on the North Korean conflict, and the assistant secretary flew to Carter's home in Georgia.

For the next few days, senior officials debated the wisdom of letting Carter go. The Bush administration, after all, had discouraged Carter from accepting earlier invitations from Pyongyang. And Clinton and his team had their own issues of face to consider. As one congressional staffer puts it, "people were appalled" at the appearance of letting someone outside government take over the administration's job. "There was a concern about who's the secretary of state here, who's the president here, who does foreign policy," concedes Gallucci. "This required a lot of maturity on the part of the president and the secretary of state, to be able to cope with the standing of a former president—and a former president who is not popular in all quarters, who is viewed as someone who makes concessions, who gives in."

Faced with ever-narrowing options, however, and with at least partial support from Vice President Al Gore, Defense Secretary William Perry, and Gallucci, Clinton approved Carter's visit to Pyongyang with the explicit condition that the former president would be going as a private citizen and not as a representative of the U.S. government. Carter came to Washington for further briefings.

## CARTER VISITS THE NORTH

Five days later, on June 15, Carter crossed the DMZ from South to North accompanied by an aide, a State Department escort, and a television crew from Cable News Network (CNN). "There is little expectation that Jimmy Carter's visit here will produce any kind of breakthrough," a CNN broadcast noted at the end of the first day. "But in a situation where there are virtually no channels of communication between Washington and Pyongyang, the mere fact of his presence may be breakthrough enough."

According to Richard Christenson, whose role as Carter's State Department escort was to make sure the DPRK-supplied interpreters translated accurately and with proper nuance, the North Koreans were predisposed to like Carter from the start—a predisposition reinforced, no doubt, by the former president's status and by his 1976 campaign pledge to remove U.S. troops from South Korea.[2] Carter's "special gift," Christenson says, was the ability to create a reasonably trusting working relationship despite animosity on both sides. "There was a respectful atmosphere and a businesslike atmosphere," Christenson recalls, "and they got right down to the business of discussing this nuclear problem and how to avoid a confrontation."[3]

> How do the skills of a great mediator differ from those of a great negotiator?

Carter's first day of discussions did not produce any breakthroughs. On the second morning, apparently unhappy with his progress, Carter sent aide Marion Creekmore to the DMZ, ready to alert Clinton to the failure of the talks if Carter gave the word. But no letter was ever sent. Kim Il Sung made an unexpected offer: pressed by Carter to freeze the DPRK's nuclear program, Kim said North Korea would put the program on hold and would consider a permanent freeze if the United States promised to provide the North with LWRs.[4]

Kim's offer came as a shock to administration officials in Washington. Indeed, Carter's call to Washington reporting a breakthrough interrupted a presentation by Secretary Perry and General Luck of their plan to send ten thousand more troops to South Korea. To the amazement of Gallucci, who received the call, Carter declared that North Korea was ready to freeze its nuclear program and that he would appear on CNN within minutes to announce the development.

> How did Carter's public announcement change U.S. perceptions of its alternatives? Was this an appropriate action for Carter to take?

Alarmed that sensitive diplomacy was being conducted in such a public way yet cautiously optimistic that a new and less dangerous course had been opened, top officials gathered around a television set. Carter appeared live from Pyongyang, telling reporters that Kim's promise was "a very important and positive step." In addition to the apparent freeze of the North's nuclear program, Carter announced that Pyongyang would not evict the two remaining IAEA inspectors and was willing to comply with NPT regulations.

"We watched the TV, and we came back in and took out the yellow legal pads," Gallucci recounts. "Then some of us were sent off to try to draft a statement of what would be acceptable to us as a freeze."

## THE ADMINISTRATION RAISES THE BAR

Wiedemann describes the immediate reaction to Carter's call as "a little skepticism," but Gallucci and others huddled to discuss how to figure out whether North Korea was serious about its offer and under what conditions the United States would return to the negotiating table. After all, by unloading the 5-MW reactor in flagrant disregard of IAEA controls, the North had apparently destroyed both the best evidence of its bomb program and any grounds for meeting again with the United States. On the other hand, the DPRK proposal offered an unexpected opportunity to redefine the negotiation in terms more favorable to the United States. "As a negotiator, I needed to go back to the table feeling I was in a position of strength," explains Gallucci. "We needed a new standard because we needed to be able to answer the question—for ourselves and for the public—'If you didn't talk to them before, what's new?'"

**Note the need for face-saving and the shifts in the issue agenda.** Both to justify a return to the table and to advance U.S. objectives, President Clinton raised the bar for what the DPRK would have to do to reengage the United States. "People talk about changes in the U.S. position," notes Daniel Poneman, the National Security Council's senior director for nonproliferation and export controls. "Well, that was the single most significant change."[5] In fact, in Gallucci's eyes, the North Korean conflict had acquired a new dimension: instead of targeting North Korean compliance with the NPT, as it had the previous fall, the Clinton administration now demanded an immediate and lasting freeze, as well as eventual dismantlement of the DPRK's nuclear program. "The negotiations from the beginning were very narrow," Gallucci muses. "They were kind of traditional nonproliferation negotiations with the bad guy. Then it changed. All of a sudden you had an opportunity to go after their whole program. It became a real international security issue."

Later on the day of Carter's CNN appearance, National Security Adviser Anthony Lake asked Carter to relay to Pyongyang the administration's conditions for resuming negotiations: an immediate freeze of the North's nuclear program, continuing IAEA inspections, and—a significant new condition—no refueling of the shutdown reactor, in effect closing down the North's production of more plutonium. While affirming the sincerity of the North's freeze offer, Lake added, the United States would continue its sanctions quest. "President

Carter thought this was a tougher position than we had had before, and we said 'That's right,'" Gallucci recounts. "And I know President Carter—this may be understating the case—wondered why that was happening now."[6] At a White House news conference that evening, President Clinton declared, "If today's developments mean that North Korea is genuinely and verifiably prepared to freeze its nuclear program while talks go on—and we hope that is the case—then we would be willing to resume high-level talks."

In the days following the freeze proposal, matters moved quickly. Friction increased between Carter and the Clinton administration when the former president told North Korea that the United States would not pursue sanctions and had already committed to new high-level talks, despite Lake's clear statement to the contrary.[7] Nevertheless, Gallucci wrote to DPRK's vice foreign minister, Kang Sok Ju, offering to resume negotiations if the North Koreans confirmed that their nuclear program was frozen. Three days later, after a positive and unexpectedly cooperative response, Clinton said that the United States would proceed with talks the following month.[8]

> Note the principal-agent issues. Was Carter an agent? A principal? What problems did his involvement create for the administration?

## LINGERING TENSIONS

Most senior officials believed the Carter-brokered deal had served U.S. interests well. Although Gallucci insists that the threat of sanctions helped bring the North back to the negotiating table, Bush administration official Arnold Kanter claims that killing the sanctions initiative may have been Carter's best achievement. "Whatever you think of Jimmy Carter's visit, he probably performed a public service by putting a bullet through the head of that horse," he declares. "Because if we had been forced to go to sanctions, we would have embarrassed ourselves and shown ourselves to be really quite weak."

Yet tensions lingered between Carter and the administration. "They're a little reluctant to attribute it to Carter, because he did this in a way that was embarrassing to Washington," explains one State Department official. In particular, Carter's involvement opened the Clinton administration—under fire for its handling of other international conflicts—to the embarrassing charge of having allowed a private citizen to conduct the nation's foreign policy.

> What did Carter's intervention let the parties do that they could not have done on their own?

But NSC aide Daniel Poneman and Gallucci rebut these charges. According to Poneman, Clinton deserves credit for allowing Carter to try his unofficial approach despite the likelihood of just such criticism. Gallucci argues that the former president's outsider status enabled him to engage the North Koreans in a manner inappropriate for an active government official. "My overall assessment of the Carter visit to Pyongyang was [that] he provided an opportunity for the North Koreans to back away in a face-saving way," he says. "And that was very useful."

According to some observers, Carter provided the U.S. government precisely the same opportunity. "Basically, he committed the administration to a new bargain for getting to a third round," states Mitchell Reiss of the Woodrow Wilson Center. "Part of what we had wanted to do was to get at North Korea's history. Now that history had been pretty much destroyed. What Carter said is, 'We will still talk to you.'" Reiss adds: "The Clinton administration had not yet made that decision, to put it mildly. They couldn't give up their ultimatum without losing a lot of face. But Jimmy Carter did it for them."[9]

Before leaving the Korean Peninsula, Jimmy Carter achieved what some Korea watchers considered another breakthrough: an agreement that the leaders of North and South Korea would meet for the first time.

# CHAPTER SIX

# Managing Conflict

In this chapter, we explore how contending parties manage conflict and overcome barriers to negotiated agreement. We look at how President Carter got involved in the negotiation process and how negotiators seek strategically to involve others in the intervention game. We examine how the involvement of outside parties, or *intervenors,* can help the parties to get to the table and reach agreement. We highlight how contending parties mediate their own disputes—a process known as *comediation.* Finally, we explore how negotiators overcome barriers to agreement by employing tools like phased agreements, confidence-building measures, and secret diplomacy.

## THE INTERVENTION GAME

The Carter mediation proved to be a critical turning point in the North Korean crisis. Following President Carter's discussions with Kim Il Sung and his announcement of a breakthrough freeze of North Korea's nuclear program on CNN, tensions eased, and the parties resumed negotiations. But how did President Carter come to be the mediator in this dispute? How did he get the parties back to the negotiating table? What had already happened that made his job easier?

President Carter was invited into the dispute by the North Koreans, over the objections of some officials in the Clinton administration. The DPRK wanted

Carter to act as intervenor because of his stature as a statesman, because they believed he had a personal interest in seeing the mediation succeed, and because his record as president and later as a peacemaker led them to believe he could help them advance their interests.

More subtly, the DPRK selected Carter because it would be very difficult for the Clinton administration to refuse to let him go, and once they allowed him to go, if would be difficult to reject the results of his mediation. Although Carter was acting as a private citizen, there was no avoiding the public perception that he represented the administration. By involving Carter, the North Koreans entangled the United States in a mediation and undercut the move toward sanctions.

The selection of Carter as intervenor was the result of an *intervention game.* In such games, contending parties and potential intervenors jockey to advance their interests through the selection and participation of third parties in dispute resolution processes. Potential intervenors with interests in the conflict decide whether to try to intervene and how to do so. Disputants seek to advance their interests by deciding which potential intervenors to try to involve or exclude.

When a dispute is ripe for settlement and the disputants are roughly equal in power, they will either negotiate over who is acceptable as an intervenor or try to preempt the selection process by unilaterally inviting someone in. Each side will seek someone sympathetic to its interests, but the final choice is likely to be a relatively neutral third party with an interest in reaching a settlement and, possibly, with some bargaining power. For obvious reasons, the parties tend to reject interested intervenors with coercive power.

In a nonripe dispute characterized by a power imbalance (such as between the North Koreans and the United States or the Israelis and the Palestinians), the weaker disputant will seek to pull in a sympathetic intervenor. One way a weaker party can do so is by putting pressure on its allies. Another is to increase spillover from the dispute intentionally, in the hope that the resulting damage will alter the cost-benefit calculations of potential intervenors. Stronger disputants try to block these efforts by pressuring their own allies, raising the perceived costs of intervention, and minimizing the impact of spillover.

When several outside parties are affected by a dispute but none has sufficient incentive or power to intervene unilaterally, some parties may try to free-ride on the efforts of others. This can make it hard to build a coalition in favor of intervention. And when competing coalitions of outside parties organize for and against intervention, the result can easily be paralysis. Effective intervention is more likely to occur in such situations if one powerful party takes on the role of lead intervenor, earmarking resources, pressuring other parties to contribute, and working to undermine blocking coalitions. The large-scale international interventions in the Persian Gulf, Somalia, and Bosnia, for example, would probably not have occurred without the leadership of the United States.

# INTERVENTION STRATEGIES

What did Carter do to get the parties to the table? Simply by going to Pyong-yang, he opened a channel for communication between the leaders of the United States and North Korea. He met directly with the leadership of the DPRK, and—to the dismay of some in the United States—built some rapport with Kim Il Sung. Carter was therefore in a unique position to build bridges between the dangerously isolated sides.

Carter also helped reframe the issues, creating an opportunity for the parties to move beyond the impasse over special inspections.[1] Carter knew from Gallucci's briefing that the Clinton administration had begun to understand the DPRK's objections to special inspections and to reconsider the North's offer to trade old reactors for new ones. Recognizing a basis for agreement in such a trade, Carter promoted Kim Il Sung's offer to freeze the program if the United States promised to provide LWRs. This formula accelerated the rethinking of interests and options within the U.S. government.

Third, Carter enabled both sides to back away without losing face. The freeze proposal gave the Clinton administration a much-needed opportunity to retreat from its public commitment to pursue UN sanctions. By responding to the DPRK's offer with a modest counterdemand—not to refuel the shutdown reactor—the administration could declare victory and get back to the negotiating table. Meanwhile, the North Koreans could maintain the face-saving fiction that they had simply been seeking a secure source of electricity all along.

President Carter employed classic mediation techniques to defuse a crisis and bring contending parties to the table. Unlike conventional mediators, however, he took actions that effectively committed the Clinton administration to resume negotiations. Although Carter was there "on his own hook," the public perception was that President Clinton had sent him as an envoy. Once he announced the breakthrough on CNN, the administration had only two options: resume negotiations based on the new formula or be viewed as having a foreign policy that was completely out of control. Although Carter's willingness to box in the Clinton administration is a controversial aspect of his approach to mediation, it worked.

# TYPES OF INTERVENORS

President Carter functioned more or less as a traditional mediator: he sought to foster communication between the sides and develop workable options while attempting to remain relatively evenhanded. Other types of intervenors in disputes include *negotiators,* who attempt to advance their own interests with respect to the conflict by bargaining with the disputants, and *arbitrators,* whose coercive power allows them to impose settlement terms on the contending parties. In intervening in the dispute between Iraq and Kuwait, for example, President George Bush certainly did not act as a mediator; instead, he functioned as an arbitrator, deciding that Saddam Hussein should be ejected from Kuwait and assembling the military, political, and economic coalition to make it so.

To understand the range of roles that intervenors can play, it is useful to explore first why outside parties might decide to intervene and to identify the sources of power on which they can draw to influence the contending parties.

## Intervenors' Interests

Outside parties who decide to intervene in conflicts may simply want to help the contending parties stop damaging each other. But they may also be seeking to advance personal or institutional goals—for example, by gaining a reputation for resolving disputes. We can only speculate about Carter's motives, but he appears to have had both an altruistic desire to prevent conflict on the Korean Peninsula and personal motivations to broker a deal. Many otherwise neutral intervenors (without a preexisting bias in favor of one of the disputants) may nonetheless have a bias toward settlement.

Outside parties may intervene because their vital interests are being directly or indirectly threatened by the conflict. If a conflict spills over, affected intervenors have a powerful incentive to minimize the damage. In seeking to prevent the Korean conflict from sliding into war, for example, both China and Japan sought to avoid spillover damage. In dealing with the war in Bosnia, the European nations worried that the dispute could spill over and trigger ethnic violence and damaging population migrations in Central Europe.

Outsiders partial to one or the other of the disputants try to influence the conflict in favor of their allies. China remained an ally of the DPRK, for example, while the Japanese were aligned with the United States. Similarly, European efforts to intervene effectively in Bosnia were seriously complicated by the long-standing relationships between Germany and Croatia and between Russia and the Serbs. Progress was made, as we will see, only when the relatively neutral (but by no means disinterested) United States took the lead in pressing for a settlement.

## Intervenors' Sources of Power

Intervenors draw on three main types of power to influence the contending parties: facilitative power, bargaining power, and coercive power.

**Facilitative Power.** Intervenors with facilitative power use their own status, legitimacy, process management skills, and interpersonal persuasiveness to help contending parties overcome barriers to agreement. These are the sources of influence most often attributed to traditional mediators such as President Carter.

These mediators can help to manage conflict and overcome barriers in a number of ways:

- *Enhancing and shaping communications among the disputants.* An intervenor may create a communication channel by shuttling between the contending parties or convening face-to-face meetings in neutral locations. The intervenor can also shape communications by serving as a conduit, softening language, or increasing the salience of potential common ground.

- *Setting up action-forcing events.* An intervenor may be able to establish deadlines that force the parties to make hard choices. One way is to impose time limits on the intervenor's own involvement. The contending parties then have to decide whether to compromise or let the intervention fail.

- *Critiquing the parties' positions.* An intervenor can act as a reality check by offering independent assessments of both sides' positions. Throwing cold water on unrealistic and incompatible aspirations may move the parties toward settlement.

- *Developing creative options.* An intervenor can suggest trades that create value for both parties. Because of strategic concerns, communication barriers, or differences in worldviews, the parties may have overlooked or failed to build on compatible interests.

- *Persuading the parties to make concessions.* Sometimes parties make concessions to the intervenor that they could not make to each other. The intervenor may be able to secure contingent commitments by asking the parties, "If the other side is willing to make the following concession, would you be willing to make a countervailing concession?" and promising not to reveal either side's response unless both agree.

- *Helping the parties to save face.* An intervenor can craft options or processes that allow the parties to back away from mutually incompatible commitments without undue loss of face. Carter did this by claiming that he had achieved a breakthrough that permitted the parties to go back to the table.

- *Absorbing anger or blame.* An intervenor can allow the parties to blow off steam and otherwise serve as an emotional buffer.

- *Serving as a witness to agreement.* Witnessing an agreement is especially important when it is feared that one or more of the parties will agree but back away from full implementation or seek to reinterpret the agreement.[2]

Mediators who rely solely on facilitative power cannot offer tangible incentives or coerce the disputants to come to the table. This means that the combatants (or at least their leaders) must have reached the point of wanting to make peace but be unable to overcome residual barriers on their own. The dispute must have become ripe, in the sense that the parties see negotiated agreement as preferable to continued contention.[3] Intervenors with facilitative power alone must also gain entry to the dispute by getting permission from the contending parties.

Contending parties seek an intervenor sympathetic to their interests. When the power differential between the parties is steep, however, the only way to move forward may be for the weaker party to accept a biased intervenor. Once involved, the intervenor automatically becomes a target of influence attempts by the parties, both of whom will try to gain sway or, if they perceive bias, to discredit the intervenor.

**Bargaining Power.** Intervenors with bargaining power possess the resources to reward the disputants for taking steps toward peace. The intervenor with bargaining power effectively becomes a party to the negotiation and can substantively shape the combatants' perceptions of their alternatives. When Richard Holbrooke offered aid to the Croats, Muslims, and Serbs if they signed a peace treaty at Dayton, he was effectively acting as a negotiator.

Intervenors with bargaining power can use it to try to buy a (often temporary) resolution to the dispute. In effect, the intervenor purchases a cease-fire or a settlement by offering incentives that make agreement preferable to continued contention. Bargaining power is also helpful when the disputants need to compensate each other but cannot make direct transfers of resources because of political barriers: the intervenor with bargaining power can become the conduit for *circular payoffs.* For example, disputant A makes a concession to disputant B, who in turn gives something to the intervenor, who compensates disputant D, completing the circle.[4]

But bargaining power has downsides. The disputants' attitudes toward an intervenor who becomes a party to the negotiations inevitably shift. If the intervenor is perceived as willing to offer them compensation, the disputants are less likely to be open about their interests and walkaways. This lack of openness may hinder a settlement, since the intervenor will be less able to explore interests and generate creative options, and more likely to be pulled into bargaining.[5] Contending parties who agree on little else share an interest in extracting a high price for peace when they know a third party has interests at stake and resources to bargain with. Thus, intervenors with bargaining power are vulnerable to disputants who tacitly cooperate to extract value from them.

**Coercive Power.** Intervenors with coercive power are in a position to impose terms of settlement by threatening to punish the contending parties or block their access to crucial resources. President Bush clearly employed coercive power in the Iraq-Kuwait dispute. Less obvious, the ability of the Chinese and Japanese to withhold key resources, such as oil and cash remittances, constituted sources of leverage over North Korea. Still less obvious, President Carter exerted a modest form of coercive power when he undercut the Clinton administration's negotiating position by announcing a breakthrough on CNN.

When intervenors possess coercive power, control over decision making shifts away from the disputants. At an extreme, the intervenor can forcibly impose terms on the disputants. If the dispute has significant spillover effects and is not ripe for settlement, outside parties may feel justified in imposing outcomes and even punishing the disputants to deter future eruptions.

Using coercive power to impose a settlement has potential costs: the expenditure of resources can be significant,[6] and a settlement that is imposed on the disputants is inherently unstable. One or more of the contending parties will view the settlement as illegitimate and feel free to violate its terms unless credible threats are made to enforce them.[7] The intervenor who uses coercive power must therefore be willing to invest in ongoing postsettlement monitoring and enforcement of the terms of agreement—in effect, to act as the guarantor and enforcer of agreements.

Intervenors with coercive power may therefore seek to use their power in indirect ways. One option is to alter the balance of power by damaging one or more of the disputants in ways that make settlement preferable to continued conflict, leaving the contending parties to negotiate a settlement. This is what happened when the North Atlantic Treaty Organization (NATO) bombed the Bosnian Serbs' strongholds. A softer option would be to threaten to impose a settlement if the parties are unable to work out their own accommodation.

## The Intervention Role Grid

Intervenors' roles are shaped by the source of their power. Intervenors with facilitative power are likely to have only as much power as the parties are willing to concede, for example, whereas intervenors with coercive power have innate power, independent of the parties. Let us look first at the three pure versions of the roles that outsiders play in disputes: mediator, negotiator, and arbitrator.

**Mediator.** The pure mediator is an impartial, mutually acceptable third party whose goal is to help the parties resolve their dispute. A mediator is not biased in favor of any of the parties or toward achieving or preventing a settlement. Mediators lack the power to coerce or bargain, but they can use facilitative power to influence disputants. A mediator must gain entry to the dispute by being accepted by the contending parties.

**Negotiator.** The pure negotiator has well-recognized partisan interests in the outcome of the dispute, either in getting a settlement (substantive interests) or in seeing one of the disputants gain a favorable settlement (relationship or coalitional interests). A negotiator lacks the coercive power to impose terms on the disputants, but may use bargaining power to buy entry into the dispute and advance self-interest.

**Arbitrator.** The pure arbitrator is an impartial third party with the coercive power to impose terms on the disputants. An arbitrator is not biased in favor of either party and subordinates personal preferences to some set of rules or values. Nor does a pure arbitrator have a sufficient stake in the outcome to bargain with the disputants.

## Mixed Mediation Roles

In practice, intervenors tend to embody some mixture of the mediator, negotiator, and arbitrator roles. Mixed roles can be usefully pinpointed by locating them on the two-dimensional intervention role grid in Figure 6.1.

On the vertical axis, the mediator and negotiator roles occupy opposite poles on a continuum of extent of stake in the outcome. At the bottom is the impartial mediator who seeks a mutually acceptable resolution to the conflict; at the top is the partisan negotiator pursuing self-interest or the interests of an ally. Neither the mediator nor the negotiator has the coercive power to impose outcomes, and both can use facilitative power to influence disputants. But the mediator is disinterested, while the negotiator is highly interested and has some bargaining power. Between the poles lie roles that combine a desire to help the contending parties resolve their dispute with an interest in achieving a particular outcome. At the center is the mediator-with-an-interest.

On the horizontal axis, the mediator and arbitrator roles are poles on a continuum of extent of ability to impose outcomes. Both mediators and arbitrators seek to resolve the conflict, and neither has a strong stake in a particular outcome or an incentive to bargain. However, the arbitrator has the coercive power to impose terms, while the mediator must be acceptable to the disputants and can use only facilitative power to influence them. In the middle ground between mediator and arbitrator are roles with varying degrees of coercive power. In the center is the mediator-with-muscle.

Intervenors at the upper right of the matrix are self-interested and possess all three forms of power: facilitative, bargaining, and coercive. As we will see, George Bush had strong interests in the outcome of the conflict between Iraq and Kuwait and exerted enormous coercive power to impose a "settlement." But the United States could also have decided to try to bargain with Saddam Hussein.

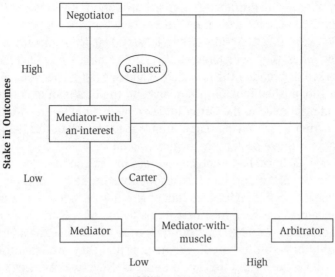

**Figure 6.1.** The Intervention Role Grid.

## Mediators with Interests and Muscle

Intervenors who employ a combination of facilitative, bargaining, and coercive power are mediators-with-interests-and-clout. Jimmy Carter acted primarily as a mediator, but he exerted coercive power when he undermined the Clinton administration's negotiating position by announcing the breakthrough on CNN. As we will see in Chapter Thirteen, Richard Holbrooke brought Serbs, Croats, and Muslims to the negotiating table in Dayton using military force to level the playing field. Although interested in helping the warring parties in Bosnia reach a settlement, Holbrooke also represented the partisan interests of the United States.

# COMEDIATION

Outside intervenors are not necessarily alone in working to manage conflict and overcome barriers to agreement. Negotiators representing the contending parties often undertake what Roger Fisher has termed *comediation* initiatives. The logic of comediation flows from Fisher's previously cited observation that "a good negotiator mediates his own disputes." Fisher argues that effective representatives of contending sides often play dual roles as partisan negotiators and as mediators.[8]

Without minimizing President Carter's contribution, it therefore is important to point out that he crystallized the parties' own efforts to get back to the negotiating table. Within the U.S. side, Gallucci, Perry, Flanagan, and others practiced comediation when they sponsored studies and seminars on the consequences of war, worked to broaden the agenda beyond special inspections and North-South dialogue, pushed the South Koreans and the IAEA not to complicate the process, and responded to the Carter initiative with a modest request for a concession to permit a face-saving retreat from sanctions. All of this helped lay the foundation for a move back to the negotiating table.

Even earlier, Gallucci had established more robust channels for communication with the DPRK. After the initial negotiations broke down, Gallucci recognized the value of better information about North Korean interests and initiated low-level meetings between members of his team and a North Korean ambassador to the United Nations. The routine nature of the meetings, and the fact that they did not result in "products," meant that they attracted little media attention or objections from the South Koreans. Nevertheless, they provided a crucial conduit for information exchange.

In addition, the basic formula for settlement had already been put on the table by the North Koreans. Although the Clinton administration had initially discounted the offer to trade old reactors for new ones, the DPRK had repeated the offer and floated variations through third parties. These successive overtures had helped to convince Gallucci and others in the administration that the offer might be serious. When the time came, they were ready to reframe the negotiations.

Thus, a foundation for a move back to the negotiating table was already in place prior to the Carter initiative. Escalation had forced both sides to reevaluate their alternatives to a negotiated agreement. Advocates for settlement within each side had begun to reframe the core issues and build internal support. But having publicly committed themselves to positions, the United States and the DPRK needed a way of backing away from confrontation, and this is what the Carter initiative provided.

More generally, representatives, either alone or in tacit cooperation with representatives of the other side, may seek to comediate in a variety of ways:

- Educating their internal constituencies about new external realities
- Reframing the issues
- Crafting face-saving compromises that permit their leaders to back away from confrontation
- Delinking entangling sets of negotiations to simplify the process
- Developing working relationships with their counterparts that moderate partisan perceptions

- Setting up momentum-building processes such as phased agreements, back-channel diplomacy, and confidence-building measures
- Bringing in outside intervenors

The first four approaches have already been dealt with in the discussion of mediators' facilitative power. External mediators and internal comediators employ similar process management techniques and may in fact work cooperatively to overcome barriers to agreement.

The final three approaches are worthy of equal attention. How can representatives develop the productive working relationships necessary to make comediation work? What processes can they set up to build momentum and overcome barriers to agreement? And how can they invite in intervenors, such as President Carter, to help manage a conflict?

## Developing Productive Working Relationships

A working relationship between the representatives of contending parties is indispensable in comediation. Without some level of interpersonal trust, representatives are unlikely to be able to cooperate tacitly or explicitly to manage their dispute. In the U.S.–North Korean negotiations, the initial contacts between the Bush administration and the DPRK would not have succeeded if Arnold Kanter had not treated the North Korean representatives with respect. Although Kanter lacked the authority to do anything but talk, the DPRK representatives nonetheless left partly satisfied. The mere fact of a meeting with the United States was a step forward, but Kanter's respectful approach mattered.

A working relationship represents a psychological buffer against shocks to the conflict system. Actions and events away from the table that would otherwise trigger escalatory responses may prove manageable if a degree of trust has been established. James Baker notes:

> If honesty and trust developed, even the most contentious talks could be brought to a successful conclusion. The negotiators feel free to set aside their formal negotiating positions and reveal their informal thinking—the assumptions, strategies and even fears—that underlie their approach. . . . But if the relationship soured—if it became infected with distrust and discord—then it mattered little how far apart the parties actually were. The perception of mistrust overwhelmed any objective reality.[9]

If the parties have a long history of contention, partisan perceptions and distrust may be the steepest barrier to moving forward. At least to some degree, productive contact between negotiating representatives can counteract the biases of the leadership. In addition to the examples cited here, consider the relationships between Abu Ala and Uri Savir in the negotiations between the PLO and Israel[10] (discussed later) and the history of the South African peace process.[11]

Leaders' choices of representatives in dispute resolution negotiations are crucial. If the objective is settlement, not delay or disruption, representatives should be selected for interpersonal insight and ability to build rapport, bridge cultural gaps, and counter stereotypes. They should learn quickly and be able and willing to educate their counterparts externally and their constituencies internally. Above all, they must be able to balance the roles of partisan negotiator and comediator, which inevitably presents the difficult choices that we explore in Chapter Fourteen on the negotiator as leader.

## Designing Momentum-Building Processes

The design of negotiation processes can also help overcome psychological, strategic, and political barriers. The goal is to build momentum by bootstrapping the negotiations; common approaches to doing this are phased agreements, confidence-building mechanisms, and secret or back-channel diplomacy.

**Phased Agreements.** The logic of phased agreements is that the parties negotiate relatively easy issues first, implement the resulting agreement, and then work toward more difficult issues. In one common variation, the parties first negotiate guiding principles for an acceptable settlement; these principles then serve as a foundation for negotiating more specific and divisive issues. Gallucci's successful negotiation of the U.S.–North Korean Joint Declaration of June 1993 is an example of this approach, as is Richard Holbrooke's successful approach to negotiating a set of principles for peace in Bosnia. The Oslo Declaration of Principles, which established a foundation for negotiations between Israel and the Palestine Liberation Organization (PLO), is a third example.

Once guiding principles are in place, attention can shift to a framework agreement and then to the details of implementation. The rationale is that the experience of forging a joint agreement alters the contending parties' attitudes toward each other and creates a sense of investment in the process. When the time comes to tackle more difficult issues, these changed attitudes represent a resource: they help build momentum to overcome the remaining barriers.

But the phased approach has its drawbacks. The hard issues remain to be worked out at the end, and the parties will find that they remain hard. Furthermore, the process may not build trust. If implementation of the first-phase agreement provokes internal opposition and sours the relationship, the contending parties may build momentum, only to run straight into a brick wall. This was the case when Israel and the PLO negotiated to implement the Oslo agreements in the late 1990s. Even so, it may simply be impossible to aim directly for a comprehensive settlement. Phased processes must therefore be undertaken with care, making certain that enough issues remain on the table to craft mutually acceptable trades later.

**Confidence-Building Measures.** In Chapter Four, we noted that contending parties who want to move toward peace can face strategic vulnerabilities in doing so. Suppose, for example, that both the United States and North Korea wanted to trade the DPRK's old reactors for more proliferation-resistant new ones but were stuck on implementation issues. How could the United States be sure that the North Koreans would really dismantle their program? What would happen to the fuel rods? At what point would sensitive nuclear technology be transferred to the North Koreans? On the North Korean side, how could the DPRK make sure that the United States would give them advanced LWRs if they dismantled their program?

Working out the mechanisms would be relatively straightforward if the two sides trusted each other. But they did not, and trust is hard to come by in bitter disputes. So how could the United States and the DPRK overcome this strategic barrier to agreement? More generally, how can contending parties have confidence in each other's good faith when they are mutually vulnerable and do not trust each other?

As we saw in Chapter Four, a number of techniques are useful for fostering cooperation—or at least compliance—in the absence of trust:

- *Verification regimes*—arranging to observe each other's actions as a way of reducing mutual uncertainty and increasing transparency
- *Mutual deterrence*—making credible mutual commitments to devastating retaliation in the event of noncompliance
- *Incrementalism*—proceeding in a series of small and mutually verifiable steps, making important future gains contingent on meeting current obligations, and, more generally, embedding current negotiations in a larger context to avoid end-game effects
- *Hostage taking*—having each side deposit resources into an escrow account supervised by an independent party, with the understanding that the proceeds will be forfeited in the event of noncompliance
- *Outside guarantors*—involving powerful external parties as guarantors of the agreement, with the understanding that they will punish noncompliance

As we will see, several of these confidence-building mechanisms were employed in the next phase of the negotiations between the United States and North Korea.

**Secret Diplomacy.** Secret or back-channel diplomacy is a common approach to managing conflict in complex negotiations. A secret channel sometimes enables leaders to present an agreement to their constituencies for ratification as a fait accompli. Secrecy temporarily transforms two-level (internal-external) negotiation processes into simpler bilateral ones, delaying the internal negotiations and marginalizing opposition. According to Fred Iklé, "Secrecy has two major effects in diplomacy. First, it keeps domestic groups ignorant of the process of negotiation, thereby preventing them from exerting pressures during successive phases of bargaining. Second, it leaves third parties in the dark and thus reduces their influence. The exclusion of the public may help overcome domestic opposition to concessions or threats before negotiations are completed."[12] Secrecy permits the parties to concentrate on substance without posturing and media dynamics. An initial agreement also constitutes a public commitment on the part of the leaders that is difficult to undo without serious loss of credibility.

Like phased agreements, however, secret diplomacy has potential drawbacks. In particular, it may legitimize violent protest on the part of opposition groups who are excluded from the process. The Oslo peace process, which we discuss in Part Two, offers a cautionary tale: secrecy appears to have been essential to the initial agreement between Israel and the PLO, but it also legitimized violent opposition within Israel and among the Palestinians, violence that eventually resulted in the assassination of Yitzhak Rabin. It is often impossible to move forward without marginalizing such groups. But agreements concluded in secret must be carefully and vigorously sold internally.

In Chapter Seven, we conclude the story of the U.S.–North Korean negotiations. Then we will look at strategies for building momentum and assessing effectiveness and outcomes.

# CHAPTER SEVEN

# The United States and
# North Korea Reach Agreement

With the third round of talks finally at hand, Gallucci was seized with a new sense of optimism. Freezing Pyongyang's entire nuclear program was a goal truly worth fighting for. Moreover, the United States' strong diplomatic and military response before Carter's visit had proven its toughness and resolve and strengthened his hand. "This president [Clinton] was not going to walk away from this, and the North Koreans had to see that," Gallucci says. "We were going into negotiations much better off." But on July 8, 1994, as U.S. and DPRK representatives began the third round of negotiations in Geneva, Kim Il Sung died of an apparent heart attack at the age of eighty-two.

U.S. negotiators feared that Kim's death would derail the process and that the DPRK might revert to a rigid stance without his leadership. But the State Department's Robert Carlin says the North Korean delegates were quick to reschedule talks and that there was a "clear softening" of the North's position when the two sides met again on August 5. The DPRK delegation no longer balked at cooperating with the IAEA on routine inspections, Carlin says. Nor did chief negotiator Kang waste time demanding the withdrawal of U.S. troops from South Korea, a red herring routinely thrown into prior negotiations. According to Joint Staff representative Thomas Flanagan, the North Korean team showed a real willingness to deal: "The very first session that I had, I remember . . . coming back to my office saying, 'I firmly believe that they're serious.'"

In some respects, the United States was also ready to deal. Officials had finally become convinced that North Korea was sincere about its more-than-year-old request for LWRs. Most experts agreed that simple coal-fired power plants would have been more cost-effective, but LWRs appeared to possess a political significance that transcended their practical value, and the United States had no desire to argue the point. "As Gallucci said a couple of times," recalls Kent Wiedemann, the senior NSC director for Asia, "if their condition for resolving the nuclear issue was to buy X number of BMWs for the people of North Korea, that's what we'd do."

**What were the key elements of the package deal?**

But although the United States was ready to deal on the big issue—LWRs in exchange for a freeze in the DPRK's nuclear program—the package that Gallucci brought to the table was tougher than ever and included demands that had stymied negotiations from the start. Special inspections were an explicit objective, as were progress in North-South talks and full implementation of the North-South denuclearization agreement. And as part of the freeze, the United States wanted something more: immediate removal of the eight thousand spent fuel rods and dismantlement of the existing nuclear program.

Carlin, who feared that the U.S. position was too hard, recalls a near-explicit plea from a North Korean delegate for the United States to match the DPRK's apparent move toward conciliation. "I can remember one of their guys, as we were breaking for lunch, saying to me, 'Please, look very carefully at what we said,'" Carlin recounts. "And we went back and looked at it, and the message that came out of it was, 'If we're willing to take some steps, you have to take some steps as well.' That took us a while to figure out—what we could do and how far we could go." Indeed, the first week-long session produced only an Agreed Statement, laying out in principle the concept of replacing North Korea's existing reactors with proliferation-resistant LWRs. All the difficult questions remained to be resolved at the next meeting, which began September 23.

By then, a distinct process had evolved. Gallucci, who had been named ambassador at large the previous month, enhancing his status, had also been granted more discretion to make offers and alter the U.S. position at the table. "The negotiating team was inevitably in front of the final policy," notes Carlin. "A lot of things will occur to you sitting at the negotiating table that you wouldn't even think about in Washington ahead of time." Nevertheless, Gallucci still relied on talking points that laid out basic positions approved by the interagency group and in some cases by the deputies committee and the principals. Whenever he modified those points, Flanagan says, Gallucci had to clear it in Washington.

As the talks dragged on into October, however, Gallucci became convinced that the United States had to make changes, beginning with its position on special inspections. His own feelings on the issue were clear. "It is our view," Gallucci had declared almost a month earlier, "that the actual implementation of special inspections, which we recognize is a serious political issue for the DPRK, need not be undertaken immediately for a settlement to be successful."[1] But some administration officials, senior to Gallucci, did not agree. Special inspections had been a central U.S. demand since the DPRK first refused to come clean on the suspected nuclear waste sites in early 1993.

Even if inspections would be of limited usefulness, as some experts now argued, they symbolized U.S. determination to uncover the true nature of the North's nuclear accomplishments and ambitions. Gallucci appealed to top officials to concede. But although Defense Secretary Perry, among others, supported him, the principals as a group would not relent.

> Note Gallucci's role in shaping perceptions of interests and BATNAs *within* his own side.

"We played hard initially, hoping that the North Koreans would come around, and we sat there and we butted heads," says Flanagan about the stalemated negotiations. "We'd make our points, they'd make their points, we'd go back [and] the interagency would say, 'No, we don't want to change our position.' So we'd go back the second time to Geneva, say the same thing, they'd say the same thing, and we'd go back to our country and say, 'We're still butting heads,' but the principals would say, 'No, we're still not going to give in.'" He adds, "We really tried. I mean, anyone who thinks that Gallucci and the administration just gave in—we sat many, many hours negotiating with them, and it was very clear after a while that, hey, we're just not going to get anywhere."

For Gallucci, special inspections paled next to such pressing objectives as disposing of the eight thousand spent fuel rods, closing down the North's reprocessing facility, and dismantling all three nuclear reactors. "We need special inspections," he says. "We need to get that somewhere in the agreement. But in terms of what's important to our security and South Korea's security, the special-inspections issue is a political issue and the others are real security issues." Adds Wiedemann, "The world knows that North Korea could have a bomb or a bomb-and-a-half, and it's clearly in North Korea's interest to keep us guessing about that. The negotiations in the end came down to reducing the amount of time that that ambiguity would be allowed to exist."

In mid-October, perhaps sensing Gallucci's willingness to deal, Kang made an important concession. In all previous negotiations, Carlin says, North Korea had been unbending in its refusal to allow access to the alleged waste sites. "Kang's position had been, 'Never, ever, special inspections. Hell can freeze over nine times, you will never get them, Mr. Gallucci,'" he says. But suddenly Kang's language changed. "Essentially he said, 'Gee, we couldn't possibly do something this difficult before we got the proper percentage of the light-water reactors,'" Carlin recalls. "I looked at my watch at that point and wrote in the margin of my notebook, 'We won the war.' They had just given the principle away."

# A DEAL IS STRUCK

With the cautious approval of Washington, Gallucci and Kang finally crafted a compromise. Pyongyang could keep intact the secrets of its suspected waste sites until the LWR project was well underway, a major U.S. concession. But North Korea also yielded: before any nuclear components for the LWRs would be delivered, probably in about five years, it would have to comply fully with its IAEA safeguards agreement, including special inspections. "I don't want to fight the point that there is a political vulnerability in the agreement on this point," Gallucci admits. "Our eyes were wide open when we were negotiating this. Our objectives were all plutonium, plutonium, plutonium, plutonium—and then you got down to what I consider a real political issue, and that was one in which, in terms of time, I had flexibility to compromise. And I did."

**Note the use of time and staged commitments to overcome barriers.**

With this issue finally resolved, North-South relations remained the biggest potential deal breaker and the final significant point to be negotiated. When the United States demanded inclusion of North-South dialogue, Carlin recalls, "It was like someone had turned the thermostat down." The final wording, negotiated over several rancorous days, called for North Korea to "consistently take steps" to implement the North-South denuclearization agreement and to engage in talks with the South "as this Agreed Framework will help create an atmosphere that promotes such dialogue." The vague stipulations pleased neither side.

Meanwhile, South Korea continued to behave, according to one Bush administration official, as "the classic dependent ally whom you can never please," publicly criticizing in Seoul the same agreement it had privately approved at meetings following each day's negotiations. "Officially, we had the South Korean government on board," Gallucci notes. "We have to be mature enough to know we will not always have them as publicly supportive of the framework as we'd like."

The final Agreed Framework, signed by U.S. and North Korean negotiators on October 21, capped sixteen months of fragmented negotiations. Praised by Clinton as "good for the United States, good for our allies, and good for the safety of the entire world," the framework had six key provisions:

1. North Korea, under IAEA supervision, would immediately shut down and eventually dismantle its entire gas-graphite nuclear program: the

5-MW reactor, its fuel fabrication facility, two larger reactors under construction, and its plutonium reprocessing facility.

2. The United States would oversee construction of two 1,000-MW LWRs by a U.S.-led international consortium.

3. Before delivery of sensitive nuclear components for the first LWR, North Korea would submit to any inspections deemed necessary by the IAEA, including special inspections.

4. As nuclear components began to arrive, the North would begin shipping the eight thousand spent fuel rods out of the country.

5. To compensate North Korea for energy lost from its closed reactor, the United States would provide a 50,000-ton shipment of heavy fuel oil at a cost of almost $5 million. Later oil shipments to replace the larger reactors that would have come on line would increase to 500,000 tons annually, financed by the international consortium.

6. The United States and North Korea would gradually normalize economic and diplomatic relations, beginning with liaison offices in each other's capitals, as progress was made on nuclear and other issues.

In some ways, the final framework resembled the settlement that North Korea had suggested the previous October and even Kang's original request for LWRs in mid-1993. Some critics, believing the United States should have compromised sooner, complained that the entire conflict could have been resolved a year earlier. But U.S. negotiators disagree, insisting that the political climate would not have allowed it. "I don't think in '93 we could have done this, because in '93 I don't think we could have generated this support for our concessions," Flanagan argues. "It took the North Koreans to defuel the reactor. It took the North Koreans to have roughly 30 kilograms of plutonium sitting in this pond of water deteriorating, with a threat that they were going to have to reprocess."

Nor were the concessions one-sided, as Gallucci points out. Without the buildup toward sanctions, preparations for possible war, and the pressure of the ongoing negotiations, he asserts, Pyongyang would not have gone beyond the requirements of the NPT and given in to Washington's increasingly ambitious nonproliferation goals. "It was a result of the negotiations that we got back to 'Sorry, folks. You want to avoid sanctions? You want to avoid an American military buildup in Japan, on the Korean Peninsula, and in the Sea of Japan? Do a deal,'" Gallucci says. "It was a wonderful mating of the military instrument being ready and the diplomatic instrument being used."

Do you agree that U.S. efforts to shape the DPRK's perceptions of its BATNA were effective?

# A CONTROVERSIAL AGREEMENT

The Agreed Framework concluded this round of negotiations between the United States and the DPRK, but it did not end criticism of how the Clinton administration had handled the conflict. The framework had strong supporters, particularly among those who believed that the United States would further its own political interests and improve regional security by engaging North Korea. And Gallucci's skills as a negotiator were praised even by those who least liked the results. Yet in the weeks following the settlement, he and his team faced challenges to the negotiated resolution, including warnings from Republican members of Congress that they might try to block U.S. participation in the deal. Most Washington observers believed that Congress would not carry out its threat, but administration officials defended the hard-won resolution at a dizzying round of hearings and briefings. "It is quite an amazing thing for North Korea to have accomplished, because it is a diplomatic agreement in which both sides give up something," notes Korea expert Bruce Cumings, an advocate of the framework. "Yet most Americans, including a lot of people in Washington, can't figure out why we need to give up anything to deal with a country like North Korea."

> *Note the institutional barriers and Gallucci's role in selling the agreement to his own side.*

Criticism of the framework, bolstered by skepticism that North Korea would honor any agreement, took a number of forms. The deal's impact on the strength and credibility of the nonproliferation treaty was unclear. According to Arnold Kanter, some European allies with no direct input to the negotiation complained that the United States had unilaterally approved an agreement that "deals a body blow" to the global nonproliferation regime. The IAEA supported the agreement, but some of its representatives disliked the staggered timetable for North Korean compliance. Moreover, countries such as Iran and Iraq, with proliferation issues of their own, complained about what they referred to as North Korea's "special treatment."

Gallucci, noting that IAEA inspectors in North Korea had already confirmed that the nuclear program was successfully frozen—by all accounts, an impressive achievement—insists that expecting all nations to follow the same path toward nonproliferation is unrealistic and impractical. Selig Harrison, a senior associate at the Carnegie Endowment for International Peace and a supporter of the framework, agrees. "We can't treat countries as monolithic, and we can't approach nonproliferation in a legalistic fashion and get the desired results," he asserts. "What we've ended up with in this case is a country doing more than it was required to do under the NPT—giving up the right to reprocess, a most

THE UNITED STATES AND NORTH KOREA REACH AGREEMENT

extraordinary concession to make. It's the greatest victory for nonproliferation that we've ever had, and it shows that, while the NPT is important, it is not the be-all and end-all of dealing with the problem of proliferation."

Oil shipments to North Korea also provoked claims that such assistance would prop up a regime ready to topple if left alone.[2] Not only was North Korea to be provided with nuclear reactors capable of producing more electricity than those it had been building, but the annual infusions of heavy oil would be a significant donation to the cash- and resources-poor country. "Clearly we are delaying the ultimate collapse of a government that we don't really like," concedes Flanagan. "But we may be contributing to greater peace on the peninsula, a more peaceful reunification, by doing it this way." In fact, Flanagan warns that if the DPRK regime failed, South Korea would pay a terrible price. "The rapid collapse of North Korea would overwhelm the South Korean economy, just overwhelm it," he adds. "And they know that."

The most biting charge was that North Korea had taken advantage of a confused Clinton foreign policy to walk away with prizes it never should have won. As the world's last superpower, some critics charged, the United States should have been able to insist on North Korean compliance without making major concessions. "I think we promised North Korea everything we could conceivably promise them," laments Brent Scowcroft. "I would have brought a few sticks along. The one tiny stick we had, Jimmy Carter gave away." Adds Robert Manning: "The North Koreans had a very weak hand, and they played it brilliantly. We had a strong hand and didn't know how to play it. We didn't know what we wanted."

Gallucci, however, challenges critics to propose a superior strategy or a more propitious outcome given the complexity of the conflict and the North's "capacity to cause great pain." The real source of discontent is not the framework, he argues, but the conviction among many observers, including members of the press, that any U.S. deal with North Korea is a bad deal. Add the strong antipathy many politicians and opinion leaders felt toward Clinton's foreign policy, he says, and the North Korean resolution was almost preordained to be unpopular. Republican congressional leaders were sending him letters of protest even before they had seen a copy of the settlement, Gallucci recalls. "We got 98 percent of what we wanted and 100 percent of the security issues. And we got a deal that allows us to verify it, and allows us at no point to be disadvantaged if they walk away from the deal," Gallucci says. "And we have no body bags yet. We have no war yet. Good outcome." He goes on: "But in the end, how does your viscera feel? Those North Koreans are getting a $4 billion reactor project. Damn!"

Not even the most optimistic members of Gallucci's negotiating team claimed the North Korean conflict was over. It would be years before the framework agreement could achieve its ends, and those who had participated in the negotiations expected ongoing challenges from the DPRK. "They will continue to fight us every step of the way to get the most they can," states Flanagan. "That's the North Korean style."

But Flanagan expects history to cast the long negotiation in a positive light. "We're not at war," he says. "We're not in the conflict. We're not spending a billion dollars a year like we are in Haiti. And we have some hope that this framework agreement is a first step to the peaceful reunification of Korea. If things go as planned, this will be viewed as a brilliant stroke of negotiation by the U.S. government." Bruce Cumings, another supporter of the framework, sums up Gallucci's accomplishment this way: "He deserves a lot of credit for pursuing the possible agreement, rather than the ideal agreement, in this whole thing."

The signing of the Agreed Framework marks the end of our exploration of these negotiations. The agreement set the stage for later negotiations over implementation and normalization of relations. Readers interested in what happened next can consult "Update of the Cases" at the end of the book.

# CHAPTER EIGHT

# Building Momentum

Now we are ready to examine strategies to build momentum. In the process, we seek to answer two fundamental questions about the U.S.–North Korea case. First, did the North Koreans play a weak hand brilliantly, as Robert Manning asserted, and did the United States play a strong hand badly? If so, what made the North Korean hand weak and the U.S. hand strong, and what made for good play and bad play? Second, was the agreement a good deal or a bad one? If good, what made it good? If bad, what would a better agreement have looked like? More generally, what criteria should we use to evaluate the outcomes of such complex negotiations?

## STRATEGIES FOR BUILDING MOMENTUM

To answer these questions, we need to look more deeply at strategies for building momentum. The breakthrough approach to developing negotiation strategies consists of a seven-element process for building momentum:

1. *Shape the structure.* Take actions to shape the structure (parties, issues, interests, alternatives, potential agreements, linkages, and action-forcing events) favorably before negotiations begin, and work to reshape the structure as they proceed.

2. *Organize to learn.* Figure out what you do not know, and develop a strategy to learn while you are influencing the other side's perceptions of your interests and alternatives.

3. *Orchestrate actions at and away from the table.* Employ an integrated strategy to learn and shape perceptions at the table while improving your alternatives through actions away from the table.

4. *Find the formula for the deal.* Frame the negotiation in ways that are favorable to you by defining the problem and identifying promising trades.

5. *Lay the foundation for your position.* Articulate rationales for your positions, and plan the sequence of concessions you will make.

6. *Channel the flow.* Use action-forcing events to get your counterparts to make difficult choices and to move beyond psychologically important resistance points.

7. *Sequence to build momentum.* Plan the order in which you will approach other players, deal with the issues, and move between linked sets of negotiations.

## Shape the Structure

By the time at-the-table negotiations begin, your counterparts will have taken actions to shape the framework within which talks will take place. They may have favorably influenced who participates in the process and defined the agenda of issues. They may have taken actions to improve their own alternatives and undermine yours. They may have linked the current negotiations to other sets of negotiations past, present, and future. They may have exerted undue influence on locations, meeting schedules, decision-making procedures, and physical arrangements.

You have to work just as hard to stack the deck in your own favor in advance and to reshape the structure as negotiations proceed. Good negotiators pay as much attention to influencing the structure of the negotiations as they do to planning for and participating in at-the-table dialogue. This is especially true of parties in relatively weak bargaining positions. Strategies for shaping the structure are summarized in Table 8.1.

One powerful way to shape the structure is by linking or delinking negotiations. To identify promising opportunities for doing so, ask the following questions:

- Do opportunities exist to create linkages that advance my interests?
- Can I short-circuit others' efforts to create linkages favorable to them?
- Can I find ways to eliminate constraining linkages?

Table 8.1. Shaping the Structure of Negotiations.

| Strategy | Tactics |
|---|---|
| Influence who participates. | Bring in parties who will support you or increase the potential for value creation. |
| | Exclude parties who will oppose you or block efforts to reach an agreement. |
| Frame the issues. | Influence the agenda early. |
| | Gain control over the agenda-setting process. |
| | Include issues that increase the potential for value creation or promote efforts to claim value. |
| | Exclude toxic issues. |
| Alter BATNAs. | Build coalitions with potential allies, including interest groups within other sides. |
| | Find stronger alternatives in case no agreement is reached. |
| | Make your counterparts' perceptions of their alternatives to agreement look less attractive. |
| Shape the decision rules and procedures. | Shape the process by which decisions will be made. |
| Control the location and atmosphere. | Shape the setting to promote particular outcomes. |
| Influence the timing of interactions. | Manage the pace of negotiations. |
| | Negotiate at times favorable to you. |
| | Structure breaks within and between rounds to facilitate analysis and reflection. |
| Link and delink negotiations. | Create linkages between past and current negotions or current and future negotiations. |
| | Create competitive linkages to improve your BATNA. |
| | Eliminate reciprocal linkages to remove constraints. |

- Can I block others' efforts to advance their interests at my expense by entangling them in linked negotiations?

To illustrate the power of linkage, consider how it can be used to build and break coalitions. Once you succeed in your negotiations to get one powerful ally on board, it becomes easier to recruit others. As you recruit more allies, your resource base grows and your likelihood of prevailing increases, making it easier to recruit still others who support your view. Sequential linkage of this kind transforms uncommitted parties' perceived alternatives. Initially, their alternatives are to join the coalition or maintain the status quo. Once you have a critical mass of support, they face a very different choice: join the coalition or be left behind.

Competitive linkage can be employed to break coalitions. (Negotiations are competitively linked if only one can reach fruition.) If you are opposed by a coalition whose members are not strongly bound by shared interests or long-standing relationships, it may be possible to drive wedges between them. One divide-and-conquer tactic is to negotiate with members of the opposing coalition, offering each an attractive deal for being the first to switch sides and making clear that others are being offered a similar deal. If the leaders of the opposing coalition cannot counter with more attractive offers or credible threats to punish defection, the opposing coalition may split.

Reciprocal linkage is also useful in coalition building. (Negotiations are reciprocally linked if all must reach fruition for any to go forward.) Suppose you are engaged in negotiations with two potential allies, both reluctant to be the first to make a commitment. You may be able to allay their concerns by requesting *contingent commitments.* Say to each, "Would you, Party X, be willing to support me if Party Y also agrees to join the coalition?" and promise not to reveal either's response unless both say yes. As a result, you effectively bootstrap the process. Alternatively, you may be able to recruit an ally by persuading a third party to provide him with needed resources.

## Organize to Learn

Having better information than your counterparts is a clear advantage. Inadequate learning can initiate a vicious cycle in which your uncertainty and awareness of vulnerability make you behave defensively, evoking a reciprocal response. By the same token, effective learning bolsters your confidence, enlarges the scope for judicious information sharing, and promotes openness from your counterparts.

As we have seen, learning in negotiation is not easy. No one will teach you, and many will seek to mislead you, so you have to organize to learn. As William Ury notes in *Getting Past No,* "Most negotiations are won or lost before talking begins, depending on the quality of the preparation. People who think they can 'wing it' without preparing often find themselves sadly mistaken. Even if they reach agreement, they may miss opportunities for joint gain they might well have come across in preparing. There is no substitute for effective preparation."[1]

**Identify the Key Levels of Learning.** In complex negotiations, learning takes place at three distinct levels: individual, team, and organizational. At the individual level, negotiators seek to acquire information as described. At the team level, negotiators figure out how to work together as a team and how to synthesize what they are learning at the table. At the organizational level, negotiators synthesize the lessons of past negotiations and share them with others in the organization who are conducting similar negotiations.

Managing team learning processes means building a team with an appropriate mix of expertise and then working out ways to integrate the differing frames of reference. It also means establishing clear roles and giving some team members explicit responsibility for observation and note taking. The resulting observations form the basis for reflection, analysis, and planning between formal negotiating sessions. You also have to instill discipline in the team to be sure that information does not leak during formal or informal interactions with other negotiating teams. We return to issues of team leadership when we describe Richard Holbrooke's efforts to end the war in Bosnia in Chapter Thirteen.

Negotiators also may represent organizations (such as the State Department) that undertake many similar negotiations over time. Overall organizational effectiveness increases if negotiators undertake postnegotiation reviews and work to distill lessons learned from them. When organizations have many negotiators undertaking similar negotiations, it makes sense to set up mechanisms, such as regular meetings, in which negotiators can share key learnings.

**Establish Learning Goals.** What do you need to learn about? First and foremost, as we saw in Chapter Two, you need to analyze the structure of the negotiating situation carefully. Next, you need to learn as much as you can about each of the parties, focusing in particular on their interests (in both substance and process), reputations, characteristic styles, and sources of power. Then you need to size up the zone of possible agreement.

Good preparation equips you to assess your strengths and weaknesses relative to those of your counterparts. The following list will help you do so:

- *Alternatives to agreement:* How strong is my BATNA? How strong are the BATNAs of my counterparts? Can I strengthen my alternatives or weaken theirs?

- *Allies:* How strong is my support among other key players, stakeholders, and constituencies? How much coalitional support do my counterparts have? How can I strengthen my base of support and weaken theirs?

- *Information:* Do I have better information about my counterparts' interests and walkaway values than they have about mine? What can I do to gain an informational advantage?

- *Expertise:* Do I have the necessary technical and negotiation expertise (either individually or as part of a team) to negotiate effectively? Do my counterparts have an expertise advantage? If so, how can I close the gap?

- *Position and status:* Is there a good match between my position or title and those of my counterparts? Are my counterparts' cultural expectations concerning the type of person they should be dealing with likely to be met?

- *Confidence:* Am I confident about my case? Do I understand the issues? Have I marshaled good arguments? Have I done a better job of preparing than my counterparts have? Can I support my offers and concessions with plausible rationales? Can I draw on powerful principles to buttress my claims?

- *Outcomes:* Do I know what a good agreement would look like? Do I know at what point I would need to walk away? Am I willing to walk away if necessary? Am I willing to make concessions if necessary?

**Learn at and Away from the Table.** Learning does not stop when negotiations begin. On the contrary, there are usually severe constraints on how much you can learn before negotiations begin. Consider, for example, the limits on what Robert Gallucci could learn prior to his first meeting with the North Koreans. It is important to be diligent about familiarizing yourself in advance with the issues, history, and negotiators and to develop options carefully. But at some point, the costs of still more preparation begin to exceed the benefits, and resources are better spent figuring out what you need to learn at the table and how to learn it. Gallucci's team's preparatory exploration of options contributed to their education but could not unlock the central mysteries.

Preparation can also go astray; erroneous assumptions can reinforce existing frames and partisan perceptions and lead you to behave in ways that result in self-fulfilling prophecies. You should therefore treat your preliminary assessments as hypotheses to be tested, not as guiding assumptions. This stance means reserving judgment, continuing to consider alternative explanations for observed behavior, and "unlearning" when necessary.

Positions that are laboriously hammered out internally may turn out to be a bad match for external realities. This was the case when Arnold Kanter first met with representatives of the DPRK. The only thing the influential players in the U.S. government could agree to was that Kanter could meet with the North Koreans. He was so constrained that he could not offer them anything of value.

In such situations, you may have to manage a difficult tension between pursuing consensus internally and maintaining flexibility in external negotiations. Sometimes you even have to teach your own side what its interests should be, or work to shift internal perceptions to reflect changing external realities. Effective learning during negotiation is a matter of continuously acquiring new information from all available sources, including the other parties, and adjusting one's expectations and strategies accordingly. Good negotiators learn not just in order to plan; they plan to learn, developing hypotheses and establishing precise goals for gathering knowledge at the table.

**How to Learn at the Table.** How do you learn at the table? Pleasantries and casual chit-chat when negotiations begin can yield insight into character and opportunities for making personal connections. Counterparts' proposals and concessions signal changes in positions, but can also convey information about their interests and walkaways.

*Active listening* is both a set of skills and an attitude. By asking open-ended questions, seeking clarification, driving for specificity, and then demonstrating your grasp of what the other party has said, you both learn and project empathy with your counterparts' point of view.[2] Typical active-listening questions include, "If I understand you correctly, you need. . . . Why is that important to you?" and "What specific concerns do you have about our proposal?"

As you gain confidence, you can experiment with offering bits of information to see if your counterparts reciprocate. You might also propose alternative packages to probe your counterparts' preferences and trade-offs. Low-level exploratory meetings, such as those that Gallucci and his team set up with the North Koreans in New York, are yet another mechanism for learning before the formal negotiations begin. Naturally, information gathered at the table should be subjected to commonsense tests for plausibility, consistency, and congruence with body language, facial expressions, voice tone, and other signals.

## Orchestrate Actions at and Away from the Table

Strong BATNAs are not just handed to negotiators; they are built. As Roger Fisher and William Ury put it, "Vigorous exploration of what you will do if you do not reach agreement can greatly strengthen your hand. Attractive alternatives are not just sitting there waiting for you; you usually have to develop them."[3]

BATNA-building strategies consist of orchestrated sets of actions: away from the table, developing your own options and altering your counterparts' perceptions of theirs; at the table, selectively sharing information to shape your counterparts' perceptions and to reinforce the impact of your away-from-the-table actions.[4]

Consider, for example, the impact of the DPRK's decision to dump the core of its reactor, a classic away-from-the-table action. This move effectively put to rest U.S. and IAEA aspirations to uncover the history of North Korea's nuclear program. It powerfully affected U.S. decision makers' perceptions of their options and channeled the negotiations away from narrow issues of compliance toward broader political issues.

**Weaken Counterparts' BATNAs.** Often, away-from-the-table actions are designed to support threats or to nullify others' threats. By reinforcing its military forces in South Korea, for example, the United States was not just preparing to win a war; more important, it was seeking to deter the North Koreans and weaken their BATNA.

Moves explicitly designed to undermine a counterpart's BATNA entail risks. If negotiators are rational, strategic actions of this sort will be viewed with pragmatic detachment—as part of the game. But in practice, direct use of power to weaken a counterpart's BATNA tends to poison the atmosphere for negotiation and can trigger an escalatory spiral, as occurred in the North Korea situation. Actions at and away from the table must be carefully synchronized to be sure they are mutually reinforcing.

**Build Coalitions.** When negotiations involve more than two parties, coalitional alignments become decisive. Your BATNA, and thus your bargaining power, may depend on the support of others. Building your BATNA may therefore largely entail efforts to build alliances with currently involved parties or to alter the party structure by bringing in others. You may also seek to weaken opposing coalitions or to exclude problematic parties. This is why a nuanced analysis of existing and potential coalitional alignments is such an important part of mapping the party structure of negotiations.

Suppose that a counterpart cannot sustain its negotiating position without the support of a linchpin party. In the U.S.–North Korean negotiations, for example, the North Koreans' avoidance of international economic sanctions depended heavily on the continued support of the Chinese. China was the linchpin in the DPRK's coalition. For this reason, the North Koreans made strenuous efforts to retain that support, and the United States attempted to weaken it. Similarly, the North Koreans were strongly dependent on hard currency remittances from Japan, a U.S. ally. They therefore tried to neutralize U.S. efforts to get the Japanese to cut off the flow of cash by means of implicit threats, such as testing missiles in the Sea of Japan.

The Bush administration's efforts to build the Gulf coalition, chronicled in Part Two, provide another example of BATNA-strengthening coalition building. When Iraq invaded Kuwait, the United States demanded unconditional withdrawal but lacked the resources to back up that position. The Bush administration then built an unprecedented political, military, and economic coalition in support of ousting Iraq while simultaneously neutralizing Iraq's traditional supporters. When Saddam Hussein refused to withdraw unconditionally, the United States went with its (now very strong) BATNA and invaded.

In all the cases examined in this book, actions away from the table were as decisive as what actually happened at the table, if not more so. In North Korea, Oslo, the Gulf War, and Bosnia, diplomacy and the actual or potential use of force went hand in hand.[5] In all these cases, too, away-from-the-table efforts to build and break coalitions proved central in shaping the eventual outcomes.

## Find the Formula for the Deal

Negotiations tend to proceed through predictable stages. Following an initial stage of feeling out the other side, the negotiators focus on identifying the basic framework or formula for agreement and then move to detailed hard bargaining based on this formula.[6] By *formula,* we mean a promising set of trades that creates value. A good formula creates a zone of possible agreement where there was not one previously or enlarges an existing ZOPA. In the case of the United States and North Korea, the formula that unlocked the negotiation was a trade of old reactors and a program freeze for new reactors and oil. Once this formula was identified, the focus of negotiation shifted to detailed bargaining: how much oil and how many reactors over what time period.

Identifying a promising formula may be a struggle. One or more of the parties may frame the negotiations in a way that makes it difficult to find good trades. The early U.S. preoccupation with special inspections and North-South dialogue narrowed opportunities to create value. It is commonplace for negotiators to focus on too few issues or the wrong ones, which shrinks opportunities for value creation. The uncertainty and ambiguity that characterize complex negotiations create additional barriers. The parties may refuse to share information, or not know what they want, or face internal differences that complicate their efforts to create value.

There are two basic ways to devise a promising formula. The first is to transform distributive negotiations into integrative negotiations by adding or subtracting issues.[7] Negotiations can sometimes be transformed by introducing issues that create new opportunities for trades. Alternatively, setting aside toxic issues, such as North-South dialogue, can create new opportunities.[8]

The second approach is to identify promising trades within the existing issue structure. Unbundling the issues sometimes reveals complementary differences in the parties' needs and resources across the issues. You can also look for complementary differences in underlying interests within issues.

Unbundling the issue structure simply means looking at the issues separately and assigning a relative importance to each.[9] Then do the same analysis from the point of view of your counterparts, asking how much weight they are likely to assign to each issue and what trade-offs among the issues they might be willing to make. The point is to identify complementary differences in needs. If you care more about issue A than issue B, and they care more about B than A, there may be a basis for a trade.

Differences in sensitivity to time, aversion to risk, and beliefs about the future also present opportunities for joint gains within particular issues.[10] In the case of the United States and North Korea, time limits on special inspections turned out to create value. By stretching out the schedule for inspections and linking them to delivery of key reactor components, they were able to craft a package deal. You can identify such opportunities by asking these diagnostic questions:

- *Are there differences in sensitivity to time?* A less patient negotiator might accept modest but prompt gains on a given issue in exchange for giving a more patient counterpart greater long-term returns.

- *Are there differences in attitudes toward risk?* A more risk-averse negotiator might accept a low but guaranteed up-front payment in return for giving a less risk-averse negotiator more upside potential (and more downside exposure).

- *Are there differences in beliefs about the future?* Negotiators may be able to forge contingent agreements whose outcomes are linked to future events, such as the price of oil one year later. If one negotiator believes prices will rise and the other that prices will fall, both may be willing to make a bet. Only one will turn out to be right, which may lead to problems sustaining the agreement.

Identifying potential sources of joint gains can generate hypotheses about core trades—that is, the formula—and productively move the negotiations on to detailed bargaining. Even under the best of circumstances, uncertainty and ambiguity—what you might think of as the *fog of negotiation*—make it difficult to find a promising formula. Hypotheses should always be treated as provisional, subject to testing and modification at the table. But a promising formula early in the game can be a tool to shape your counterparts' perceptions and to learn, through their reactions, about their interests. This is the case even if your formula initially is rejected.

In the U.S.–North Korean negotiations, the timing of special inspections and resumption of North-South dialogue activated interests on both sides: sovereignty and survival for North Korea and the integrity of the global nonproliferation regime and stability in Northeast Asia for the United States. Of the two issues, the United States was probably more concerned about special inspections than about North-South dialogue. The core trade embodied in the final agreement reflected this emphasis.

# Lay the Foundation

By identifying a good formula for detailed bargaining, you and your counterparts create a pie of potential value. You then start to divide the pie by taking positions or exchanging proposals.[11] If a ZOPA exists, this exchange should eventually converge on an agreement. If there is no ZOPA, you may revert to seeking a better formula or altering your own and your counterpart's BATNAs—or the negotiations may reach an impasse. What do good negotiators do in the detailed bargaining phase to make sure they end up with favorable agreements? How do they establish initial positions and then make concessions? How do they support their positions with persuasive rationales?

Keep in mind that negotiators accept only terms that they perceive to be better than their BATNAs and only when they believe that the costs of continuing to negotiate exceed the benefits. The art of position taking therefore consists of figuring out what your counterparts' ultimate walkaways will be, identifying a target deal that gives them an acceptable margin of value and you a favorable margin, and convincing them that the costs of trying to get a better deal exceed the benefits.

Your immediate goal is to put forward a *supportable position*—a position that is acceptable to them, allows you to claim your desired share, and, crucially, is supported by rationales and actions that convince your counterparts you have no more to give. To lay the foundation crafting a supportable position, you should undertake four tasks: (1) hypothesize about their walkaway values, (2) judiciously take an opening position, (3) plan a series of concessions, and (4) craft plausible supporting rationales.

**Hypothesize About Your Counterparts' Walkaways.** A shrewd assessment of your counterparts' walkaway positions will stand you in good stead as you hammer out a supportable position and craft a process. Looking at the negotiating situation from your counterparts' perspective requires you to, as William Ury put it, "step to the other side."[12] Ask yourself: What would I care about if I were standing in their shoes and seeing the world through their eyes? What would my constituents accept, and how would I sell it to them? Stepping to the other side is especially difficult in long, entrenched conflicts in which negotiators have deeply held biases about the other side.

There are two caveats here. First, as we have seen, uncertainty and ambiguity can make it difficult to assess others' walkaways accurately. You may have to learn at the table, pushing and probing and continually revising your assessments. The obvious risk is that your counterparts will be working to shape your perceptions, so your assessments should always be treated as provisional. This inescapable cut-and-thrust is evident throughout the U.S.–North

Korea negotiations, for example, in how the North Koreans worked to maintain ambiguity and generate anxiety about whether they already had nuclear weapons.

The second caveat is that your counterparts' perceptions of their walkaways may shift in response to BATNA-changing moves away from the table or shifts in aspirations. They may perceive that no zone of agreement exists or become more anxious to do a deal and move on. The goal, therefore, is not to assess your counterparts' current aspirations but to make sound predictions about what they will ultimately accept.

**Take a Judicious Opening Position.** The ultimate agreement is likely to split the difference between opening positions roughly, a phenomenon known as the *midpoint rule*.[13] This is the case because negotiators' initial positions establish the upper and lower boundaries of the bargaining range. Then the powerful psychological norm of reciprocity kicks in: the expectation that one's concessions will be reciprocated leads to agreements situated close to the midpoint of the bargaining range.[14] Your initial position shapes the final outcome by anchoring perceptions of the bargaining range.[15] Your goal is a position that anchors your counterparts' perceptions such that the midpoint between their opening offer and yours approximates your target agreement.

An opening offer that is perceived by the other side as extreme, arbitrary, or unreasonable will trigger defensive counter-anchoring and lead to unproductive positional bargaining.[16] The U.S. demand that the IAEA get full access to suspected North Korean waste sites, for example, was designed to anchor the negotiations. But the DPRK counter-anchored with a refusal to consider such inspections. The ensuing process remained futile until the basic formula was modified. Defensiveness in response to clumsy anchoring also short-circuits the information sharing necessary to capitalize on potential joint gains. An artful initial offer therefore favorably shapes the other side's perceptions of the zone of possible agreement without sparking defensiveness. Successful anchoring also depends, as we will see, on the rationales you offer to support your position.

Whether to make the first offer or try to elicit one from your counterparts depends in part on expectations. Sellers of goods, for example, are customarily expected to declare what price they are seeking. In other contexts, this decision boils down to whether it is more important to learn about your counterparts or to shape their perceptions. If you are uncertain about your counterpart's walkaway position, you can learn a lot from their opening offer; that information may offset the potential risk of having your perceptions anchored. But if you have a good sense of your counterparts' walkaway position, a carefully crafted first offer can powerfully shape their perceptions.

**Plan Your Pattern of Concessions.** Once a formula is established and initial positions are declared, detailed bargaining gets under way. The parties progressively make adjustments in their proposals that either converge to an agreement or lead to impasse. Howard Raiffa characterized this mutual jockeying in *The Art and Science of Negotiation* as the "negotiation dance."[17] In the process, the potential value that got created in the formula stage gets divided among the parties.

To reiterate, the parties' initial positions tend to define the boundaries of the perceived bargaining range. But negotiators also influence perceptions through the pattern of their concessions.[18] In effect, negotiators signal each other how far they are willing to go. One way they do so is by supporting their concessions with plausible rationales or commitments that make it costly for you to back away. Another is to signal increasing resistance by making progressively smaller concessions and taking more time to make them.[19] Such a pattern of concessions can be used strategically to shape your counterpart's perceptions of your walkaway position.

Good negotiators plan their concessions carefully, with an eye to the signals they are sending. A judiciously crafted sequence of concessions can powerfully shape counterparts' perceptions of the zone of agreement and help you to claim value.

At the same time, you have to be careful not to set yourself up for impasse. The art of concession making consists of giving up something and simultaneously making it clear that further concessions will be much harder to extract. How do you make a concession without signaling that you have still more to give? The resulting dilemma often contributes to impasse as negotiators dig themselves into irreconcilable positions. Both the United States and the DPRK found it very hard to make concessions to the other. This is why, in part, the Carter mediation was so important in breaking the logjam. The North Korean offer to trade new reactors for old can also be seen as a tactic for moving beyond the positional stalemate.

**Craft Plausible Supporting Rationales.** If both initial positions and subsequent concessions are to be credible, they have to be supported by either coercive power or plausible rationales. Arbitrary positions and unsupported concessions tend to be credibility busters, triggering defensive reactions. How can you support your positions in ways that shape perceptions? How can you convince your counterparts that the cost of seeking better terms from you outweighs the benefits?

One obvious way to support your position is to use coercive power and, in particular, threats of harm. In its most basic form, one negotiator says to the other, "You will accept my position, or I will cause you harm." If this threat is perceived as credible, it may work. But recourse to power carries the risk of provoking irrational reactions and escalation, as we saw in Chapter Two. The resulting agreements may also prove difficult to implement or sustain.

Several softer tools are available to support your positions. Paradoxically, as Tom Schelling has noted, negotiators sometimes support their positions by imposing limits on their own flexibility.[20] For example, labeling an offer "last and final" indicates that you would rather walk away than concede another inch. If your credibility is truly at stake, this statement precludes further concessions.

Alternatively, representatives can claim that they will lose credibility with their constituents if they make further concessions. The subtext of such a claim is, "If it were up to me, I would give more. But the people I represent are not so understanding." This stance permits a representative to maintain productive relationships with counterparts while hewing to hard positions. Negotiators may even deliberately raise constituents' expectations to support their commitments. For example, a union leader could intentionally inflate members' expectations about the expected size of a wage increase as a way of constraining his own ability to make concessions.

*Commitment tactics* of this kind are like a game of chicken between two cars on a narrow mountain road.[21] If you see the other driver throw the steering wheel out the window, you would be well advised to get out of the way. If both drivers constrain themselves in this way, of course, a crash is unavoidable.

Precedents, guiding principles, and standards can be cited to explain the impossibility of giving more. The undesirability of establishing a precedent is sometimes invoked to justify refusal to make a concession. Similarly, a commitment to specific principles may be cited to shape the other side's perceptions of the bargaining range.[22] In negotiations with the United States, for example, the Chinese have traditionally insisted on a set of principles that includes noninterference in internal affairs.[23] This principle is intended to blunt U.S. insistence on improvements in China's human rights record as a condition for other agreements.

Negotiators may try to establish objective standards of fairness by invoking precedents or data on comparable situations, and they may commit themselves to certain standards to convince their counterparts that they cannot make more concessions.[24] But because standards of fairness can never be truly objective, arguments over the standard tend to become part of the fabric of the negotiation.

**Put It All Together.** The bottom line is that you do not merely take a position; you craft it, putting in place multiple mutually reinforcing planks. The process of crafting a supportable position does not necessarily occur in the order we have outlined. You might begin by shaping your counterparts' perceptions of your constraints and then work to establish principles and standards for an acceptable agreement. You might then take a soft initial position, consistent with this frame, and make a sequence of concessions, each supported by a rationale that does not undermine your core principles and standards. Ultimately, you commit yourself by saying, "This is as far as I can go." The net effect is to convince your counterparts that the costs of trying to get better terms from you would exceed the benefits.

In position taking, there is a fundamental tension between asserting that you can give no more and retaining flexibility in case the zone of agreement is smaller than you expected. Good negotiators are adept at finding ways to escape their own commitments and to help their counterparts do the same. Typically, this involves reframing the negotiations, perhaps by arguing that the situation is unique, and hence unlikely either to set a precedent or to be governed by particular principles or standards. In the U.S.–North Korean negotiations, for example, the two sides' incompatible commitments to positions on special inspections were ultimately overcome through a combination of reframing and a phased agreement.

## Channel the Flow

Momentum toward agreement is built in two interrelated ways: by shaping counterparts' perceptions of time-related costs and by structuring action-forcing events. Suppose you and a counterpart each make an initial offer, and then your talks deadlock. You jockey to see who will make the next move. If your counterpart is incurring substantial costs and you can get across that delay is practically costless for you, you should be able to extract large concessions in return for closing the deal. Note that no specific event broke the deadlock. Instead, rising tensions caused by cumulating costs eventually led to movement.

Contrast this process with the impact of a deadline, a classic action-forcing event. Action-forcing events are clear breakpoints, imposed by outside forces or by the actions of the negotiators, that force some or all of the participants to make hard choices or incur substantial costs. Whether the instrument is slowly ratcheting pressure or an action-forcing event, the ultimate goal is to break a stalemate and build momentum in a favorable direction.

**Shape Perceptions of Time-Related Costs.** Time pressure produces faster concessions and faster agreement.[25] Sometimes time pressure acts equally on all the negotiators. Often, however, time pressure is asymmetrical and results from negotiators' or outside intervenors' strategic actions. In *The Art and Science of Negotiation,* Raiffa cites the following examples of strategic efforts to shape perceptions of time-related costs:

> When the United States negotiated with the North Vietnamese toward the close of the Vietnam War, the two sides met in Paris. The first move in this negotiation game was taken by the Vietnamese: they leased a house for a two-year

period. The party that negotiates in haste is often at a disadvantage. The penalties incurred in delays may be quite different for the two parties, and this discrepancy can be used to the advantage of one side. . . . In some negotiations, the tactic might be to delay negotiations indefinitely. For example, environmentalists can often discourage a developer through protracted litigation. In a civil liabilities suit, an insurance company can use delays in bringing a case to court in order to get the plaintiff to accept a more favorable (to the insurance company) out-of-court settlement.[26]

In both of the cases Raiffa cites, the objective was to ratchet up pressure gradually until the other side reaches a breaking point. The method is to find a way to let time pass, and then to convince the other side that the relative cost of permitting time to pass is unfavorable to them. There are many ways to dam the flow of the process. Clarifying meetings and internal ratification discussions serve the cause of delay admirably. The environmentalists and the insurance company that Raiffa referred to used such procedural barriers. Or, as we have seen, negotiators can intentionally engineer an impasse.

There are two ways to shape your counterparts' perceptions of time-related costs: by convincing them that you have all the time in the world or by making them alarmed about their own costs. During the 1969–1973 Paris Peace Talks designed to end the Vietnam War, the North Vietnamese delegation rented a house in Paris for two years, thereby sending a powerful signal: We're in no rush. . . . What about you? The Vietnamese knew that U.S. leaders were facing growing domestic opposition to the war and that time in that sense was on their side.

Cumulating transaction or opportunity costs also generate time pressure on negotiators. That is, delay may be costly because it consumes valuable resources or because it prevents participants from moving on to other activities.

Negotiators who believe that their alternatives to agreement (BATNAs) will get worse as time passes or that those of their counterparts will get better also experience time pressure. Dean Pruitt and Peter Carnevale cite a negotiation over the sale of fruit that will spoil if much time passes; the fruit is a "wasting asset."[27] Another example is a small company with dwindling funds negotiating a make-or-break financing deal with a venture capitalist. The passage of time may also permit the other side to accumulate resources, such as the support of allies, that strengthen its bargaining position.

Actions can be taken away from the table to influence perceptions of time-related costs. In seeking to end the war in Bosnia, as we will see, NATO initiated a bombing campaign aimed at punishing the Bosnian Serbs for their attacks on civilians in Sarajevo and crippling their military capacity. As damage accumulated, the Serbs became anxious to end the bombing lest it fundamentally alter the balance of power in the region. They became receptive to negotiations, and the resulting talks ended the siege of Sarajevo.

Inaction at the table combined with actions away from the table are a time-honored way to increase time-related pressure. At the table, you delay, engineer impasses, and seek to persuade your counterparts you are in no rush; away from the table, you work to strengthen your own BATNA and weaken your counterparts'. Naturally, you have to be cautious in applying this strategy. If all the participants managed to convince each other that delay is costless, the result would be . . . delay. If, in reality, everyone is accruing time-related costs, this result is undesirable. You can also end up overcommitted to a "you concede first" position that contributes to impasse.[28] In situations of bitter conflict, the contending parties may not care that they are suffering high costs themselves if they are inflicting damage on the enemy. As a result, collective value is destroyed.

**Structure Action-Forcing Events.** Action-forcing events are cost breakpoints. Prior to the event, the cost of inaction may be low. But permitting the event to pass without taking action causes some or all negotiators to incur substantial costs.

Like time pressure in general, the impact of an action-forcing event can be symmetrical or asymmetrical. Consider a union threat to strike if there is no settlement by a given date. In symmetrical situations, both the company and the union incur high costs if the deadline passes without agreement. But if the company can maintain operations with nonunion labor or if the union has accumulated a large strike fund, costs may be asymmetrical.

When time limits are externally imposed, one set of negotiators may face the prospect of losing options or resources. In international negotiations, for example, presidential elections often serve as action-forcing events. A president approaching the end of his term may seek closure to solidify his legacy; an example is President Clinton's efforts to negotiate a deal in the Middle East before the end of his term. And other players may seek to reach closure if they believe that the next president is likely to be less sympathetic to their arguments.

In conflict situations, outside parties may impose deadlines on contending parties; intervenors with coercive power may back up these deadlines with threats to impose a settlement. The NATO bombing of the Serbs in Bosnia is an example. Even if they lack coercive power, mediators can establish deadlines that force contending parties to make hard choices. In announcing a breakthrough on CNN, for example, Carter forced action in Washington.

Mediators can also set time limits on their own involvement. The contending parties then have to decide whether to permit the mediator to withdraw, and the process to fail, or to make compromises. Like all other threats, this works only if it is perceived as credible and if the associated costs to the combatants are high. A deal was struck in the Northern Ireland peace process mere hours after a deadline set by George Mitchell, the U.S.-senator-turned-peacemaker. Worried that the parties would not make the target date for completion of talks and fearful that splinter groups would undermine the talks if they had time, possibly by resorting to assassination, Mitchell set a firm cutoff point for his own involvement. "I had plenty of practice listening to long debates, seeing people waste time, stall and delay," he was quoted as saying about his experience in the Senate.[29] Backed by the governments of the United Kingdom and Ireland, Mitchell set as his deadline the last workday before the Easter holiday. He later told reporters that scheduling Senate votes just before the summer break had effectively focused senators' attention.

*Spoilers*—outside parties that seek to undermine negotiations—also use action-forcing events to advance their goals. Terrorist groups stage attacks, for example, with the intention of undermining moves toward peace. More generally, action-forcing events can cut both ways: they can be used to promote movement toward agreement or to provoke a breakdown.

Sometimes action-forcing events emerge consensually from the negotiation process or are unilaterally imposed by some negotiators on others. You and your counterparts could agree on deadlines, for example, as a way of forcing yourselves to reach closure. This form of mutual commitment can help force action within each side. It works, of course, only if both sides will incur costs if the deadline is missed.

You can also unilaterally bring about action-forcing events to constrain your counterparts' choices. A notable example is North Korea's announced withdrawal from the NPT. The announcement effectively forced the United States into direct high-level negotiations. The North Koreans were legally permitted to withdraw, but doing so would have undermined upcoming negotiations over renewal of the NPT and weakened U.S. efforts to prevent proliferation of weapons of mass destruction. Crucially, the United States was given time to react to the North Korean move: the ninety-day time limit allowed for pressure to build and negotiations to resume. The deadline also focused media attention, increasing pressure on the Clinton administration to react.

## Sequence to Build Momentum

We have already discussed the importance of sequencing in negotiation in several previous sections, but sequencing is so important that it deserves a more in-depth, unified discussion.[30] Because some sequences of actions are better than others, in the sense that they increase the likelihood of achieving desired objectives, good sequencing is a very important source of power in negotiation. This power is grounded in the negotiator's skill at shaping the process and building momentum.

Three types of sequencing deserve emphasis here: interaction sequencing, issue sequencing, and sequencing in linked negotiations.

**Sequence Your Interactions with Other Players.** When negotiations involve more than two parties, you can build momentum by planning the sequence in which you will interact with others.[31] When building a supportive coalition, for example, you will approach others in a particular sequence in an effort to recruit or neutralize them. Of course, your counterparts will simultaneously be trying to build or buttress their own coalitions. As a result, your sequencing plans may interact, resulting in competition for the support of pivotal players such as China in the U.S.–North Korean negotiations.

**Sequence the Issues.** How you parse complex sets of issues into subsets and the sequence in which you deal with them can have a powerful impact on your ability to create momentum. You will need to decide whether to proceed issue by issue or to construct packages. As we have seen, breaking up an intricate negotiation into a series of subnegotiations, tackling easier issues first and deferring harder issues for later, can build momentum. On the other hand, the broad and thorough initiative proposed by the United States was an effort to break a deadlock by putting a package deal on the table, as was the effort by the DPRK to trade old reactors for new ones.

**Sequence Your Moves Between Linked Negotiations.** You may also have to plan the order of your moves in linked systems of negotiations. If you set up a competitive linkage, for example, you may be able to improve your BATNA progressively by skillfully playing off one party against another. You will also have to decide what information you will carry from one negotiation to another, as Gallucci did, in the reciprocally linked negotiation between the United States and the DPRK and the United States and South Korea.

In summary, effective negotiation strategies consist of sequences of moves taken at and away from the table. Good negotiators develop sequencing plans that spell out a particular sequence of actions intended to build momentum in desired directions. Research suggests that the best negotiators are more fluid and flexible in working out the sequencing of issues and interactions than their less successful counterparts.[32]

# ASSESSING EFFECTIVENESS

Now we will return to the questions we posed at the beginning of the chapter about the effectiveness and outcomes of the U.S.–North Korean negotiations. Table 8.2 uses the seven principles spelled out in this chapter to evaluate both sides' strategies.

Clearly, the DPRK did a better job early on of managing these negotiations. The leadership of North Korea was fully focused on the crisis; meanwhile, the United States struggled through a change of administration, got caught in a reactive mode, and lacked a coherent strategy and sense of objectives. Once Robert Gallucci and his team were in place full time, the United States was, in

Table 8.2. Assessment of Negotiation Effectiveness.

| Prescription | Assessment |
|---|---|
| Shaping the structure | The DPRK clearly did a better job of shaping the structure at first. Its efforts to engage the United States in direct negotiations and to sideline the ROK were largely successful. North Korea also initiated Carter's involvement and reframed the negotiation. Later, the United States did a good job of delinking negotiations between the DPRK and the IAEA and ROK to simplify the structure. |
| Organizing to learn | The transition from Bush to Clinton led to substantial forgetting on the U.S. side. Until Gallucci was assigned to the brief full-time, the United States was not well organized. The DPRK, by contrast, was highly focused. |
| Orchestrating moves at and away from the table | The DPRK did a better job early: threats to withdraw from the NPT and to unload the reactor yielded gains at the negotiating table. The DPRK was also largely effective at preserving its core coalition and intimidating Japan. U.S. efforts to rally support for economic sanctions bore little fruit, but later efforts to build up military options contributed to eventual movement. |
| Finding the formula | The formula that unlocked this negotiation was proposed by the DPRK with the help of President Carter. The United States, hobbled by reactive devaluation and internal differences over North Korea's intentions, accepted the reframing of the negotiations late in the game. |
| Laying the foundation for a supportable position | The United States was ultimately successful at using power to support its position. The DPRK's position combined threats of destruction and commitments to the principle of no special inspections, but it eventually backed away from this commitment. |

| Prescription | Assessment |
| --- | --- |
| Channeling the flow | The DPRK largely controlled the pace until late in the game. By means of action-forcing events like a threat to withdraw from the NPT and defueling of the reactor, the DPRK altered U.S. assessments of alternatives and forced particular choices on the part of the United States. |
| Using sequencing to build momentum | The DPRK appeared to do a good job of sequencing actions at and away from the table. Information is lacking to assess which side did better at issue sequencing and sequencing in building coalitions. |

Gallucci's words, "organized to negotiate," and its effectiveness improved dramatically.

In hindsight, the United States could have assigned a full-time team and point person to the problem earlier. It could also have framed the negotiations in regional terms, rather than in terms of nonproliferation, early on. The negotiations eventually evolved into a four-power undertaking, directly involving the ROK and China. Could the United States have pulled China into the negotiations earlier? Would it have made a difference? The answer is not entirely clear, but doing so would have made the North Korean situation China's problem as well, changing the coalitional structure and discouraging the North Koreans from making threats or driving a wedge between the United States and the ROK. On the other hand, unilateral action on the part of the United States would also have been constrained. This is a tension to which we will return in our discussion of the Gulf War case in Part Two.

## ASSESSING OUTCOMES

The process was messy, but the outcome was arguably a good one: value was preserved, and war was avoided. Neither side claimed excessive value. The agreement, which was not completely secure, has largely withstood the test of time. Critics of the agreement should be prepared to pass the *plausible alternative test*—that is, to specify what they would like to have seen happen and, crucially, how they would have gotten there. Could the DPRK's nuclear program have been eliminated through military strikes? Probably not, and almost certainly not without triggering a wider conflict. The agreement effectively capped North Korea's efforts to build additional nuclear weapons, at least for now.

Because the regime's ability to sustain itself was slowly crumbling, deferring confrontation was valuable in and of itself. Although it might have been desirable for the United States to realize additional gains—involving, for example, control of missile technology or conventional arms—it is not at all clear how these ends could have been accomplished. The bottom line is that the agreement bought time. At the time this book is being written, it appears to have paved the way for a soft landing in the Korean Peninsula.

# PART TWO

# BUILDING THE BREAKTHROUGH TOOLBOX

You are now ready to look more deeply at the approaches that skilled negotiators use to manage conflict and build momentum. Part Two presents three more case histories of breakthrough negotiations, each with an accompanying conceptual chapter. In Chapter Nine, we examine how the Israelis and Palestinians got to the table in Oslo. Chapter Ten presents a general approach to getting to the table in complex negotiations, which is often in and of itself the key breakthrough.

Chapter Eleven is an account of how the Bush administration built the coalition to fight the Gulf War. The breakthrough here was assembling an unprecedented international coalition to confront an aggressor. Chapter Twelve analyzes and discusses the building of supportive coalitions.

Chapter Thirteen examines Richard Holbrooke's efforts to negotiate an end to the war in Bosnia. Notable here is the finely tuned orchestration of force and diplomacy by outside intervenors and the difficulty of building and sustaining a coalition in support of intervention. Chapter Fourteen looks at the complex and difficult set of roles that negotiators play in international negotiations, particularly when acting as an intervenor in conflicts and as a representative in negotiations.

As you read Chapter Nine on the Oslo negotiations, think about the four major elements of the breakthrough approach to negotiation:

- What is the structure of this negotiation?
- What are the structural, strategic, psychological, institutional, and cultural barriers to agreement?
- How is conflict being managed?
- How did the parties build momentum?

# CHAPTER NINE

# Getting to the Table in Oslo

Ever since the 1948 war between the new state of Israel and its Arab neighbors, Israelis and Palestinians have battled for ownership of the sanctified ground known once as Palestine and now as Israel.[1] Both the Israelis, granted a homeland by the world community in the wake of Nazi atrocities, and the Palestinians, driven from their villages during the 1948 war, were willing to die for their right to live there. For fifty years, enmity between the two peoples ran deep. Fear and distrust permeated their interactions. The Palestine Liberation Organization (PLO), the political/military group formed to fight for a free Palestine, vowed to wipe Israel off the face of the earth and backed its pledge

This is an abridged version of "The Oslo Channel: Getting to the Negotiating Table," a case written by Kirsten Lundberg for Professor Michael Watkins of the Harvard Business School, Harvard University. Funding was provided by the Peres Center for Peace. Copyright © 1998 by the President and Fellows of Harvard College. Reprinted with the permission of the Kennedy School of Government Case Program, Harvard University.

Note to the reader: Given that the road to peace in the Middle East since Oslo has proven to be very rocky indeed, why did we choose to include this case in a book on breakthrough negotiation? Because the Oslo negotiations forever changed the political landscape of the Middle East, bringing Yasser Arafat and the PLO back to Palestine and irreversibly transforming the no-agreement alternatives of the Israelis. In this sense, at least, these negotiations were a breakthrough. At the same time, there remains the question of whether the Oslo process, with its incremental logic, was flawed from the outset. One's assessment of this depends crucially on what one thinks the alternatives were and are.

with bombs. Israel drove the PLO leadership out of the Middle East, refused to recognize the PLO as the legitimate political representative of the Palestinians, and branded PLO members as terrorists.

Israel reached a peace agreement with Egypt in 1978, but the unresolved fate of the Palestinians proved an intractable obstacle to peace with its other Arab neighbors. Countless mediators had failed to reconcile the Palestinians and Israelis as a first step toward a comprehensive regional peace.

**Diagnose the barriers to agreement in this conflict. What were the toughest barriers? Why did the parties decide to negotiate at this time?**

By the early 1990s, however, conditions seemed propitious for peace in the Middle East. The Soviet empire had fallen, leaving the PLO without a superpower sponsor. In the 1991 Gulf War, PLO leader Yasser Arafat had sided with Saddam Hussein of Iraq, eroding Arab support and funding for the PLO and possibly leaving Arafat more conciliatory. In mid-1992, meanwhile, Israel elected a Labor-led government for the first time in 15 years. Traditionally the Labor Party had been more pro-peace than the Likud Party, and Prime Minister Yitzhak Rabin pledged a settlement with the Palestinians within nine months. Finally, the Palestinians' *intifadah* uprising in the Israeli-controlled territories of Gaza and the West Bank had given the Palestinian cause new international prominence.

However, much-publicized Middle East peace talks—begun in Madrid in 1991 and continued in Washington—had produced mostly grandstanding on both sides. Among the many barriers to a breakthrough was Israel's adamant opposition to the participation of the PLO. Yet the PLO played a decisive role behind the scenes, making a mockery of the Israeli stance.

Sentiment was growing on both sides that a *back channel*—a secret communications route—might offer the best hope for productive negotiations. Nonetheless, even insiders were surprised when it was revealed that a small group had created a functioning and effective back channel. Israel's unofficial spokesmen were two academics. The Palestinians' representatives were three high-ranking PLO members. In only three meetings, held in Norway between January and May 1993, this small group had crafted a draft Declaration of Principles for interim Palestinian self-rule—a goal that had eluded official negotiators for years.

In May 1993, Israel decided to upgrade the Oslo talks to official—but still secret—status. The outcome, while never a foregone conclusion, is now history. On September 13, 1993, the world watched as Israeli Prime Minister Yitzhak Rabin and PLO Chairman Yasser Arafat—sworn enemies for five decades—shook hands on the White House lawn and signed the Oslo Accord, an agreement on principles for a first-stage peace settlement.

The official negotiations that led to the breakthrough in Oslo lasted three months. It is often forgotten, however, that those meetings followed five months of unofficial talks, a delicate dance of "pre-negotiations." For years, efforts to bring together Israeli officials and PLO representatives had failed. What confluence of circumstances fostered these talks? How necessary were the five months of prenegotiations to the success of the official negotiations? And what role did the third party, Norway, play in bringing the two sides together?

## ALIGNING THE STARS

From its birth in 1948, Arab states regarded Israel as an interloper. The Arab countries had rejected as unjust a 1947 UN partition plan creating an Israeli and a Palestinian state. They attacked Israel in 1948 in the hope of regaining all of the former British mandate of Palestine. Instead, the Arabs lost the war, and waves of Palestinian refugees fled areas that fell under Israeli control.

Between Israel and its Arab neighbors, decades of skirmishes and three more wars—in 1967, 1973, and 1982—ensued. After each war, mediators achieved cease-fires but not a more durable peace. Meanwhile the conflict grew more dangerous as the superpowers took sides: the Soviet Union backed the Arabs, the United States supported Israel.

Throughout the first 25 years of Israeli statehood, the United Nations was the chief mediator in the region. Though it failed to secure peace, the UN Security Council did pass two resolutions that created a political framework for a comprehensive Arab-Israeli settlement. Resolution 242, adopted in 1967, established terms for "a just and lasting peace." The carefully worded document called for an end to all armed conflict, respect for each state's right to exist, and a solution to the refugee problem. The resolution also introduced a "land for peace" settlement formula. Six years later, after the 1973 war, UN Resolution 338 required mandatory and binding negotiations between the warring parties. In 1975, however, Israel lost faith in the United Nations as an impartial arbiter when the UN passed a resolution equating Zionism with racism.

> Why was the UN unable to mediate a settlement? Why was U.S. mediation acceptable to the Palestinians?

The United States then took over the mediator's role. President Jimmy Carter enjoyed notable success as sponsor of the 1978 Camp David peace accord between Egypt and Israel. Camp David set a critical precedent: that peace was possible between Arab and Jew, and that peace was more readily attainable bilaterally than multilaterally. The Camp David agreement also established a Palestinian right to autonomy, with a proposed interim period of self-rule to be followed by a permanent-status agreement. The autonomy talks that followed, though fruitless, constituted recognition that the fate of the Palestinians—both those in the growing diaspora and those in the Occupied Territories that Israel had won—had become the most persistent obstacle to a regional peace.

Israel's military victories also generated quandaries. After 1967, to the dismay of many Israelis, the country found itself functioning as an occupying force on the West Bank and in Gaza, with responsibility for 2 million Palestinian refugees. While Israel sought peace with the Arab states, many Israeli citizens concluded that true reconciliation would also require a settlement with the Palestinians.

The refugees languished in a stateless limbo. The more fortunate lived on the West Bank, adjoining Jordan, where they developed relatively thriving communities. The teeming refugee camps of the Gaza Strip, with their open sewers and poverty, were far grimmer. (See Figure 9.1 for a map of the region.) Palestinians had few civil rights and lived under a form of military dictatorship. Thousands held menial jobs in Israel, but the government could close the borders at will and prevent them from working.

## The PLO

Arab leaders created the Palestine Liberation Organization in 1964 to lead the struggle to recapture the Palestinian homeland. Their cause was dealt a decisive blow by the 1967 Six-Day War, when Israel captured the Gaza Strip, the Sinai, the Golan Heights, the West Bank, and East Jerusalem. These lands became known as the Occupied Territories.

**How had the Palestinians' perception of their BATNA changed over time?**

Defeat only made the PLO more belligerent. The 1968 Palestinian National Charter bluntly called for "an armed popular revolution for the liberation of [our] country and [our] return to it." Zionism, the Charter asserted, is "racist and fanatic in its nature, aggressive, expansionist and colonial in its aims, and fascist in its methods." The PLO, it said, "aims at the elimination of Zionism in Palestine."

Among the factions within the PLO, Yasser Arafat's Fatah (Palestine National Liberation Movement) emerged predominant. Initially headquartered in the West Bank, the PLO leadership moved to Jordan after the Six-Day War. In 1970, worried about domestic instability, Jordan's King Hussein forced the organization to leave. The PLO eventually found safe haven in Tunis, far from the people it claimed to represent. Its fears that rival leadership would spring up in the Occupied Territories created a new set of tensions.

**Inside vs. Outside.** The PLO's apprehension was justified. For years, Israel's government had nurtured an indigenous Palestinian leadership it hoped would replace the PLO. Israel refused to negotiate with any Palestinians not resident

**Figure 9.1.** The Middle East Region.

in the West Bank or Gaza, and the PLO was outlawed in Israel. Aided by rivalries among the Palestinians, Israel succeeded in creating a deep rift between "inside" Palestinians in the territories and "outside" Palestinians in Tunis.

Among the spokespersons for the West Bank Palestinians were Faisal Husseini, one of the original founders of the PLO, and the academic Hanan Ashrawi. Both felt keenly the irony of being mistrusted both by Israel and by their colleagues in Tunis. "We ('the inside') became the umbilical cord of the PLO, at once linking it to the rest of the world while granting it the legitimacy of a constituency in the land of Palestine," Ashrawi recalls. "Yet the 'outside' often questioned our motives, concerned that we were trying to set up an alternative authority that would ultimately usurp their power."[2]

**The *Intifadah*.** It was an uprising by the Palestinian people that gave insiders and outsiders a common cause. The year 1987 marked the start of the *intifadah*, a revolt by angry young Palestinians against their Israeli occupiers and the world's indifference to their plight. Stunned by the uprising, the PLO quickly took steps to orchestrate it. The *intifadah* advanced the Palestinian cause as television viewers worldwide saw stone-throwing Arab youths face Israeli soldiers in full battle gear.

The *intifadah* also gave rise to a radical Palestinian organization, Hamas (Islamic Resistance Movement), with roots in fundamentalist Islam. Hamas leaders rejected talk of peace; its tactics were kidnappings and killings. Moreover, Hamas dismayed insiders and outsiders alike by rejecting the PLO as ineffectual.

The *intifadah* confounded Israel. "It was clear that this uprising was on a new scale," explained Ehud Barak, then deputy chief of staff in the Israeli Defense Ministry, "and that these people were not 'terrorists,' but the population itself."[3] The *intifadah* revealed profound differences on peace policy within Israel and caused many Israelis to question retaining total control over the Occupied Territories.

## The View from Israel

Deep political and religious differences divided the Israeli public on the desirability of pursuing peace with the Palestinians. All agreed that guaranteeing the security of Israel was vital, and most Israelis also opposed division of Jerusalem (sacred to Jews, Christians, and Muslims). But opinions differed sharply on such questions as what constituted security, what advantages or disadvantages might ensue from peace with the Palestinians, whether Palestinian autonomy was acceptable, how to define autonomy, and who legitimately represented the Palestinian people.

> What might a package deal have looked like? What were the potentially toxic issues?

The chief Israeli political parties—Labor and Likud—reflected the central political divide.

**The Labor Party.** Over time, and especially with the rise of the *intifadah*, many secular Israelis began to look pragmatically at the difficulty and costs—not to mention ethics—of military occupation of the West Bank and Gaza. The Labor Party came to represent Israelis willing to consider trading day-to-day control over Palestinian affairs (autonomy) for the stability and prosperity that peace would bring. Labor factions led by longtime rivals Yitzhak Rabin and Shimon Peres disagreed over which enemy should be approached first: Syria, Jordan, Lebanon, or the Palestinians. But peace was the party's aim.

In the early and mid-1980s, party policy was to negotiate with Jordan as a surrogate for the Palestinians, in the hope of an eventual Jordanian/Palestinian confederation. But in mid-1988, King Hussein declared that he was no longer interested in the confederation. From then on, the Labor Party—at least the Peres wing—was prepared to negotiate directly with the Palestinians. But which Palestinians, and in what forum?

> Note the structural and institutional barriers to agreement.

**The Likud Party.** The Likud Party, which had dominated Israeli politics since 1977, took a harder line. Likud feared that peace would pose an unacceptable threat to Israeli security. In the Knesset (parliament), Likud needed the support of the religious right and endorsed its goal of resettling "the Biblical land of Israel," which included the West Bank and Jerusalem. The religious right systematically established Jewish settlements on the West Bank, and Likud encouraged this process with tax breaks and subsidized mortgages. Likud rejected any contact with the PLO. In 1986, a Likud-dominated Knesset passed a law (the "Law of Association") banning communication between Israelis and members of the PLO.[4]

# AN AGREEMENT THAT WASN'T

The political cost of Israeli differences on peace policy was vividly illustrated during the period (1984–1990) when the two leading parties shared power in a coalition government of "national unity." Labor had stipulated that it would remain in the coalition only so long as progress was being made toward peace. In 1987, Likud leader Yitzhak Shamir was serving as prime minister with Labor's Shimon Peres as foreign minister. In April 1987, Peres and King Hussein of Jordan agreed to an international peace conference, to be followed by direct bilateral negotiations between Israel and its adversaries. Hussein accepted

Israel's proposal to create a joint Jordanian-Palestinian delegation without PLO participation. The United States agreed to play an active role.

But Shamir, who had been fully informed about Peres's negotiations, rejected the formula; Likud feared that international peace talks would impose unwelcome demands on Israel. Shamir informed the United States that support of the Hussein-Peres proposal would be construed by Israel as gross interference in Israeli affairs. Peres felt humiliated and betrayed, and the London agreement died. But both covert and overt attempts to find a path to peace with the Palestinians intensified.

## TRYING FOR TALKS—BUT WITH WHOM?

After the 1978 Camp David agreement, opportunities for Israeli-Palestinian dialogue had multiplied. Egypt was newly able to function as an intermediary, and U.S. and European academic institutions hosted

**How did prior linked negotiations influence this negotiation?**

seminars at which representatives of the two sides could meet in unpressured settings. Prominent American Jews promoted contacts. Such meetings gradually helped both camps grasp the constraints under which the other side operated.

But even for Israelis who favored settlement with the Palestinians, the deceptively simple question continued to be: with which Palestinians should the government negotiate? On it hinged such critical issues as the framework for a Palestinian election and the degree of autonomy for a Palestinian entity. In the early 1980s, peace-minded Israelis hoped that West Bank Palestinian leaders would mature into a viable alternative to the PLO. By the end of the decade, that hope had been eroded by the PLO's clear dominance over all aspects of Palestinian affairs. Cautiously, and usually secretly, both Labor and Likud sought contact with the PLO.

### Labor Contacts

The Peres branch of the Labor Party led the effort to find common ground with the Palestinians. Since the collapse of a Jordanian-Palestinian confederation, Peres had concluded that "the only chance is the Palestinians." He resurrected an idea he had conceived after the Six-Day War: to give Gaza to the Palestinians to "self-administer." Self-rule for Gaza would not be controversial; nobody else wanted it. "While the Jordanians annexed the West Bank [until 1967], the Egyptians did not [annex Gaza]," says Peres. "I thought this was an important difference . . . that Gaza has a special status. I was simply looking for an opportunity."[5]

Peres's deputies were even more eager. A group of young Labor politicians, including Peres's deputy Yossi Beilin and Beilin's close associate Yair Hirschfeld, a lecturer on Middle East affairs at Haifa University, had already made contact with West Bank residents. Their agenda was at first economic—to study the Occupied Territories' potential for self-sufficiency—but it quickly became political. "In the course of conversations with [Faisal Husseini and Hanan Ashrawi]," wrote Beilin, "we were made aware of a picture vastly more complex than what we had previously envisaged. We were exposed to the divisions among themselves, to their conceptions of future solutions, and to the manner in which they analyzed Israeli policy."[6]

Such meetings grew more sensitive after passage of the 1986 law banning Israeli-PLO contacts, because leading West Bank Palestinians had close ties to the PLO. Husseini was a founding member. It was also increasingly clear that real decision-making power resided in Tunis. Israelis eager to promote peace were led inexorably toward the PLO. Ostensibly, Likud found this unacceptable. An Israeli peace campaigner was jailed for contacts with the PLO, and Shamir expelled a Cabinet minister for meeting a PLO member in Geneva.[7]

### Likud Contacts

But Likud members—especially Shamir—were less implacable than they wanted the public to believe. As early as 1985, Shamir consented to contact with the PLO to trace missing soldiers.[8] A secret negotiation channel was maintained for a year. It led nowhere, but marked a turning point—the first direct talks between Israelis and the PLO.[9]

Meanwhile, other Likud members pursued secret contacts with Palestinians and, indirectly, the PLO. In 1987, Moshe Amirav (a close associate of Shamir) had a series of encounters with Faisal Husseini to outline steps for establishing an unarmed Palestinian entity. But Shamir once again proved unforgiving toward the initiatives of others and torpedoed the arrangement.[10] Amirav was expelled from Likud; Husseini was jailed for contact with the PLO.

## THE PLO ACCEPTS ISRAEL

Barely a year later, Yasser Arafat took a step that made it harder for Israeli officials to bypass the PLO: the PLO's ruling body finally agreed to the 1947 UN partition plan for Palestine and endorsed UN Security Council Resolutions 242 and 338. These moves meant that the PLO accepted Israel's right to exist.[11] The PLO also called for an international peace conference.

> Note the removal of an institutional barrier to agreement.

The PLO thus threw down the peace gauntlet to Israel and freed its own officials to pursue contact with Israelis. It also reinforced its dominance in Palestinian affairs by making it likely that overtures toward Palestinians would lead back to the PLO. It had made itself an acceptable partner within the community of nations.

The United States was gratified by the PLO overture. Washington had made discussions with the PLO contingent on three conditions: acceptance of Resolutions 242 and 338, recognition of Israel's right to exist, and renunciation of terrorism. The United States now opened a formal channel to the PLO and proposed a plan for Israeli-Palestinian negotiations. But Shamir rejected the U.S. plan as he had the Peres-Hussein proposal of 1987. Then in March 1990, the United States again suspended relations with the PLO after a terrorist attack on Israel.

## SECRET CONTACTS

But the 1988 PLO decision opened the door to ever-bolder contacts between Israelis and Palestinians. Most of the contact focused on West Bank Palestinians, but increasingly they were seen as a conduit to the PLO in Tunis.

**Note the efforts at comediation.**

Peres's associate Yossi Beilin, then deputy minister of finance, was eager to reach out to peace-minded Palestinian leaders. Beilin's confederate Hirschfeld explains that "we knew that we wanted to use the inside Palestinians as a stepping-stone towards the outside [PLO]."[12] In early 1989, Beilin led a group of dovish Labor Party members to a confidential meeting with leading Palestinians. Discussion focused on Palestinian elections, recently proposed by Rabin. Under the Rabin plan, Palestinians in the West Bank and Gaza would elect representatives to negotiate with Israel for "expanded autonomy." The elections would exclude PLO representatives.

The Palestinian contingent was led by Faisal Husseini, recently released on Rabin's order from nearly 14 months of "administrative detention." Husseini opposed elections on the grounds that they would freeze the *status quo* to Israel's advantage. He also asserted that "at the very least, you need to understand that we are part of the PLO."[13] News of the meeting leaked to the press and further contact was suspended, but Beilin felt both sides understood each other's position better.

Four months later, Beilin pursued an opportunity for direct contact with the PLO. The Dutch had offered to host secret "proximity talks" (the two sides would not meet face-to-face). Beilin accepted the offer and took Yair Hirschfeld to the Hague with him. The PLO representatives were Hassan Asfour, Abdullah Hourani, and Afif Safiyeh.[14] A former Dutch foreign minister shuttled between the hotel rooms of the Israeli and PLO participants. The participants agreed on principles for opening negotiations between the PLO and Israel, but the document foundered on PLO reservations. Nonetheless, says Hirschfeld, "this opened up a lot of things. The proximity talks were enormously useful—not necessarily successful, but useful. Because they were sending a message, a very clear signal, that we will speak to the PLO."

| Note the use of initial agreement on principles to try to build momentum toward broader agreement. |

For Beilin, the Holland talks crystallized a vital personal decision: Beilin believed that it was willful blindness to pretend that Palestinian power lay anywhere but with the PLO, and in July 1989 he called openly for negotiations with the PLO.[15] Likud was outraged, but Peres refused a request from Shamir to fire Beilin.[16]

By early 1990 even Rabin, who had tried to hold together the coalition government, admitted that Likud was obstructing peace efforts. Labor quit the government. In mid-1990 a Likud-dominated right-wing/religious coalition took office with Shamir as Prime Minister.

In August 1990 Beilin, now a member of the opposition, and fourteen other members of parliament met with local Palestinian leaders. The resulting joint protocol for negotiations was released three days after Iraq invaded Kuwait, and events rendered it moot. But Beilin calls this the most important meeting yet with Palestinians. Husseini seemed to speak for both sides: "Peace will not be built on a balance of forces, such as leads to a balance of fear. Genuine peace and security will be built only on the shared interests of the two peoples."[17]

The Iraqi invasion would have far-reaching effects on the Middle East peace process. When the dust cleared, the geopolitical landscape had changed dramatically.

## DESERT STORM YIELDS MADRID CONFERENCE

After Iraq's invasion of Kuwait, an international coalition that included the United States and the Soviet Union ejected the Iraqi troops. Building on their military cooperation, the USSR and the United States co-sponsored a Middle East regional peace conference in Madrid in October 1991. Another sign of the new era was Moscow's

| How did the Gulf War alter the parties' perceptions of their BATNAs? |

reestablishment of diplomatic relations with Israel, broken off in 1967. Sponsorship of the Madrid Conference was one of the final acts of the Soviet state, which dissolved in 1991. The Arab states and the PLO thus lost the superpower sponsor on whom they had depended. The stage was set for a new era in

Middle East politics, but there were few signs that for the PLO it would be a better era.

The PLO participated in the Madrid peace conference from a position of weakness. Arafat had cheered Saddam Hussein's invasion of Kuwait, and Arab leaders punished the PLO: its subsidies from Arab states tumbled from $350 million a year in 1988 to only $40 million by 1993.[18] The PLO faced bankruptcy. It appeared possible that the Palestinians would decide not to participate in the Madrid Conference at all, and many Israelis would have applauded their exclusion. Thanks to the judicious diplomacy of U.S. Secretary of State James Baker, the Israelis agreed to a Palestinian presence, but the Likud-led government set stringent conditions: Palestinians would represent only half of a joint Jordanian-Palestinian delegation, and no PLO representative could join the delegation.[19] The Israelis also won Baker's agreement that bilateral and multilateral negotiations proceed separately (but concurrently).

The Madrid Conference thus opened two parallel negotiating tracks, bilateral and multilateral. Multilateral working groups took up thorny regional issues—water, the environment, arms control, refugees, and economic development. Bilateral negotiations began between Israel and Syria, Israel and Lebanon, and Israel and the Jordanian-Palestinian delegation. The groups that convened first in Madrid and continued in Washington met in a variety of locations, but the process became known as the Washington talks. With Syria and Lebanon, the goal was peace treaties. With the Palestinians, participants foresaw two stages of talks aimed at some form of Palestinian autonomy. The first stage would establish a five-year interim self-government; the second would deal with the permanent status of a Palestinian entity.

**Note how the media contributed to creating institutional barriers to agreement. Were secret negotiations a better option?**

Within months, however, talks with the Palestinians bogged down both bilaterally and multilaterally. The ban on PLO members meant that Palestinians were represented by leaders from the West Bank or Gaza.[20] But these delegates would agree to nothing without consulting a PLO representative—who often occupied a nearby hotel suite. Media scrutiny was intense. Negotiators were reluctant to agree to anything that could not be instantly explained to the TV audience at home. Positions hardened, and procedure and process consumed more time than substance. As Palestinian delegate Hanan Ashrawi remembers with some bitterness, "The negotiations took on a double vision, with one eye on our constituency and another on our counterparts, all under the scrutiny of Tunis. Our press briefings became debates by proxy, and the substance of our talks the public property of all interested parties and individuals."[21] Highly placed individuals on both sides of the conflict believed another avenue for dialogue had to be found.

# TENTATIVE CONTACTS

By early 1992, unofficial contacts between Israelis and the PLO had multiplied. Abu Mazen (Mahmoud Abbas), a top PLO official, wrote that the PLO pursued these contacts deliberately: "When we reached the conclusion that the Israelis were here to stay, we hoped that they too would reach the conclusion that dialogue with their neighboring States was no substitute for dialogue with us—the owners and people of the land, a people who yearned for an identity and an address."[22]

That year, according to Abu Mazen, the PLO established tentative communication with representatives of Likud leader Ariel Sharon, Labor leader Rabin, and then–Prime Minister Shamir. Sometimes West Bank Palestinians served as go-betweens; sometimes the Egyptians conveyed messages; sometimes the contact was direct. These meetings, though ultimately inconclusive, demonstrated to both sides that discreet communication was possible.

> An entrepreneurial mediator worked to create a secret channel. How did he gain entry? What were his sources of power?

Among the third parties eager to promote rapprochement was Terje Roed-Larsen, a Norwegian social scientist who had studied living standards in Gaza and in the process met many leading Israelis and Palestinians. In April 1992 Larsen offered Yossi Beilin Norway's assistance in setting up an unofficial channel of communication between the Israelis and the Palestinians. Beilin proposed that Larsen contact Beilin's longtime associate Yair Hirschfeld to pursue a meeting with Husseini.[23] Neither man suspected, says Beilin, that "a cordial meeting such as this was to engender a process which would influence Israel, the region, and the world."[24] Hirschfeld's initial impression was positive but guarded:

> My impression was that he's sincere, that he will keep a secret, that he will not run and that he is reliable. [But the Norwegians] had very little experience. We could tell them all kinds of stories which they would take at face value. . . . [For example] we didn't say we really want to move towards the PLO. We said we're not moving towards the PLO, that we are with the "inside."

Larsen arranged a meeting with Beilin, Hirschfeld, and Husseini to discuss a proposal that Norway host secret Israeli-Palestinian negotiations. Husseini praised the idea of a "laboratory" with the potential to yield a speedy agreement. But before any further moves along the track to peace could be contemplated, the Israelis had to elect a new government. National elections were scheduled for June 1992.

## A NEW DAY FOR LABOR

Yitzhak Rabin emerged from bitter primaries ahead of his lifelong rival Shimon Peres as head of the Labor Party and candidate for prime minister. Running on a platform of peace, Rabin pledged that his gov-

> **What roles did Rabin and Peres play in this negotiation? Whose contribution was more critical?**

ernment would reach an autonomy agreement with the Palestinians within six to nine months. The public responded by electing a Labor government for the first time since 1977. As foreign minister, Rabin appointed his defeated rival Shimon Peres. Peres's longtime assistant Yossi Beilin was made deputy foreign minister.

The two men—both nearing 70 years old—had competed personally for nearly 50 years. Uri Savir, a protégé of Peres who came to know Rabin well, observes, "[The two men] had traveled a long road together in fierce competition and mistrust. They were almost perfect opposites: Rabin, a guarded analyst of the present, obsessed by details; Peres, a cosmopolitan conceptualist who sees history in terms of processes and is obsessed by the future."[25] Peres was a diplomat who spoke several languages and moved with ease in global circles. Rabin was a soldier, blunt and principled. Eitan Haber, an aide and confidante to Rabin, muses, "You can write, not a book—you can write a bible about their relations and how their relations affected the Israeli story, in politics, in every field you can choose. From art to the army to everything."[26]

Terje Larsen was delighted with the election results. A potentially academic discussion with an opposition leader took on a new aspect when Beilin assumed high office. In September, Norway sent Deputy Foreign Minister Jan Egeland to Israel to pursue a Norwegian back channel for Palestinian-Israeli negotiations.

## NORWAY: SMALL AND GENEROUS

At a secret meeting in September 1992, Egeland renewed Larsen's offer. Beilin says they agreed to "a series of conversations between myself and Faisal Husseini, with the intention of dismantling the obstacles currently blocking progress in the Washington talks."[27] The talks would remain secret, and breakthroughs would be presented to the official delegations in Washington to claim as their own.

Egeland's belief that Norway could help advance the Middle East peace process was consistent with the Scandinavian country's self-image and history. It had long provided generous aid to the developing world, and benefited as a potential mediator from a neutral public image.[28] As Egeland puts it: "We either have no image, because nobody knows we exist, or we have a good image."[29]

Norway's geostrategic insignificance also meant that other countries did not suspect it of a hidden agenda. A national consensus in favor of promoting world peace, plus the 50-year dominance of its Labor Party, allowed the government to take a long view of its commitments abroad. "If you work to promote peace, democracy, development of human rights, you can't think in one presidential period," says Egeland. "You have to think in terms of at least two or three, and that is one of our strengths."

> **What made Norway a good candidate for sponsoring the secret talks?**

Norway had long taken an active interest in the Middle East, and supported the state of Israel from its inception. Later, to even the balance, Norway strengthened its contacts with the PLO and permitted a PLO office in Oslo. Now, its eagerness to build contacts seemed on the verge of paying off. Perhaps Norway could help engineer a breakthrough in Palestinian-Israeli relations. After all, Rabin had pledged peace with the Palestinians within six to nine months. The clock was ticking.

## WHOSE CHANNEL WHERE?

Rabin was indeed committed to finding a road to peace, but he intended any solution to redound to his own credit. Peres, he made clear, was to stay out. Beilin soon discovered this for himself. As Beilin prepared to tell Peres about the Norwegian offer, Peres informed him that Rabin had forbidden Peres to meet with Husseini.[30] Beilin was dumbfounded: if Peres was prohibited from meeting with Husseini, Beilin himself could not ask for permission to do so. But, he says, "I couldn't tell anyone the reason for canceling the Oslo track, since this would expose the relationship between the Prime Minister and the foreign minister and the vulnerable status of my immediate superior."[31] Instead, Beilin told his colleague Professor Hirschfeld that he should consider going to Oslo in Beilin's stead. Beilin left it up to Hirschfeld whether to go, and whether to meet with Husseini or someone else. Both men remembered Husseini urging them that Israel contact the PLO directly.

> **Note the use of informal representatives to build momentum and overcome institutional barriers.**

Meanwhile, West Bank Palestinians and the PLO were disappointed to see little new or bold coming from the new Labor government. Hanan Ashrawi recalled that Palestinians had "looked forward to the end of ostrich politics and mercurial negotiations and to the beginning of genuine engagement."[32] But no new proposals were put on the table in Washington. In mid-1992, Rabin froze

Israeli settlements in the Occupied Territories, but finessed the decision by allowing work to proceed on some 11,000 units already under construction.[33] Instead of discussing Palestinian claims to Jerusalem, Rabin referred to "the eternal capital of Israel forever and ever."

But Rabin was officially committed to reaching a settlement with the Palestinians, and his government pursued opportunities. The Egyptians became a favored channel of communication. In October 1992, for example, Egyptian Foreign Minister Amr Moussa told the PLO's Abu Mazen about his encouraging recent conversations with Rabin, in which Rabin had declared himself ready to hold elections soon for a Palestinian Council.

# GAZA FIRST?

Meanwhile Peres visited Egypt to float a trial balloon of his own. Peres had a trusting relationship with the Egyptians, earned in the 1980s when he had returned part of the Sinai to Egyptian control. Peres suggested to Mubarak that Israel might be willing to test Palestinian autonomy first in Gaza. If Arafat accepted autonomy in Gaza, Peres indicated, the PLO leader could return to govern it. Peres's lieutenant Uri Savir comments: "That was the strategic move that made a difference. . . . 'Gaza first' would never have happened without Arafat knowing that he was part of the deal."[34] Peres also made a second, equally important offer. Aware that Palestinians feared "Gaza first" would mean "Gaza last" (that there would be no further autonomy), Peres suggested that Israel might be willing to grant autonomy to Jericho or Jenin, largely Arab West Bank towns—a concept that came to be known as "Gaza Plus."[35] For unclear reasons, the PLO rejected the proposal and the offer languished.

> The move to a package deal helped to open up a ZOPA.

But Peres did not stop with that. He had already told Rabin privately that Israel needed to deal directly with the PLO.[36] Now he went public with that belief. In December 1992, Peres told the newspaper *Yedioth Aharanot*, "We must speak with the PLO." In January, he took an arguably even more daring step: he told Rabin that Israel should invite Arafat to return to Gaza. Avi Gil, the aide to whom Peres dictated notes of the conversation, was shocked by Peres's suggestion: "Peres told me that he had told Rabin, 'There's no hope for the talks in Washington. We have to make a big step in the PLO's direction. We actually have to talk with the PLO. We have to offer them Gaza First, and we have to bring Arafat and his people to Gaza.'"[37]

Peres urged Rabin to think about it. The suggestion to allow Arafat to return "was what horrified [Rabin] the most," notes Peres. Gil considered Rabin's dismay justified. "To bring Arafat to Gaza—I told [Peres] at that moment, 'You've lost your mind, lost your political sense!'" But Peres felt the PLO connection was inevitable. "I was seized with the fear of what would happen if Arafat were to fall," he explains. "The conclusion was that he would be replaced by Hamas. We came to the conclusion that it was preferable to save Arafat."[38] At the same time, Peres notes, "In my heart, I had a lot of hesitations about Arafat."

Peres's longtime preference for dealing with "inside" Palestinians had shifted toward a recognition that the PLO called the shots. But if Israel wanted negotiations with the PLO, where should they be held? Who should participate? And how would a negotiator gain the support of the Israeli public—not to mention Rabin's endorsement? Answers to some of these questions were already in the works.

## BIRTH OF THE OSLO CHANNEL

In 1991 and early 1992, the PLO had sent delegations to Oslo to seek financial support for the Occupied Territories. One delegation included Abu Ala (Ahmed Suleiman Qurei), the PLO minister of economy, who had risen to prominence as director of the investment fund for the PLO. Terje Larsen met with Abu Ala and recalls "a fantastic conversation. . . . He was very different from anything I thought the PLO was all about. A very charming, very sophisticated man, and I could see sparks in this guy, a very rich personality."[39] The two met again through the Working Group on Refugees, a multilateral group affiliated with the Washington talks. Both men represented their governments, although as a PLO member Abu Ala could not attend sessions. Larsen observed that the West Bank Palestinian delegates "were just puppets on a string. The PLO in Tunis were steering absolutely everything."

Meanwhile Larsen wondered why Beilin was being so elusive about Norway's offer of a secret venue for frank Palestinian-Israeli talks. His frustration would not last much longer. In December 1992, Abu Ala was to attend a London meeting that Yossi Beilin, the Israeli deputy foreign minister, also planned to attend. Beilin had continued to argue that the most constructive path to peace was Israeli contact with the PLO, and to make that legal he had sought repeal of the 1986 "Law of Association" banning communication. A first reading of a bill revoking the law passed the Knesset on the eve of the London meeting. Prime Minister Rabin emphasized that government sponsorship of the bill did not mean that Israel meant to negotiate with the PLO.

But Beilin's unofficial West Bank Palestinian contacts were urging their Israeli associates to pursue this very course. Ron Pundak, an academic colleague of Hirschfeld's, remembers that "the message we always got from Hanan [Ashrawi] and Faisal [Husseini] was: 'Go to the PLO. [The Washington delegation] can't deliver [a peace agreement].'"[40] Ashrawi suggested that Hirschfeld and Pundak establish contact with Abu Ala. "She knew exactly what we were doing," says Pundak, "and she saw a very interesting possibility . . . maybe a meeting can bring something in order to get the PLO engaged. It was illegal, but we were academicians and we thought maybe we could get away with it."

Hirschfeld had felt jubilant at the Labor Party election victory. Over the years of meeting with West Bank Palestinians, he believed the two sides had developed a three-step approach to reaching workable negotiation proposals.[41] He had hoped that, with Labor in power, he and his Palestinian counterparts could function as an unofficial channel for pursuing a peace settlement. But Rabin's injunction against a Peres-Husseini meeting had put an end to that process. "My conclusions were simple," says Hirschfeld. "The entire back-channel concept was basically in a deadlocked situation, as were the negotiations."

**Why wouldn't the Israelis simply agree to official negotiations? What barriers did the unofficial talks help them to overcome?**

Hirschfeld had not forgotten the Norwegian offer to host confidential meetings. Aware that Abu Ala would be in London, he decided to meet the Palestinian. Ashrawi called Abu Ala and asked him to meet Hirschfeld. Hirschfeld did not inform Beilin. "We didn't want to tell Yossi [Beilin] that we were going to meet Abu Ala," says Pundak. "The reason was we wanted neither to receive a yes nor a no. A yes could make problems for him; a no could make problems for us. So this was probably the first and last time we did something connected to the process without telling him."

Hirschfeld took what he acknowledges as a risk and told Larsen of the meeting with Abu Ala: "I said, 'I'm about to meet Abu Ala. If this works well, I will want to meet him again. Can you help me?' His answer was, 'I'll get you any help you want from the Norwegian government. We will do everything you need.' He couldn't have been clearer."

Abu Ala had been reluctant to meet Hirschfeld. He says he told Ashrawi: "'But I never met an Israeli before!' And that's true. I met with Jewish [people], but never with an Israeli."[42] After the meeting, Abu Ala felt encouraged. For his part, Hirschfeld was aware that he was walking a thin line: "I had to give two contradicting impressions. The first is that I'm not an official, I'm speaking for myself, I'm speaking for nobody else. Whatever I say is what I think, but it has nothing to do with the government of Israel. On the other hand, I wanted to give the impression also that I had to be taken seriously, that what I say has relevance and weight, it is connected to the government."

That evening, Hirschfeld told Beilin about the meeting. Beilin had just told two U.S. State Department officials that they should start a back channel to the PLO. They had said they could not—but that someone should. Continues Hirschfeld: "Then I come five minutes afterwards and say, 'You know, I've established a back channel.'" Beilin encouraged him to pursue it.[43]

At a second meeting with Abu Ala, Hirschfeld suggested that they meet again in Oslo. Abu Ala recalls asking him: "'For what to meet, to waste time?' I told him: 'With whom you are here?' He said alone. I told him: 'You know Yossi Beilin?' He said, 'Of course, he's my close friend.' I said Aha, perhaps they coordinate." The two men agreed in principle to meet again in Oslo.

## THE LEAD-UP TO OSLO

Back in Tunis, Abu Ala asked Arafat whether to accept the invitation to Oslo. "Of course. Why not?" responded Arafat. Abu Mazen concurred. Notes Abu Mazen:

> The thought flashed through my mind that a door for a secret dialogue was opening, that this man [Hirschfeld] could not have acted on his own initiative . . . that he must have received authorization from his bosses, Peres and Beilin, that he had been sent to sound us out and that this faction in the Israeli Cabinet wanted to open a channel other than the Washington channel.[44]

Norway, says Abu Mazen, had skillfully positioned itself to host the upcoming talks: "We realized how perfectly the Norwegians had played their hand in bringing about a meeting between the two adversaries on their soil."[45] Beilin remembers approving Norway as a rendezvous because the Norwegian government could finance the meetings and set no preconditions. Other governments had wanted assurances that Rabin and Peres were behind the secret initiative. "The most important role of the Norwegians was that they were ready to take part in such an effort knowing it was only me behind it," says Beilin. "I tried to convince two other governments [U.S. and Britain] to do this and . . . they were afraid."[46]

According to Uri Savir, an Israeli who would later work with Abu Ala, events unfolded in keeping with PLO plans. Arafat wanted the Washington talks to fail, Savir says, to prevent the West Bank Palestinian negotiators from gaining ground. The PLO had sought to forge direct contacts with Israel instead. Moreover, adds Savir, Abu Mazen and Abu Ala shared an ideology—that salvation for the Palestinians "would be realized through cooperation with Israel and not through cooperation with the Arabs. . . . They were looking for a suitable track to express this."[47] Above all, the PLO wanted an agreement with Israel because peace would discredit Hamas, which posed the greatest threat to PLO authority. As Abu Ala would later concede: "If you quote me, I won't admit it, but as far as we are concerned your [Israel's] battle with Hamas is our battle, because the strategy of Hamas is a greater threat to the Palestinians than it is to Israel."[48]

The entire Oslo project could have foundered in December when Rabin expelled over 400 Hamas militants to Lebanon in retaliation for the deaths of eight Israeli soldiers. International reaction was swift. The United Nations voted for the return of the Hamas fighters. Arab governments, at the behest of the PLO, broke off the Washington talks. The talks remained stalled for months.

Surprisingly, the PLO did not cancel the Norway meeting. As Abu Mazen recalls, it was too good an opportunity to lose. "In spite of its unofficial and humble beginnings, at least on the Israeli side, we depended on it," he says, "since to us it was a glimmer of hope that was not to be squandered."[49] The Norwegians decided to disguise the meeting as a seminar on living conditions in Gaza. The PLO would send three participants. For the Israelis, Hirschfeld would attend with his colleague Ron Pundak. Beilin says his instructions were specific: "The most important thing was to make clear to Abu Ala that these talks were not taking place in the conventional framework of pyramidal power—that only I was aware of them—and the objective at this stage was to study ways of overcoming obstacles in the Washington talks."[50] If the two teams could resolve outstanding differences, the plan was to inform the U.S. State Department, which would introduce the compromise into the Washington talks as an American-sponsored measure. The two sides would then give it formal approval.

> **Note the removal of a barrier to agreement.**

The night before Hirschfeld and Pundak left Tel Aviv, the Knesset finally repealed the "Law of Association" banning contact with the PLO.[51] They would not have to break the law to attend the Norwegian seminar.

## THE SPIRIT OF NORWAY

The first meeting took place at a manor house outside Oslo. The organizers were at pains to establish the right tone for the initial encounter. Larsen recalls:

> What I wanted was a prenegotiating phase, because I thought there had to be confidence established on an emotional basis. . . . I thought if they were to get to know each other, they had to be in a remote place and they should be with one another around the clock. . . . I also decided to treat the Israelis and the Palestinians exactly the same way: they should have the same cars, the same hotel rooms, the same food.

Abu Ala brought with him Hassan Asfour, who had taken part in the 1989 "proximity talks" with Hirschfeld and Beilin in The Hague. The third member of the PLO team was Abu Ala's economic advisor, Maher el-Kurd, who spoke fluent English.

Deputy Foreign Minister Jan Egeland joined the group for lunch on the first day, which Pundak recalls as a critical signal: "It put the whole session at the ministerial level. It told the Palestinians that the Norwegians are taking the Israelis very seriously. After all, the PLO were ministerial level. We were no level. They were officials, we were nonofficials." After lunch, the Israelis and Palestinians secluded themselves for an eight-hour marathon session. The negotiators chose to sit at a round table rather than on sofas. They spoke English, which as a second language for all put them on an equal footing.

> What techniques did Larsen use to help overcome psychological barriers? What role did he play in the negotiations and why?

From the start, the Norwegians were facilitators, not mediators. Larsen understood that the Norwegian role was to let the two parties get to know one another:

> In prenegotiations, the parties have to gain confidence. It's like a love story. You can't have a chaperone with you if you try to seduce. That's why I thought they have to sit alone, they have to fight, they have to scream, they have to cry, they have to do everything. But I'll be there when it collapses to pull them together.

Abu Ala opened with a document from Arafat proposing a close variant of the "Gaza first" concept that Peres had suggested two months earlier. The proposal called for Israeli withdrawal from Gaza within three years, leaving it in trusteeship under Egypt or an international authority while negotiations continued on an interim autonomy scheme for the West Bank. Abu Ala was both wide-ranging and specific. He suggested a free-trade area, a maritime canal, and a gas pipeline. He also advocated a "mini–Marshall Plan" of global economic assistance for the Palestinians. "Why has there not been a withdrawal if Gaza gives you all these headaches?" he asked. "If that happens, it will herald the beginning of cooperation with Israel, because Gaza needs a Marshall Plan, and it could be made a free zone."[52] Such language was well calculated to win points with the Israeli officials who presumably stood behind the two academics. According to Uri Savir, Abu Ala was "speaking Peres's language. Abu Ala had read Peres's books. The whole thing with a Marshall Plan, etc., these were buzzwords." Abu Ala also urged those present to put aside the past:

> Look, we can speak about the past. You will never convince me; I will never convince you. I will continue to say it's Palestine and from the sea onwards it's ours. And you will continue to say that the same land is Israeli. We will not reach an agreement. Let's look to the future. . . . What's the basis [for negotiations], the principles?

Both sides agreed on more discussion as soon as possible.

# DELIBERATIONS AT HOME

The PLO was encouraged by the first meeting, though Abu Mazen notes that Tunis worried about "the extent to which these Israeli negotiators represented the Israeli political establishment, their ability to commit themselves to whatever was agreed, and to subsequently promote these agreements in Israel."[53] The PLO saw little indication, however, that the Oslo talks would be any more successful than previous attempts to reach agreement with Israel. Recalls Abu Ala, "This channel has been created by accident. It was never designed, it was never planned. . . . Negotiations, particularly secret negotiations—there should be there some results. Otherwise it's a talk, like two friends—"How are you, how's your son, how's the weather? It's nothing.""

Abu Mazen, by contrast, had a vision for the Oslo channel and persuaded Arafat to pursue the opportunity it presented.[54] As Peres later noted, "The central figure, the sharp one, was Abu Mazen. . . . Abu Mazen absolutely played a constructive role. I think he is a constructive individual." PLO hopes clearly outweighed their doubts.

In Israel, the two professors reported to Beilin. "The partners [the Palestinian team] were very serious," Hirschfeld told Beilin, "and taking the track with alarming and possibly excessive seriousness."[55] But Hirschfeld was buoyed by the furthering of what he saw as the talks' true purpose: "The real purpose was to check what are their positions. The real purpose was to go and see where are the real red lines? What do they really want? What do they really not want?"

When the Washington talks broke off in December, the Israelis and Palestinians were still far apart. The Palestinians, afraid that any interim solution would turn into a *de facto* final settlement, wanted guarantees about the form of a permanent arrangement. At bottom, they wanted a Palestinian state. The Israelis were unprepared to accept such a state or to commit to final settlement details.

**The basic outlines of a package deal emerged.**

Hirschfeld offered to draft a bridging proposal for the second meeting in Norway that would favor neither side. Pundak characterized it as "a kind of integrated paper, not representing anybody's first positions but already almost the last position, close to an agreement." The document consisted of principles for negotiations on interim Palestinian self-rule and supplements on Israeli-Palestinian cooperation in such matters as water and Abu Ala's "Marshall Plan" project. Hirschfeld's paper incorporated a concept that had emerged from years of conversations with West Bank Palestinians: 'graduality'—the gradual transfer of authority from Israeli to Palestinian institutions. It proposed that the Palestinians accept interim self-government even without the guarantee of an eventual state—a proposal that had been rejected in Washington—and argued that the

Palestinians needed time to build their institutions. The interim government would have the authority to conduct final status negotiations, at which time the Palestinians could draw any lines in the sand they wished. The document also incorporated Abu Ala's suggestion of a temporary trusteeship. Graduality would reassure the Israeli side as well, giving both parties some authority but leaving in Israeli hands any powers not explicitly transferred to the Palestinians. Many thorny questions, including the status of Jerusalem, were postponed, and Hirschfeld's paper avoided the contentious issue of mutual security.

## REACHING A DRAFT AGREEMENT

Meanwhile, Beilin informed Peres about the first Oslo meeting, and in February 1993, Peres took the momentous step of informing Rabin about the overtures coming out of Oslo. Peres says he "made sure to tell Yitzhak everything I knew. Because I thought that if he found out about something that I didn't tell him, it would make him unusually suspicious."[56] Peres laid out Abu Ala's proposals, including the mini–Marshall Plan and economic cooperation. To Peres's relief, Rabin did not halt the meetings in Oslo. He did insist that Oslo in no way supplant the Washington talks; Rabin continued to prefer dealing with West Bank Palestinians. Rabin's grudging acquiescence can be attributed, say Peres and others, to his belief that the Oslo talks would lead nowhere. Remarks Peres:

> He agreed to the connection with Oslo in the beginning because he thought nothing was going to come of it. I must say that he even admitted this frankly. He was asked why he didn't tell [close aides]. He said, "I didn't tell them because I didn't think anything was going to come of it." He thought to himself: It's good that Shimon will keep himself busy with that.[57]

Rabin, Beilin, and Peres agreed that the talks must remain both secret and deniable. A "belt of deniability" between the government and the two academics allowed the government to disavow the talks should they become public. Peres says that without secrecy, the talks would have failed:

> The minute it becomes public, it becomes a public polemic. When you begin to negotiate, you discover very soon that you have to negotiate with your own people more than you negotiate with [the adversary]. . . . They would say "Why are you making concessions, why are you making compromises? Are you crazy?"

The politicians were particularly anxious to keep the Oslo negotiations secret from the Israeli intelligence service, AMAN. The normal give-and-take of bargaining would inevitably have been distorted by AMAN, says Peres: "After going through the laundry at AMAN, every bluff becomes truth and every kibbitz [translation: suggestion] becomes serious."[58]

With Rabin in on the Oslo secret, the nascent negotiations took on a new level of solemnity. With their draft of negotiating principles in hand, Hirschfeld and Pundak returned to Oslo in February 1993. The meeting focused on Hirschfeld's bridging proposal. The two sides discussed such intractable problems as the status of Jerusalem and Israeli settlement policy, deportees, and elections. The Palestinians also reported, says Pundak, that the leadership in Tunis had decided "to turn Oslo into the exclusive channel, into a clearinghouse for all [other] channels." Hirschfeld gave the Palestinians what he called a travel plan—an overview of the stages they could expect to traverse together: fact-finding, authorization, legitimization, and breakthrough. He pinpointed their joint position as well into the second stage.[59]

**What were the pluses and minuses for the Israelis of negotiating in secret through unofficial representatives?**

The session made speedy progress. The participants hammered out a compromise draft of a Declaration of Principles (DOP), for which they agreed they would seek initial approval in the secret track. Then Warren Christopher would be alerted and, in a spurt of shuttle diplomacy, secure the public agreement of Husseini and Rabin. On the eve of the signing, Israel would begin transferring powers to Palestinian councils. Elections a few months later would create a Palestinian Assembly (legislature), which would sign an interim agreement with Israel. Israel would fully withdraw from Gaza within two years, to be replaced by Egyptian or international trustees.[60]

**Note the use of stages and agreement on principles to build momentum.**

Larsen informed Beilin within days that the PLO had accepted the draft DOP in principle, which put new pressure on Hirschfeld and Pundak. Abu Ala had pressed them repeatedly for proof of official backing. Hirschfeld had put him off, but knew he could not do so for long. Wrote Beilin: "We came to the conclusion that all the potential for informal [probing] had been exhausted." It was time to submit the draft to higher authority.

## PROGRESS BEHIND THE SCENES

Beilin gave Peres the draft DOP but did not characterize it as a breakthrough. At the time he did not consider it an historic achievement: "It was not a surprise for us that we had an agreement," he says, "because we had had it in the past, a common document.[61] I believed and Yair believed, all those years, that it was possible to have a final agreement."

Peres convened what would become the "Oslo headquarters" team: himself, Beilin, Hirschfeld, Pundak, Beilin's aide Shlomo Gur, and Peres's office manager, Avi Gil. Peres's first reaction was not heartening. Ironically, it was the Palestinians' cooperation that disturbed him. "The thing that surprised me, and also worried me a little," he explains, "was Arafat's unexpected flexibility. The whole time I had doubts about whether they were pulling our leg, or whether it is possible to work with them."[62] Peres was also uneasy about how well the two professors were representing Israeli interests. "I thought [the draft] was not professional," he says. "With the trusteeship and all this." Among his chief reservations was that "I thought that Yair and Ron were too eager. . . . I would have liked to have seen our side being a bit more to the point, because I understood that we had to sell the deal to two sides, and not just to one side."

Hirschfeld and Pundak, however, were well aware of the responsibility that rested with them. Says Pundak: "Yair and I all the time [asked ourselves], 'If Yossi [Beilin] and Shimon [Peres] were sitting here, what would they have said?' In other words, we didn't speak based on the feelings in our own hearts at all."

"My problem," responds Peres, "was to find out whether there was a partner, not whether there was a program. . . . Programs don't make partners. Partners make programs." But several aspects of the document gave Peres grounds for optimism. He was pleased that discussion of the status of Jerusalem and Israeli settlements had been postponed; he also welcomed the agreement that self-rule and Israeli withdrawal from the Occupied Territories would be gradual. He was puzzled, however, by an omission. Why had the Palestinians not picked up on his own suggestion to add Jericho or Jenin to the Gaza First proposal? Was Arafat not involved?

> **Note the efforts at mutual confidence building that led to official talks.**

Both the Israelis and the Palestinians were uncertain about the legitimacy of the Oslo channel. Peres asked himself with whom he was dealing. Did Abu Ala have the ability and authority to implement difficult political decisions? Did Arafat support him? And the Palestinians had ample cause to wonder who stood behind Hirschfeld and Pundak. Larsen had assured Abu Ala that the two academics had high-level backing, but he could not supply proof. There were even signs that Larsen was wrong. Abu Mazen knew Rabin had recently dispatched other envoys to seek indirect dialogue with the PLO, but could not decide whether Rabin was in the dark about Oslo or playing a complex double game.[63] When other Israelis invited Abu Mazen to meet, he refused: "[I] refused such proposals because of the possibility in my mind that Rabin's government was testing us and our commitment to the Oslo channel, to see whether we might hedge our bets and contact more than one group or open more than one channel."[64]

Both sides tested the channel by seeking concessions that had proven unattainable in Washington to see how influential the Oslo participants were. The Palestinians wanted Husseini admitted as a delegate to the Washington negotiations. Rabin wanted resumption of the Washington talks, suspended since his expulsion of the Hamas activists. He asked Peres to request in Norway that the talks be restarted. It was not an auspicious moment for such a request. On March 2, two Palestinians from Gaza killed two Israelis in Tel Aviv. Rabin sealed off the Gaza Strip indefinitely, preventing 35,000 Palestinians from commuting to jobs in Israel. More violence followed, with deaths on both sides. But Hirschfeld and Pundak returned to Norway with the explicit charge of asking the PLO to call off the Arab boycott of the Washington talks.

## WHO ARE YOU, ANYWAY?

The five negotiators reconvened in Norway for the third time in March 1993. Hirschfeld, aware of the Palestinians' doubts about his authority, opened with a strong hint that he and Pundak had highly-placed supporters. Peres had authorized him to ask Abu Ala at what stage during the proposed interim settlement talks Arafat would return to Gaza. "From that point on," says Hirschfeld, "I personally felt that Abu Ala was mine. We gave Abu Ala the ability to say to Arafat: 'Listen, you're going home.'"[65] Hirschfeld also requested resumption of the Washington talks. After consultations with Tunis, the three PLO members promised to try to get the Palestinians back to the table in Washington.

Meanwhile the negotiators refined the draft DOP. The Israelis wanted to omit references to international supervision of Palestinian elections. The Palestinians were willing to modify rules on eligibility to vote in return for earlier Israeli withdrawal from Gaza. Neither side raised the status of the PLO, still outlawed under Israeli law. And the Palestinians still did not refer to Peres's "Gaza Plus Jericho" formula. In two days, the group produced a document that would have to be scrutinized by the leadership of both sides. But the draft DOP was a proud achievement for its five authors. If both Israel and the PLO signed off on the draft, they would ask Secretary of State Christopher to present the agreement as if it had been a U.S. initiative all along. The official delegations in Washington would then sign—and take credit for—the statement of principles.

The Norwegian foreign minister had already told Christopher that unofficial talks were under way in Norway. No one wanted Washington to consider the Oslo effort subversive; the participants viewed Oslo as a complement to the larger peace process in Washington. Accordingly, Hirschfeld and Pundak showed a copy of the DOP to the State Department's Dan Kurtzer. Nevertheless, the Israelis say, the Americans never took the Oslo channel seriously. Even when the Washington talks resumed, the Americans did not give the Oslo channel credit. For the Israelis, however, resumption of the Washington talks cast the Oslo connection in a new light.

# TRUST VINDICATED

The renewed Washington talks increased Peres's esteem for Abu Ala—the apparent engineer of the return to Washington. Peres sanctioned a fourth round of talks in April, at which much discussion was devoted to the channel itself: its status compared to that of the talks in Washington, and its secrecy. Abu Ala also broached for the first time granting Jericho autonomy simultaneously with Gaza. This proposal was the same "Gaza Plus Jericho" option that Peres had first floated to Egyptian President Mubarak with instructions to notify Arafat. Peres and Beilin had been puzzled by the PLO's failure to introduce the concept to the Oslo channel. Now Abu Ala had done so, but without referring to Peres as its source.[66] He must have known that the formula was heatedly opposed by Rabin.

> In working out the package deal, how were complementary interests being integrated?

Only two weeks earlier, Mubarak and Rabin had met in Egypt, and Mubarak had responded on Arafat's behalf to Peres's "Gaza Plus Jericho" proposal. It was unusual that the response was made to Rabin when the proposal had come from Peres. Perhaps Arafat chose to deliver his answer to Rabin rather than Peres to test Rabin's reaction. Arafat told Mubarak to inform Rabin that he would accept the addition of Jericho but wanted control over the bridges connecting Jericho with Jordan. Whatever Arafat's motivation, Rabin had been furious—he had given grudging private approval to the Gaza Plus Jericho concept, but had no intention of relinquishing Israeli control over such a strategic position.

In Norway Abu Ala stressed that acceptance of Gaza Plus Jericho "was not a condition for agreement, only a private proposal."[67] In other words, agreement could be reached without it. Abu Mazen wrote later that the Israelis "were absolutely livid when they heard our demand for an Israeli withdrawal from Jericho too. At first they refused to even discuss the matter."[68] But he says they listened to the Palestinians' reasoning "that Jericho was the gateway to the West Bank, that a withdrawal from there would be a symbolic gesture for the people of the West Bank, that anyway withdrawal from Jericho would not be problematic, seeing there were no Israeli settlements in that area."

Hirschfeld and Pundak do not recall expressing dismay. They were more conscious of intense awkwardness over Israel's failure to decide how to react to the draft DOP submitted in March. They put off PLO members' urgent inquiries with assurances that Israel would take a firm position within a week. The group's fifth meeting was accordingly scheduled for barely a week later. "How long could we delay our response?" Beilin recalled wondering. "In Israel we hadn't even got as far as discussing it with the prime minister and the foreign minister."[69]

# FISH OR CUT BAIT

When the negotiators reconvened in early May, Pundak and Hirschfeld's instructions were to apologize for continued indecision and to try to move on to issues such as Jericho, the Washington talks, and refugees. This fifth meeting was attended—to the participants' surprise and appreciation—by Norway's new foreign minister, Johann Juergen Holst. Despite Holst's presence, or perhaps emboldened by it, Abu Ala declared that PLO patience with their low-level Israeli counterparts was at an end. He had nothing against Hirschfeld and Pundak as individuals, he said, but they were not Israeli officials. The Palestinians considered the draft Declaration of Principles a document that could be signed. Abu Ala wanted officials on both sides to at least initial it. Larsen remembers Abu Ala's frustration. On the way to the airport, the PLO leader told his Norwegian friend, "I will never come back. This is a charade, this is a bluff, the Israelis are exploiting us and using all this time for nothing. . . . I want to have proof, and the only proof I will accept is that Beilin comes." Hirschfeld and Pundak reported Abu Ala's position to Beilin. They were convinced, Beilin later wrote, that "they could proceed no further with the apparatus as it then was."

> No way could they go back to the Palestinians without referring to the draft agreement, and no way could they pass the time chattering about the importance of the Washington talks, when everybody knew nothing was happening there. . . . If it was decided to kill it off [the Oslo track], it would be a mistake but a logical one; if the decision was to continue—we must make up our minds on the statement of principles.[70]

The mounting pressure reminded Beilin once again how *ad hoc* the process was:

> This whole business really was not conducted in an organized fashion, where there's a captain who has an approach and has authority and works together with his employee, and together they can administer the deal, and there are technocrats who conduct the negotiations in their name. It was just an upside-down story.[71]

# THE TALKS TURN OFFICIAL

At stake for Israel was a larger issue than whether officials would replace academics at the Oslo talks. Upgrading the negotiations to official status would require a reversal of nearly 30 years of Israeli policy, constituting implicit recognition of the PLO. Peres's political aide Avi Gil elaborates:

> We had had channels to the PLO throughout the years. It was no great novelty, no big deal. I don't mean we had a formal channel. But when you engage daily with Palestinians in the West Bank and Gaza, when they have their contacts with the PLO, when you have international statesmen visiting Israel the day after meeting Arafat and vice-versa, when you have members of the Knesset flirting with people from the PLO—then the PLO contact itself is not striking. . . . The element which in my view was the most important was the government decision to say, "Yes, we are ready for formal discussions with the PLO." And the moment that decision is taken, you know, it ultimately will lead to formal recognition of the PLO, with all the consequences that involves.

By May, Peres concluded that Israel must send an official representative to Oslo. To persuade Rabin, Peres argued that the Americans supported the progress made so far, and that "Gaza First" was in Israel's self-interest. He compared the Oslo team favorably to those in Washington: "I stressed that the PLO men in Oslo were more flexible, more imaginative, and more authoritative than the West Bank–Gaza team negotiating in Washington."[72] He also pointed out that Arafat, with all his faults, was preferable to a Hamas leader who might take his place if he were weakened. Peres had an Israeli negotiator in mind—himself.

> **Why did the Israelis decide to move to official negotiations at this juncture?**

Rabin, Peres says, was skeptical but willing. He vetoed Peres as the Israeli representative, however, for fear that Peres's participation would commit the Cabinet to a process about which it knew nothing. Peres suggested, and Rabin agreed, that Israel send Uri Savir, the 40-year-old director general of the Israeli Foreign Ministry. Savir, says Peres, was "young, he was a good negotiator, he was not a member of the cabinet." Adds Gil: "He is a brilliant diplomat, full of humor, wise, clever, shrewd. . . . You can trust his assessment."

Savir attended one meeting in Oslo with Hirschfeld and Pundak, marking the first time that an authorized Israeli official met with the PLO face to face. The meeting was a watershed: Savir and Abu Ala, initially wary, developed a rapport that was to prove enduring. In early June, lawyer Yoel Singer also joined the team. Singer subjected the proposed DOP to thorough and legally exacting scrutiny. He came up with forty questions to which he wanted PLO answers.

On June 13, 1993, after five months of unofficial negotiations, the entire Israeli team assembled in Oslo, carrying for the first time the full force of Rabin's and Peres's official—though still secret—endorsement. The pre-negotiation, the first act of what would become known as the Oslo Accords, was over.

# REACHING AGREEMENT

Once the Israelis upgraded the back-channel negotiations to official status in May, and added a hard-nosed lawyer to the team in June, the talks became more difficult and the stakes became higher. The June session ended dramatically when a small news item published by Agence France-Presse reported rumors of Middle East peace talks in Oslo; it looked as if the talks might unexpectedly lose their all-important secrecy. But the Foreign Ministry was able to head off follow-up interest by asserting that the stories must have referred to a May meeting of the official multilateral peace talks in Oslo.

In July brinkmanship grew more intense on both sides of the secret talks, and at one juncture negotiations were broken off. Norwegian Foreign Minister Johann Juergen Holst, in Tunis on an official visit, met with Arafat and persuaded him to compromise on a territorial corridor between Gaza and the West Bank. At the same time, it became clear to both sides that no agreement could be reached on a Declaration of Principles without mutual recognition of each other's authority. After decades of enmity, there was considerable political risk that the Israeli public would find acceptance of the PLO unacceptable.

But it was also at this juncture that Rabin finally began to imagine that the Oslo talks might yield a serious accord. He confessed to surprise at the number of concessions the PLO was prepared to make:

> On four or five major issues, they agreed to [things] I had doubted they would agree to. First, [keeping all of] Jerusalem under Israeli control and outside the jurisdiction of the Palestinians for the entire interim period. Second, [retaining all Israeli] settlements. . . . Third, overall Israeli responsibility for the security of Israelis and external security. Fourth, keeping all options open for the negotiations on a permanent solution.[73]

Meanwhile Rabin and Arafat exchanged secret letters, for security reasons neither signed nor addressed to one another, in an effort to clear up the final contested points in Oslo. Rabin's letter indicated Israeli willingness to recognize the PLO if the matter was considered separately from the Declaration of Principles. While this correspondence was under way, Israel launched a week-long bombardment of southern Lebanon. At the same time there were signs that Israel and Syria (with U.S. urging) might make progress in their bilateral negotiations—a prospect long feared by Palestinians who doubted that their own concerns would be fully addressed.

As a result of the Rabin-Arafat correspondence, and the potential Syrian-Israeli progress, the PLO softened its position and agreed to resume the Oslo talks. Israel's position too became more conciliatory when a domestic crisis threatened the government with collapse. Securing an agreement took on a new urgency. August 19, the date of a long-scheduled visit Peres was to make to Oslo, became a target for the Oslo group.

Norway's Holst met Peres in Stockholm to stage-manage final negotiations of the DOP directly with Arafat. In a seven-hour telephone conversation with Tunis, where Abu Ala stood next to Arafat, the participants hammered out the last details. On the night of August 19, after Peres's official duties in Oslo were concluded, the exuberant negotiators signed the Declaration of Principles in a secret ceremony at a Norwegian government guesthouse. The Norwegian secret service taped the proceedings for posterity.

The final business at hand was to inform the Americans, which Peres and Holst did in a meeting with Secretary of State Warren Christopher on August 27. Christopher rejected the option of presenting the agreement as a U.S.-sponsored document. Instead, he applauded the Norwegians for their role and insisted on giving them full credit.

The Israeli Cabinet approved the agreement after heated debate. The PLO leadership also gave its stamp of approval, despite the strong resistance of many members of the official Washington negotiating team. A signing ceremony was scheduled for Washington on September 13. The final details of the DOP were not agreed on until the audience had assembled on the White House lawn. Thunderous applause greeted the historic handshake that President Clinton engineered between Rabin and Arafat.

Euphoria was quickly supplanted by the nitty-gritty reality of implementing the DOP. The implementation talks missed deadlines, were undermined by terrorist attacks (notably a murderous assault on worshippers at a mosque in Hebron by an extremist Israeli settler), and bogged down in disputes—but moved forward. On May 4, 1994, an implementation agreement for Gaza-Jericho was signed in Cairo. In the wake of the signing, PLO Chairman Yasser Arafat returned to Gaza to head a newly created Palestinian Authority.

# CHAPTER TEN

# Transforming the Balance of Forces

In bitter disputes like the conflict between the Israelis and the Palestinians, getting to the table is often the key breakthrough. The apparently simple act of sitting down with "the enemy" profoundly altered the dynamics of the conflict. Resolution of this dispute remains elusive (for reasons that will become clear), but the Oslo negotiations changed the playing field forever.

Why did these avowed enemies decide to enter into negotiations in 1993? How did the path to the negotiating table—the process of prenegotiation—unfold? More generally, what are the implications of the Oslo experience for the theory and practice of international dispute resolution?

## EQUILIBRIUM AND CHANGE IN SUSTAINED CONFLICTS

Kurt Lewin, a pioneer in the field of group dynamics, observed that human social systems—groups, organizations, and nations—exist in a state of dynamic tension between forces pressing for change and forces resisting change. The behavior of a social system, he wrote, is "the result of a multitude of forces. Some forces support each other, some oppose each other. Some are driving forces, others restraining forces. Like the velocity of a river, the actual conduct of a group depends upon the level . . . at which these conflicting forces reach an equilibrium."[1] When there is a rough balance between driving forces and restraining forces, social systems remain in equilibrium. The system may fluctuate within narrow limits, but attempts to move beyond these limits (driving forces) trigger rapid increases in restraining forces. As the forces driving for change mount, so do the forces resisting the change. If the pressure becomes great enough, the system may become ripe for revolution, leading to a new equilibrium. Otherwise, it will tend to return to the status quo.

Sustained conflicts are social systems that tend to remain stuck in states of cold war—that is, low-level contention and friction that is neither all-out war nor durable peace. Forces driving the system toward violence exist in tension with forces restraining violence and seeking conciliation. Resolution of such conflicts (when it occurs) comes about through some combination of changes in the balance of driving and restraining forces and the operation of channel factors to overcome residual barriers.

## Driving and Restraining Forces

Conflicts stuck in cold war equilibria are stable but not static; periodically, a driving force will trigger a bout of escalation. The escalation does not usually result in full-scale violence, because restraining forces such as mutual deterrence or outside intervention act to moderate the dispute. In family disputes, periodic fights flare and then die out. In adversarial union-management relationships, strikes give way to less contentious times. In international border conflicts, skirmishes and bellicose rhetoric alternate with periods of relative quiet.

In a similar way, efforts to make peace (another type of driving force) often run afoul of powerful barriers to negotiated settlement. Attempts to reconcile feuding family members fail; apparently promising initiatives to redefine workplace relations fade; efforts at international mediation produce meaningless statements of intent. Sustained conflicts therefore remain locked in extended states of cold war, punctuated by occasional escalatory episodes and failed efforts at peacemaking.

An uneasy equilibrium results from tensions between, on one hand, escalatory forces and forces resisting escalation, and, on the other hand, forces pushing for resolution and forces opposing negotiated settlement. The conflict system model in Figure 10.1 illustrates the forces that make disputes self-sustaining. The valleys represent stable states—peace, cold war, and war; the hills represent forces that resist change in one direction or the other. The ball at the bottom of the valley labeled "Cold War" represents the equilibrium state of a sustained conflict.

Events that propel the conflict out of the cold war valley in the direction of either war or peace are driving forces. Escalatory actions push the conflict up the hill to the right, toward all-out violence. Conciliatory actions push the conflict up the hill to the left, toward peaceful coexistence. But sustained conflicts have internal regulatory mechanisms that resist change: driving forces in either direction are met by restraining forces that act to maintain the cold war equilibrium. These forces are represented in Figure 10.1 by the slopes surrounding

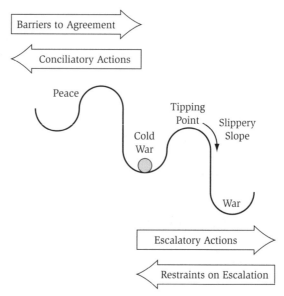

**Figure 10.1.** Conflict System Dynamics.

the cold war valley. Escalatory forces driving the system toward war are moderated by restraining forces such as outside intervention. Conversely, efforts at peacemaking are undermined by forces that act as barriers to settlement. Conflicts thus tend to be resistant to both escalatory efforts that could lead to all-out violence and conciliatory efforts to make peace.

This is not to say that change cannot take place. As the forces driving a conflict system toward war or peace gather strength, so do the restraining forces—at least at first. With rising tension, however, the conflict could reach a tipping point beyond which only a small additional push would be needed to propel it rapidly into a new state. Tipping points are represented in the figure by the tops of the hills. As long as escalatory forces fail to reach some threshold, restraining forces will tend to return the system to its cold war equilibrium. Beyond the threshold, a small incremental impetus can set in motion an accelerating slide down the slippery slope to full-scale violence.

The dynamics of a particular conflict depend on the relative balance of driving and restraining forces. If restraints on escalation are weak, the hill on the right will be low and violence will be easily ignited. If there is no effective regime of mutual deterrence, for example, and outside parties wield insufficient power to intervene, the conflict will flare frequently and often escalate to violence.

If the forces resisting settlement are weak, the hill to the left will be low, and peace will be easier to achieve. The parties could realize, for example, that their hurting stalemate is causing unacceptable damage to everyone. Or a powerful outside party could intervene to alter the balance of forces in the conflict, such as when NATO bombed the Bosnian Serbs in 1995.

## Channel Factors

Powerful forces pressing for change are necessary but not sufficient to bring about change. As driving forces gather strength or restraining forces weaken, pressure in the system mounts. At this point, the presence or absence of what Lewin calls *channel factors* becomes decisive. Channel factors are small but critical expeditors of change—pivotal events that can seem inconsequential until one understands the forces they unleash. In his study of the genesis of European revolutions, Charles Tilly observes that the acts of a single rebel—a good example of a channel factor—may signal the possibility of successful rebellion to others, leading latent opposition to coalesce: "The unpunished defection of one visible member [of a ruling coalition] sends a whole barrage of signals: the very possibility of defection, the decreasing capacity of the central executive to maintain its commitments and keep others in line, the opportunity to seize assets formerly under central control, the chance for cooperation with other defectors, and the probable increased costs of loyalty to the center."[2]

Channel factors act as catalysts for new behavior. They tunnel through residual barriers to change, initiating chain reactions that progressively build to seemingly disproportionate results.

Even when the balance of forces shifts strongly in the direction of peace, channel factors remain decisive in overcoming residual barriers to negotiated settlement. In dispute resolution, two classes of channel factors are noteworthy: leaders and momentum-building processes. Leaders of the contending parties can play crucial roles in tunneling through the remaining barriers, as can external mediators and facilitators. Leaders who have built credibility as guardians of their groups during times of struggle may be able to build the internal political consensus necessary to make peace. And processes like secret diplomacy, mutual confidence building, and phased agreements can help overcome residual barriers by building momentum toward agreement.

## Getting to the Table in Oslo

The twin concepts of a shifting balance of forces and facilitating channel factors shed an interpretive light on the events that led to official negotiations between Israel and the PLO—and on prenegotiation processes in general. To understand why the PLO and Israel decided to pursue a negotiated settlement, we examine the changing balance of driving and restraining forces in the Middle East conflict system. To understand how it happened that formal negotiations began in Oslo in June 1993, we focus on the channel factors introduced by unofficial representatives and third-party facilitators and momentum-building processes like secret talks, confidence-building measures, and phased agreements.

There was nothing inevitable about the way the Oslo process unfolded. Other paths might have led to the signing of a Declaration of Principles by the contending parties, or the Oslo talks could have been exposed prematurely, triggering internal strife within Israel and the PLO and renewed conflict between them. But this is not to say that the Oslo peace process was either random or idiosyncratic. The core dynamics can be understood in terms of changes in driving and restraining forces and in the types of channel factors that helped the parties overcome barriers to agreements.

## THE CHANGING BALANCE OF FORCES IN THE MIDDLE EAST

To analyze changes in the forces acting on the Israelis and the PLO, we recast three of the five types of barriers to agreement discussed in Chapter Four—strategic, institutional, and psychological—as forces that either propel or restrain moves toward negotiation.

### Strategic Forces

In deciding whether to negotiate, contending parties make strategic assessments of their prospects of reaching a mutually acceptable agreement. If any party believes that others' aspirations are unrealistic or views its own best alternative—which may be the status quo—as preferable to negotiation, a move to the table is unlikely. Changes in strategic assessments occur when parties reevaluate their interests, recalibrate their aspirations, or find that their alternatives to negotiation have become (or will become) less attractive. For example, recognizing that the conflict has become a hurting stalemate and is likely to remain so can push the parties toward the table.

On the Israeli side, the end of the Cold War and the defeat of Iraq made a land-for-peace deal less risky. Meanwhile, the internal groups opposed to dealing with the PLO had been weakened by the rise of Hamas; by the PLO's public commitments to negotiate a land-for-peace compromise; and by failed Israeli efforts to build an alternative Palestinian leadership, crush the *intifada,* or bypass the Palestinians through direct negotiations with Jordan or Syria.

On the PLO side, the cutoff of financial support by moderate Arab states following the defeat of Saddam Hussein, the challenge posed by Hamas, and worry that the Palestinians would be bypassed by independent negotiations between moderate Arab states and Israel made the future look increasingly bleak and a negotiated settlement more attractive. These changes in the balance of strategic forces are summarized in Table 10.1.

Table 10.1. Strategic Forces.

| | Strengthening of Forces Supporting Negotiations | Weakening of Forces Resisting Negotiations |
|---|---|---|
| PLO | The PLO, stuck in Tunis, feared that alternative Palestinian leadership, either Hamas or moderates from the Occupied Territories, would undermine its authority. | |
| | The decision to back Saddam Hussein in the Persian Gulf conflict proved disastrous. The PLO faced bankruptcy when the Gulf states cut off financial support. | |
| | Worry grew that Israel might enter into bilateral negotiations with Jordan or Syria, bypassing and marginalizing the PLO. | |
| Israel | The rise of Hamas threatened to undermine the authority of the PLO in the Occupied Territories, raising the specter of further radicalization of the Palestinians. | Moderates in the PLO signaled that they were ready to acknowledge Israel's right to exist and to negotiate to trade land for peace. |
| | | Efforts to build a moderate alternative Palestinian leadership in the Occupied Territories were acknowledged to have failed. |
| | | Iraq was defeated decisively in the Gulf War, and its ability to build weapons of mass destruction was curtailed. |
| | | The collapse of the Soviet Union deprived Israel's Arab adversaries of their superpower sponsor and improved the security situation, raising concerns about the future of U.S. support and the post–Cold War Israeli economy. |
| | | Efforts to bypass the Palestinians and negotiate peace treaties with Jordan and Syria did not make progress. |

## Institutional Forces

Institutional forces—organizational and political factors—include the presence or absence of communication channels between the sides, internal political constraints on leaders, and the involvement of external players with stakes in the outcome.

As conflicts escalate between groups, communication channels between them tend to break down. Often the result is a vicious circle in which each party comes to view any communication as a concession or unwarranted recognition of the legitimacy of the other side. Without channels for communication, however, the parties cannot begin to explore opportunities for a negotiated settlement. And reestablishing communication can result in a virtuous circle: as the parties begin to communicate, stereotypes and false assumptions progressively dissolve.

The internal coalitional dynamics of each side are an important institutional factor of another kind. As conflicts escalate, strongly polarized subgroups are likely to develop within each side. Such groups' zeal and organizational capabilities may equip them to exert a disproportionate influence over internal politics, in support of or in opposition to negotiations.

Finally, external parties with interests in the outcome of the conflict may use their influence to stoke the fires of conflict or push the parties toward settlement.

On the Israeli side, the Labor victory in the 1992 elections represented a profound institutional shift, leading to repeal of legal restrictions on communication with members of the PLO, the weakening of right-wing and religious political groups opposed to trading land for peace, and concerted pursuit of peace by the new leadership. On the PLO side, the most significant institutional shifts were the 1988 decision to recognize (at least implicitly) Israel's right to exist and to accept UN Security Council resolutions 242 and 338 and the subsequent loss of superpower sponsorship and support from moderate Arab states.

Shifts in institutional forces that moved Israel and the PLO toward negotiations are summarized in Table 10.2.

## Psychological Forces

Most people desire a secure and peaceful existence, and living in a state of siege is corrosive. But in protracted conflicts, powerful psychological forces discourage moves toward settlement. In the conflict between the PLO and Israel, moderates on both sides experienced psychological transformations that helped open a window for negotiated agreement. The PLO suffered important setbacks following the defeat of Iraq, the breakup of the Soviet Union, and the rise of Hamas. At the same time, the *intifada* settled into a grinding stalemate that took an increasing toll on Israeli security forces and their families and tarnished Israel's image abroad.

Table 10.2. Institutional Forces.

| | Strengthening of Forces Supporting Negotiations | Weakening of Forces Resisting Negotiations |
|---|---|---|
| Israel | The 1992 election replaced the hard-line Likud party with a Labor government committed to negotiating a land-for-peace settlement—a shift that reflected a shift in Israeli public opinion.<br><br>Shimon Peres took the position of foreign minister with the explicit objective of advancing the peace process. | The collapse of the Soviet Union left the United States as Israel's sole strong ally and forceful advocate for a comprehensive settlement.<br><br>The Labor's Party's election victory weakened the religious right and settler groups that viewed the Occupied Territories as biblical lands promised to the Jewish people by God.<br><br>Legal restrictions on communication between Israelis and members of the PLO were repealed.<br><br>The Labor government acknowledged that the formal Madrid-Washington talks would not be productive. |
| PLO | The PLO's ruling body in 1988 agreed to the 1947 UN partition plan and endorsed the UN Security Council Resolutions 242 and 338 and its land-for-peace formula. | The PLO suffered the loss of superpower sponsorship with the collapse of the Soviet Union.<br><br>Moderates in the PLO established multiple channels of communication with Israelis.<br><br>The PLO's relations with moderate Arab states soured in the aftermath of the Gulf War. |

# CHANNEL FACTORS

After the 1992 Israeli elections, the leadership of the PLO was ready to begin formal talks, but the Labor government of Yitzhak Rabin faced potent barriers to doing so. The time seemed ripe: Israeli decision makers had concluded that they could not negotiate with moderate Palestinians in the Occupied Territories, and they did not want to see the PLO usurped by a more militant Hamas. But the government was not prepared to recognize the PLO, and open official negotiations would have led to serious internal political problems, because such talks would have implicitly constituted recognition.

At a deeper level, the Israelis confronted a classic dilemma of learning and bargaining. They did not want to enter into formal talks with the PLO without reasonable certainty that they could get an agreement that could be sold inside Israel. But how could they know whether such an agreement was possible without first negotiating with the Palestinians? And if they did not talk directly to the PLO, how would they know that the people to whom they were talking were authorized representatives of the PLO? At the same time, they wanted to maintain secrecy and surround the talks with a belt of deniability. For their part, the PLO wanted to sit down with Israeli negotiators who had the authority to make commitments on behalf of the government. They were justifiably worried that the Israelis were seeking to maintain an escape hatch or were simply not serious.

The resulting need to learn about whether there was a zone of possible agreement without prematurely revealing that negotiations were underway constituted a potent residual barrier to negotiated agreement. How could they negotiate without negotiating? It is here that channel factors became important. The parties get to the point of willingness to enter into official negotiations through the combined actions of (1) leaders, inside and outside the contending parties, who played varied roles, and (2) the use of momentum-building processes.

## Leadership Roles

At various points in the process, leaders acted as comediators, guardians, unofficial representatives, legitimizing sponsors, and neutral facilitators.

**Comediators.** In the 1980s and early 1990s, leading Palestinians and Israelis undertook comediation initiatives. In comediation, moderate partisans seek to advance the process by building relationships with moderates on the other side and by generating centering proposals that pull the sides together. These efforts help break down the parties' accumulated misconceptions and distorted images of each other. Because comediators are viewed as dovish within their own groups, they can rarely act alone. Instead, as we will see, they often act in concert with more conservative "guardians."

Several notable examples of comediation contributed to the success of the Oslo process. In the early 1980s, Shimon Peres began to develop the idea of "Gaza First" as a basis for a comprehensive settlement. An expanded Gaza-Plus-Jericho proposal was presented to Yitzhak Rabin by Yasser Arafat through Egyptian president Hosni Mubarak. Gaza Plus Jericho was eventually enshrined in the Oslo Declaration of Principles as the basis for the first stage of Palestinian self-rule.

Other Israelis, mostly from the Labor Party, tried to build relationships with West Bank Palestinian leaders, whom they hoped could become an alternative to the PLO. In the early 1980s, Yossi Beilin had established contact with leading Palestinians in the Occupied Territories, including the academic Hanan Ashrawi and Faisal Husseini, a founding member of the PLO. In spite of subsequent legal restrictions on contacts with the PLO, Beilin and Husseini continued to meet throughout the late 1980s and early 1990s. These connections were crucial in creating the Norway Channel.[3]

**Guardians.** *Guardians* are top leaders who have established credibility as protectors of their respective groups during periods of danger and struggle. Their credibility becomes a resource when these leaders decide to make peace. Consider the role played by Yitzhak Rabin in the Oslo process. Rabin, a former general and war hero, had a reputation as remote but strong and judicious. As a leader, he personified caution and a conservative stance on protecting Israel's security. When he decided that the time had come to make peace, he could carry many others with him. Yasser Arafat similarly played the role of guardian within the PLO.

Cooperation between guardians and entrepreneurial comediators helped shape the Oslo process. Shimon Peres could push the envelope, developing options and floating proposals, while Yitzhak Rabin played the role of conservative protector of Israeli security. Rabin was trusted by a large portion of the Israelis, but Peres was not. As events have revealed, Peres could not play the role of guardian and sell the agreement after Rabin's death. At the same time, Peres could do things that Rabin could not to move the process forward. A similar guardian-entrepreneur relationship existed between Arafat and Abbas. Such relationships, we hypothesize, arise in many peace processes.

**Unofficial Representatives.** Comediators and guardians officially represent their sides. But unofficial representatives were also instrumental in setting up the Oslo channel. On the Israeli side, academics Yair Hirschfeld and Ron Pundik became de-facto representatives of the government in the prenegotiation talks. Hirschfeld and Pundik embodied a useful combination of connections to important officials and unofficial status. Hirschfeld was a longtime associate of Yossi Beilin, a favorite of Shimon Peres, and a strong advocate of a negotiated settlement. As Deputy Foreign Minister following the Labor victory in 1992, Beilin could not afford to meet with the PLO, but Hirschfeld and Pundik had the necessary cover to do so. They could legitimately travel outside Israel to participate in conferences and seminars without attracting attention.

On the Norwegian side, Terje Roed-Larsen became the unofficial link between the Israelis, the Palestinian negotiating team, and the Norwegian government. Larsen's assets were unofficial status, institutional backing, connections with all sides, and strong ideas about resolving the conflict.

**Legitimizing Sponsors.** The resulting prenegotiation discussions, organized as seminars under the auspices of a nongovernmental organization, were actually funded and supported by the Norwegian government. As Beilin later noted, Norway distinguished itself from other potential small state sponsors by its willingness to commit resources to such a risky venture. As a sponsor, Norway had three significant advantages over the United States: it was perceived as neutral by both sides, it had the flexibility to fund prenegotiation discussions quickly and discreetly, and it could provide a secure environment for secret talks.

Unlike the United States, Norway had few (if any) strategic interests in the Middle East. The Norwegian Labor party, in power for forty of the previous fifty years, was able to take a long view and had sought to be even-handed in the conflict. Norway had also earned the PLO's trust by arranging secret contacts between the Israeli Labor Party and PLO moderates. Throughout the Oslo process, the Norwegian Foreign Ministry tapped sources of funds much more flexibly and discreetly than would have been possible in the United States. The compactness and coherence of the Norwegian government and a national consensus about promoting peace reinforced Norway's ability to support the talks.

Norway kept the talks secret in a way that would have been impossible had the United States been the sponsor. The negotiations remained secret because no one was looking for them and because Oslo was a media backwater. The country's closely knit executive branch, flexible funding mechanisms, and history of working through nongovernmental organizations also helped maintain secrecy. All of these factors contributed to making this small nation a central player in this drama.

The Norwegians also actively worked to legitimize the talks. Legitimization was important because the playing field was not level. The PLO was represented by official representatives, while the Israelis were academics with uncertain connections. The Norwegians were also concerned about power imbalances between the two sides and took great care to treat the Israeli and PLO representatives identically.

**Facilitators.** Once the informal talks began, Terje Roed-Larsen played an indispensable role as facilitator. Trained in conflict-resolution theory, Larsen explicitly sought to break down the perceptual barriers between the parties by isolating them together. He facilitated and shaped communications between rounds of negotiation, when the parties returned to consult with their respective leaders.

Unlike Carter in North Korea, Larsen decided not to act as an activist mediator, on the grounds that the parties themselves must own the conflict. He did work with both parties during breaks between sessions, fostering the development of a shared set of experiences that helped to buffer the process during difficult times.

Although his style was quite different from Carter's, Larsen's role in negotiations was equally critical. It allowed the sides to communicate more effectively, to vent, and to make concessions that they would not otherwise have been able to make.

In summary, leaders playing an array of distinct conflict management roles helped both of the parties learn and negotiate prior to committing themselves to formal talks. Guardians like Rabin and Arafat oversaw (and were influenced by) the work of entrepreneurial comediators like Peres and Abbas, but they retained the capacity to distance themselves if things did not work out. The entrepreneurs in turn worked through (and were influenced by) unofficial representatives Hirschfeld and Pundik, while maintaining a measure of deniability. The small state sponsorship of Norway legitimized the negotiation, and Larsen's skilled facilitation helped move it in productive directions.

## Designing the Process to Build Momentum

The architecture of the process helped build momentum to overcome residual barriers. As we saw in Chapter Six, momentum-building processes include secret diplomacy, confidence-building measures, and phased agreements.

**Secret Diplomacy.** Setting up a secret channel enabled the parties to conclude an agreement that could be presented as a fait accompli for ratification by their constituencies. Secrecy permitted Rabin and Arafat to negotiate without triggering "how-can-you-talk-to-those-criminals" internal opposition that would have killed the discussions. As Peres put it, "If it would be exposed ahead of time, it would expire the very same day." Free of the posturing and media dynamics that had plagued the Madrid-Washington talks, the parties could concentrate on the substantive issues. In addition, an initialed agreement constituted a public commitment on the part of the leadership of the PLO and the Israeli government that was difficult to undo.

**Confidence-Building Mechanisms.** The parties also built confidence through mutual testing. In April 1993, for example, Israel pressed for resumption of the Washington talks as a test of the authority of the PLO representatives in Oslo. Before Yitzhak Rabin and Shimon Peres would sanction another meeting in Norway, they demanded a concrete display of influence by the PLO representatives. In response, Abu Ala engineered the Palestinians' return to the bilateral negotiations in Washington. For Shimon Peres, this was a turning point. "I formed the distinct impression that Abu Ala was a man of his word, a man with whom we could do business," he recalled.

Testing also occurred between the Norwegians and the disputants. In his first meeting with Terje Roed-Larsen, Yossi Beilin asked whether Larsen could engineer a meeting with Faisal Husseini. Beilin made this request even though Yair Hirschfeld had been meeting with Husseini almost weekly for four years and Beilin himself saw the Palestinian every few months.

**Phased Agreements.** A third approach to building momentum is the use of phased agreements. The structure of the Oslo process allowed the parties to make progressively bigger and more difficult commitments. The initial price of admission was low: agreement to participate in one exploratory, deniable meeting in Oslo at the Norwegian government's expense. Only when the meetings began to bear fruit did the Israelis need to decide to send official representatives. The still more difficult commitment to mutual recognition was deferred until after the Declaration of Principles was initialed.

At the first meeting in Oslo, the parties agreed to work on a Declaration of Principles—essentially a framework agreement—which itself defined a multiphase negotiation process. In the resulting document, limited self-rule in Gaza and Jericho would be followed by negotiations on expanded Palestinian self-rule in the Occupied Territories. The most difficult issues, such as borders, Jerusalem, and settlements, were deferred to "permanent-status" negotiations.

# FATAL FLAWS?

Analysis of the Oslo experience through the lens of driving forces and channel factors leaves many questions. One question is how and why changes in the balance of forces take place within conflict systems. These changes may occur endogenously within the system, as they did in the Oslo peace process, leading to a classic ripening. In other cases, powerful outside parties may intervene and alter the balance of forces, using their resources to push contending parties toward the negotiating table. In Bosnia, as we will see, coercive diplomacy by the United States and its NATO allies brought the warring parties to the table *and* produced a peace agreement. However, U.S. efforts to strong-arm Yitzhak Shamir's Likud government into participating in the Madrid negotiations ultimately proved counterproductive: the Israelis could be led to water but could not be made to drink. So which characteristics of the contending parties and which circumstances of the conflict make external coercion more or less effective in advancing the cause of peace?

The events since the signing of the Declaration of Principles (summarized in "Update of the Cases" at the end of book) raise difficult questions about the use of secret diplomacy and phased agreements to build momentum. The use of secrecy appears to have been essential in reaching the initial agreement, but it also apparently legitimated violent forms of opposition—violence that eventually resulted in the assassination of Yitzhak Rabin. Would it have been possible to move forward without marginalizing such groups? Are there better ways to sell agreements concluded in secret? To neutralize extremists?

Phased agreements too have drawbacks. By settling the easy issues first, the contending parties built momentum toward agreement. But this left the hard issues—Jerusalem, settlements, refugees, borders—to be worked out at the end. The logic was that increasing trust would make these issues easier to manage, but this has not proven to be the case. How do those who seek to build momentum in dispute resolution processes avoid this trap?

Finally, the Oslo experience underlines the importance of individual leadership in international dispute resolution. Leaders in the PLO, Israel, and Norway took personal risks to initiate and conclude the negotiations, driving others to undertake the painful changes necessary to embrace peace. The individual personalities of the key actors and their histories, drives, and abilities must figure prominently in any balanced account of the Oslo process. The role of the individual as a channel factor is often lost in theories of conflict resolution that focus on the inevitable forces of history and overlook leadership and personality.

In the next two chapters, we shift our focus from conflict dynamics to coalition building. In every case in this book, building coalitions—both externally and internally—was essential to achieving breakthroughs. But the process of building winning coalitions and preventing the formation of blocking coalitions is far from straightforward. The efforts of the Bush administration to build the Gulf coalition provide a powerful template for effective coalition building. As you read the case, think about the techniques Baker and Bush used to recruit key allies. What coalitions were they trying to build, and why? What were the bases of these alliances? How were they working to build momentum?

CHAPTER ELEVEN

# Assembling the Persian Gulf Coalition

On August 2, 1990, Iraqi President Saddam Hussein invaded tiny neighboring Kuwait. Iraqi troops had been massed at the border for weeks, but most military and intelligence experts had dismissed the buildup as a scare tactic or, at worst, the prelude to a limited land grab. Within hours, denunciations poured forth from around the world. In Washington, the initial reaction to the invasion was firm but restrained. Hussein had done wrong, but the United States' stake in redressing it was not immediately clear.

But within days, the U.S. response became urgent and purposeful. President George Bush seized on the conflict as a flagrant challenge to "the new world order"—the harmony between nations that many hoped would follow the end of the Cold War. The Husseins of the world had a lesson to learn, particularly if they sat on vast oil reserves and threatened to seize more. Over the next several months, the Bush administration labored to piece together an international coalition with the political and military muscle to drive Hussein out of Kuwait.

---

This is an abridged version of "The Gulf Crisis: Building a Coalition for War," a case written by Susan Rosegrant in collaboration with Michael D. Watkins, assistant professor of public policy, for use by the National Security Program, at the John F. Kennedy School of Government, Harvard University. Copyright © 1994 by the President and Fellows of Harvard College. Reprinted with the permission of the Kennedy School of Government Case Program, Harvard University.

# STEPS TOWARD AN INVASION

Mutual opportunism and mistrust characterized relations between the United States and Iraq in the decade before the invasion of Kuwait. The Soviet client state had severed relations with the United States in 1967 after the Six Day Arab-Israeli War, and until 1980 the two nations held each other at arm's length. In the eyes of the United States, Iraq was one of the more unpredictable and radical Arab nations, and Saddam Hussein's consolidation of power as leader of the socialist Baath Party in 1979 did nothing to dispel that image. Saddam confirmed his ruthless reputation by purging hundreds of military and government officials, many of them his own friends and relatives.

> What factors contributed to escalation of the conflict between Iraq and Kuwait?

But when the fundamentalist Islamic followers of Ayatollah Ruhollah Khomeini overthrew the pro-American Shah of Iran in 1979, the Western attitude toward Iraq began to shift. Saddam's oppression of Iraq's minority Kurd population continued, as did executions of his domestic opponents. But viewed in the light of Khomeini's hostage taking and condemnation of the Western world, the Iraqi leader appeared the lesser of two evils. Moreover, Saddam's war against Iran, launched in 1980, promised to keep Khomeini in check.

During Ronald Reagan's presidency, the United States began offering agricultural credit guarantees to Iraq, and diplomatic relations resumed in 1984. Even after evidence surfaced that Iraq was funneling money freed up by the credits into military purchases, including parts and supplies for chemical and nuclear weapons, the program continued. Many in Congress protested the warming relationship with Iraq, because of apparent irregularities in the credit-guarantee program and Saddam's record of human-rights violations. But others ardently supported the credit guarantees, which had helped make Iraq a major purchaser of American farm products. By the end of the Iran-Iraq War in 1988, most policymakers in the incoming Bush administration were convinced that continuing the diplomacy initiated under Reagan would moderate Saddam's behavior.[1] Iraq faced massive reconstruction after the war, and U.S. businesses hoped for their share of the contracts. Saddam, for his part, was doing his best to convey a message of cooperation to Iraq's near-neighbors and to the international community. The war had shackled Iraq with debts estimated at $80 billion, and he would need large-scale loans and debt forgiveness to keep the shaky economy on its feet.

But by early 1990, the Iraqi dictator's message had changed. He demanded that fellow Arabs raise oil prices, stepped up his anti-American rhetoric, and threatened Israel with chemical attack. Saddam's ruthlessness was believed to be driven in part by fear that he would be forced from power and die violently, like his predecessors. These fears took on new urgency when several attempts were made on his life. The decline of Iraq's old ally, the Soviet Union, and the growing influence of the United States, where Saddam was still widely viewed as an irrational tyrant, heightened his anxieties.

Meanwhile, Iraq's failing economy was causing internal discontent. The country could no longer service its debt. Oil revenues, which accounted for 95 percent of Iraq's income, were dropping, in part due to overproduction by Kuwait and another small Gulf kingdom, the United Arab Emirates (UAE). What the country needed, Saddam reasoned, was an influx of money to salvage the economy and keep him in power. If getting that money called for armed confrontation, that too could have rewards. A quick military victory promised to boost the nation's morale while solidifying Saddam's leadership.

Kuwait made an ideal target for Saddam's aggression. The testy relationship between the two neighboring states was colored by grievances dating back to the dismantling of the Ottoman Empire by the Western powers at the end of World War One. Iraq ended up with a paltry 37-mile coastline on the Persian Gulf, crucial for exporting oil. Kuwait, though less than one-twentieth Iraq's size, boasted an almost 120-mile-long coastline and some of the richest oilfields in the Middle East. Since Kuwait's independence from Britain in 1961, Iraq had threatened invasion twice and repeatedly contested the legitimacy of its borders with the tiny sheikhdom. (For a map of the region, see Figure 11.1.)

As Iraq's financial situation grew more desperate, Saddam took action. His threats against Kuwait escalated in early 1990; when he demanded that Kuwait give up two islands blocking Iraq's access to the Gulf, the Emir of Kuwait did not respond to his satisfaction. In mid-July, Saddam charged that Kuwait and the UAE had crippled Iraq's economy by ignoring oil-production quotas, thus forcing down prices. Saddam also claimed that Kuwait had stolen $2.4 billion of oil from Iraq's Rumaila oilfield, at the border of the two countries. He demanded that Kuwait and the UAE cut production and raise oil prices, forgive Iraq's war debts ($10 billion, in Kuwait's case), and compensate Iraq for some of its wartime losses. This rhetoric was accompanied by a buildup of Iraqi troops on the Kuwaiti border.

The U.S. State Department responded to Iraq's initial threats by asserting "that disputes be settled peacefully and not by threats or intimidation."[2] When the UAE requested two refuelling aircraft, the United States supplied the aircraft and scheduled a joint naval exercise to demonstrate its support. But alarm at the apparent escalation eased off in late July after Saddam summoned U.S. Ambassador to Iraq April Glaspie for an emergency session. Saddam was angry at perceived wrongs against Iraq by the Gulf states and the United States, Glaspie reported, but he had pledged not to attack Kuwait except as a last resort.[3] Glaspie's report was seconded by Arab leaders, who had received similar pledges and who urged the United States to stay out of the conflict.

**Figure 11.1.** The Persian Gulf Region.

With these assurances, the United States pinned its hopes on an Arab resolution. On July 31, delegations from Iraq and Kuwait met to discuss their differences. The summit fell apart, however, only hours after it began. Resigned Kuwaiti representatives began to prepare for the next scheduled meeting on August 4. But on August 2, at 1 A.M. Gulf time, Iraqi troops began to drive deep into Kuwait.

# THE BUSH ADMINISTRATION RESPONDS

Though U.S. intelligence experts had been tracking the movements of Iraqi troops for days, the invasion and occupation of all of Kuwait shocked the Bush administration. When word of the invasion reached Washington, D.C., at 7 P.M. on August 1, officials—already seasoned by conflicts such as the invasion of Panama—reacted swiftly. The deputies committee, a crisis-management group of sub-Cabinet-level representatives from State, Defense, and other agencies, convened to craft a diplomatic response to Saddam's aggression. At 11:20 P.M., the White House publicly called for "immediate and unconditional withdrawal of all Iraqi forces."

> Why did the United States decide to intervene? What enabled the Bush administration to respond so quickly?

Meanwhile, the State Department directed U.S. Ambassador to the United Nations Thomas Pickering to convene a special session of the Security Council to consider a resolution condemning Iraq. The Security Council, whose members then included the Soviet Union, Cuba, and Yemen, was an unlikely vehicle for speedy diplomatic action, particularly a U.S.-led resolution. But after an all-night meeting, the Council passed a draft largely written by the State Department. Resolution 660, condemning the invasion and calling for Iraq to withdraw its forces "immediately and unconditionally," was approved without dissent, with only Yemen abstaining. Pickering attributes the swiftness and unanimity of the response to the "outrageous" nature of the invasion, which he describes as "very much contrary to what people had come to expect the end of the Cold War might mean."[4] By the time Bush met with the National Security Council the morning after the invasion, the UN resolution was in place, and the United States had frozen Iraqi and Kuwaiti assets—to keep Iraq from plundering Kuwait's foreign accounts—and begun to look at the question of U.S. deployment. Bush and his key advisers—a group dubbed the "Gang of Eight" and consisting of Bush, Vice President Dan Quayle, National Security Adviser General Brent Scowcroft, Secretary of State James Baker, Defense Secretary Richard Cheney, Chief of Staff John Sununu, Chairman of the Joint Chiefs of Staff Colin Powell, and Deputy National Security Adviser Robert Gates—had also begun to call leaders in Europe and the Middle East, both to gauge and to help coordinate the international response.

But what to do next was not as obvious as the initial acts of condemnation. The United States had asserted its right to intercede militarily against threats to the Persian Gulf since 1980, when President Jimmy Carter declared the oil-rich region a "vital" American interest. Clearly, the invasion of Kuwait was just such a threat. Saddam had already taken control of 20 percent of the world's known oil reserves, and his troops were poised at the Saudi Arabian border. If Iraqi forces captured the Saudi capital of Riyadh, just 275 miles to the south, Saddam would double his reserves and his power over the economically critical market.

Yet Saddam's intentions toward Saudi Arabia were impossible to discern. Moreover, Saudi Arabia's King Fahd might not allow U.S. troops to defend his country. And it was unclear how much domestic support the Bush administration could muster for military involvement in a far-away conflict that posed no immediate threat other than higher oil prices. The August 2 meeting, which National Security Adviser Brent Scowcroft describes as "lackadaisical," adjourned with these questions unanswered.[5]

> Note the impact of key external allies. How did Scowcroft manage internal coalition building?

Later that day, however, Bush's resolve began to harden. The president flew to Aspen, Colorado, with Scowcroft for a long-planned session with British Prime Minister Margaret Thatcher. Thatcher, a hawk on international conflicts, was from the start the only Western leader to be as outspoken about the invasion as Bush. Some commentators later claimed that it was this meeting that fired up the president. But British and American officials present at the Aspen session describe it as a meeting of like minds that gave both Bush and Thatcher a chance to shape their emerging ideas.

Because of the Thatcher encounter and careful preparation on Scowcroft's part, the second National Security Council meeting the next morning exhibited an urgency the first had lacked. Scowcroft had enlisted the aid of Defense Secretary Richard Cheney and Deputy Secretary of State Lawrence Eagleburger to push things to a head. All three urged a hard look at U.S. options, arguing that far more was at stake than the independence of a tiny Gulf emirate: possible disruption of oil supplies, and repercussions through world markets; imbalance of power in the region, particularly if Saddam marched on Saudi Arabia; danger to Americans and other foreigners caught inside Iraq and Kuwait; and the threat that Israel might be drawn into the conflict by an Iraqi attack. All three spoke in support of sending forces to Saudi Arabia. "The first meeting was, 'Well, it's a *fait accompli,* and how do we adjust to it?'" Scowcroft recalls. "The second was, 'This is an event that affects vital American interests. What are we going to do about it?'" Bush and his advisers began discussing how to win King Fahd's acceptance of American troops to defend his nation.

The next day at Camp David, Bush was briefed on military options by a team including Cheney, Chairman of the Joint Chiefs of Staff Colin Powell, and General Norman Schwarzkopf, commander of Central Command, responsible for the Middle East. The plan Schwarzkopf presented had been crafted in the 1980s as a defensive option to protect the Persian Gulf's oil reserves against such potential antagonists as Iran or the Soviet Union. To mount any operation would be an enormous undertaking, Schwarzkopf warned. Because American military bases were unwelcome in the Gulf, Central Command would have to transport troops and equipment to the region. To move the 200,000 to 250,000 troops required by the plan could take four months. Moreover, Saudi cooperation would be essential for the operation to begin.

> What was the intended audience of Bush's "This will not stand" statement? Whose BATNAs got altered as a result?

Bush returned to Washington the next day. As he climbed from his helicopter onto the White House lawn, the press questioned him about the likelihood of a U.S. military response. "I view very seriously our determination to reverse out this aggression," Bush declared heatedly. "This will not stand. This will not stand, this aggression against Kuwait."

## AN UNFORESEEN LINK WITH THE SOVIETS

When Iraq invaded Kuwait, Secretary of State James Baker was meeting with Soviet Foreign Minister Eduard Shevardnadze in Siberia. Iraq was not on the agenda, and in fact Shevardnadze had reassured Baker that despite the Iraqi troop buildup an invasion was highly unlikely. Just hours after the invasion, Baker left for home via a long-scheduled stopover in Mongolia. Dennis Ross, director of the State Department's policy planning staff, went on to Moscow with the returning Soviets. Ross was sent with no instructions, but when an aide suggested a joint U.S.-Soviet statement condemning the invasion, Ross seized on the idea. "If we and the Soviets were not together right away, . . . there would be potential for Hussein to create a difference between us and then exploit that within the Middle East," Ross recalls. "If he had a sense that the superpowers weren't together, it would create a great degree of ambiguity about whether in fact the international community was aligned against him."[6]

In the wake of the crumbling of the Berlin Wall and Soviet President Gorbachev's bold moves to strengthen ties with the West, the United States and the Soviet Union were groping toward a new relationship. The invasion of Kuwait represented an opportunity to see how the two countries could respond to an international crisis that didn't find them automatically on opposite sides. Shevardnadze and Ross's Soviet counterpart Sergei Tarasenko both strongly favored a joint statement. With a good draft in hand, Ross urged Baker to return through Moscow. For the foreign ministers of the two former Cold War adversaries to denounce Iraq's aggression side by side would send a powerful message to the world—and to Hussein. But by the next day, with Baker still in transit, the joint-statement concept began losing ground. Old-line Arabists in the Soviet government wanted to weaken the language and keep condemnation private. "The traditionalists didn't want to cut their ties with Iraq," Ross explains.

> How did the Bush administration enlist the support of the Soviets? What were Gorbachev and Shevardnadze being asked to do? In return for what?

Ross and Tarasenko went back and forth on drafts, with Ross rejecting the "emasculated" Soviet rewrites. Ross was unable to contact Baker about the ongoing stalemate, but told Tarasenko that he would tell Baker not to bother to come, a warning Ross now admits he used as a device. "I was arguing with Tarasenko that either we're going to have a partnership or we aren't. If we can't cooperate and engage as partners on something like this, then all this is a charade." Ross's hard line worked. The joint draft he handed Baker on August 3 condemned the invasion and called for an arms embargo of Iraq. The only significant deletion from his original, Ross recalls, was a threat to resort to additional steps, including the possible use of military force, a threat Ross concedes he was in no position to deliver on.

One top State Department official marvels not only that this seminal moment of cooperation came about so quickly but that it happened at all. "Had Baker not been in a position to stand up there in Moscow . . . and have the foreign minister of the Soviet Union and the American secretary of state condemning the action of a Soviet client state, it could have been different," he muses. "We still had substantial work to do, but it certainly locked the Soviets into condemnation of the action." National Security Adviser Scowcroft saw the joint statement more simply. "That's when I first thought the Cold War might be over," he recalls.

## ASSEMBLING THE ARAB COALITION

Meanwhile, Middle Eastern leaders were calling for restraint. President Hosni Mubarak of Egypt and King Hussein of Jordan together called President Bush to urge him not to press for Arab denunciations of Hussein nor to act before they had a chance to mediate the issue. "I'll leave it to you," Bush reportedly responded. "You've got it."[7] Such calls for restraint did not indicate lack of alarm on the part of the Arab countries. True, Kuwait elicited little affection in the region. The wealthy sheikhdom, whose 600,000 citizens were served by a working class of almost 1 million drawn from poorer nearby countries, was viewed with envy and contempt. But Iraq's seizure was seen as an alarming act of aggression, particularly by Saudi Arabia, whose oil reserves might be Hussein's next target. Arab leaders had been as surprised by the attack as had President Bush. Immediately before the invasion, in fact, Mubarak had reassured Bush of Hussein's peaceful intentions.

**Why was the Arab coalition the place to start? Who were the key players, and how were they brought on board?**

But most Arab nations were anxious to avoid outside interference. Foreign intervention had often exacerbated tensions in the region. Moreover, some Arab leaders believed that Hussein would be open to a negotiated withdrawal if not confronted with a direct demand to get out of Kuwait. Hussein had confirmed this belief on the day of the invasion, when he told Jordan's King Hussein that he would begin withdrawing troops within days but asked the king to "do whatever you can with the Arabs to persuade them that condemnation and threats don't work with us."[8] The UN Security Council resolution demanding Iraq's unconditional withdrawal had already complicated efforts at a regional solution. But most Arab nations regarded the resolution as redeemed by its call for Iraq and Kuwait to begin "intensive negotiations" under the auspices of the League of Arab States. Hours after the invasion, the Arab League met in Cairo. Kuwait pressed for immediate action against Iraq, a demand unintentionally bolstered by Iraq's deputy prime minister, who asserted that the conflict with Kuwait was "not negotiable."[9] But the League postponed a vote until King Hussein—who offered to serve as an intermediary—could meet with Hussein on August 3. King Hussein's goal would be to arrange an Arab mini-summit to discuss Hussein's "claims" against Kuwait and attempt to procure Iraq's withdrawal.

But this progress fell victim to conflicting agendas. King Hussein asserted that the meeting went well. Saddam Hussein had repeated his willingness to withdraw—given an appropriate settlement with Kuwait—and agreed to the mini-summit. After returning to Amman, however, King Hussein claimed to have been stunned that Egyptian President Mubarak had issued a blunt condemnation of Iraq, in violation of the Arab pledge to withhold comment. Mubarak insisted that the condemnation followed his discovery that King Hussein had failed to obtain assurances from Saddam Hussein on two critical points: commitment to withdraw from Kuwait and willingness to allow the emir to return to power. Some Egyptian officials claimed that Mubarak's censure of

Iraq followed a U.S. State Department threat to cut off arms shipments to Egypt if Mubarak didn't speak out. In any event, the mini-summit was cancelled, and the Arab League condemned Iraq and called for its immediate and unconditional withdrawal from Kuwait.

The State Department denied any role in Mubarak's response. After all, President Bush had assured Mubarak and King Hussein of a few days' grace in which to work with Saddam Hussein. But U.S. officials had had reason to hope that an "Arab solution" would not succeed. For one thing, the Bush administration feared that an Arab-negotiated settlement would grant concessions that would provoke Hussein to make future territorial grabs. There had been talk of offering Hussein one of the two Kuwaiti-controlled islands that Iraq had seized. And it was rumored that the Saudis were considering a payoff of billions of dollars—either to pave the way for a withdrawal or to buy safety from invasion.

The threat to Saudi Arabia was an even more compelling reason for the United States to play a role in the conflict. Administration officials discounted Hussein's claims that he would soon leave Kuwait. They saw his apparent receptivity to Arab proposals as a ruse to gain time, both to strengthen his hold on Kuwait and to regroup for a strike into Saudi Arabia. Although better armed than Kuwait, Saudi Arabia could not defend itself against an Iraqi invasion. Bush and his advisers concluded that the only way to protect Saudi Arabia was to persuade King Fahd to accept U.S. troops right away.

That the United States would need a base of operations for military action in the Gulf was never in question. But winning King Fahd's blessing for a U.S. deployment, even with the express purpose of defending Saudi Arabia, would not be easy. American military bases were largely shut out of the Gulf, for cultural and religious reasons and because of America's pro-Israeli stance on Arab-Israeli disputes. Most Arab countries avoided military alliances with the United States, and requests for short-term U.S. military support were often cloaked in secrecy.[10] Some Arab leaders suspected that the United States would establish permanent bases and refuse to leave.

> Note the use of private information and expertise to help bring potential allies on board. What role did Prince Bandar play in this process?

After the second National Security Council meeting, Brent Scowcroft invited Saudi Arabia's ambassador in Washington, Prince Bandar Ibn Sultan, to the White House to review classified U.S. intelligence photos of Iraqi troops massing at the Saudi border. Bandar, a powerful emissary to the king, agreed to lobby for U.S. deployment. The next day, President Bush called King Fahd to impress on him both the danger of an invasion and the United States' willingness to help. At Fahd's invitation, Bush agreed to send a team immediately to discuss deployment. Fahd requested a technical team, but Bush feared that a low-level group would be disregarded. The king agreed to a group led by Defense Secretary Richard Cheney and including Deputy National Security Adviser Robert Gates and General Schwarzkopf.

Cheney expected King Fahd to insist on a guarantee that U.S. troops would leave once they were no longer needed. But, Cheney says, Fahd's worry was just the opposite—that the United States would respond with insufficient strength or leave before the job was done. "The concern that some of our friends in the region had wasn't that we were going to go too far," Cheney says.

> Why would Syria agree to support this U.S.-led initiative? What were its interests?

"It was that we wouldn't go far enough."[11] Once Cheney showed the Saudi king U.S. intelligence photos and promised at least 200,000 troops, Fahd accepted the offer of American forces. Less than forty hours later, U.S. F-15s were on the ground in Saudi Arabia. Only then did King Fahd risk Hussein's wrath by shutting down the Iraqi oil pipeline through Saudi Arabia.

Cheney's group continued on to Cairo to enlist the support of Egyptian President Mubarak. Mubarak granted permission for the nuclear aircraft carrier USS *Eisenhower* to pass through the Suez Canal, the first indication that Egypt would cooperate. Many Arab League members denounced the acceptance of outside intervention and continued to argue for an Arab solution. At a League summit on August 10, only a slim majority endorsed the arrival of foreign forces. But Egypt, Morocco, and Syria agreed to send troops to defend Saudi Arabia and the Gulf, critical proof of regional support for the U.S. deployment. Arab mediation efforts continued, but success was unlikely. The arrival of U.S. and other foreign troops signaled a change in the stakes and the "internationalization" of the Gulf crisis.

## DESERT SHIELD BEGINS

President Bush announced Desert Shield, the deployment of U.S. troops to protect Saudi Arabia, on August 8. The mission was wholly defensive, Bush emphasized. "No one commits America's armed forces to a dangerous mission lightly," he said. "But after perhaps unparalleled international consultation and exhausting every alternative, it became necessary to take this action." Cheney and Powell refused to discuss the size of the deployment, but the actual figure of up to 250,000 troops was soon leaked to the press.

The early days of the deployment were tense. For one thing, it would take a couple of weeks for enough troops and equipment to arrive to resist an Iraqi attack. "There was nothing to stop Hussein," recalls Richard Clarke, the State Department's assistant secretary for military and political affairs. "Even after the 82d Airborne deployed . . . , they essentially deployed with the bullets in the rifles that they carried, and they didn't have anything much beyond that for days."[12] And except for the British and a couple of Arab nations, it was unclear how many nations would participate in the military coalition, particularly when it came to supplying ground troops. "So far," one columnist wrote, "[the] multinational label is largely a gleam in America's eye."[13]

In truth, the United States expected to shoulder the lion's share of the defensive operation. Once Saudi Arabia made its bases available, the United States needed only enough time to pull together an adequate defense. The Arab League vote condemning Iraq and committing troops had been sufficient to cast the conflict as an international response, rather than a U.S. vendetta. But politically, the United States still needed the legitimacy that would flow from a broad-based multinational operation. President Bush, whose years in govern-

> Note the importance of established relationships in rapidly building a coalition.

ment had put him on a first-name basis with many foreign leaders, stepped up the "telephone diplomacy" that had earned him the nickname "the mad dialer" among State Department foreign-service officers. "Bush's personal relationships with a lot of people really helped," asserts Richard Haass of the National Security Council staff. "You don't want to make your first call to someone be the time you need them."[14]

Within days the military coalition began to grow, aided by Iraq's decision to retain as hostages thousands of Western and Soviet nationals trapped in Iraq and Kuwait when the borders were sealed.[15] Belgium, Greece, Spain, the Netherlands, and Italy announced that they would contribute naval units. Egypt, which was evolving into a key coalition ally, sent 5,000 troops. Britain expanded its commitments to include an armored brigade. And France—which had initially preferred to respond independently—agreed to send 4,200 ground troops. These early efforts to stitch together a military coalition focused strictly on defending Saudi Arabia, Cheney says. "It wasn't in our interest to talk publicly about offensive military action," he explains. "We didn't have enough forces over there to defend Saudi Arabia at the outset. If Hussein had figured out that we were going to get after him, he might have been smart enough to go ahead and move another 250 or 300 miles and take the Saudi airfields and the ports that we needed to get in there."

In fact, the president had not shown his hand on liberating Kuwait even to his "Gang of Eight" advisers. Most Americans still viewed an attack by U.S. troops as unlikely. But by the end of August, Cheney says, he and others were thinking about offensive action. From the day Bush declared, "This will not stand," administration officials insist, war was a possibility. "You can't use words like that lightly," notes Haass, who interpreted the remark as a policy declaration. "Did we think at that time that we would have to mount a military operation?" asks Brent Scowcroft. "Not necessarily. But by then we'd decided it was basically up to Hussein how he got out."

## THE UN SECURITY COUNCIL: ADVOCATE OR ADVERSARY?

In the weeks after the invasion, the United States continued to push resolutions through the Security Council. Hussein's blatant acts of aggression, and his inability or unwillingness to turn world opinion in his favor, eased passage of a resolution imposing full economic sanctions against Iraq.[16] When Hussein announced a Kuwaiti "provisional government" whose ministers were all Iraqi, even Cuba and Yemen voted to declare the annexation null and void.

That the Security Council would continue to support the U.S. position and take a forceful role was by no means a foregone conclusion, however. The Council's rules, as well as the differing political agendas of its members, made it difficult for a single country to engineer a sustained response to an international crisis. For a resolution to pass, nine of the fifteen members had to approve it, and all five permanent members had to either approve or abstain. For the United States to win passage of a resolution, in other words, it needed nine votes and the support of the other four permanent members—China, France, Great Britain, and the Soviet Union. In the past, the Soviets routinely rejected U.S.-led resolutions, and the Chinese usually followed their lead. But with relations between the United States and the Soviets thawing, and with the joint condemnation of Iraq in hand, UN Ambassador Thomas Pickering says there was a nearly unprecedented opportunity for cooperation among the permanent five. "Those traditional recalcitrants on the Council who were normally galvanized by the Soviets were left to drift by the fact that the Soviets were immediately with us," he explains.

> How did the Bush administration recruit a critical mass of support on the Security Council? What techniques were employed?

The White House and the State Department made the most of the new political landscape. "The Gulf crisis brought the Security Council to center stage in Washington, directly involving the president and the secretary of state in unprecedented ways," explains John Bolton, the assistant secretary of state responsible for U.S. policy toward the United Nations. "Both were involved in the direct negotiation of strategies, resolution texts, and all manner of things that their predecessors probably had never even heard of."[17] Even before the Gulf crisis, Washington had begun to take a more activist role in the Security Council as the Council's potential as a serious player in world events grew. With the Iraqi invasion of Kuwait, however, the U.S. approach to Security Council diplomacy changed dramatically. Resolutions, once drafted in New York, were now crafted by the State Department, passing through a laborious multibureau clearing process before Pickering began negotiations.

Even more revolutionary was the State Department's decision to push U.S.-backed resolutions at three levels simultaneously. Pickering consulted with his counterparts in New York while the State Department met with the same nations' ambassadors to Washington. At the same time, American ambassadors to Security Council nations and other major capitals presented the U.S. position to their foreign ministers. "It demonstrated that we wanted attention paid to these issues at the highest political levels, and that we expected a clear decision by those levels," Bolton explains. "Implicit was the notion that a 'wrong' vote would be noticed in Washington."

> Note the use of sequencing to build momentum.

This multilevel diplomacy required careful strategy in wooing allies and pursuing Bush administration goals. "The essence of our strategy in winning in New York depended first on getting Britain and France with us, and then the Soviets. And the Soviets were really critical, because without them we had no chance of China," Pickering explains. With the permanent five members on board, Pickering could largely count on the votes of Canada, Romania, and Finland.

That left one final obstacle: the so-called Nonaligned Caucus of countries that rotated membership on the Council. This group—which in 1990 consisted of Colombia, Cuba, the Ivory Coast, Ethiopia, Malaysia, Yemen, and Zaire—got its political strength from deliberating and voting as a bloc. "The nonaligned had never fractured on an issue of significance since the '60s," Pickering notes. The Caucus represented a potential veto, which gave it clout and bargaining power. To minimize anti-American sentiment on the part of the nonaligned, Pickering downplayed the role of the United States as chief architect of the Iraq resolutions. "We attempted never to face the nonaligned with a U.S. product, but with a permanent five or permanent four [excluding the Chinese] product," he explains. "Often when we presented resolutions of the permanent five to them, . . . the Brits or the Russians and I would take a different part of the presentation."

Despite the State Department's growing involvement in Security Council diplomacy, and Pickering's success with the first three resolutions, some in the administration opposed making the United Nations the implementing agent and de-facto final arbiter in the crisis. Haass acknowledges the value of the Security Council's "Good Housekeeping seal of approval" but recalls fretting over the precedent being set. "The idea that before you could ever do anything you have to go to the Council was not an approach to international relations that filled me with great confidence," he says. And the Pentagon worried that the United

States might eventually find itself shackled if the Council opposed the use of force.

The question of whether to continue to work through the Security Council came to a head less than two weeks into the crisis. When the Council voted to impose full economic sanctions, ending all trade with Iraq, it did not address enforcement. According to President Bush and Prime Minister Thatcher, the United States and Britain had the authority under Article 51 of the UN Charter to enforce the embargo and stop Iraqi ships—using force if necessary. This article, affirming "the inherent right of individual or collective self-defense," could be invoked once Kuwait asked for help, and the United States, Britain, and France had all received formal requests for assistance.

> Bush and Thatcher worked to keep the option for unilateral action alive. Why was it important to do so?

But when Bush, invoking Article 51, declared that the United States had the right to take unilateral action against Iraqi tankers, he set off a firestorm of criticism among allies and at the Security Council. Angry Council members claimed that such a move would amount to an act of war. And UN Secretary General Perez de Cuellar claimed that "only the UN, through Security Council resolutions, can really bring about a blockade."[18] Thatcher and some administration officials, including Scowcroft and Cheney, continued to push for decisive action. "Inside the U.S. government there were people who said, 'Haven't we run the UN string out?'" recalls Robert Kimmitt, undersecretary of state for political affairs. "'Isn't now the time just to take matters into our own hands?'"[19]

But Kimmitt and Baker were convinced the United Nations was too important to abandon. They were confident that the United States could achieve its goal—bringing force to bear on Iraq—under the protective mantle of the United Nations. "We sat and talked [to skeptics in the administration] about the fact that the Council had now become the centerpiece of the effort to take action under the UN Charter, as a matter of international collective security. And therefore Council members bore a particularly important responsibility," explains Pickering. The United States also did its best, he says, to portray Hussein's "totally recalcitrant" actions as a direct challenge to the Council.

The argument that a Council vote authorizing force would represent an international consensus was compelling, since Security Council resolutions were binding on all 158 UN member nations. "Baker's and my position was we *do* have the unilateral authority to stop the ships," Robert Kimmitt recalls. "But if we can get a resolution at the UN that puts the Security Council behind that action, then we have taken yet another step in the direction of keeping that coalition together." He adds: "The rap against us in earlier crises, both at home and abroad, was always, 'Why did you act unilaterally? Why didn't you go to the UN?'"

The State Department drafted a resolution that would not constitute a declaration of war, nor appear to allow the United States to take any action it pleased. At the same time, the United States rejected Moscow's proposal to place military enforcement under direct UN control. "We did not want the UN to take charge of this operation," Scowcroft declares. "We wanted them to provide the political backing for us, and that's all."

By August 22, the permanent five—except China—were largely comfortable with adding a threat of force to give more bite to the embargo. Meanwhile, Pickering encountered opposition from representatives of the nonaligned countries who thought the United States was resorting to force too quickly. "The U.S. was just driving the whole effort towards war without any interest in making peace," said Colombia's Ambassador to the UN Enrique Penalosa. The nonaligned also objected to the lack of UN authority over the military action being contemplated, and considered vetoing the resolution or insisting on radical changes in its text. Ultimately, opposition to the U.S. draft was abandoned when Ethiopia, the Ivory Coast, and Zaire broke with the group to support it. Penalosa thinks that the United States coerced the three. "The only explanation for the fact that they split the group at that moment was that they were subject to tremendous pressures from the U.S. and maybe other permanent members," he declares.[20]

With only Cuba and Yemen in opposition, the Security Council approved what amounted to a naval blockade against Iraq. Resolution 665 allowed member states, in cooperation with Kuwait and maritime forces in the area, to use measures "commensurate to the specific circumstances" to enforce the embargo. The resolution's deliberate ambiguity discouraged antiwar rhetoric in the United States and was also crafted to avoid a Chinese veto. As Pickering explains, "The Chinese finally abstained on the thesis that the resolution text didn't authorize the use of force in their view, a statement . . . we had agreed we would not try to counter." Even Colombia and Malaysia voted in favor.

> A deal was crafted carefully to avoid creating a blocking coalition.

The U.S. position prevailed, but not without bruised feelings. According to one diplomat, "Many of us felt the Americans lost a lot of goodwill" due to the Bush administration's aggressive diplomacy.[21] But U.S. officials were pleased. An American-run military operation was taking shape in Saudi Arabia with unprecedented Arab backing; the Soviets were criticizing Iraq, almost in unison with the United States; and an international embargo—backed by a UN-sanctioned threat of military force—had isolated Iraq economically and militarily. A multinational coalition was coalescing, just as the United States had planned.

# THE "TIN-CUP TRIPS": CASH AND FAVORS

When President Bush first decided to send forces to Saudi Arabia, the international support he sought was political, not economic. But when the average daily cost of the deployment reached $28.9 million by the end of August, raising money—or, as Baker put it, "responsibility sharing"—became a practical and political necessity. The domestic economy was weak, and Congress, though relatively passive about the deployment itself, was vocal about sharing the cost. "The Hill at that point was just hammering the administration about 'Well, what are the Germans putting up? What are the Japanese putting up?'" recalls an aide to Baker. "In order to get domestic support, you needed to make sure other people were putting up money." Republican Congressman Mickey Edwards agrees: "There was a sense that came out of Vietnam that we don't want to do this alone anymore. We either do things multilaterally and other people help share the burden—costs, lives, and so forth—or we're not going to do it."[22]

> **Note the framing. How is *responsibility sharing* different from *burden sharing*?**

Administration officials also wanted to help coalition members harmed by the sanctions against Iraq. Higher oil prices, inflated by the disruption of supply, and the breakoff of loan and trade agreements with Iraq and Kuwait were taking a toll. If the price of the embargo proved too high, some of the allies might break with the coalition. The countries hurt most by the sanctions—Egypt, Jordan, and Turkey—were critical for political support and, in the case of Jordan and Turkey, for their ability to seal Iraq's borders.

Around Labor Day, Baker went to the Middle East while Treasury Secretary Nicholas Brady flew to Europe and Asia on what came to be known as "tin-cup trips." The Kuwaiti government-in-exile was already bankrolling the U.S. effort.

> **Identifying complementary interests and making trades helped secure support.**

Now the administration targeted Saudi Arabia and other Gulf countries that stood to gain directly. The United States also solicited aid from Germany and Japan, whose national constitutions precluded military participation in the Gulf. The fundraising effort was highly successful. By November, a $13-billion aid package had been arranged. The United States eventually collected $53.7 billion from allies, leaving $7.4 billion to absorb itself.[23]

The Bush administration also offered indirect forms of support to hold onto allies. Some officials deny the importance of *quid pro quos* —"It wasn't a bargaining thing, where we had to go out there and sell chairs in the coalition," asserts Haass—but others insist that "sweeteners" were critical to coalition building. "You knew you could order up whatever it took," recalls Richard Clarke of the State Department. "You could talk about debt forgiveness for Egypt. You could talk about doubling the trade quota for Turkey. As soon as you had the idea, you knew you could get away with it."

The administration doubled the quota of textiles Turkey could export to the United States, and arranged with 16 other creditor nations to forgive half the $20.2 billion Egypt owed them. But most coalition members weren't looking for anything so tangible. The Soviet Union wanted U.S. support for Gorbachev's shaky domestic reforms and the promise of future economic assistance. China hoped to rebuild a relationship with the United States badly damaged by the Tiananmen Square massacre. And Syria hoped that membership in the coalition would help it shed its outlaw status. "We wanted Syria in the coalition not so much for its military contribution but for the political legitimacy it would give," explains a former White House official. "It was as much in their interest to align themselves with us as it was in our interests to have them in there." Adds a top State Department official, "We were in the process of seeing the collapse of the Soviet Union and the end of the Cold War. Everybody wanted to be close to the United States of America."

## PARRYING PRESSURE TO NEGOTIATE

The multinational coalition served U.S. interests well. Its size and geopolitical diversity signified a world united in outrage. But this same diversity made for a lot of work. "One of the real challenges was creating and holding together the coalition over a multi-month period," says Robert Gates, the president's deputy national security adviser. "People were in it for very different reasons."

The "Gang of Eight" remained responsible for policy, led by President Bush, whose involvement, Assistant Secretary of State Bolton says, is "impossible to overstate." Managing the Gulf conflict had become the Bush administration's top agenda item. "Everything else was secondary," declares Haass. "The U.S. government, for better or worse, revolved around this set of issues."

Hussein did little to exploit differences between coalition members or to influence public opinion. His announcement that "foreign visitors" would be stationed at likely target sites strengthened

> Note Hussein's effort to drive wedges into the coalition and to create constraining linkages. How did the United States respond?

resolve against him and bolstered the terrorist image of him the Bush administration was eager to foster; by October, more than 600 hostages had been detained at such sites. But Hussein succeeded in making Israel an issue by portraying the invasion of Kuwait as a tool to redress old wrongs and seizing every opportunity to implicate Israel. He claimed that the first troops in Saudi Arabia were Israeli soldiers wearing U.S. uniforms. He repeatedly declared his intention of attacking Israel should a battle begin, thus transforming the conflict into an Arab-Israeli war. But most damaging to the United States diplomatically was Hussein's August 12 "peace plan." In order for Iraq to discuss Kuwait, Hussein declared, other regional occupations must first be addressed, including Israel's occupation of Arab territories. Only then would Iraq come to the table.

The Bush administration hoped to avoid any linkage between the U.S. response and Israel, and cautioned strict restraint on Israel's part. If Israel got involved, even the moderate Arab states would surely drop out of the coalition. The United States took pains not to appear to favor Israel over its new Arab allies. This resolve was put to the test in early October when Israeli police killed 22 stone-throwing Palestinians at Jerusalem's Temple Mount. The Security Council began debating a resolution to condemn the action. In the past, the U.S. response would probably have been a veto or an abstention. But this time, the United States had other interests to balance. "We were acutely concerned about not losing the consensus against Iraq," UN Ambassador Pickering recalls. The eventual compromise resolution, condemning the Israeli response as "excessive," won unanimous Security Council approval.

Hussein's linkage of his invasion of Kuwait with the Israeli occupation of Arab territories remained troubling. It became harder for the United States to take the moral high ground when critics insisted that Israel had illegitimately occupied Arab territories since 1967 and had largely escaped Security Council condemnation. "To recover its independence, there is no reason for Kuwait to wait for the Arab-Israeli conflict to be resolved," Colombian Ambassador Penalosa declared. "But at the same time, it is clear that for the Arabs there is a connection, because they see that the West is in this case determined to . . . prevent the acquisition of territory by violent means, whereas in the Palestinian case the West has shown little desire to go beyond mild verbal condemnations of the occupying power, while giving that power economic and military aid."[24]

Most troubling was the way that linkage was adopted as a negotiating wedge by countries anxious to avoid military confrontation with Iraq. The Soviets and the French, in particular, had compelling reasons to embrace negotiation. Both had long-term ties to Iraq as investors, advisers, and arms suppliers, and both had a stake in being seen as important and thoughtful players in the conflict, independent of America's lead. Hence both countries continued to search for common ground with Hussein, even while cooperating with the coalition. French President François Mitterrand shocked U.S. officials and some other allies by proposing a comprehensive regional peace conference to follow an Iraqi pullout from Kuwait. Nor were the Soviet Union and France alone in pursuing a compromise. Colombia and Malaysia pushed within the Security Council for a less confrontational approach. UN Secretary General Perez de Cuellar was also sympathetic to seeking a negotiated settlement with Iraq and to addressing the broader Palestinian issue. But U.S. officials made clear their distaste for such proposals. There could be no hedging, they declared, on the "unconditional withdrawal" demanded in the first Security Council resolution. "This was not a traditional negotiation," asserts a White House official. "I was not looking to save Hussein from himself, I was simply looking to get him out—bottom line. He was going to choose the method of his leaving Kuwait. That was the choice we gave him."

## DOUBLING OF FORCES: THE OFFENSIVE OPTION

Iraq, whose income had been choked off with the closing of its pipelines, appeared vulnerable to an economic embargo. Moreover, the embargo appeared to be holding solid, with more than 100 countries participating. But after two months, the Bush administration grew impatient with the lack of concrete results. "What we hoped was that the presence of 250,000 U.S. forces, plus worldwide political solidarity, plus economic sanctions, would make Hussein realize that he had misstepped, and he would find some way to pull out," says Robert Kimmitt of the State Department. "But by about the end of September, we started making plans for the eventuality that this guy was never going to get the message and that we were going to have to bring the message to him."

> Why was it important for the administration to be seen giving sanctions a good try?

Publicly, the administration continued to praise the effectiveness of the economic embargo, but belief that sanctions and diplomacy could prevail had faded. In late August, Deputy Treasury Secretary John Robson had presented a sobering historical assessment concluding that sanctions alone rarely compel a country to change course. "I don't think we ever believed sanctions would do the trick," declares Richard Clarke, "but . . . we had to be seen to be exhausting our remedies."

Throughout October, as Hussein continued to snub overtures at negotiation, the Bush administration began planning seriously for war. Schwarzkopf, Powell, and others produced the rudiments of a plan. An offensive option would require twice the number of troops currently deployed; most could be pulled from Germany. Ideal timing would be after January 1—when sufficient troops and equipment would be in place—and before February 15, when bad weather and a series of Muslim holidays would complicate logistics. Militarily, only Saudi Arabia's cooperation was vital, for its bases. "The bottom line," one senior Pentagon official asserts, "was that the war was going to be run by the United States and was going to involve primarily U.S. forces."

Bush met with advisers on October 30 to reach a decision on an offensive to retake Kuwait. Alarmed by evidence that the coalition might break down, and convinced that only the threat of military action would convince Iraq to withdraw, the president approved the buildup. Bush decided to hold the news for at least a week to avoid influencing the upcoming congressional elections. Meanwhile, Baker began a series of visits to inform allies of the doubling of forces, to ask for more troops and money, and to test Security Council reaction to a use-of-force resolution. "The November trip was laying the basis for intense coercive diplomacy," says a Baker aide, "namely, building up forces large enough to go to war if necessary." Baker hoped to solidify the allies' support before the troop buildup was made public. Congress and the American people, he believed, had not been prepared to accept escalation. But word began to leak out, and Bush called a news conference on November 8. "After consultation with King Fahd and our other allies, I have today directed the secretary of defense to increase the size of U.S. forces committed to Desert Shield to insure that the coalition has an adequate offensive military option should that be necessary to achieve our common goals," the president announced. "Iraq's aggression is not just a challenge to the security of Kuwait and other Gulf nations, but to the better world that we all have hoped to build in the wake of the Cold War."

## CHALLENGES BACK HOME

The doubling of forces took Congress by surprise. The president had met with congressional leaders shortly before the announcement but had given no hint that it was imminent, which they found galling. More troubling was the message itself. For many administration officials, the troop increase was simply the next logical step. But for many in Congress, and for a significant percentage of the American public, neither the timing nor the need for a military buildup was obvious. Senator Sam Nunn, chairman of the Senate Armed Services Committee, described the increase as a "fundamental change" in U.S. policy. No longer, it seemed, was the Bush administration willing to give sanctions a chance. No longer was international pressure considered adequate. Suddenly, a U.S.-led war had become a real possibility. Both the Senate and the House announced hearings on the nation's Gulf policy.

**Note the importance of timing and the role of action-forcing events.**

Representative Mickey Edwards describes Congress as "an afterthought" during the crisis. "Most presidents consider foreign policy to be their arena," he notes. "Only rarely does somebody think to say, 'Oops, I think we better go ask Congress what they feel about that.'" But Scowcroft describes Congress's exclusion from the loop as more calculated: "I didn't want to have a precise time where it looked like we turned from a defensive to an offensive strategy, because we didn't have the Congress on board yet. We thought we could just get away with it and nobody would notice. But it didn't work."

The outcry confirmed Baker's fears. Public opinion, which had been strongly supportive of the president, took a nosedive. A *New York Times* poll found that 47 percent of the public considered the administration "too quick to get American military forces involved rather than seeking diplomatic solutions." In late November, a *Los Angeles Times* poll measured support for the president's policies at just over 50 percent, down from 75 percent in August. As one columnist put it, "an anti-war movement is afoot."[25]

Those who testified at the Congressional hearings included ardent advocates of the president's policies, but also critics Bush found difficult to ignore. Admiral William J. Crowe, Jr., who had served as chairman of the Joint Chiefs of Staff under both Ronald Reagan and Bush, made a strong plea for restraint:

> Whether initiating conflict against Iraq will moderate the larger difficulties in the Gulf region and will put Washington in a better position to work with the Arab world in the future, is in my estimation, the . . . important question. . . . It would be a sad commentary if Saddam Hussein, a two-bit tyrant who sits on 17 million people and possesses a gross national product of $40 billion, proved to be more patient than the United States, the world's most affluent and powerful nation.[26]

As the White House reacted to the fallout, some officials faulted Bush for lavishing attention on foreign allies but not reaching out to the American people. "The administration didn't begin selling the war until well into November," charges Richard Clarke. "I remember the constant criticism within the administration that the White House hasn't begun laying the psychological groundwork."

But there had been no shortage of explanations for why the United States should send troops to Saudi Arabia. The problem was the

> The administration searched for a compelling rationale to support its position.

variety of messages. At first Bush had emphasized Hussein's violations of international law. Then the accusations had become more personal, as Bush detailed Iraqi atrocities against the Kuwaiti people, spoke of the need to protect American hostages, and compared Hussein to Hitler. The attention focused on atrocities was heightened by a Kuwaiti woman who testified before Congress on such Iraqi soldier misdeeds as throwing Kuwaiti babies from hospital incubators. The specific incident was later challenged, even before the woman was identified as a member of the Kuwaiti royal family under the tutelage of public relations firm Hill & Knowlton, Inc.

In mid-November, Baker raised the economic consequences of the Gulf conflict, concluding that "for the average American citizen, let me say, that means jobs." This assertion, however confusing, came closest to acknowledging what many observers considered the real reason for the United States to be in Saudi Arabia—to protect the region's oil supplies. "There was a feeling nobody really wanted to address or put out publicly on the table, which was: we were going to war over oil," says Representative Edwards.

As public support eroded, Bush began working with his pollster, Robert Teeter, to develop a more coherent message. Their solution: to portray Hussein as a nuclear threat. In a speech to U.S. troops in Saudi Arabia, Bush declared that "every day that passes brings Saddam Hussein one step closer to realizing his goal of a nuclear weapons arsenal—and that's another reason, frankly, why our mission is marked by a real sense of urgency." Intelligence agencies had in fact warned that Hussein might be close to producing a nuclear bomb. Nevertheless, Bush's warning provoked cynicism, even within the White House. After all, recent government estimates had predicted that Iraq wouldn't have nuclear capability for at least five years.[27] Nevertheless, the president kept returning to Hussein's potential to initiate a nuclear confrontation. Bush's pollster had found that this was one threat the American public really cared about.

## THE EXPANDED AGENDA

As President Bush deliberated over the offensive option, a shift was occurring in the administration's thinking. Liberating Kuwait was the first goal of any military action. But according to one White House official, consensus was growing that "a narrow return to the *status quo ante* was inadequate." Even before Bush had committed to the buildup, CIA Director William Webster had asserted that Hussein should be "disassociated from his weapons of mass destruction."[28] Before long, the phrase "nightmare scenario" had been coined to describe any outcome that did not cripple Hussein's political power or military strength. "There was an argument," says Philip Zelikow of the National Security Council, "that not only must he fail, he must be seen to have failed in a humiliating way."[29]

**Why did this transformation of the administration's goals occur?**

The emerging U.S. plan called for bombing raids on nuclear, military, and communications targets deep in Iraq. One official who claims there was "a punitive element" to the plan also insists that there were sound short- and long-term reasons to hit Iraq so hard: any battle to liberate Kuwait must also disable Hus-sein's ability to strike back or to lash out at Israel. Though many in the admin-istration doubted that Hussein had already produced nuclear weapons, no one doubted that he intended to do so. "People began thinking, 'We don't want to be in a situation where we bloody him and kick him out of Kuwait, and then he goes away and sulks and builds his nuclear weapons to come back at us,'" recalls Richard Clarke. "So people talked seriously about an air campaign to eliminate his weapons of mass destruction."

In late November, an internal directive was drawn up articulating two goals: to remove Iraq from Kuwait and to destroy Hussein's offensive war-making capabilities. An additional objective—changing the regime in Baghdad—was rejected as politically unsupportable and militarily unachievable. The expanded agenda was never debated either domestically or internationally. "We never thought it was necessary to go to the Security Council to say, 'Please approve our tactical blueprint,'" observes Haass, though Defense Secretary Cheney says Hussein's close neighbors quietly supported plans to inflict as much damage as possible on Iraq. Cheney recalls that the defense minister of a small Gulf coun-try privately revealed his eagerness for decisive American action: "The guy wanted to know if we were going to use nuclear weapons on Saddam."

# BACK TO THE SECURITY COUNCIL: GAMBLING ON THE COALITION

When Baker began drumming up support for a UN resolution authorizing force, some in the administration considered it politically unwise. Scowcroft and Cheney feared that, in the event of a Security Council veto, the United States would be hobbled or subject to paralyzing international and domestic criticism if it went ahead with a unilateral attack. "The key risk was that we might fail" to get the UN vote, Ambassador Pickering states bluntly. "Once hav-ing failed, the entire structure on which our activ-ity was based would have become insufficient, at least in the minds of many people."

> Note the interplay between unilateral and multilateral options.

Many in the administration were also convinced that Security Council authorization was a mere gesture. The United States had the legal right under Article 51, they believed, to move unilaterally to liberate Kuwait. Defense officials predicted that the most skittish Arab states, such as Syria, might back down without a UN umbrella, but that the allies that mattered most militarily, such as Saudi Arabia and Britain, would stick with the United States. "We did not need Security Council action," Cheney declares. "Partly what made the coalition successful was the fact that it became clear over time that we would do it whether we had anybody else on board or not."

But Baker and Bush pressed forward, convinced that the United States had a good chance of winning the vote. Pickering thought the United States would be helped by the growing belief that the Americans would eventually launch an attack even without a resolution: "This underlying current meant . . . that members of the Council had to decide whether they would rather have the U.S. operating inside the Council, and somewhat subject to Council consensus, or outside the Council, acting in ways they might not really like or approve of." The president began calling the heads of state of Security Council countries, and Baker began another diplomatic trek. In Moscow, he found that the Soviets were determined to put their imprint on the resolution. Gorbachev wanted to prove his commitment to peace, both to Hussein and to conservatives in his own government. Baker and Shevardnadze agreed to eliminate language specifying use of force, and instead to call for "all necessary means," a phrase that both sides found comfortably vague. But Baker left with no guarantee of Soviet support.

Baker assured Scowcroft and Cheney that he would not bring the resolution to a vote unless he knew he could win. When questioned by reporters, Baker denied that a Security Council resolution was even under consideration. According to Representative Edwards, the administration's caginess was a smart approach. "The president knew enough to keep his mouth shut, work quietly behind the scenes, get people lined up, and then come back and tell us," Edwards notes. "If Gorbachev or the president of Argentina laughed at him and said, 'No way,' we wouldn't know it."

## How was support solidified and opposition neutralized?

By mid-November, it was still unclear whether Baker would garner enough votes. France, like the Soviet Union, was still talking about negotiation. And the Colombian ambassador had submitted an alternative proposal on behalf of Colombia, Malaysia, Cuba, and Yemen, seeking to clarify the consequences of Iraq's withdrawal and offering such carrots as an end to economic sanctions, suspension of the threat of military attack, and a negotiation process to settle the dispute with Kuwait. The four nonaligned countries were also pressing for a resolution creating a UN peacekeeping force in the Israeli-occupied territories, which Pickering feared could stir up anti-U.S. sentiments among Arab allies.

After regrouping in Washington, Baker returned to Europe for a final push. Ethiopia, the Ivory Coast, and Zaire all agreed to support the U.S. position, reportedly in return for promises of Western aid, and Finland and Romania indicated their likely agreement. Baker and Bush kept working on their French and Soviet counterparts. In meetings with Gorbachev, Bush argued for the UN effort as a model of cooperation for the post-Cold-War world. Finally Gorbachev and

Mitterrand announced their readiness to consider a resolution authorizing force.

The United States now appeared to have the necessary nine votes, but Baker continued to seek the broadest possible support, even from the most unlikely quarters. When he appealed to Yemen, the one Arab member of the Security Council and a consistent critic of U.S. policy, Baker got a public lecture from Yemen's president on the mistakes being made in the Gulf. A U.S. official warned in response that "everything has its price."[30] A meeting with Cuba's foreign minister produced similarly disappointing results, but Baker successfully used pressure and *quid pro quos* to convince Colombia and Malaysia to support the U.S. draft. Finally China declared that it would not veto the resolution. Explains Robert Kimmitt, "We just mentioned to the Chinese that we needed to keep our dialogue going on Tiananmen Square and other issues and that, obviously, when they were prepared to support us, it would be easier to receive them in Washington."

The draft resolution put before the Council on November 29 was jointly sponsored by the United States, the Soviet Union, Canada, and Great Britain. Resolution 678 called on Iraq to take advantage of this "one final opportunity, as a pause of goodwill," to comply with all eleven previous UN resolutions by January 15, 1991. If it did not, "all necessary means" could be used to enforce the resolutions and "to restore international peace and security in the area." The resolution did not give the United Nations jurisdiction over an offensive operation, but granted the right to take military action to "Member States cooperating with the Government of Kuwait." In effect, this left military coordination in the hands of the United States.

Baker's travelling diplomacy paid off: the final vote was twelve in favor, with Cuba and Yemen opposed and China abstaining.[31] But the hard work was not over. The Bush administration still had to prove to Congress and the American public that, if it came to war, the United States would not be fighting alone. In the wake of the Security Council vote, Representative Les Aspin, chairman of the House Armed Services Committee, asserted, "The vote for the UN resolution is, in effect, a vote by the members of the Security Council to let the United States fight Iraq."[32]

# WAR: THE PREFERRED ALTERNATIVE

One day after the Security Council approved the use of force, President Bush made a controversial televised offer. To "go the extra mile for peace," Bush said, he was inviting Iraqi Foreign Minister Tariq Aziz to Washington. In the United States, the diplomatic overture was a coup. Though congressional hearings on Gulf policy continued to air anti-administration views, Bush's approval rating began to rebound. A movement for a congressional vote on Bush's right to use force against Iraq lost momentum. "We were saved from ourselves," jokes one administration official who had opposed the Bush offer. "It looked like we were going the extra mile."

**Why was the administration doing this? Who was the audience?**

But many coalition members, and Arab allies in particular, heard the invitation with astonishment and dismay. Hussein would conclude, they said, that the United States lacked the will or ability to use force. Brent Scowcroft, who had opposed the offer, feared that Aziz would use his visit to strengthen the case against war. That Baker and Scowcroft were on opposite sides of this issue was no surprise. A split had developed in the administration: Baker and General Colin Powell were still anxious to work sanctions and diplomacy, but Cheney, Scowcroft, and—by and large—Bush had concluded not just that force might be needed but that war was the preferred alternative. "Saddam had demonstrated that he had strong intentions about Kuwait," asserts Scowcroft. "If he pulled back intact, we would be in a very awkward situation because he would be there as a constant threat. . . . The best way to do it was to deal with it now."

Those who favored going to war feared that the invitation to Aziz would give Hussein an opening to offer conditional withdrawal—which one official took to calling "a half-loaf proposal." And even if the United States turned down a half-loaf offer, other allies would probably grab at it. "It would have stretched our coalition-management capabilities to the limit," the official says. "The Soviets or the French would have said, 'Aha, this is great.'" Moreover, if Hussein made an offer—no matter how contrived—before January 15, it would have to be dealt with before the United States could launch an attack.

To prepare for such a contingency, the White House hammered out detailed responses to any possible proposal on Hussein's part short of unconditional withdrawal. "The bottom line was that we were not going to play that game," Haass recalls. "Anything less than full compliance with the basic 660 Resolution was unacceptable." White House insiders admitted, though, that any pullback on Hussein's part could shut down the offensive option—at least temporarily. "If he had moved back to a situation where he was only occupying the Rumaila oil field and maybe the islands," notes Richard Clarke, "I think it would have been very hard for us to launch a military attack."

Hussein did not take advantage of the opportunity Bush had handed him, though he appeared to have interpreted it, as some allies feared, as evidence of last-minute American cold feet and openness to negotiation. Iraqi newspapers gloated that the United States had submitted to Hussein's demand to resolve the Palestinian issue before addressing Kuwait. A week after Bush's announcement, Hussein released all foreign hostages, perhaps to solidify the United

States' apparent move toward peace. But the likelihood of substantive talks faded as the two sides bickered over logistics.

As Baker had hoped, however, the U.S. offer discouraged other countries from pursuing their own diplomatic efforts, and Baghdad offered no concrete proposal for a partial withdrawal. "Rarely," says Gates, "has anyone been so fortunate in the clumsiness and stupidity and incompetence of the enemy."

## THE UNWIELDY MILITARY ALLIANCE

With the UN vote in place, war preparations began in earnest. General Schwarzkopf's daunting task of coordinating the international military effort was further complicated by Baker's enthusiasm for coalition building. The State Department was eager to enlist participants for the political legitimacy they would lend the coalition; then the Defense Department had to scramble to find space, supplies, and food for the often ill-prepared foreign troops. As Richard Clarke puts it: "There was not an easy fit between our State Department's desire to get a lot of countries involved and the Defense Department's desire not to."

> Efforts to build a political coalition complicated military operations. Was there any alternative?

Some military assistance was crucial. Saudi contributions and British troops and equipment became integral to the offensive plan. NATO sent troops to protect Turkey—encouraging that country's continued cooperation—and served as a clearinghouse for Western European operations. In general, though, defense organizers saw the potpourri of forces as a necessary evil. "Most of the coalition partners were more trouble than they were worth in terms of actual military effectiveness," Gates states bluntly. "The British were worth having. The French to a lesser extent were worth having. But most of the rest were a drain, so the fewer the better from the U.S. military standpoint." The clash between political needs and military expediency led to a few awkward standoffs. Clarke recalls "beating on" several countries to contribute aircraft, only to be told by the Pentagon that there were no airfields available. "Eventually," Clarke adds, "we got them an airfield."

But Baker's argument ultimately prevailed. "There were a lot of people you needed to impress, not the least of which were the Congress and the American people," he explains. "But you also needed to impress any people who might have had misgivings about signing on." Small gestures could be politically significant. One State Department official, recalling that the Czechs sent a chemical-detection unit, notes, "It was really symbolically very important to have an East European, formerly communist country sending a medical unit to the Gulf. It was important in making it clear that this was an undertaking that had unprecedented international support from around the world."

The State Department paid particular attention to Arab representation. With the switch to an offensive mission, membership in the U.S.-led alliance had become politically sensitive, especially for less moderate countries like Syria. "Putting troops in the field against another Arab was really a big bump for all these guys, especially under the umbrella of the United States," Gates says. "They might kill each other to a fare-thee-well, but partnering with us was a big problem." Baker was determined that Arab troops play a visible role. Scant Arab involvement would confirm Hussein's charge that the international coalition represented a Western-led vendetta against the Arab world. Meanwhile domestic critics questioned why the United States had to play cop for the world and resolve a far-away Gulf dispute. The claim that U.S. troops had become mercenaries for the oil-rich Gulf states was one the administration particularly wanted to avoid. This charge was reignited in January when the *Wall Street Journal* quoted a senior Gulf official as saying: "You think I want to send my teen-aged son to die for Kuwait? We have our white slaves from America to do that."[33] As one State Department official puts it: "It was important . . . that when the casualty count started to come in, that they not all be American or Western European."

Still unresolved was whether the Soviet Union should be invited into the coalition, as Baker believed, or limited to a symbolic role, as Scowcroft insisted. "We didn't want Soviet troops on the ground in the Gulf," Scowcroft says. "We've been spending thirty years trying to keep them out of the Middle East." Scowcroft feared that continued intelligence links between the Soviet Union and Iraq could threaten the security of allied military operations. Baker had obtained Saudi and Egyptian support for Soviet troop involvement, but it became a moot point. The Soviets might have considered military action under a UN flag, but going to war under U.S. command was unthinkable.

The final allied force in the Gulf consisted of units from 36 countries, but 85 percent of the troops were American. As one Pentagon official put it, "It was primarily a U.S. show from beginning to end."

## BAKER AND AZIZ MEET AT LAST

After weeks of haggling, Baker and Tariq Aziz met in Geneva on January 9. Baker and others in the administration believed that Hussein's stubbornness might arise in part from ignorance of the forces uniting against him. If the United States could communicate through Aziz the seriousness of its resolve, Iraq might still withdraw. Although there was no evidence that either side would bring fresh offers to the table, Scowcroft viewed the exercise with alarm. "I personally was concerned that it might work," he confides. He needn't have worried. Despite Baker's warnings about the resolve and technological superiority of the forces united against Iraq, Aziz insisted that Iraq would win if it came to war. "Never has an Arab regime entered into a war with Israel or the United States and lost politically,"[34] he asserted. Kimmitt observes, "Ultimately, Saddam was his own worst enemy. If Aziz had walked in and said, 'We screwed up. We will be out by the deadline,' or 'We'll have started full withdrawal by the deadline,' maybe that would have disappointed some people. But that is an offer that we would have had to accept."

> Did the administration want this peace initiative to bear fruit? If not, how might it have helped provoke a rejection by Iraq?

Baker emerged grim-faced from the meeting with Aziz. "I heard nothing today that suggested to me any Iraqi flexibility whatsoever on complying with the United Nations Security Council resolutions," he declared. "The choice is Iraq's. If it should choose to continue its brutal occupation of Kuwait, Iraq will be choosing a military confrontation which it cannot win, and which will have devastating consequences for Iraq." Bush professed himself discouraged and described the Iraqi response as "a total stiff-arm. This was a total rebuff." The Baker-Aziz meeting proved to be an ideal prelude to the congressional vote on use of force. According to one Democrat, Baker's press conference alone was worth 20 votes.[35] The next day Congress began debating a resolution authorizing the president to go to war.

## COURTING CONGRESS

It had still been unclear a week earlier whether Bush would ask Congress for authorization. Since the doubling of forces, Congress had been threatening to take matters into its own hands by calling a vote unilaterally. Some Democrats regretted that they had not acted sooner, when support for the president's policies was still low. But the issue's explosiveness had discouraged congressional action. "Congress doesn't want to have to vote on any military endeavor," says one top official. "They want to sit back there, and if it works they say, 'Terrific, Mr. President. Wonderful for the nation and God bless America.' But if it doesn't work, they want to dump all over him."

After the Baker-Aziz session, it appeared that Congress would take up authorization on its own. But within the administration, the question of

> Note once again the interplay of unilateral and multilateral options.

going to Congress remained, in Scowcroft's words, a "strong, sharp debate." Cheney, convinced that the president had the constitutional authority to go to war, advised against involving Congress: by asking for a vote, Bush would appear to be relinquishing that authority. Scowcroft and Lawrence Eagleburger also opposed a vote, mainly because they feared Bush wouldn't win. If the United States attacked Iraq after Congress had refused authorization, it would be "disastrous" for the president, Eagleburger said, adding, "I can see impeachment resolutions."[36] Scowcroft agreed: "It would have been a firestorm."

The risk that Bush's agenda would fail in the Democratic Congress was real. In the end, however, Bush concluded that ignoring Congress posed a greater risk than losing the vote. Vice President Dan Quayle had insisted on the importance of involving Congress, and some Republican stalwarts on the Hill had confided that they would oppose a war on constitutional grounds unless Bush sought congressional authorization. Bush was also swayed by the erosion of public support for Lyndon Johnson during the Vietnam War, in part due to congressional opposition. The day Baker met with Aziz, Bush requested congressional support to use "all necessary means" to remove Iraq from Kuwait, the same language used in the UN resolution.

> Note the sequenced use of the international coalition to build domestic support. Did Congress have any choice but to support the administration? What were its alternatives?

Bush's decision kicked off a lobbying blitz. Administration officials invoked the Security Council resolution condoning force and the backing of the multilateral alliance. "There has been some criticism of us for, in effect, pressuring Congress by building an international coalition and then making the argument, 'You mean, Congressman, you're not going to support the president, but the president of Ethiopia is supporting him?'" notes one top official. "But I don't think we should be apologetic about it. You build consensus in whatever way you can, and when this thing first started we didn't have support from Congress, and we didn't have support from the American people."

After three days of debate and an overnight session, both Houses approved a joint resolution effectively authorizing Bush to go to war. The resolution relied almost exclusively for its justification on the Security Council actions that had preceded it. "We couldn't have gotten the Congress earlier, I don't think," says Scowcroft. "And if there had been no coalition and no UN vote, we would never have gotten Congress."

Even had Congress voted no, according to Gates, the outcome would have been the same. "As long as Saddam was adamant [about staying in Kuwait], there was going to be a war, with or without the UN sanction, with or without congressional sanction," he declares. "George Bush was going to throw the son of a bitch out of Kuwait and there was never any doubt about it."

## THE LAST PROPOSALS FOR PEACE

The United States made final preparations. A delegation had already gone to Tel Aviv to reiterate the U.S. commitment to defend Israel. Prime Minister Yitzhak Shamir indicated that he would not make a preemptive strike, but remained noncommittal about responding to a direct attack. However, the United States' refusal to deconflict—to exchange the codes necessary for each side to identify and avoid the other's aircraft—made it virtually impossible for Israel to participate in the offensive.

On January 12, Hussein told the Russians that Iraq was prepared to relinquish Kuwait. The Soviets feverishly pressed for Iraqi withdrawal for two days before finally abandoning hope. "The Soviets wanted to find a way to have their cake and eat it too," Gates observes. "To be supportive of the coalition, but at the same time to get credit with Saddam for having prevented the conflict."

UN Secretary General Perez de Cuellar, whose earlier negotiating efforts the United States had discouraged, made a final trip to Baghdad on January 12, this time with the administration's blessing. The mission was destined to fail, the Bush administration believed. After meeting with Hussein, Perez de Cuellar commented simply, "I don't see any reason for hope."[37]

The French also made a last effort, drafting a new UN resolution promising UN participation in resolving other regional differences once Iraq withdrew. But the British countered with their own resolution. "Keeping the coalition together, against the natural inclination of all of these countries to want to see a war avoided, was not easy," one State

> Note the avoidance of an entangling linkage.

Department official says. "But we were of the view that we really didn't have any room to negotiate down from the UN resolutions we had sponsored." Adds a top aide: "That was an added benefit of going the multilateral route, in that the resolutions became a baseline that made it hard for members of the coalition to defect backwards from us."

## IT COMES TO WAR

Bush and his advisers continued to wonder if Hussein would surprise them with a last-minute parry. "There was no way we could have launched anything if it looked like he was finally fulfilling the resolutions," Haass explains. "We could never appear not willing to accept yes for an answer." He adds: "Saddam never gave us anything but no."

One day after the deadline, administration officials notified allies and congressional leaders that the war would begin that night. At 7 P.M. Washington time, 3 A.M. in the Gulf, White House spokesman Marlin Fitzwater announced, "The liberation of Kuwait has begun." Two hours later President Bush addressed the nation. After describing the rudiments of the air war, Bush continued, "Some may ask, why act now? Why not wait? The answer is clear. The world could wait no longer. . . . We have before us the opportunity to forge for ourselves and for future generations a new world order, a world where the rule of law, not the law of the jungle, governs the conduct of nations."

> What would have happened if Hussein had staged a partial withdrawal, perhaps keeping the disputed islands and oilfield?

The war lasted just 42 days. Only 240 allied soldiers were killed, including 148 Americans. Estimates of the Iraqi dead ranged from 35,000 to 100,000. "I think Saddam never thought we would do it," muses Gates. "I think right until the very end he never thought that this would actually happen."

# CHAPTER TWELVE

# Building Coalitions

Few goals in life are attainable without the help of others. The objective could be as ambitious as containing the Iraqi threat or as modest as lobbying city hall for a new stop sign in your neighborhood. In these and a host of other situations, the ability to build coalitions is a basic skill for those who wish to attain, and maintain, power and influence.

Coalition building was imperative in the Persian Gulf crisis because the Bush administration lacked the military, political, and economic resources to achieve its objectives independently. The administration had to be able to threaten credibly to drive Iraqi forces from Kuwait. It also had to alter Hussein's perception of his alternatives—from a choice between consolidating control over Kuwait and negotiating terms of withdrawal to a choice between unconditional withdrawal and destruction of Iraq's military capabilities. To achieve its objectives, the Bush administration assembled a winning coalition of domestic and international supporters and prevented the formation of blocking coalitions. In the process, the administration successfully sought access to bases in Saudi Arabia; financial support from Kuwait, Saudi Arabia, Japan, and Germany; international legitimacy in the UN Security Council; a commitment from Israel not to respond if attacked; and domestic political support from the U.S. Congress.

## MAPPING THE LANDSCAPE

The first step in coalition building is to identify who needs to be persuaded and (critically) who can be persuaded. Time and energy should not be wasted on those who are irrelevant or irrevocably opposed. At the outset, aspiring coalition builders should identify potential winning and blocking coalitions and pinpoint supporters, persuadables, and opponents. Resources should then be devoted to persuading the persuadable and consolidating and deepening the commitment of supporters. Courting supporters helps ensure that allies do not slip away in the night and expands the coalition builders' persuasive reach, as Owen Harries notes in "A Primer for Polemicists": "Preaching to the converted, far from being a superfluous activity, is vital. Preachers do it every Sunday. The strengthening of the commitment, intellectual performance, and morale of those already on your side is an essential task, both in order to bind them more securely to the cause and to make them more effective exponents of it."[1]

Because coalition building typically involves pursuing the support of groups (or organizations or nations), coalition builders need to understand the forces that bind those groups together. This means probing their internal structures by mapping influence networks, analyzing patterns of deference, and identifying the channels along which information is shared.[2] Such analysis pinpoints authority figures and opinion leaders—those who exert disproportionate influence on others.[3] Convincing these pivotal people typically translates into broader acceptance; their resistance can be a severe impediment. In the Gulf crisis, the Bush administration had to understand the internal political situations of the foreign leaders whose support it was seeking.

Relationships among groups (or, in this case, nations) deserve equal scrutiny. The history of conflict and cooperation can offer insight into how to build coalitions. Who characteristically lines up with whom on a given set of issues? It is important to remember, however, that coalitions can be fluid. The same groups may cooperate on some issues and not on others.

After identifying pivotal recruits, the next step is to assess their interests and how they are likely to perceive their alternatives—the set of options among which they believe they must choose. As a rule, people evaluate costs and benefits only when they face decisions. Coalition builders can thus influence decisions by structuring choices that activate certain interests and options and not others.

## TRANSFORMING THE BALANCE OF FORCES

Armed with insight into what the people in question care about, coalition builders can devise persuasion strategies likely to get them on board, or at least out of the way. A productive point of departure is a thorough analysis of driving and restraining forces. People facing a tough decision experience psychological tension caused by internal conflicts (Do I want X more than I want Y?

Should I do as I want or as I think I should?), or by external pressures, such as competing commitments or worry about what others will think.[4] The tension that a potential ally experiences is usefully viewed in terms of opposing forces: driving forces push them in the direction the coalition builder favors (toward joining the coalition or remaining neutral), while restraining forces pull them toward an opposing coalition or inaction.

Moving persuadables in the desired direction calls for strengthening driving forces or weakening restraining forces, or both. In other words, coalition builders recruit by enhancing the attractiveness of the alliance or by making the alternatives—to do nothing or to join an opposing coalition—appear less attractive. Of course, opposing coalition builders try to do the same thing, leading to a competition to influence pivotal people.

The tension between driving and restraining forces can be illustrated in a force-field diagram. Figure 12.1a illustrates the hypothetical forces in effect if Congress had been asked to send troops to the Gulf at the start of the crisis, just after Iraq's invasion of Kuwait. Clearly, powerful forces opposed such a deployment. Figure 12.1b illustrates the driving and restraining forces at work on Congress just prior to the war, after the Bush administration had built an international coalition. The balance of forces has been profoundly transformed in favor of intervention.

## BUILDING WINNING COALITIONS

How did the Bush administration achieve this remarkable transformation? And how can aspiring coalition builders do likewise? The answers lie in the techniques that coalition builders use to achieve their desired ends:

- *Mobilize compatible interests:* Identifying alignments that can serve as a basis for short- or long-term alliances
- *Alter incentives:* Using carrots and sticks to transform potential allies' and adversaries' perceptions of their alternatives
- *Eliminate options:* Making the status quo unsustainable and allowing unattractive options to play themselves out
- *Frame choices:* Constructing favorable definitions of the problem and the options
- *Use social influence:* Analyzing and using characteristic patterns of deference on pertinent issues
- *Use sequencing to build momentum:* Approaching other players in a sequence likely to elicit resources and make it easier to recruit others

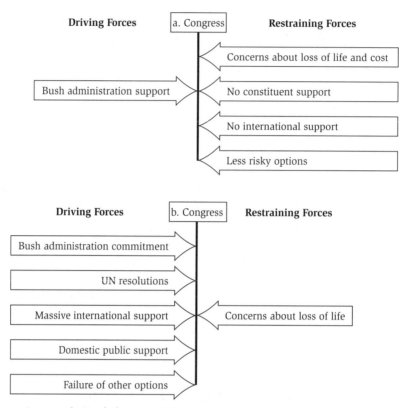

**Figure 12.1.** Analysis of Changing Balance of Forces.

## Mobilize Compatible Interests

What motivates people to join coalitions? A straightforward, if tautological, answer is that people join coalitions when they perceive that it is in their interests to do so. To put it another way, parties join coalitions when they have interests—either shared or compatible—that can be advanced by trading support. The United States and Japan, for example, shared an interest in preserving access to Persian Gulf oil supplies. The United States and Syria had very different long-term interests, but both wanted to weaken a common enemy. The interests of the principal members of the Gulf coalition are summarized in Table 12.1.

Compatible interests alone do not create a coalition. Potential allies must first recognize that they could act collectively, and then they must communicate and ultimately agree to cooperate. Coalition builders therefore have to make potential allies aware of their compatible interests. Sometimes potential allies immediately recognize the benefits of collaboration and communicate freely to build a coalition. The United States and Japan, for example, could openly discuss preserving access to Middle East oil supplies. But barriers can prevent direct communication. Internationally, moderate leaders of contending nations who reach out to each other invite attack by internal hard-line factions.

If parties with compatible interests cannot communicate openly, they may work in secret or through trusted intermediaries. If this is impossible, they may engage in signaling. Examples of signaling include an announcement of intent to raise prices, a threat to veto a given bill, and increases in the readiness of military forces. During the Gulf crisis, for example, the Bush administration's actions to reinforce Saudi Arabia signaled its resolve to other Arab states.

Sometimes parties fail to recognize their compatible interests. The United States and Syria, for example, may not have recognized immediately that both stood to gain by cooperating to oppose Iraq. In such situations, a coalition builder may press potential allies to recognize their compatible interests (while forestalling such awareness among adversaries, possibly by acting to prevent an opposing coalition from mobilizing).

Coalition builders also use privately held information, such as intelligence assessments, to shape, reinforce, or change beliefs and attitudes. The United States, for example, provided classified intelligence information, including satellite photographs of Iraqi formations, to the Saudis to help win their support. As Jowett and O'Donnell note in *Propaganda and Persuasion,* control of information takes the form of "withholding information, releasing information at predetermined times, releasing information in juxtaposition with other information that may influence . . . perception, manufacturing information, communicating information to selective audiences, and distorting information."[5]

## Alter Incentives

Sticks and carrots are time-tested tools for altering the balance of forces in coalition-building situations. A coalition builder may threaten harm if support is withheld or withdrawn. Threats are also used to neutralize potential members of opposing coalitions. Because coercive power (money, military forces, connections) effectively transforms others' perception of their alternatives, coalition builders who can make credible threats have an advantage over those whose threats lack credibility: they may never have to expend scarce resources to gain compliance. A reputation for toughness is therefore an important asset in coalition building. Failure to follow through on threats undermines credibility and paradoxically increases the likelihood of having to spend resources to enforce compliance.

Warnings can serve a similar function, but with different implications for relationships. Warnings point out the damage likely to result from a failure to get on board, but the coalition builder does not threaten to be the instrument of harm. The Bush administration appears to have made extensive warnings but

Table 12.1. Interests of Key Players.

| Party | Interests |
|---|---|
| United States | Energy security |
| | Maintenance of position as a superpower |
| | Security of the Gulf region |
| | Alarm that unchecked aggression creates a dangerous precedent |
| Kuwait | Restoration of sovereignty and power of ruling elites |
| United Kingdom | Energy security |
| | Alarm that unchecked aggression creates a dangerous precedent |
| | Fulfillment of preexisting pledges of mutual support |
| France | Energy security |
| | A voice in international response to Iraq |
| | Preservation of traditional influence in region |
| Soviet Union | Closer relationship with the United States, and U.S. economic support |
| | Demonstration of independence and influence in world events |
| | Control over treatment of Iraq |
| | Preservation of traditional influence in region |
| Saudi Arabia | Reduction or elimination of Iraq's threat to ruling elites |
| | Regional stability |
| | Leadership in the Arab world |
| Belgium, Greece, Spain, Netherlands, Italy, Canada | Energy security |
| | Alarm that unchecked aggression creates a dangerous precedent |
| Egypt | Maintenance of good relationships with the United States and other nations |
| | Maintenance or increase in foreign aid and other support |
| | Restoration of prestige following Iraqi invasion |
| | Aspirations to regional leadership |

| Party | Interests |
|---|---|
| Israel | Reduction of threat from Iraq |
| | Maintenance of close relationship with the United States |
| | Aggressive self-defense and maintenance of reputation for toughness |
| Turkey | Closer economic connections with European community |
| | Improved trade relations with the United States |
| | Increased foreign aid |
| Syria | Aspirations to regional leadership |
| | Closer connections with the United States, Saudi Arabia, and Kuwait |
| Ethiopia, Ivory Coast, Zaire | Improved economic relations with the United States |
| | Demonstration of autonomy and maintenance of relations with nonaligned nations |
| Colombia | Continued good relationship with the United States |
| | Demonstration of autonomy and maintenance of relations with nonaligned nations |
| Japan | Energy security |
| | Maintenance of good relationships with the United States and other nations |
| Germany | Energy security |
| | Maintenance of good relationships with the United States and other nations |
| China | Improved relationships with the United States and the international community following the Tiananmen Square incident |
| | Autonomy and maintenance of relations with nonaligned nations |

limited use of threats during the Gulf crisis. Only the cutoff of aid to Yemen and a rumored threat to Egypt received publicity. Of course, threatened parties do not advertise that they can be intimidated, nor does the stick wielder always want its threats made public. But the lack of evidence of other threats may signify that none were made. Threats are risky; they can provoke resistance and poison future relations. Threats also elicit counterthreats, leading to an escalating spiral of conflict and entrapment.

Thus, carrots are sometimes preferable to sticks. Inducements are commonly traded for open or covert support (or inaction). China, for example, agreed to abstain in critical UN Security Council votes in exchange for a measure of international political rehabilitation following Tiananmen Square, and the Bush administration offered Egypt debt forgiveness and Turkey expanded trade opportunities. The carrot may be an up-front quid pro quo, a share in the spoils of success, or a future favor.

Carrots are also used to fracture opposing coalitions by inducing those of its members who are not bound to the others by strong shared interests or long-standing mutual support to switch sides. A variant of this tactic is to drive a wedge between two or more members of an opposing coalition. Each party is offered an attractive deal for being the first to switch sides and told that others are being offered a similar deal. Each therefore has an incentive to preempt the others—a version of the prisoner's dilemma. If the leaders of the opposing coalition do not counter with a more attractive offer or a credible threat, the opposition may fracture.

The size of an inducement depends on the extent of support sought. The price of China's abstention on the use-of-force resolution, for example, was much lower than it would have been for an explicit vote of support. If open rather than covert support is required, the recruit may demand a premium for sharing the risks of failure.

## Eliminate Options

Eliminating alternatives to joining a coalition is another way to transform the balance of forces. If people see their choices as maintaining the comfortable status quo or setting off in an unfamiliar new direction, we should not be surprised when the status quo wins out. But what if the status quo is no longer an option? As we have seen, even people with good intentions defer decisions and delay committing scarce resources. When success requires the coordinated actions of many parties, delay by one party can have a cascading effect, giving others an excuse for not proceeding. Doing nothing must therefore be eliminated as a viable alternative.

The power of eliminating the status quo as an option is illustrated by the true story of a worker on an offshore oil platform who realized that the platform was on fire. He ran to the edge and gazed at the churning ocean eighty feet below.

Then he turned and saw a ball of fire racing toward him. He jumped—and survived. The point is not that coalition builders should set fires to build support. Manufactured crises sometimes spur action, but they can backfire or fuel a reputation for crying wolf. The point is that eliminating the option of staying put is powerfully persuasive.

One way to deliver this message is to make it clear to potential recruits that the train will leave with or without them. Once the core of a coalition is in place, the alternatives of those who remain sitting on the fence are transformed. Originally the choice was to support change or preserve the status quo, but now they must choose between getting on board and watching from the sidelines.

A related strategy is to threaten unilateral action. Suppose a coalition builder can either recruit further or act alone (or with existing allies). If the probability of succeeding alone is low, the potential recruits' support is necessary and they can extract value in exchange for it. The fence sitter can thus claim a disproportionate share of the spoils of success or water down the goals of the coalition. But if the coalition builder has a reasonable probability of succeeding with existing support, that option functions like an implicit threat to attract potential recruits to the coalition. Consider France's participation in the Gulf coalition. The French had longstanding military and political relationships with Iraq. Saddam Hussein was one of the French arms industry's best customers, and Iraq owed France substantial sums. Important factions of the French political-military establishment did not want to see Iraq suffer a humiliating defeat. France also zealously maintained independence from the United States in foreign policy matters. Yet France still voted for the UN Security Council resolution authorizing use of force.

France's reasons for its vote included the blatant nature of Iraq's aggression, a desire to perpetuate its position as a world leader, alarm about energy security, and solidarity with its European allies. But there was also the likelihood that the United States, the United Kingdom, and other allies would proceed under Article 51 of the UN Charter even if France withheld support. Thus, refusal to support the U.S.-led coalition would not have prevented Iraq's defeat, and France would have lost influence over what happened to Iraq after the war. In effect, the viability of unilateral action enabled the United States to recruit a coalition to pursue a multilateral option. Potential recruits had to choose between participating in the coalition and watching it go forward anyway, with consequent loss of control over the situation.

When unilateral action is repeatedly threatened but never materializes, credibility suffers. If a coalition builder does not maintain the credibility of a unilateral option, in other words, that option may become a wasting asset. Coalition builders thus have to act unilaterally from time to time simply to bolster their credibility. Overuse of unilateral action can lead to *isolating unilateralism*, but underuse can result in *paralyzing multilateralism*.

A related approach is to eliminate less desirable options progressively, funneling potential recruits toward the desired choice. People are rarely willing to make difficult decisions before they have exhausted less painful options. Letting other options play themselves out (while acting to accelerate the process) is often necessary to provide a defensible rationale for a decision, spread responsibility for possible unpleasant outcomes, and bring others to the point of readiness to commit. The Bush administration, for example, could not have persuaded Congress to authorize the use of military force before giving economic sanctions a chance. Congressional support for the offensive option also rose after President Bush agreed to the meeting between Secretary of State James Baker and Iraqui foreign minister Tariq Aziz, although the administration may not have been genuinely committed to going the extra mile for peace. By January 1991, Congress was ready to commit American lives to Operation Desert Storm. Actions that would once have been unthinkable were made palatable by the passage of time and the apparent inadequacy of less forceful alternatives.

## Frame Choices

*Framing* is shaping potential recruits' perceptions of reality—specifically, of their interests and options. In essence, the coalition builder creates a framework to promote "right thinking." When two contending sides vie to persuade a recruit, the contest is often primarily a language game. Each tries to link its objective to the target recruit's preexisting mental models. Secretary of State Baker's designation of his requests for allies' financial support as responsibility sharing rather than burden sharing is a superb example of framing. Aware that Congress would not support the administration unless allies shared the economic costs of the conflict, Baker emphasized that Congress would interpret failure to provide ample support as shirking, which would have negative implications for future relations with the United States.

To develop resonant messages, a coalition builder should analyze the situation in the light of the target audience's needs, desires, beliefs, attitudes, and values. The coalition builder can then work to achieve the following goals:

• *Shape the agenda for debate.* Decisions can be influenced early in the course of a series of preliminary processes, in particular those that define the agenda.[6] By the time the problem, the alternatives, and the criteria for evaluating costs and benefits have been defined, the final choice may be a forgone conclusion. As Owen Harries notes, this means that coalition builders have to work to control the agenda: "Pay great attention to the agenda of the debate. He who defines the issues, and determines their priority, is already well on the way to winning. . . . Diplomats, at least when they are performing effectively, understand this well, which is one reason they often appear fussy and pedantic to outsiders who have not grasped the point at issue. It is just as important, and on the same grounds, to deny your opponent the right to impose his language and concepts on the debate, and to make sure you always use terms that reflect your own values, traditions and interests."[7]

Thus, one key to successful framing is simply being present during the formative stages to define the terms of the debate before momentum builds in the wrong direction, or irreversible decisions get made, or too much time passes. Throughout the case, we see the Bush administration striving (sometimes struggling) to keep control of the agenda and frame the terms of debate.

• *Link the current issue to other issues.* Saddam Hussein tried to fragment the Arab coalition by linking its conflict with Kuwait to the Israeli-Palestinian conflict. This linkage was echoed in France's campaign for a comprehensive regional peace conference. The Bush administration blocked this linkage and prevented a split in the coalition by carefully crafting resolutions criticizing Israel for the Temple Mount incident and blocking proposals to create a UN presence in the Occupied Territories.

• *Invoke self-defining values.* Marketers and propagandists long ago learned the power of linking a desired choice to deeply held values. That is why cigarette companies sought to associate smoking with independence and the freedom to choose. In the United States, values that are often invoked for their persuasive power include freedom, equality, justice, fair play, choice, and patriotism. The Bush administration used patriotism to pressure Congress by saying, in effect, "You mean, Congressman, you're not going to support the president when even the president of Ethiopia is supporting him?" President Bush also stressed that Saddam Hussein denied basic rights and freedoms to the people of Iraq and now planned to do the same in Kuwait.

• *Draw analogies to formative experiences.* Using analogy to link the current situation to formative experiences can be compelling. Memories of definitive experiences like wars and depressions are easily triggered and come bundled with potent emotional responses. Once evoked, the remembered experience can shape one's response to a new experience, even if their similarities are limited.[8] The Bush administration summoned the ghost of Hitler in its efforts to build a coalition. George Bush explicitly labeled Saddam Hussein a new Hitler, and the failure of appeasement before World War II was invoked to argue for forceful action. Atrocity stories, such as the congressional testimony of a young woman (later revealed to be a member of the Kuwaiti royal family) that Iraqi soldiers had taken babies from their incubators, helped cement these associations.

• *Play up threats to assests.* People's fervor to preserve their existing endowments—wealth and property, position, authority, status, rights, and privileges—is another wellspring of resonant messages. Coalition builders often rely on *loss aversion*, presenting the desired course of action in terms of potential gain and undesirable choices in terms of potential losses. Similarly, because people tend to be *risk averse*—preferring guaranteed gains over risky choices, even those likely to yield significantly larger gains—it pays to characterize your desired course of action as less risky than the undesirable choices.[9] Thus, the Bush administration had trouble rallying public support for conflict with Iraq until the threat of Iraqi nuclear weapons was emphasized. The prospect of devastating future losses was sufficient to overcome the public's aversion to smaller, more immediate losses.

• *Inoculate against expected challenges.* Finally, coalition builders can inoculate the target audience against the foreseeable arguments of their opponents.[10] The inoculation process works exactly like inoculation against an infectious disease: the audience is vaccinated by exposure to a weak form of expected counterarguments, which are then decisively refuted ("He will tell you X is true, but it is not—and here's why"). The audience is thus immune to the argument when it is later trotted out in its stronger form. Successful framing provides the immediate target audience with a script for resisting counterpersuasion and for convincing others.

## Use Social Influence

Techniques of social influence represent another set of persuasive tools. People rarely make important choices alone. When deciding whether to support a coalition builder's initiative, potential recruits will be influenced by their relationships with others. The opinions and expectations that prevail in this network will strongly influence their assessments of costs and benefits. Analyzing the driving and restraining forces that operate on key people calls for identifying the full range of social pressures that could impinge on them. Research in social psychology has established that people prefer to make choices that allow them to do the following:

• *Remain consistent with their prior commitments.* Failure to follow through on commitments tends to lead to social sanction. People prefer not to make choices that require them to reverse themselves. They also avoid commitments that constrain their future choices by setting undesirable precedents.

• *Preserve a sense of control.* Choices that threaten people's social positions and sense of control provoke anxiety.

• *Repay obligations.* Because reciprocity is a very strong social norm, people tend to seek opportunities to repay their debts. They are vulnerable to appeals linking current support to past favors.

• *Preserve reputation.* People worry about the impact of their choices on their reputations. Choices that preserve or enhance reputation are viewed favorably; those that could jeopardize reputation are viewed negatively.

- *Gain the approval of respected others.* People look to respected others (opinion leaders and mentors) for clues about "right thinking." Choices that have the approval of respected others tend to be viewed favorably.

- *Defer to experts and authority figures.* From childhood, people are taught to defer to those in authority and those with superior expertise on technical issues. This reflexive deference has been weakened somewhat by distrust of government and other institutions, but it remains operative.

In seeking to influence recruits, coalition builders therefore attempt to:

- *Make irreversible commitments that constrain others.* The high price of backing away from public commitments can be used opportunistically by employing a method known as the "commitment tactic."[11] A coalition builder employs the commitment tactic by making an irreversible commitment to a course of action that limits the options of other parties. The party making the commitment will lose face, suffer damage, or disappoint its constituencies if its objectives are not attained. The interdependent parties thus face a difficult choice: they can either allow the committed party to have its way, or they can trigger a mutually damaging failure.

The interdependence of domestic politics and international relations provides opportunities for use of commitment tactics.[12] During the Gulf crisis, for example, the Bush administration and Congress were interdependent in that both had a stake in the United States' reputation as a superpower. Once George Bush had committed the nation to liberating Kuwait and assembled an international coalition, Congress could not oppose the president without undermining U.S. credibility in international affairs.

- *Practice progressive entanglement.* Most people feel a need to maintain external consistency between their commitments and their subsequent actions and internal consistency between their beliefs and their public behavior. Our actions, especially our public actions, create images of us in other people's minds. Our subsequent actions are then molded in part by a desire to maintain consistency (or the appearance of consistency) with this image. As psychologist Robert Cialdini notes, "Once we have made a choice, or taken a stand, we will encounter personal and interpersonal pressures to behave consistently with that commitment."[13]

This need to remain consistent can be exploited by coalition builders. A target recruit who can be persuaded to make inconsequential early commitments and to follow through on them is headed down a slippery slope toward larger commitments. This process is *progressive entanglement,* whose core principle is that people can be led in a series of small steps from point A to a point B they never would have reached in a single leap. The apparently innocuous initial commitment takes them down a path that is difficult to reverse. If James Baker had gone to Eduard Shevardnadze right after Saddam Hussein's invasion of Kuwait to request Soviet support for a resolution authorizing a U.S.-led multinational force to wage war on Iraq, Shevardnadze almost certainly would have refused. Yet five months later, the Soviet Union supported the use of "all necessary means" to liberate Kuwait. The Bush administration achieved this transformation through progressive entanglement. The Soviet Union was asked first to sponsor a joint resolution condemning Iraq's aggression, and then to support economic sanctions, next a defensive military operation, and ultimately the offensive military operation.

The implication is that involvement engenders commitment. A potential recruit who becomes "voluntarily" involved (or implicated) in publicly undertaking small but supportive actions may conclude that it is imperative to continue to support the coalition builder's agenda. Once Bush's team had gotten Gorbachev and Shevardnadze to condemn Iraq's aggression, the Soviet leaders had a stake in continuing to act as protectors of "the new world order."

Public commitments carry more weight than private commitments. A commitment made in private offers wiggle room; people can argue that they were misunderstood or misquoted. When commitments are made in front of others, the scope for backing away is narrowed.

Because commitments are so powerful, it is very important to get there first. It is an uphill battle to undo a recruit's prior commitments of support to one's opponents; in addition to making a good case, one must help the recruit find a graceful way to back out of the commitment.

• *Draw on the power of reciprocity.* Most societies have strong social norms that obligate people to repay debts and return favors when requested to do so.[14] Failure to reciprocate can seriously damage one's reputation. Cialdini notes that "each of us has been taught to live up to the rule, and each of us knows about the social sanctions and derision applied to anyone who violates it."[15] Appeals to repay favors or meet obligations thus exert a strong influence on people's behavior.

Obligations between nations accumulate over time—particularly through provision of military, political, and economic support—and the rule of reciprocity can powerfully affect how nations behave. For example, Egypt was indebted to the United States for large foreign aid payments and support for regional stability. The resulting sense of obligation probably contributed to Hosni Mubarak's early willingness to support the United States against Iraq (though other factors were also at work). More generally, the United States had a strong network of obligations to draw on. The special relationship between the United States and the United Kingdom—a longstanding mutual obligation to provide support in times of crisis—was the starting point on which the coalition was built. And President Bush drew on decades of investments in personal relationship building during the Gulf crisis.

Reciprocity also underlies legislative logrolling. Politics makes for strange bedfellows in part because legislators operate within a web of mutual obligations and favors. The impact of special-interest gift giving on the behavior of elected and appointed officials is another example.

• *Employ experts.* People readily defer to experts. Experts have superior access to information through their sources and networks of connections. They are also trained to use powerful conceptual frameworks to interpret complex issues and events, and they can therefore help nonexperts make sense of the world. Experts also have *source credibility* because of their credentials, their confidence and certainty, and their track records of providing valuable advice or direction.[16]

Authoritative analysis resembles expertise in its properties and persuasive power. Even analysis that frames issues in ways that favor its sponsors comes bundled with the credibility of the analyst and the methodologies employed, such as statistics.

The Bush administration made good use of expertise and analysis in assembling the Gulf crisis coalition. Early in the crisis, for example, Prince Bandar was shown satellite photos of Saddam Hussein's troop dispositions near the Kuwait-Saudi border. The photos had been enhanced by the most advanced image-processing systems and interpreted by military experts.

• *Find pressure points in hierarchies of authority.* A mastery of hierarchies of formal authority, and the powers vested in each office, is useful in building coalitions. Faced with opposition in the Security Council from Colombian Ambassador to the United Nations Enrique Penalosa, the Bush administration persuaded the president of Colombia to instruct Penalosa to vote for the use-of-force resolution. The president had the authority to direct Penalosa's vote, leaving the ambassador two alternatives: comply with instructions or resign.

• *Leverage influence networks.* It is usually possible to identify someone from whom a target recruit receives advice or to whom he or she defers or is obligated.[17] By analyzing recruits' webs of relationships, it is often possible to discern who possesses influence over them and who, in turn, influences the influencers. Using relationship networks dramatically increases a coalition builder's persuasive ability.

A coalition builder who has not built a direct relationship with a potential recruit may still be able to work indirectly through *bridging parties*—those who have some influence over the potential recruit and are in turn open to influence by the coalition builder. To convince King Fahd of Saudi Arabia to accept U.S. forces, the administration worked indirectly through Prince Bandar (while President Bush used his direct relationship with the king).

Once recruited, new allies activate their own relationship networks to accelerate coalition building. Saudi Arabia's extensive network of relationships with other Arab states was activated once the United States gained King Fahd's support. In effect, the recruitment of allies acts as a kind of force multiplier in coalition building.

A coalition builder with a thorough mastery of relationship networks can also convey information through multiple channels. Throughout the Gulf crisis, the Bush administration sought to influence Security Council member nations at several levels simultaneously. Drafts of resolutions were presented not only to each country's UN ambassador in New York, but also to its ambassador in Washington and its in-country foreign ministry. This approach ensured that the U.S. message got through ungarbled to the highest levels and also underlined its urgency.

## Use Sequencing to Build Momentum

The Bush administration made skilled use of sequencing. A striking example is Thomas Pickering's description of U.S. actions at the United Nations: "The essence of our strategy in winning in New York depended first on getting Britain and France with us, and then the Soviets—and the Soviets were really critical, because without them we had no chance of China." The administration also applied many of the rules of thumb for sequencing we have already discussed:

- *Approach parties with whom you have established mutual support relationships early,* both to affirm those relationships and to ensure that a core base of support is in place. The Bush administration consulted early with traditional allies like the United Kingdom to project a common front against Iraqi aggression.

- *Identify the resources (economic, political, and military) critical to success, and focus on the parties that possess those resources.* The Bush administration knew that Saudi Arabia's support was critical to developing a credible military option, and it worked hard to convince King Fahd to agree to the deployment of U.S. troops.

- *Approach parties with strongly compatible interests early,* unless such recruitment efforts will alienate important parties whom you will approach later. The special relationship between the United States and the United Kingdom was crucial from the start.

- *Work with relationship networks,* using the recruitment of respected parties as a resource for recruiting others. By working with key allies in Congress, for example, the Bush administration was successful in building a supportive coalition and in neutralizing opponents.

# PUTTING IT ALL TOGETHER . . . AND TAKING IT APART

By mobilizing interests, altering incentives, eliminating options, framing choices, mobilizing social influence, and sequencing to build momentum, coalition builders can transform the balance of forces in a favorable way. As in the case of the U.S. Congress during the Gulf crisis, the impact can be quite extraordinary. In fact, it is worth asking whether Congress was left with any choice but to support the administration. The forms and rituals of debate were observed, and the vote was close, but was the outcome ever really in doubt?

It is also revealing to ask what Hussein could have done to prevent the United States from building such a powerful coalition to oppose him. The answer lies in identifying the weakest links in the chain—in this case, Russia and France—and then identifying the best levers for prying them away from the core coalition. Suppose Hussein had pulled his forces out of most of Kuwait but retained the disputed oil fields and islands in the Gulf. And suppose he had appealed to Russia and France to convene a regional conference to examine not just the Iraq-Kuwait dispute but others, including that of the Israelis and Palestinians. What would have happened?

The war might have gone forward anyway, but it seems unlikely that Congress and key allies would have bought into waging war over scraps of territory. International and domestic opposition to the use of military force would probably have begun to build. Hussein's actions since the war, summarized in "Update of the Cases" at the end of book, suggest that he learned some lessons about coalition breaking. Subsequent efforts to disarm and contain Iraq have been confounded by the difficulty of maintaining a coalition of strange bedfellows.

In the final two chapters, we explore the difficult challenges negotiators face when they intervene in disputes or represent diverse, potentially divided internal constituencies. Both situations demand that the negotiator play multiple roles, in the process managing classic tensions between short-term and long-term goals and between ends and means. Chapter Thirteen presents the final case history, about Richard Holbrooke's efforts to end the war in Bosnia. As you read the case, think about the structure of the negotiation and the barriers to agreement. Focus in particular on the range of roles Holbrooke plays and the dilemmas he confronts.

# CHAPTER THIRTEEN

# Ending the War in Bosnia

In August 1995, Richard Holbrooke, Assistant Secretary of State for Canadian and European Affairs, flew to the Balkan Peninsula to try to end the war in Bosnia—the bloodiest European conflict since World War II. The former Yugoslavia's most multiethnic republic, Bosnia had declared independence three years earlier. Since then, nationalist uprisings within its borders, aided by its covetous neighbors Serbia and Croatia, had resulted in deaths estimated at more than one hundred thousand. But despite Bosnian President Alija Izetbegovic's pleas for Western intervention and regular reports of atrocities, Europe and the United States had refused to enter the war, opting to send UN peacekeeping forces and to seek a settlement through diplomacy.

Fruitless efforts at a negotiated agreement generated intense criticism of the United States and the European powers, and raised anew the question of whether the world's great powers are responsible for resolving regional conflicts in the post–Cold War era. Now, changed circumstances and a reported massacre of Muslim civilians had convinced the United States to take the lead with a new

This is an abridged version of "Getting to Dayton: Negotiating an End to the War in Bosnia," a case written by Susan Rosegrant in collaboration with Michael D. Watkins, associate professor of public policy, John F. Kennedy School of Government, Harvard University. Copyright © 1996 by the President and Fellows of Harvard College. Reprinted with the permission of the Kennedy School of Government Case Program, Harvard University.

diplomatic plan. It would be up to Richard Holbrooke to convince the parties that peace—even a peace requiring the abdication of long-held goals—was a better option than war.

## A NEGOTIATOR'S CHALLENGE

Holbrooke, whose extensive foreign-service experience included difficult negotiations with North Vietnam, China, and the Philippines, seemed ideally suited to the task. It would be his charge to overcome the bitter legacy of the three-year war and the history of ineffective international policies and interventions. Even for someone as seasoned as Holbrooke, however, bringing a quick end to the war would be a tall order.

The Balkans had witnessed hundreds of years of bloodshed.[1] Ethnic strife had erupted most recently during World War II, when a Nazi-backed fascist regime in Croatia murdered hundreds of thousands of Serbs. Fundamentally, however, the war in Bosnia had its roots in the breakup of

> What were the principle barriers to agreement in this conflict?

Yugoslavia—a gradual process of disintegration that began in the late 1980s—and in the rising nationalism, particularly Serbian, that had hastened Yugoslavia's end. Marshal Tito, the communist partisan who ruled Yugoslavia from 1945 until his death in 1980, had suppressed nationalism in the country's six republics to prevent domination by any one of them and to solidify his own control.[2] (See Figure 13. 1 for a map of Yugoslavia.) But economic hardship and the absence of a unifying leader in the decade following Tito's death fueled calls for independence from some ethnic groups and republics.

Slobodan Milosevic, then leader of the Serbian Communist Party, capitalized on growing nationalism and on tensions in Kosovo, a semiautonomous Serbian province that was 90 percent Albanian. Just one year after Tito's death, ethnic Albanians had called for the province's independence. The public outcry was silenced, but fear of secession by Kosovo—seat of the Serbian church—helped spark a Serbian nationalist movement within Kosovo that gradually grew in numbers and radicalism. By 1987, when Milosevic declared his support for the Kosovo Serbs, he had realized that nationalism offered the leverage he needed to lead Serbia to a dominant role in Yugoslavia. Milosevic promptly orchestrated the ouster of Serbian President Ivan Stambolic, his long-time mentor, and maneuvered himself into the presidency. By 1989, after a series of purges (aided by Serb police and the Federal Army of Yugoslavia), Milosevic had gained the allegiance of Montenegro and authority over both Serbian provinces.

Serbia's increasingly overt nationalism, and Milosevic's growing power base, alarmed and intimidated Yugoslavia's smaller republics, particularly as the Serb

**Figure 13.1.** Bosnia and Surrounding Region.

leader tightened his grip on the Federal Army. The first to react was Slovenia, the republic most distant from Serbia, which began to prepare for independence in 1990. Croatia, led by its first democratically elected president, Franjo Tudjman, soon followed Slovenia's lead. Tudjman too was a nationalist, although his ambitions were less grandiose than Milosevic's; he wanted Croatia to be a nation-state.

The two presidents shared another goal: both had designs on Bosnia. At a secret 1991 meeting, Milosevic and Tudjman discussed how Serbia and Croatia might divide Bosnia between their two republics.[3]

Muslims constituted 44 percent of Bosnia's population, and a Muslim president, Alija Izetbegovic, had been elected in 1990. But Bosnia was also home to substantial Serb and Croat communities that Milosevic and Tudjman hoped to make part of their own countries.

> What were the shared and differing interests that underpinned this alliance? Was timing important here?

The alliance between Milosevic and Tudjman would not last long: Milosevic was also eyeing Croatia's Krajina region, which had been a Serb enclave for centuries. Milosevic had accepted the dissolution of Yugoslavia, but he had no intention of letting large populations of Serbs remain under the rule of independent nations. He planned to annex them to what remained of Yugoslavia—creating, in effect, a Greater Serbia.

In June 1991, Slovenia and Croatia both declared independence. The Federal Army, whose leaders were determined to enforce a united Yugoslavia, and who considered Milosevic the only leader committed to that cause, quickly rolled into Slovenia to crush the rebellion and bring the former republic back into the federal fold. But the Slovenians turned out to be well armed and organized, and the army ignominiously retreated. More to the point, Milosevic was willing to let go of the republic, whose largely homogeneous population included few Serbs. Slovenia had broken free, but its rash move had begun a chain reaction that was to have far bloodier results.

Slovenia's declaration of independence served as a call to arms for Serbs within Croatia. Milosevic wanted the Krajina as part of a Serb-dominated rump Yugoslavia, and most Krajina Serbs were equally anxious to break from an independent Croatia. Their fears were heightened by Tudjman's inflammatory statements and policies that undermined the power of Serbs in Croatia.[4] Battles between the Croatian army and Krajina Serb forces—backed by a Federal Army still trying to save Yugoslavia—gradually escalated into full-scale war.

Bosnia had counseled the republics of the former Yugoslavia to stay together, and had tried to remain neutral. But when the European Community prepared to recognize Croatia and Slovenia as independent nations in 1992, Bosnian President Alija Izetbegovic had little choice but to seek independence as well. The decision provoked a revolt of nationalist Bosnian Serbs. Already allied with Serbian President Milosevic, they called for a boycott of Bosnia's independence referendum and declared that international recognition of the new country would amount to a declaration of war. When the United States and the European Community (EC) recognized Bosnia in April, the leader of the Bosnian Serbs, Radovan Karadzic, took action. Karadzic declared himself president of an independent Bosnian Serb republic and lay siege to the capital city of Sarajevo.[5]

**How are linkages contributing to moving the situation toward a crisis?**

Though many observers had predicted a violent fallout from Yugoslavia's dissolution, the rapid downward spiral in Bosnia caught the EC and the United States by surprise. The Serbs made land grabs, and by late 1992 had captured 70 percent of Bosnia, forcing some 750,000 Muslims from their homes.[6] The term "ethnic cleansing" came into use to describe expulsions, mostly by Serbs, of people of other ethnicities to create regions that were ethnically "pure." Reports emerged of brutal Serb-run concentration camps and of the systematic rape of Muslim women. In 1993, the war became even grimmer when Bosnian Croats seeking an alliance with Croatia began seizing Bosnian territory and attacking Muslim civilians. By April, the Muslim-Croat conflict had escalated into another all-out war.

For two years after the 1992 offensive, Muslim and Serb conflict in Bosnia centered on six so-called safe areas established by the UN Security Council—Muslim towns where UN peacekeepers provided a measure of safety from Serb and Croat assaults. The Serbs continued their steady siege of Sarajevo—itself a safe area—with only occasional internationally brokered cease-fires. Despair subsided slightly in early 1994 when the Muslims and Croats agreed to a shaky federation, ending most of the fighting between the two groups. But the country remained partitioned into a patchwork of warring ethnic enclaves. At the end of 1994, eight months before Richard Holbrooke would begin his shuttle negotiations, the war between Bosnia's Muslims and Serbs seemed as grim as ever.

## THE RESPONSE OF THE WEST: A LEGACY OF FAILURE

To negotiate an end to the Bosnian war, Holbrooke would have to overcome deep ethnic divisions and the distrust and cynicism of all the combatants. The United States and Europe had repeatedly failed to act, bringing shame on the European Union and shaping up as a foreign-policy disaster for President Clinton. In 1995 Holbrooke described the faltering international response to the war in Bosnia as "the greatest collective failure of the West since the 1930s."

From the start, the international community had fumbled for an appropriate response. The U.S. position had been simple: the two republics should not break away, nor should Serbia or any other country challenge existing borders. The Bush administration did not threaten military intervention, however, and the spreading war did not change this stance. The European Community wanted to take charge in the regional dispute, and the United States was all too eager to let it do so. In the words of Luxembourg's foreign minister, often quoted later for ironic effect, "The hour of Europe has dawned."

In late 1991, the UN Security Council imposed an arms embargo on the entire former Yugoslavia, and the European Community imposed trade sanctions, including an oil embargo.[7] The international community was optimistic when the United Nations negotiated a Croat and rump-Yugoslavia cease-fire in January 1992, and sent peacekeepers to Croatia in March. But hope soon faded as Bosnian Serb forces, with direct aid from Milosevic, began to carve up Bosnia.

> What were the barriers to creating and sustaining a European coalition in support of forceful intervention? Was this paralyzing multilateralism?

Bosnian President Alija Izetbegovic made repeated appeals to the United States and Europe, but the international community seemed unprepared to respond forcefully. The dissolution of the Soviet Union was raising alarm about stability in that part of the world. The Gulf War had strained the military budgets of the United States and other countries, and dampened enthusiasm for another intervention. Moreover, the Bush administration continued to view Bosnia as a European problem, and had maintained a largely hands-off policy in the region.

Many observers expected a change of policy from the Clinton administration. Clinton had faulted Bush's hands-off stance, and had declared his intent to help preserve Bosnia as a multiethnic state. Unlike the Europeans, who had been painstakingly evenhanded in their negotiating efforts, the new administration explicitly viewed the Serbs as aggressors and the Muslims as victims. That the change of direction promised by Clinton's campaign might not come to pass became evident, however, when Secretary of State Warren Christopher went to Europe to sell a new approach to the Bosnian conflict. Like the Bush regime, the Clinton administration had already concluded that neither Congress nor the American people supported sending troops to fight in Bosnia. But the United States was still looking for a way to help the Bosnian Muslims.

Christopher's proposal was to lift the arms embargo against Bosnia—widely believed to be crippling the Muslim government's ability to defend itself—and to employ strategic NATO air strikes against Bosnian Serb targets.[8] Christopher was reportedly far too tentative, however, and the Europeans bluntly rejected the "lift-and-strike" plan. Even had Christopher argued more compellingly, the Europeans would probably have rejected the plan. Normally the United States would have had considerable clout with NATO and the

## How were the current negotiations linked to prior ones?

United Nations. But the Clinton administration was hamstrung by the U.S. decision not to contribute troops to the UN Protection Force in Bosnia, UNPROFOR, established in 1992.[9] The British, the French, and other troop contributors argued that lift-and-strike would endanger the peacekeepers. Only if UNPROFOR were withdrawn would they consider allowing additional arms into Bosnia or conducting NATO air strikes. "There was a lot of criticism about the U.S. not being on the ground, but giving advice from the sidelines," says one senior U.S. defense official. "There's a lot of validity to that statement."

Although Christopher failed to sell the plan to the Europeans, the administration adopted lift-and-strike as its official stance. But lift-and-strike remained a mere policy statement. Had the Clinton administration unilaterally lifted the arms embargo, it would have violated a Security Council resolution that the United States itself had supported, creating a dangerous precedent and undermining UN authority. Nor could it conduct air strikes in Europe's backyard without NATO support. To do so could have provoked "the biggest crisis in NATO since its founding," according to an official at the National Security Council (NSC). So the policy had little effect, other than to serve as a constant reminder of differences between the United States and Europe, and perhaps to give the Bosnian Muslims false hope that the Clinton administration would soon intervene. Frustration over U.S. inaction led to the resignations of four foreign-service officers in a five-month period, including a former ambassador to Yugoslavia.

After Christopher's abortive trip, the United States again took a back seat on Bosnia. The United Nations and NATO, though, with U.S. support, tried to protect the Bosnian Muslims without military intervention. In early 1993, the UN Security Council established the Hague International War Crimes Tribunal to prosecute war crimes in the former Yugoslavia. The Council also created the six safe areas of Srebrenica, Zepa, Gorazde, Tuzla, Bihac, and Sarajevo. The safe-area concept, however, was botched. UN Secretary-General Boutros Boutros-Ghali called for 34,000 UN peacekeepers, but the Security Council authorized only 7,600 troops and fewer still arrived.[10]

NATO, meanwhile, began enforcing a UN-imposed no-fly zone over Bosnia to prevent air bombardment of civilian targets, and the UN authorized NATO to provide protective military air support to UN troops if under attack. In August 1993, under pressure from the United States, NATO threatened air strikes against the Bosnian Serbs if they did not ease the siege of Sarajevo. The threatened air strikes, however, came at a price. To make sure such action was not taken precipitously, the European allies insisted on a "dual key" approach, requiring approval from both the United Nations' conservative civilian leadership and NATO before strikes could occur.

By late 1993, the Europeans had failed three times to negotiate peace plans for Bosnia. First the Muslim government blocked a confederation of Swiss-style ethnically based cantons united by a weak federal government. British diplomat Lord David Owen and UN envoy Cyrus Vance then proposed a new canton-based plan that briefly appeared promising: Croatia embraced it and Bosnia reluctantly accepted it. But the Bosnian Serbs refused to return land or to have their holdings split into isolated pockets.[11] A third plan that emerged from meetings between Muslims, Serbs, and Croats would have partitioned Bosnia into three ethnic republics. This time Bosnian President Izetbegovic rejected the plan, which would have given only 30 percent of Bosnia to the Muslims.

> Is there a ZOPA here? What might have been done to create one?

Meanwhile, world leaders distanced themselves from the killing and chaos. Some declared the fighting in the Balkans a civil war—ethnic hatred unleashed by the collapse of Communism and the destabilizing breakup of the former Yugoslavia. Early in 1993, Christopher and other administration officials began to abandon the goal of preserving Bosnia's multiethnic identity in favor of a policy of "containment" that would keep the war from spreading to more economically and politically important neighbors. For some, however, containment was an abdication of responsibility in the face of genocide. Marshall Harris, one of the foreign-service officers who resigned from the State Department in protest in 1993, faults the Bush and Clinton administrations for failing to challenge the weaknesses of the EC approach. "Had we had a stronger administration in either the Bush era or the Clinton era," Harris insists, "we would have said to the Europeans, 'We tried it your way, we were there for the hour of Europe, and it was an abominable failure. Now it's time for you to get out of the way.'"

In early 1994, a mortar fell on a Sarajevo marketplace, killing at least 68 people. The carnage led to a flurry of international action.[12] The United States insisted on NATO intervention and pushed through an ultimatum threatening air strikes unless the Serbs agreed to a cease-fire at Sarajevo and withdrew their heavy weapons from the city. The same month, NATO shot down four Bosnian Serb planes for violating the no-fly zone, the alliance's first offensive operation.

For a time NATO finally appeared to be getting tough. But the alliance was still constrained by cautious NATO and UN leaders, and its responses—often referred to as "pinprick" retaliations—had limited effect. The Bosnian Serbs briefly complied with the Sarajevo cease-fire but soon shelled the safe area of

Gorazde. They retreated after NATO's first two air strikes, but Sarajevo was under siege again by July. Despite NATO threats and occasional bombings, Bosnian Serb violations continued. "The Bosnian Serbs' initial inclination was to take NATO seriously," notes Alexander Vershbow, senior director for European Affairs at the NSC. "But the dual key and the strains within the alliance—which they were all too aware of—quickly made them realize that NATO was less of a menace to their war aims than they first thought."[13]

The United Nations' reputation was also tarnished. Many U.S. officials believed UNPROFOR was doing more harm than good. Critics say that General Sir Michael Rose, commander of UNPROFOR, insisted on treating all parties as equally responsible in the conflict despite Security Council resolutions branding the Serbs as aggressors. Rose's mantra was that UNPROFOR should never "cross the Mogadishu line," a reference to a flawed UN operation in Somalia in which it abandoned impartiality. In the bitter words of one U.S. official, many European troops were "inculcated with evenhandedness in the face of genocide."

> **What made the role of the UN intervenors complex and difficult? Was there an alternative to neutrality?**

Though critical of this disappointing record, the Clinton administration remained unwilling to send troops to Bosnia or to break with NATO or the United Nations. Nevertheless, officials were looking for strategies that would sidestep the issue of U.S. military intervention. Before the marketplace attack, U.S. officials had begun negotiating behind the scenes to create an alliance between the warring Muslims and Croats. The advantages for Bosnia's Izetbegovic were clear: if the two groups could settle, Muslim troops would be freed up to combat the Serbs more effectively, perhaps even with Croat assistance. Croatia's Tudjman, who would have had to abandon his designs on northwest Bosnia, was harder to convince. He relented after U.S. officials warned that he could not seize land in Bosnia and still expect international support if he tried to oust the Serbs from Krajina.

In March 1994, Croat and Bosnian officials agreed to a Muslim-Croat Federation, which the NSC's Vershbow calls "the first real diplomatic breakthrough" since the war began. For both sides, it was a marriage of convenience. Other than ending most of the fighting between them, few bridges were built between Muslims and Croats.[14] The agreement did stipulate, however, that at future peace talks the Muslims and Croats would negotiate as one delegation, reducing the number of parties at the table. And the Federation improved Bosnia's military standing: Croatia revived a pipeline of third-country arms shipments to Bosnia through Croatian territory, in violation of the UN arms embargo.[15] Few heavy weapons got through, but the pipeline helped equalize the military balance in the Balkans.

Another promising development followed. Representatives of the United States, France, Britain, Germany, and Russia formed a new entity called the Contact Group to address the Balkan crisis, raising the diplomatic profile of the United States and forcing some consensus on U.S. and European efforts to settle the war.[16] Meetings of the Contact Group were often divisive, but the group proposed a new territorial split, giving 51 percent of Bosnia to the new Muslim-Croat Federation and 49 percent to the Bosnian Serbs. The Muslims would have to share their territory with the Croats, but the Contact Group plan gave the Bosnian government more land than had most previous offers, and all-important access to the sea. The allies rejected a U.S. recommendation that the map be accompanied by inducements, such as a threat to lift the arms embargo on Bosnia if the Serbs refused to accept.

> How did this effort to build coalitions alter the structure of the game?

The Muslim-Croat Federation accepted the plan, but Radovan Karadzic, head of the Bosnian Serbs, rejected the proposal and the substantial Bosnian Serb concessions that the new map would entail. U.S. officials saw a silver lining in the failure of the Contact Group's plan: Serbia's Milosevic was experiencing economic and political pressure from international sanctions; anxious to settle the Bosnian war, he had supported the plan and encouraged Karadzic to do the same. When Karadzic refused, in keeping with his pattern of insubordination, Milosevic appeared to break with the Bosnian Serbs, closing the border between Bosnia and Serbia and cutting off most Serbian support. U.S. officials saw the discord as a positive sign.

Otherwise, though, the situation in Bosnia was discouraging at the end of 1994. The international community's two-and-a-half years of diplomatic and "peacekeeping" interventions had achieved only the highly volatile federation between Bosnia's Muslims and Croats. As Izetbegovic's pleas for military intervention went unanswered, leaving the Bosnian president bitter and disillusioned, the United States and the European Union became desperate to end the bloodshed and to resolve the appalling conflict that was making the Western powers appear uncaring and ineffectual.

## A CHANGED SITUATION ON THE GROUND

In early 1995 during the months preceding Holbrooke's appointment as lead negotiator, the pattern persisted: the Bosnian Serbs would harass a safe area, NATO would slap their wrist, and the Serbs would pull back briefly and then resume. If NATO began to get hard-nosed, the Bosnian Serbs would threaten UN peacekeepers, and thus keep the alliance at bay.[17] The qualms that had prevented U.S. intervention all along—refusal to deploy the military in a region not vital to national security, and unwillingness to take actions that might undermine NATO or the United Nations—continued to stymie U.S. officials.

In May, in response to blatant Bosnian Serb shelling of Sarajevo and other safe areas, the new UN commander in Bosnia, Lieutenant General Rupert Smith, ordered NATO air strikes of an ammunition dump near Pale, the Bosnian Serb capital.[18] The Bosnian Serbs promptly seized more than 350 UN hostages and chained some to likely bombing targets. In response, the United Nations shut down Smith's air strikes. The UN hostages were eventually released unharmed, but the Bosnian Serbs had again stopped NATO cold.

The hostage-taking was another blow to the reputations of the United Nations and NATO, and at last the United States and the European Union both realized that the status quo was no longer possible. "It was after this debacle with the hostages that the tide began to turn," the NSC's Vershbow recalls. To help protect the peacekeepers, Britain and France deployed a 12,500-member Rapid Reaction Force authorized by the United Nations. And NATO's willingness to fight back against Serb aggression got a boost with the election of France's new President Jacques Chirac, who urged the international community to shake off its paralysis. The French change of heart left Britain largely alone in advocating a continued soft response. "Chirac and Clinton spoke a lot at that point on Bosnia," notes Ivo Daalder, NSC director for global affairs.[19]

In May and June, President Clinton began pressing for a new approach. "We began here at the White House to develop what we called 'the endgame strategy,'" Vershbow recalls. "How can we break out of the impasse and solve this? Not just muddle through better, but get to a real diplomatic solution." The State Department's chief Bosnia negotiator, Robert C. Frasure, had been urging Milosevic to abandon the Bosnian Serbs and to recognize Bosnia as a state in exchange for sanctions relief. Frasure had also been trying to persuade U.S. officials to deal directly with Milosevic. Officials at the White House now began to embrace the Milosevic channel, but instead of incremental steps they debated how to go straight to a comprehensive settlement by combining more assertive U.S. diplomacy with more aggressive use of NATO air power as leverage.

Before the new strategy was in place, another atrocity occurred. On July 9, Bosnian Serb forces closed in on the safe area of Srebrenica. The commander of the area's peacekeepers urgently requested NATO air strikes, but UN Force Commander Bernard Janvier turned down the request as too dangerous. The following day, as 400 Dutch peacekeepers stood by helplessly, Serb forces took the town. NATO planes eventually bombed a few Serb tanks, but Srebrenica was already lost. A second small safe area nearby fell about two weeks later. "By the summer of '95," says one U.S. official, "UNPROFOR had become a cancer on the UN." Information later implicated Karadzic and Bosnian Serb Commander General Ratko Mladic in the massacre of as many as 7,000 Muslim men and boys from the captured town.[20]

Even before the slaughter became public, the Bosnian Serbs had finally pushed the international community too far. "When Srebrenica fell . . . , the terms of the debate began to shift in favor of the hard-liners and also with our European allies," says Vershbow. "They realized the jig was up—that UNPRO-FOR was really in tatters, even with the Rapid Reaction Force. Something had to be done to restore Western credibility." According to Walter Slocombe of the Department of Defense, the British and French were considering canceling the UN mission. "They made it perfectly clear that unless things got a lot better fast, they were prepared to pull out," he says.[21] Now U.S. policymakers had two choices: send troops to help with a humiliating and dangerous UNPROFOR retreat—a move that could have crushing political consequences for the Clinton administration—or pursue a negotiated solution so that the U.S. troops would be implementing peace, not helping back away from failure.

On July 21, the NATO allies met to hammer out a new agreement. Pressed by the United States and France, the group took a new stance on Serb aggression. If Gorazde, the last and most important of the eastern safe areas, was seriously threatened, NATO would conduct preemptive air strikes using disproportionate force.[22] The dual-key arrangement so hated by the United States was also changed: the UN key was delegated to military officers on the ground instead of the more cautious civilian leadership. With this military stick in place, the United States prepared to launch its new diplomatic initiative.

> **Was this threat more credible than the previous one?**

The fall of the two safe areas had unquestionably made things easier for a diplomatic push. It was, Slocombe says, as if the ultimate bad thing had finally happened, leaving nothing with which the Bosnian Serbs could threaten NATO and the United Nations. And the territorial grab of Srebrenica—an isolated Muslim holding near the Serbian border—simplified the task for negotiators, who would ultimately have to piece together an implementable map.[23]

In early August, one more event convinced the United States that the time had come for a negotiated settlement: Croatian soldiers drove a Serb population estimated at over 100,000 from the Krajina and reclaimed the land for Croatia. The expulsion of Serbs from an area that had been their homeland for hundreds of years drew little outcry from the international community. Once the State Department concluded that Milosevic would not join the fray, officials made it clear to Croatia's Tudjman that the United States had no plans to intervene. Milosevic's decision not to interfere was evidence that the sanctions against Serbia were taking a toll, and that he was ready to settle even if it meant abandoning his vision of a Greater Serbia. Allowing the Krajina to fall, moreover, widened the growing gap between Milosevic and Karadzic. Critics protested the region's latest round of ethnic cleansing—including ethnically motivated killings that the War Crimes Tribunal would later investigate—but many observers considered Tudjman to be largely justified in retaking the land.

As the Krajina was falling, the United States laid out the fundamentals for a new negotiation. Congress had cast its most assertive vote on Bosnia yet, authorizing lifting the arms embargo unilaterally in the event of an UNPROFOR withdrawal.[24] The administration had a broader plan: to launch an intensive diplomatic effort—backed by NATO's new threat to use air power decisively—that might finally end the war.

> **How had the United States become the primary intervenor?**

Several factors distinguished the initiative from earlier efforts. It would be the first comprehensive negotiation headed by the United States, but the plan would incorporate two premises the Europeans had long advocated. First, in addition to endorsing the 51–49 percent split of Bosnia proposed by the Contact Group, the United States announced a change in its staunchly pro-Muslim negotiating stance. The Clinton administration was still committed to a generous deal for the Bosnian Muslims, but all sides would have to make concessions. If the Muslims blocked a deal, the United States would "lift and leave"—lift the arms embargo but provide no arms, training, or support.[25] Second, instead of presenting the Contact Group map as a take-it-or-leave-it offer as before, the United States now argued that both the Muslim-Croat Federation and the Bosnian Serbs should focus on securing more compact, militarily defensible territories. Furthermore, if the diplomatic initiative did not succeed and the Serbs were to blame, an international force would help UNPROFOR withdraw and the United States would initiate lift-and-strike. "We were going to go with peace and we were going to do it at the highest level," says Ivo Daalder of the NSC. "The President was going to be involved, the Secretary of State would be involved, and we would put all the resources of the U.S. government on this."

National Security Adviser Anthony Lake visited seven European capitals to sell the new U.S. approach. Lake made clear that the United States would press forward with or without a European endorsement, and the European allies, numbed by Bosnia policies to date, accepted the plan. Lake then handed off the negotiating effort to Richard Holbrooke, whose job it would be to sell the new principles to the Balkan leaders. With Holbrooke's appointment as lead negotiator, a new era in Balkan diplomacy began. "Certainly the administration would not want to go through the process of choosing a negotiator, a senior person like an assistant secretary," says one State Department official, "and then have nothing behind the negotiation, have no prospects for success."

But there were questions about Holbrooke's mission. Some critics insisted that only by helping the Muslim government retake seized territory and restoring Bosnia's former multiethnic makeup would the Western powers fulfill their obligation to the besieged nation. Others, who had reconciled themselves to partition of Bosnia, feared that a peace built on the wrong foundation might lead to renewed war. Holbrooke's challenge was twofold. To end the war would not be enough. He also hoped to cobble together the structure, incentives, and international support to allow a new Bosnia—encompassing Muslims, Serbs, and Croats—to emerge.

# HOLBROOKE STEPS IN

Not everyone saw Richard Holbrooke—one of Washington's most assertive personalities—as the ideal negotiator to insert into the Balkan morass. No one denied that he had the requisite experience: he had served on the U.S. delegation to the Paris peace talks with the Vietcong in 1968, and conducted sensitive negotiations with the Chinese and with former Filipino President Ferdinand Marcos. Yet some top officials had reservations, including National Security Adviser Lake. Holbrooke and Lake had been close when both served as foreign-service officers in Vietnam in the 1960s. But their relationship had cooled over the years, and Lake reportedly viewed Holbrooke as an unpredictable and often difficult showman. Holbrooke had also been publicly critical of the U.S. failure to intervene in Bosnia, and there were questions about whether he would toe the party line.

Still, many considered Holbrooke the logical choice once the United States decided to launch a serious negotiation. "Frasure and I had always agreed that when the time was right he would call me," Holbrooke says, "and I would be in Belgrade within 48 hours."[26] Even Holbrooke's critics conceded that his very flaws might make him the perfect choice for the job. "Holbrooke was probably the most forceful personality we could possibly find for this kind of negotiating effort," states one top NSC official. "He's both brilliant and has a bullying personality, but that was seen as the combination we needed." With Holbrooke as the negotiator, one State Department official adds wryly, the diplomatic initiative was assured high visibility.

Accompanied by Frasure, Holbrooke and a small team began crisscrossing the Balkans, laying groundwork. Within a few days, Holbrooke visited Milosevic in Belgrade twice and Tudjman in Zagreb once. Unable to secure safe passage into the surrounded city of Sarajevo to see Izetbegovic, he instead met with Muslim officials in the Croatian cities of Split and Zagreb. On August 19, Holbrooke and his team made a second effort to reach Sarajevo by a precarious mountain road. Holbrooke and military representative Lieutenant General Wesley Clark rode in a Humvee—a stable all-terrain Army jeep—while the rest of the team traveled in a French armored personnel carrier. Attempting to pass a French convoy, however, the personnel carrier tumbled into a ravine and burst into flames. Frasure and two other members of the team died in the crash. The accident, which Holbrooke still calls "unbelievable," devastated officials involved in the Balkan conflict. It also dealt a profound blow to the nascent diplomatic effort. "We lost our historical continuity with Bob Frasure," says team member Lieutenant General Clark.[27]

However, President Clinton was determined that the team not lose momentum. Christopher Hill, director of the State Department's Office of Balkan Affairs, was appointed as regional expert and adviser to Holbrooke. To help on constitutional issues, the State Department recruited Roberts Owen, a Washington lawyer who had arbitrated Federation issues between the Muslims and Croats. The Department of Defense also sent two representatives. Holbrooke believes the new team was "pulled together by the tragedy," and some observers assert that the accident intensified the team's dedication.

The new team left for Paris to meet Izetbegovic and the Contact Group. "If this peace initiative does not get moving, dramatically moving, in the next week or two, the consequences will be very adverse to the Serbian goals," Holbrooke declared to the press. "One way or another, NATO will be heavily involved, and the Serbs don't want that." In truth, Holbrooke did not foresee NATO playing a direct role soon, though he hoped its recent threats of air strikes had readied the Bosnian Serbs for negotiation. But the next day Holbrooke's words appeared prescient: the Bosnian Serbs lobbed a mortar into a marketplace in Sarajevo, killing thirty-seven people. This time there was no ambiguity about the origin of the mortar. UN investigators soon found evidence pointing to the Bosnian Serbs. "With the new rules of engagement that were then in place, the decks were cleared for action," says Holbrooke. "We instantly recommended massive NATO retaliation."

**How did Holbrooke shape the Serbs' perceptions of their alternatives?**

## PINPRICKS NO MORE

The mortar attack in the face of NATO threats perplexed observers. Most speculated that it was a test of both the new diplomatic initiative and NATO's trumpeted shift in resolve. After all, NATO's warnings had been meaningless in the past. Would things be different now? "They [the Bosnian Serbs] had a three-year record of getting away with anything they wanted," notes Daalder of the NSC. "If I were Mladic [the Bosnian Serb commander], I wouldn't have believed it." Daalder speculates that the Bosnian Serbs were also trying to disrupt the relationship Milosevic was building with the United States. "They were saying, 'Milosevic, are you with us or are you against us?'"

But significant changes enabled NATO to stand by its word. Not only were the NATO allies agreed that the bombing of Sarajevo could not go unpunished, the fall of the safe areas a month earlier had also created conditions conducive to a forceful military response. The United Nations had only to pull some 80 peacekeepers from Gorazde to protect almost all its troops from attack or hostage taking.

NATO bombing began two days after the attack, first targeting Bosnian Serb positions near Sarajevo and gradually expanding to targets near Gorazde and Tuzla. To end the bombing, it was agreed, the Bosnian Serbs would have to move heavy-artillery pieces out of Sarajevo, open the airport, and allow safe access by road. The United States had been pushing for strategic air strikes for years, but not everyone in the Clinton administration believed bombing would achieve its largely unspoken goal: to push the Bosnian Serbs back from Sarajevo and to convince their leaders to engage in serious peace negotiations. "There was a huge argument inside our country as to how much effect bombing would have," says one team member, "because of the experience in Vietnam where we just bombed the hell out of them for months on end, only to have very little effect at the negotiating table."

But Holbrooke's team was agreed. The bombing campaign was not only essential, it was a dramatic assertion that there would be no more business as usual. The biggest concern, they say, was what reception they would get from Milosevic, whom the team would meet one day after the bombing began. Holbrooke was convinced that Milosevic was key to influencing the Bosnian Serbs. But if the Serbian president was enraged, or found it politically untenable to meet with Americans during bombing, it could be weeks before negotiations would pick up speed. It was a risk they were eager to take. "I always believed that it was necessary to back diplomacy with military power," says Lieutenant General Clark. "Whether it scuttled the negotiations was a tactical issue, not a strategic issue."

Holbrooke's team arrived in Belgrade on August 31 fearing the worst, but their reception was almost warm. Milosevic expressed sympathy over the deaths of the three diplomats. Then, Holbrooke recounts, Milosevic announced, "I've been very busy while you've been gone," and pulled a piece of paper from his breast pocket. The document, signed by Milosevic, Karadzic, Mladic, and other Yugoslav and Bosnian Serb leaders and witnessed by the Serbian Orthodox Patriarch, announced that the interests of Serbia and the Bosnian Serbs would be represented in future negotiations by a six-person delegation, three of whom would be chosen by Milosevic. In the event of a deadlock, Milosevic would cast the deciding vote. Holbrooke, stunned by the document, soon dubbed "the Patriarch Paper," says it's difficult to overstate the importance of Milosevic's masterstroke. "We had spent sixteen months arguing over who spoke for the Bosnian Serbs, and here we had the answer in writing. . . . The answer . . . was

Slobodan Milosevic." Adds Christopher Hill: "That was an absolute breakthrough. It was the rock upon which every other negotiation had been shipwrecked."[28]

Like the marketplace bombing, the Bosnian Serbs' action baffled the team. Why would they agree to reduce their own control, particularly given the growing rift between Karadzic and Milosevic?[29] Moreover, the Patriarch Paper had been signed before the NATO bombing began. "We still don't know what the deal was, or what promises Milosevic may have made to them that day," says Holbrooke. Most likely, officials say, is that the Bosnian Serbs were responding to recent shifts on the ground. The fall of the Krajina had shattered the dream of a Greater Serbia. "When the Krajina fell, that was a tremendous change in the entire regional strategic equation," notes Hill. And if the Bosnian Serbs had begun to accept the wisdom of a settlement, they may have concluded that the only way to achieve it was through Milosevic. Both Karadzic and Mladic had been indicted by the War Crimes Tribunal, and Holbrooke had declared that he would not negotiate directly with indicted war criminals.[30]

**Why was the Patriarch Paper so important?**

As exciting as the Patriarch Paper was, it was still just a piece of paper. Dozens of agreements had been signed but few had been realized. Holbrooke described it to the press as a "procedural breakthrough" so as not to create "too big an expectation."[31] Nevertheless, he dates the opening of negotiations to Milosevic's presentation of the document. "As soon as he produced that paper," Holbrooke says, "I knew we were started."

## THE SHUTTLE PICKS UP SPEED

Over the next week Holbrooke and his team flew from city to city. "I had come to the conclusion that you had to approach this negotiation piecemeal, step by step, locking in your gains," Holbrooke recalls. "But you couldn't lock in your gains simply by shuttling, because whenever you were in City A, whatever you agreed to, City B wouldn't agree to." The solution, Holbrooke concluded, was to bring representatives of the Balkan countries together. Lieutenant General Clark remembers the idea coming to Holbrooke in a flash. "Dick called us aside and he said, 'Let's set up a two-day negotiation in Geneva,'" Clark says. "'We'll come up with an agreement. We'll agree on principles. We'll call it basic principles! We'll get something and we'll make them agree to it!'"

**What techniques did Holbrooke use to build momentum?**

It was too early to bring the presidents together, but Holbrooke thought the time was ripe for the foreign ministers to meet. Convening such a meeting while NATO bombs were falling would, he thought, project a strong message about U.S. leadership. His team was not convinced. "We had a ferocious argument within our delegation as to whether we ought to set up a foreign ministers' meeting in Geneva," Holbrooke says, "since we had no idea what we would agree to in Geneva." Clark, in particular, was worried about the danger of negotiating a partial agreement. Holbrooke prevailed, though he accepted his team's advice to limit the meeting to a single day. He wasn't sure what basic principles would be presented, but he won a commitment from all of the Balkan presidents to send their foreign ministers. Hill thought the strategy a sound one. "We started with the idea that we'd get a few principles, lock them in place, go announce them to the world, and begin to build up some momentum," he explains. "The theory was that if you got a piece of the mosaic in place, then announced it, it couldn't be taken away." On September 1, one day after the session with Milosevic, the Clinton administration announced the first meeting of the Balkan foreign ministers in two years.

Meanwhile, NATO and the United Nations were trying to gauge the early response to the NATO air strikes, within Bosnia and internationally. On the third day of bombing, NATO declared a 72-hour pause to allow Bosnian Serb General Mladic and UN Commander Janvier to talk, and Mladic to comply with NATO's demands. If the Bosnian Serbs refused to cooperate, NATO would intensify its assault. But when Mladic showed no sign of caving in to NATO's demands, Holbrooke says, some members of the UN command tried to prevent resumption of bombing. They feared that the United Nations and NATO would be accused of siding with the Bosnian Muslim government and essentially declaring war on the Bosnian Serbs. In Washington, meanwhile, some officials argued that NATO had already proven its resolve, and that further bombing would be punitive.[32]

Holbrooke had been careful to deny a direct link between the bombing and the negotiations. But he believed NATO's actions to be critical to his own effectiveness, and was horrified that NATO might halt the assault before any of its goals were achieved. As the deadline passed without resumption of bombing, Holbrooke pleaded with Washington to intervene. "I said, 'History hangs in the balance here. This is an historic night. You must get the bombing resumed in order to give us the best chance for negotiations.'" After strained negotiations with UN and NATO officials, the U.S. officials succeeded. "We went to sleep," Holbrooke says, "and in the morning the bombing was started again."

Holbrooke's team undertook one other negotiation that weekend. Macedonia and Greece had been at a standoff since the former Yugoslavian republic had declared independence four years earlier. Greece objected to Macedonia's use of the same name as a region of Greece and to the Greek symbol on its new flag.

The retaliatory Greek embargo had severely strained landlocked Macedonia, and some Clinton administration officials feared ethnic unrest and an extension of the Balkan conflict. Holbrooke, who believed the barriers to settlement had more to do with posturing than substance, had sent a team to Macedonia a few days earlier to begin mediating the dispute. Milosevic, with whom the team met Sunday night, scoffed that they would "never solve that problem down there." Hill recalls: "I turned to Milosevic and I said, 'Watch us in the next 24 hours.'" Holbrooke flew to Macedonia the next morning. That afternoon, he announced that Greece and Macedonia had resolved their differences and would reopen their shared border. Hill says, "It was important . . . to build up this aura of a negotiating team that in its spare time is able to rush off and resolve something that had been festering—and festering is the right word, believe me—for 16 months." He adds: "This was the negotiating team that was going to win this thing."

**How did Holbrooke orchestrate actions at and away from the table? How did he build credibility?**

Reporters covering the progress of Holbrooke's team were impressed. "Everyone knew there was something incredible going on," Hill says. "We'd be sitting in Sarajevo and Holbrooke would lean over to me and say, 'I think we ought to go back to Belgrade tonight.' I'd say, 'Dick, we were just there yesterday.' He'd say, 'Trust me, I know what I'm doing. We ought to go back to Belgrade.' So off we'd go, back to Belgrade. We'd have one more conversation with Milosevic, there may be some little nugget there that we didn't have before." He adds: "Could it have been done on the phone? I don't know. The point is, the journalists were simply dazzled by this energy, and it showed that this American team was going to get this thing done."

**What techniques did Holbrooke use to work with the media?**

Some journalists began to suggest that the effort exceeded the demands of the situation. Holbrooke, who says the "whole charge about publicity-seeking was at its core wrong," insists that the team's brutal pace had everything to do with successful diplomacy. "The plane was our great secret weapon," he insists. "These people are intensely suspicious of each other. Even in more civilized negotiations, no one negotiates by telephone."

The team met often with Izetbegovic and Tudjman. But because the U.S. and Serb positions were farthest apart, meetings with Milosevic took longer and produced more news. "Holbrooke had a more open and almost comradely relationship with Milosevic after a while than he did with Izetbegovic," muses team member Roberts Owen.[33] That Milosevic—long viewed by the United States as the primary instigator of the Balkan wars—should prove so ingratiating was an irony not lost on the negotiators, who felt it necessary to steel themselves against Milosevic's advances. "Some of the great villains of the world," Owen says, "have had a certain amount of personal charm."

# THE FOREIGN MINISTERS' MEETING

As NATO resumed its air strikes, Holbrooke and his team honed the presentation they would make to the foreign ministers. In previous discussions with the Balkan leaders, territorial issues had always frozen discussion. "We learned that the map was going to be very hard, very specific, very concrete," Clark recalls. "You can't dodge problems. You can't draw a ten-kilometer zone and say, 'We will generally divide it this way.'" Owen agrees: "We knew the map was going to be a horror when we got to it. And we didn't think we could make much progress on the map until we had other things straightened out, so we worked on these basic principles first." But they continued to pull out the map and to broach difficult issues, Clark says, both to get a better grasp of the obstacles and to "make the ideas more acceptable to the parties by constant repetition and familiarity."

Owen drafted a single page of relatively uncontroversial principles. The document had to represent real progress, yet not be so bold that the ministers would refuse to sign. Meanwhile Holbrooke's attention to detail extended beyond the document. In what Hill calls "the trick of the table," Holbrooke dictated the size of the negotiating table to accommodate only the five Contact Group representatives, a European Union negotiator, and the foreign ministers of Bosnia, Serbia, and Croatia. Bosnian Serb representatives would have to sit on the periphery. "He did not want any delegation to feel they had room to bring a second person to the table," explains Hill. "He wanted Milosevic to speak for the Serbs."

The meeting on September 8 was tense. The Muslims, Hill says, objected strenuously to giving the Bosnian Serbs their own semiautonomous entity within Bosnia. The Serbs opposed all provisions that buttressed Bosnia's powers as a state. And the subject of eastern Slavonia, the last sliver of Croatia still occupied by Serbs, provoked so much dissension that it was dropped altogether. But, at the end of the day, Holbrooke presented a page of Agreed Basic Principles. "It was a very risky thing to do" because of the possibility of a complete stalemate, Holbrooke says, "and it came very close to a disaster, but we got out of it with an agreement which was word for word what Roberts Owen had drafted." The principles agreed to by the foreign ministers:

- Recognized Bosnia's existing borders.
- Created two entities within Bosnia—the Federation of Bosnia and

Herzegovina and a Bosnian Serb region to be known as the Republika Srpska—relying on the Contact Group split of 51/49 as "the basis for a settlement."

- Allowed both entities the right to establish "parallel special relationships" with neighboring countries.
- Asserted a commitment to basic human-rights standards.

According to Hill, the meeting was most significant for jump-starting the process and producing a tangible agreement. Holbrooke disagrees: "At the time, the most important thing was the momentum," he says. "But of course, in retrospect, it's the words in the agreement."

Not everyone approved of those words. Some critics objected that the principles omitted "connective tissue" to unite Bosnia's two entities, and thus did more to promote partition than union. Some administration officials were disappointed that Holbrooke had not negotiated a cease-fire. Holbrooke insists that the basic principles went as far as any first agreement could go. Seeking a cease-fire that early in the process, he says, could have complicated the ultimate goal of a lasting peace.

It hadn't taken long for the team to grasp Holbrooke's style. "Don't expect to find a piece of paper with a plan on it," explains one team member. "It was not there. It was very much 'make it up as you go along.'" Adds Clark: "I wrote a paper to try to help Dick think about things, but he rejected the paper. Dick operated on a heuristic basis. It was purely intuitive and pragmatic." Holbrooke describes his approach this way: "It's a situation where you know what your long-term objective is, but you don't know what route you're going to take to get there. You have to be very flexible on tactics, but firm on goals."

**What made Holbrooke's style a good match for the situation? Would he be effective in any negotiation?**

Holbrooke's risk-taking and opportunistic style particularly jolted the military experts on the team, who were accustomed to more planning, more carefully calibrated options, and more control.[34] The culture clash between "Holbrooke style" and normal bureaucratic operating procedure created tensions, particularly at first, but Holbrooke's team began to appreciate his capabilities. According to the Defense Department's Walter Slocombe, who tracked the negotiation from Washington, "He was prepared to be as seductive when it was appropriate to be seductive, and as brutal when it was appropriate to be brutal, as it took. He's an operator . . . a deal maker."

Holbrooke's was not the only strong and seductive personality. One team member describes Milosevic as a "personality boy" who typically welcomed the negotiators with warm words and drinks.[35] "From the first time we went there, we were charmed by Milosevic. That was his intent, at least, to charm us—to make us feel welcome." As the Americans tried to keep up their guard against Milosevic, the Serb leader was undergoing a transformation of sorts in the U.S. press. Op-ed pieces noted his metamorphosis into a champion of peace. The Clinton administration seemed to reinforce this perception. A State Department spokesman told reporters, "President Milosevic is a respected leader among the Serbs, and for him to come out and dedicate his government to a peace process is a positive sign."[36] At least one writer suspected a strategy on Holbrooke's part to cast Milosevic in a new light. If Milosevic was to serve as a conduit for set- tling the dispute, it was preferable to depict him as a charming rogue than as the mastermind of the Bosnian war. Holbrooke acknowledges the media trans- formation, but insists it was not his doing. "There was a Milosevic-centered strategy, there's no question about that," he says. "But not to make him out to be a good guy." The source of the revisionism, Holbrooke says, was Milosevic himself.

## THE HUNTING LODGE

On September 10, two days after the meeting in Geneva, NATO expanded its air strikes against Serb radar and missile sites. Initial skepticism over whether the bombing would bite was giving way to gratified surprise at its apparent effec- tiveness. "Those air strikes were amazing," exclaims Owen. "The United States just looked like not only the strongest kid on the block, but the brightest, most democratically minded, and well-intentioned, and I was terribly impressed." The Bosnian Serbs, though publicly defiant, seemed desperate to bring the bombing to a halt. "It was heavily, heavily psychological," says one team mem- ber.[37] Milosevic, who wanted lifting of economic sanctions and renewed inter- national respectability, was similarly distressed.[38] As one team member recalls, "One night he was talking about the bombs falling and I said, 'You do under- stand that sixteen of the most powerful nations in the world—the sixteen nations of NATO, the heart of Europe—are at war with you right now?' And he said, 'Yeah, unfortunately I know that all too well.'"

Despite its apparent effectiveness, however, many NATO and UN officials were anxious to end the air campaign—with or without concessions. NATO was running out of military targets, such as ammunition depots and command-and- control centers. So-called Level Three targets, including power plants, roads, and railways, would harm more civilians. Such targets might alter the military balance between the Federation and the Bosnian Serbs to the point that NATO would appear to be on the side of the Muslims, and would almost certainly break the fragile alliance with Russia, whose pro-Serbian officials were already condemning the military action.

For Holbrooke, who did not want the bombing to end without Bosnian Serb compliance, the stakes were rising. He doubted that the British or the French would support an expansion of NATO targets. And, he says, the team was "under some pressure from Washington to produce some movement." Holbrooke painted a gloomy picture for an interviewer, declaring, "Nothing is agreed upon until everything is agreed upon,"[39] and pointedly invoked the billions of dollars in international aid that would probably flow into the region in the event of a settlement.

> **Why was it so important not to stress the alliance with Russia?**

A day later, on September 13, Holbrooke and his team met Milosevic at a hunting lodge outside Belgrade. The Serbian president got right to the point, Hill says: "Milosevic said, 'The bombing has got to be stopped,' and Holbrooke said, 'The terms are very clear.'" Holbrooke insisted that he didn't control the bombing—that it was in the hands of the United Nations and NATO—but Milosevic clearly believed otherwise. Holbrooke, meanwhile, though an advocate of further bombing, expected NATO to halt it shortly. He thus had a strong incentive to push for an immediate settlement. "We knew when we were sitting in that villa," he says, "that the bombing would stop within hours of us telling NATO it should stop."

Once again, Milosevic sprang a surprise. Would Holbrooke be willing, he asked, to meet with the Bosnian Serb leaders, who were gathered in a villa about 200 meters away? One team member, who describes the night at the hunting lodge as "one of Holbrooke's finest hours," says, "I can just see Holbrooke collecting his thoughts and seeing how he was going to proceed here."[40] Milosevic's request was a bombshell, but Holbrooke says he had expected the Bosnian Serbs to be produced at some point. "We were totally prepared for it," he says. "It was the moment we were unprepared for."

The Americans' official position had been that they would not negotiate directly with the Bosnian Serbs. Now Holbrooke pulled his team aside. "We had a brief private conversation for about three-and-a-half minutes in which we decided that this was a golden opportunity to lift the siege of Sarajevo," says Owen. "We also debated whether we would shake hands with them, and Holbrooke said, 'If Raoul Wallenberg could shake hands with Himmler in trying to get the Jews out of Germany, we can shake hands with these characters.'"[41] Holbrooke agreed to the meeting under certain conditions. The U.S. delegation would not meet with the Bosnian Serbs as individuals, but as Milosevic's delegation. Nor would Holbrooke listen to a harangue. Only if the Bosnian Serb leaders were serious about

> **How did Holbrooke manage this means-ends dilemma? Should he have handled it differently?**

discussing an end to the siege did he want to talk to them. "I wanted to establish ground rules at the outset," says Holbrooke. "I wanted to show that we weren't salivating to meet with these people, and I wanted to put Milosevic on the spot."

Clark drafted a withdrawal offer that would satisfy NATO demands. In a scene that one negotiator describes as "bizarre," Clark stood under patio lights with the Bosnian Serb leaders gathered around him; Holbrooke and Milosevic sat under a tree. As Clark read the statement aloud, Karadzic shook his head. When Clark finished, Karadzic denounced the agreement, and Mladic declared that the Bosnian Serbs would not allow themselves to be humiliated. One team member recalls thinking they should bolt from the ugly confrontation. Instead, Holbrooke laid out the choices in stark terms. "Holbrooke, who had been sitting down, got out of his chair and rose to his full six-feet-one and said, 'That's enough,'" recalls Owen. "'Either you agree to negotiate on the basis of this document or we are going home and the NATO bombing will continue.'" After a dead silence, Owen says, Karadzic agreed to work with the draft.

The sticking points, Owen says, were which roads into the capital to open, which military units to move, and which weapons to ban from Sarajevo. At about 2 A.M., the Bosnian Serbs signed a withdrawal agreement that would end the siege of Sarajevo. "What the bombing campaign proved beyond a reasonable doubt," says the NSC's Ivo Daalder, "is that Milosevic controlled the Serbs."

For the U.S. negotiators, deliverance of Sarajevo from the shelling and sniper fire estimated to have killed ten thousand people over three years was a great step forward. The Bosnian Muslim leaders saw it differently. Holbrooke's team, meeting with them the next day, was greeted not with praise but with anger. "From their perspective, they had been suffering in that city for a long time, and a little bit more suffering was not nearly as big a deal as watching those NATO planes go over and bomb the hell out of the Pale Serbs," says one negotiator. "This was something they'd been waiting for a long, long time."[42]

Holbrooke's meeting with Mladic and Karadzic also drew criticism back home about the wisdom and morality of dealing with indicted war criminals. Some observers said the United States had no business negotiating with such people. Owen insists that direct contact was the price of progress. The alternative, he says—laborious shuttling back and forth—would have been at best time-consuming and at worst a failure. "It would have taken

> How did domestic politics operate as an institutional barrier to agreement?

weeks," Owen exclaims, "and we got it all done in one night." With the siege of Sarajevo lifting at last, he says, the negotiators began to talk about a presidential peace conference to negotiate an end to the Bosnian war.

# DISCOURAGING THE MUSLIM-CROAT ADVANCE

As Holbrooke made progress at the negotiating table, the Muslim-Croat Federation was making unexpected advances on the battlefield. Izetbegovic had allowed Tudjman to send Croatian troops into Bosnia to help Bosnian Croat forces reclaim land from the Bosnian Serbs. The combined forces mostly retook towns with majority Croat populations but also captured villages that had been primarily Serb or Muslim. Meanwhile Bosnian Muslim forces intensified their efforts to reclaim land from the Bosnian Serbs' Republika Srpska, sometimes fighting alongside Croat troops.

In many areas, the Muslim-Croat Federation forces met with little resistance. The once-dreaded Bosnian Serb forces appeared to have been seriously demoralized by the NATO bombing attacks, as well as the ever-more-apparent fact that Milosevic would not intervene. "The whole myth about them was they were ten feet tall," says Hill. "They were not ten feet tall after that campaign." Some observers speculated that the Serbs preferred losing towns on the battlefield to relinquishing them in an eventual negotiation.

As Muslim-Croat gains mounted, officials in Washington watched in alarm, fearing a chain reaction and widening of the war. "There was a very sharp dispute within the U.S. government about what to do about this, with the majority of people in Washington arguing that we should put the brakes on, give them a red light," explains Holbrooke. He believed otherwise. "Our view was the opposite, that the negotiation was beginning to take place on the battlefield in a very advantageous way." Team members agree that the Federation advances were like a gift to them: land won back in battle that brought the map closer to the envisioned 51-49 percent split would not have to be painfully exchanged at the table. "Since we were not given a firm instruction [from Washington], but only suggestions," Holbrooke adds, "we chose to just let [the Muslims and Croats] go, cautioning them to be careful, but not telling them to stop."

|  |  |
|---|---|
| **How did Holbrooke influence the balance of forces acting on the parties?** | But by late September, the Federation advances began to alarm even Holbrooke. Muslim forces were closing in on Banja Luka, the largest Serb city in Bosnia, whose population of 200,000 was thought to have been swollen by 100,000 refugees from the Krajina and formerly Serb-controlled parts of Bosnia. "If Banja Luka fell," says one negotiator, "several things could happen and |

most of them were bad." A Federation conquest of the city could create 250,000 new refugees. Some observers believed that Banja Luka's fall could cause Serbia to intervene, or even destabilize Milosevic at a critical moment in the negotiating process. If the Federation took the Serb city, Holbrooke believed, it would simply have to be given back after peace. Alternatively, allowing Banja Luka to fall could, in effect, commit the United States to an abrupt change in strategy—from seeking a negotiated settlement to taking a chance on a military victory.

Those monitoring the military advance had an even bigger fear: that further fighting could destroy the shaky Muslim-Croat Federation. It was unclear whether the Muslim forces approaching Banja Luka could hold the city. According to Hill, the commander had a reputation for giving up ground he had previously taken. If this happened, it was likely that Croat forces would intervene. Already, most of the important victories were not Muslim but Croat or combined Croat-Bosnian Croat victories. Hill, who describes the Federation's dynamics as dangerous, says, "At some point, when you have so much Croatian success and so little Muslim success, you create further tensions within the Muslim-Croat alliance."[43] The NSC's Daalder puts it more bluntly: "I think Tudjman was trying to take over half the country." Holbrooke notes a "very disturbing" episode when Bosnian and Croat forces turned on each other. "Sometimes they worked together, sometimes they worked separately, and sometimes they fought each other," he says. "That's the Balkan way."

On September 19, Holbrooke told Tudjman and Izetbegovic not to take Banja Luka. He offered no concrete incentives for backing off, he says, but said further fighting would displease the United States. After a good deal of yelling, mostly at each other, the two leaders asked Holbrooke to announce the decision on their behalf. "The parties didn't dare get in the way of Holbrooke," says Hill. "He'd run them over. And the parties could make concessions to Holbrooke that they would not make to each other." Some observers speculate that the two presidents wanted to back off from the Serb stronghold and used U.S. pressure as an excuse. Others say that Izetbegovic was deeply disappointed. Holbrooke describes the Banja Luka intervention as a "controversial decision" that would be subject to criticism throughout the negotiations. Adds one Pentagon official: "The Muslims to this day think that if we'd let them continue to fight, they would have captured Banja Luka and a lot of other places."

> Why was Holbrooke able to exert so much influence over Tudjman and Izetbegovic?

The U.S. negotiating team was still operating under the auspices of the Contact Group. "Unless the United States wishes to pay all the bills itself, which we no longer can do as we did in the '40s and '50s, we have to involve the Europeans as partners," notes Holbrooke. But tensions were rising on both sides. Holbrooke chafed at the time demands of Contact Group meetings. And, despite what Holbrooke calls "constant briefings," the Europeans were not satisfied. "It wasn't their show," he notes. "They were being humiliated." The Contact Group rarely approved of Holbrooke's tactics or his goals.

# THE FOREIGN MINISTERS MEET AGAIN

Owen and the team had been trying to build on the basic principles from the foreign ministers' meeting to describe what Bosnia would look like after a peace settlement. Those principles had shown how Bosnia would be divided; the next set would define a governmental superstructure to bind the two entities together. With these constitutional arrangements in place, Hill says, it would be time to turn to the map.

As the team wrestled a set of principles through the approval process, Holbrooke scheduled a second meeting of the Balkan foreign ministers for September 26 in New York and flew back to prepare. Meanwhile, Owen and others shepherded the draft to Sarajevo for approval, and then to Belgrade to show to the Bosnian Serbs. After minor changes, they faxed the draft to Sarajevo and boarded a plane for the United States. But Bosnian Prime Minister Haris Silajdzic, who had objected to the principles from the start, rejected the Serbian changes, and declared that Bosnia's foreign minister would not attend the New York meeting. Holbrooke reached the three U.S. negotiators in flight, "raised hell," according to Owen, and sent them back to renegotiate. "We didn't lie down in a bed for three consecutive nights," Owen recalls. Holbrooke acknowledges that the trio was "reeling with fatigue" and "so mad at me that night they didn't want to talk to me," but says the extra trip was typical of the handholding and face-to-face contact the negotiation required.

The Bosnian Muslims continued to threaten to boycott the talks, and the State Department prepared two statements in advance, one announcing the accord and the other conceding failure. Nevertheless, the Muslims did attend and the meeting produced a set of principles defining the unifying structures to govern all of Bosnia, notably a parliament, a presidency, and a constitutional court; a commitment to free democratic elections under international supervision in both parts of Bosnia "as soon as social conditions permit"; and a pledge to allow the international community to monitor compliance.

**Was it a mistake to leave major issues unaddressed at this stage?**

But the meeting did not achieve everything the U.S. team had wanted. The specifics of how the new Bosnian government would function, and how the Federation and Republika Srpska entities would interact, had proven too divisive. Among the many untackled issues was the map, as well as the handling of foreign trade, currency, citizenship and passports, and protection of borders.

The time for confronting the map was approaching. The idea of convening the Balkan leaders for a peace summit had been gaining momentum since mid-September. After the agreement in New York, Owen says, "It was clear that there was going to be a peace conference somewhere." The team was convinced that the United States would be the only effective location, but officials in Washington were reluctant to link the Clinton administration directly with the difficult negotiations. "There were still people who were concerned that this thing wasn't really going to jell, and that therefore we should not do a U.S. venue," recalls Hill. "We felt that it would only work if there was a U.S. venue." But the debate was still academic. "We did not feel we could announce a peace conference," Hill says, "while people were still shooting at each other."

## LOCKING IN A CEASE-FIRE

The U.S. team turned its attention to a cease-fire. Muslim and Croat forces were still advancing. Despite signs that the Bosnian Serb line was stiffening, and despite fewer declarations of victory by Federation troops, Bosnia's Izetbegovic insisted that his troops would not lay down their arms. "It was clear that Izetbegovic was the biggest obstacle to peace," says Daalder. "He had the most to lose. The fact that the war was going well made it even more difficult to get him on our side—on the side of negotiations."

Izetbegovic was not alone. Many supporters of the Bosnian Muslim cause believed that the Muslims should be permitted to regain land seized from them. But direct aid for this effort was unlikely, from the United States or any other country, and, without outside help, further fighting might fail to oust the Bosnian Serbs and would almost certainly put the Croatian army in a more dominant position. "The prospects for a complete military victory on the part of the Muslims were remote," asserts one Pentagon official. "A lot of people would have died on both sides, civilians would have been displaced, and there would have been more refugees created. And we were still going to have to sort out a peace process at the end of the day."

Although Holbrooke now acknowledges that it was an "arguable decision and a close call," he met with Izetbegovic on October 4 to persuade him that the time to seek a military solution had passed. With a flourish, Holbrooke presented team member Brigadier General Donald Kerrick as a top intelligence officer with superb battlefield information. Kerrick played his part to the hilt, analyzing the relative strength of the Bosnian Serb and Muslim forces, and downplaying the Bosnian government's likelihood of success. "They knew that we were not visceral, knee-jerk, stop-the-war-immediately people, because we had gone now for close to two months letting the war proceed," notes Holbrooke. "So we had a lot of credibility when we finally said, 'Look, this is the first time we've suggested a cease-fire. We're worried. We think it's time.'"

Convincing Izetbegovic wasn't easy. Holbrooke didn't offer economic incentives. "You couldn't trade peace for aid," he says. "It just doesn't fly."[44] What won the Muslim leader over, suggests Slocombe, was fear that his country would be abandoned to a questionable fate. "They understood that if they were responsible for there not being a peace, they would forfeit the support that they'd gotten from the U.S. and from the Europeans," Slocombe explains. "They were also genuinely concerned that, with Croatia, they were allied with a tiger.

> Do these tactics raise ethical questions concerning the role of the intervenor?

And it was very much in their interest to get a peace agreement which—while far short of what they, in some sense rightly, think they deserve—stabilized the situation and got them a deal." If the Muslims had continued fighting, Slocombe insists, "it would not have been their military solution. It would have been Tudjman's military solution."

That afternoon, Izetbegovic and his government negotiated terms for a cease-fire that Tudjman also found acceptable. Holbrooke and Owen took the two-page agreement to Belgrade, and the negotiators traded demands by phone until Milosevic signed late that night. The eight-point cease-fire—to begin five days later—ended 42 months of fighting. It also included such conditions as the restoration of all utilities to Sarajevo. As part of the agreement, the Balkan presidents consented to attend a peace conference. "We could not go to the map without the guys being in the room together," says Hill. "You couldn't do shuttle diplomacy with a map. It was just not practical."

That afternoon, President Clinton announced with fanfare both the cease-fire and the plan for peace talks in the U.S. at the end of the month. Contact Group representatives, who had not been informed ahead of time for fear of news leaks, were reportedly enraged. Izetbegovic remained ambivalent to the end.[45] When the time came to sign, he balked and said to Holbrooke, "I don't see your signature on this paper." Only after Holbrooke signed did Izetbegovic do the same. When the date for the cease-fire arrived, the Muslim government refused to stop fighting, insisting that electrical power had not been restored in Sarajevo as specified. The cease-fire was delayed for six days, which Muslim forces devoted to one last military campaign. By the time of the cease-fire, an estimated 100,000 to 200,000 people—mostly civilians—had died in the three-year war.

## FREE-FLYING SHUTTLE

By mid-October, Holbrooke and his team were cautiously optimistic, though far from certain, that they could achieve a settlement in Bosnia. In six weeks they had lifted the siege of Sarajevo, negotiated ground rules for a settlement, mediated a countrywide cease-fire, scheduled an international peace conference, and gotten proof that Milosevic could negotiate on behalf of the Bosnian Serbs. In the process, the team had become unusually cohesive. Holbrooke could make his teammates "madder than hell," says Owen, adding, "Everything that is written about him in the press is true." But Owen recalls the shuttle with Holbrooke as one of the most rewarding experiences of his life: "He can be very tough on people, but he's a spectacular character to watch in action."

Holbrooke describes the team members as "totally committed public-servant patriots," and attributes the group's closeness to "the intensity of it, the small airplane, the smallness of the delegation, the trust that we had in each other, and the tragedy we were carrying with us." The team also took extraordinary steps to avoid the agency infighting that can characterize government negotiating teams. Clark and Kerrick showed Holbrooke the daily telegrams they sent to Washington, for example, even though the Joint Staff and the NSC usually communicate confidentially with their representatives on interagency missions.

In keeping with the mission's sensitivity and need for confidentiality, Holbrooke left it to officials in Washington to deal with the press.[46] But when the White House got tired of questions, the State Department asked the negotiators to handle the press themselves. According to Holbrooke, this represented an opportunity to shape news coverage. Each day the team would agree on a phrase that captured the shuttle's latest accomplishment or communicated a particular message. "We began to

> What did Holbrooke do to help build and maintain internal cohesion within his team?

decide, OK, today's headline is going to be 'Important Procedural Breakthrough,' or 'We Come on a Mission of Peace at a Moment of War,'" Holbrooke says. "I remember saying that one day and getting on every network in the world."

Critics and supporters agree that Holbrooke operated with an unusual degree of freedom. "There are very, very few traditional foreign-service officers who would have dared to go off the reservation the way he did," says one team member. "They would have felt they couldn't make any decision without checking back, because if the decision was wrong, then they would have to take the blame." Even so, Holbrooke checked in with Washington every day. He also returned every few weeks to update officials and argue specifics. By and large, though, he was not seeking advice or approval. "They gave me parameters," he says, "but left the details to us." Free rein was particularly important at the negotiating table, says Hill, where calling Washington would have destroyed Holbrooke's momentum. "When you're trying to bring this thing to a halt, this terrible war," Hill asserts, "you had to be empowered to make decisions on the spot, to move very quickly, and to assess the mood of people and the feel for the situation." Holbrooke vehemently agrees. "You cannot run a negotiation long-distance," he declares. "Tactical considerations for negotiation must be left to the negotiator."

The lack of accountability alarmed some. One NSC official complains that little information on the negotiations was available during the daily interagency teleconference on Bosnia. "We'd ask the State Department, 'So what's Holbrooke done?' and they just wouldn't know," he recalls. "Now maybe at the higher level decisions were being vetted. And certainly there were tons of deputies' and principals' meetings to go over basic decisions, but the focus of most of those was not on negotiations. It was on the success of the negotiations."

> How did Holbrooke achieve and maintain this level of independence? What were its pluses and minuses?

Holbrooke had earned the confidence placed in him. As he himself puts it, he had "as much negotiating experience as anyone in the U.S. government, at least on the Democratic side." Besides, the Clinton administration wanted badly for the war to end, and Holbrooke was providing regular proof that he was the right person to bring that about. "Senior people knew that this was really make-or-break for the administration," says Hill. "They felt very comfortable with the idea that Holbrooke was there trying to negotiate the best deal he could."

Finally, there was truth to the charge that the United States wanted a settlement and that its specifics were of secondary importance. "When you're negotiating over what the line is going to be on the Posavina Corridor, within very broad limits you're on your own," says Slocombe. "Anything the parties will agree to is fine with us. The United States does not have a position about who ought to own the Posavina Corridor." He adds: "What was critical was to persuade the [Balkan] parties that *they* had to close this deal." That, says Hill, was precisely what Holbrooke was good at. "You know the sort of hysteria of people whipping themselves up for war?" Hill asks. "Basically what he did was he whipped people up for peace. He turned peace into a very exciting thing. No one dared say, 'No, no. We're in favor of going back to war.'"

## PREPARING FOR PEACE TALKS

Getting the parties to agree to attend peace talks, especially talks to be held in the U.S., was one of Holbrooke's greatest achievements. Indeed, the willingness of the Balkan presidents to sign a cease-fire and attend an international peace conference astonished some observers. Those in regular contact with the leaders, though, say they were all deeply war-weary. In addition, each had an incentive to settle.

Milosevic was now championing peace, since the United States had promised to suspend sanctions against Serbia once an agreement was signed, and to lift them once it was implemented.[47] Tudjman had achieved most of his goals with the taking of the Krajina and the broadening of Bosnian Croat influence within Bosnia. The promise of a strengthened relationship with the United States, accompanied by a pledge to put the issue of eastern Slavonia on the negotiating table, was icing on the cake. As for the Bosnian Serbs, U.S. officials speculate that they were afraid of military defeat, primarily at the hands of the Croatians, and under severe pressure from Milosevic to settle.[48] As indicted war criminals, Mladic and Karadzic could not attend the peace talks, but a delegation of Bosnian Serbs would accompany Milosevic and depend on him for representation.

Most reluctant, team members agree, were the Bosnian Muslims. "I don't think they knew how far they could trust us," says one. "I don't think they particularly trusted Holbrooke." Izetbegovic had agreed to peace talks grudgingly, perhaps convinced, one negotiator speculates, that "this was the best chance they were going to get, and they needed to take it." Many U.S. representatives saw the Muslim president as difficult and distant, and his disagreements with other members of his government had become a source of frustration. Izetbegovic's withdrawn manner was accentuated by Milosevic's gregariousness, which even those who mistrusted him found compelling.

Managing these relationships remained difficult, but the negotiators' pace slowed considerably after the cease-fire. "The first eight weeks we flew more than 100,000 miles," says Owen. "After that we slowed down." The focus now shifted to Washington, where the State Department was drafting an agreement for the Clinton administration to present to the Balkan leaders on their arrival. State was also churning out annexes covering such issues as elections, the constitution, human rights, and refugees. "The idea was to present people with a complete package," says Hill. Meanwhile, the United States was refining its plan for an international military force in Bosnia after a peace agreement, with input from the British, French, and other contributors. By the time talks began, U.S. officials hoped, NATO would have accepted the military concept.

Finding the right setting for peace talks was critical, Holbrooke believed. The site should be secluded and secure, easy to close off to the press (to control leaks and to prevent the Balkan leaders from holding mini–press conferences), able to provide equivalent accommodations for all the presidents, and far from Washington. "We didn't want to have them continually saying, 'Bring the President and the Secretary of State in here and we can talk about it,'" notes Owen.[49] The administration's choice, Wright-Patterson Air Force Base near

Note the attention to detail concerning location, accommodations, and seating arrangements. What was Holbrooke trying to accomplish?

Dayton, lacked cachet but was "sufficiently remote so that you could actually imprison them in this place, but sufficiently large that they didn't feel imprisoned, " according to Daalder. Milosevic felt differently. "You want to lock me up in Dayton, Ohio?" *The New York Times* quoted him as protesting. "I'm not a priest, you know." Holbrooke oversaw everything, including outfitting participants' rooms to look presidential. "He thought through virtually anything that could have an impact on the negotiations," Owen notes.

While preparations moved forward, hostility among the Balkan leaders remained high. The cease-fire was to last 60 days or until peace talks ended, a duration the U.S. team had insisted on. Yet the negotiators were all too aware that more than 50 cease-fires had already failed. "You were always worried about the cows getting out of the barn," recalls one member of the team. "They would drift off into their own little interests, and that could cause problems." Several issues threatened to derail the talks. An apparent Bosnian Serb massacre of thousands of Muslim men and boys after the fall of Srebrenica cast doubt on the possibility of a settlement in the wake of such atrocities. A notorious Serb commander whom many suspected of reporting directly to Milosevic had apparently slaughtered Muslims in the Banja Luka area. Tudjman was threatening to retake eastern Slavonia if it wasn't handed to him in a peace settlement. And the relationship between the Bosnian government and Croatia remained edgy and unstable. A week before the talks were to begin, Clinton met with Tudjman and Izetbegovic in an effort to lessen the strains between the Federation partners.

In Washington, also, tensions were rising over the U.S. role in an eventual settlement. The Republican-controlled Congress passed a resolution declaring that the Clinton administration should not commit U.S. soldiers to an implementation force in Bosnia without Congress's permission. The resolution had no legal force, but it signaled to the international community—and the Balkans in particular—the potential for ongoing discord over U.S. military involvement.

> ## How did Holbrooke work to sell the agreement within the United States?

The resolution, Holbrooke declared, "grievously interferes with the negotiating processes of peace. I think any member of the Congress who supports that kind of resolution on the eve of an historic and important negotiation is doing grave damage to the national interests."

Finally, it was unclear if the Balkan leaders—particularly Izetbegovic—cared enough about settling to make wrenching compromises and tradeoffs. Holbrooke and his team had identified 50 divisive issues, including return of refugees, the election, war crimes, and the Federation. And there was always the map. "We have a pretty good idea of 90 percent of the territory," Holbrooke announced, "but the remaining 10 percent . . . those are really tough." If no middle ground could be found, Holbrooke warned, the consequences would be dire.

# THE DAYTON ACCORD

The Dayton talks began on November 1. Despite earlier threats, all three presidents arrived with a pledge to get results. "Holbrooke got them to agree to come and stay for as long as it took to reach an agreement," says Owen. "Now that's an amazing concept. Because they knew there were going to be some terrible disagreements." Milosevic, who seemed blithely ready to deal on behalf of the Bosnian Serbs, continued to dispense charm. "He took over the Officers' Club at Dayton," one team member recalls. "He'd be sitting at this big table saying, 'Bring more wine. Bring, please, for my friends. Bring lobster.' It's the Godfather. He's the perfect Godfather."

But for most of the participants, the Dayton negotiations were grim. Those who were there scoff at reports of a convivial atmosphere. "There was no collegiality amongst the delegations," declares Paul Williams, director of a London-based legal-aid nonprofit, who served on the Bosnian government's team at Dayton. Meetings were tense and often stalemated. Initially, the three presidents did not meet; U.S. negotiators shuttled among them with drafts and revisions. The Americans circulated during meals, but the three Balkan delegations kept to themselves.

Williams recalls sighting balls on the grass. "We read in the newspaper the next day that the Americans had provided the different delegations with footballs and soccer balls, and they were all out there playing soccer together and overcoming through sports what they couldn't overcome through diplomacy," says Williams. "We thought, what are they talking about? We were all walking back and forth between the housing complex and the negotiating center in the rain in our trenchcoats, looking at these balls laying on the ground." Adds Hill: "I barely got any sleep, let alone played soccer. It's a very deadly serious subject, war."

The scant principles agreed on before Dayton still served as a foundation. "One side or another would argue for a proposition inconsistent with the general principles, and we would say, 'No, you can't do that,'" Owen recalls. "'It's already been agreed to in the three pages [the agreement on principles].'" Even so, trying to conduct a negotiation among the parties in Dayton—the Bosnian Muslims, the Bosnian Serbs, Serbia, Croatia, the United States, and the European Union—was terrible, says one negotiator: "It was just day after day of grinding on the same people on the same issues. Moving two steps forward and one step back. Reaching agreement, and the agreement falls apart." Holbrooke calls the Balkan leaders the most difficult heads of state he had ever dealt with. "They're thugs, they're murderers, they're entrenched," he declares. "They represent very small countries and movements that are beleaguered."

Surprisingly, political issues that Holbrooke feared might topple the negotiations proved less contentious than expected, though U.S. negotiators had to accept concepts they viewed as divisive and foolhardy.[50] The Balkan leaders insisted on a rotating presidency similar to that of Bosnia before the war, filled alternately by a Muslim, a Croat, and a Serb. "They built a tribal ethnic concept into their constitution that I think is undemocratic," Owen says. Holbrooke also felt it essential to resolve the explosive issue of eastern Slavonia before addressing the Bosnian map. At Holbrooke's request, Warren Christopher came to Dayton, and the two convinced a reluctant Milosevic to settle. After intense negotiations, the Croatian and Serbian presidents agreed to a UN Transitional Authority to oversee a phased return of eastern Slavonia to Croatia. Tudjman, who wanted the region back after just one year, and Milosevic, who argued for two, agreed to Christopher's suggestion—largely a semantic trick—to call it "12 months of transitional rule, plus a second period not to exceed the first period."[51]

But territorial disputes over Bosnia remained deadlocked, each side insisting on control of areas claimed by others. "There were threats to leave," Owen recalls. "They would say, 'I've had enough. I'm packing up. I won't be here tomorrow.'" One of the most emotional battles erupted over Sarajevo, which the Bosnian Muslims wanted to keep unified, and the Bosnian Serbs wanted to split into Serb and Muslim cities on the model of Berlin. "There was a point where I had resigned myself to the fact that I'd risked my life and wasted months of my life—gained weight and lost hair—and this damned thing wasn't going to work," says one U.S. negotiator. "We just couldn't drag them across the finish line."

Holbrooke hammered at the delegations, arguing that Dayton was their last chance to end the war with the help of the United States and the international community. "He browbeats people," says one NSC official. "He talks until they're tired. Everything was geared to getting this agreement, and he was working 21, 22 hours a day on this stuff." After two weeks of haggling, some obstacles finally gave way. Milosevic agreed that the Bosnian Muslims had "earned" Sarajevo after years under siege, and gave them the city along with four suburbs. A crisis arose when the Serbs discovered that the last-minute dealmaking had left them with only 45 percent of Bosnia, rather than the 49 percent promised in the principles. Most of the land to make up the difference came from the Croats, who only relented after Clinton called Tudjman to plead for cooperation.[52]

Then a final snag threatened to kill the settlement. Almost three weeks into the talks, Izetbegovic demanded that Brcko—a Serb-held town in the corridor connecting Serbia with the Republika Srpska—be returned to Bosnia's control. Faced with the unlikelihood of resolving this demand, Christopher and Holbrooke distributed a "failure statement" to the Balkan leaders at midnight. The statement declared that the talks would end the next morning, when the United States would turn the negotiations back to the Europeans. The announcement, Holbrooke says, was no bluff. President Clinton had authorized the shutdown. Still, Holbrooke was not ready to give up: he sent team members to tell Milosevic that, unless he could think of a solution, the negotiations were over.[53]

The next morning, after talking to Tudjman, Milosevic offered to break the deadlock. "In the interests of peace, I will walk the last mile," he told Holbrooke. "I will agree to arbitration for Brcko. I won't give it away, but I'll agree to arbitration." Christopher and Holbrooke took the offer to Izetbegovic. "There was this long pause," Holbrooke recounts, "and Izetbegovic said, 'This is not a just peace.' Another long pause. 'But my people need peace. Let's go ahead.'" Holbrooke and Christopher hurried to notify Clinton. Once the president had announced the breakthrough, they reasoned, it would be harder for the Bosnian government to renege.

> **How did the United States lock the parties into an agreement? Why was this important?**

As Clinton declared the talks' success on national television, Christopher and Holbrooke instructed Owen to draft an arbitration provision for Brcko. The provision was hustled around to all the participants, signed, and slapped into the Dayton accord. "The initialing ceremony was half an hour late, and we got it in," Owen says. "Now that was not done the way it is supposed to be done. But if we hadn't gotten it done, the whole thing would have fallen apart. And we had 30 minutes to do it, so we did it in 30 minutes."

At the end of twenty-one days, the Balkan leaders signed the peace agreement. Izetbegovic and his delegation remained angry and reluctant to the end. "It was very hard for them to accept this," says one team member. "Izetbegovic described this as a bitter and unjust peace, even in the signing ceremony." The Bosnian Serbs, who reportedly only saw the agreement minutes before the signing, refused to attend. For Holbrooke's team, all of whom call the accord imperfect, the ceremony brought profound relief. "Holbrooke is a closer, and that's what it takes," says one member. "Sometimes that's a brutal process. You can have people come up with the greatest negotiating scheme in the world, but if you can't bring it to closure, it doesn't go anywhere."

The agreement included the following key provisions: Sarajevo would remain united as the capital of Bosnia; free elections would take place under international supervision; Bosnia's estimated 2.2 million refugees would have the right to return or obtain just compensation; and entities within Bosnia could establish links with neighboring countries, namely the Bosnian Serbs with Serbia and the Bosnian Croats with Croatia. NATO's implementation force, IFOR, would keep the peace for one year, overseeing withdrawal of troops behind cease-fire lines and enforcement of a 2.5-mile-wide zone of separation between Bosnia and Republika Srpska. Other international groups, including the UN High Refugee Command, would monitor human rights and the return of refugees. Mladic, Karadzic, and other indicted war criminals would not be allowed to campaign for or hold public office, and all signers agreed to cooperate fully with the War Crimes Tribunal. Soon after the signing, 20,000 U.S. troops began arriving in Bosnia as part of the 60,000-member NATO force.

The Dayton agreement was a foreign-policy coup for the Clinton administration. Holbrooke and his team had ended the terrible Balkan conflict, allowing refugees to return and reconstruction to begin. But even Holbrooke would not predict whether the accord could satisfy the second part of his challenge—to craft a sustainable peace incorporating Muslims, Croats, and Serbs within Bosnia's borders.

## AN UNEASY PEACE

With the agreement signed, questions about implementation still abounded. If NATO troops withdrew after one year, the tenuous peace between the Republika Srpska and the Federation might deteriorate into war. IFOR's narrow mandate had left critical tasks—such as protection of returning refugees—to local police, who were unlikely to be free of bias or to be equipped to manage volatile situations. As long as such notorious figures as Mladic and Karadzic remained free, the Bosnian Muslims might refuse to participate in elections. And danger remained that the Bosnian Serbs might break away and link up with Serbia and Montenegro, and that the Bosnian Croats might do the same with Croatia, resulting in the very partition of Bosnia that the international community and the Muslim government had hoped to avoid.

A year later, most of these questions still generated deep uncertainty over Bosnia's destiny. Clinton administration officials were quick to point out what had gone right and to note small steps toward cooperation. IFOR had met little resistance, and most of the military provisions of the accord, such as troop withdrawals and weapons removals, had been implemented. It also appeared likely that an IFOR follow-on operation after the one-year NATO commitment expired would provide a continued international presence. But critics of the Dayton accord found ample evidence to predict eventual partition of the troubled nation. Refugee resettlement had gone badly, with some refugees barred from their old homes, others killed outright, and most afraid to return. Freedom of movement between Bosnia's two entities, guaranteed by the accord, was in many areas a sham, and almost no progress had been made in integrating Bosnian Croat territories into the Muslim-Croat Federation. Mladic, Karadzic, and other war criminals were still at large, and NATO forces had ignored international appeals to arrest them, fearing rioting or hostage-taking.

Encouragingly, national-level elections provoked only scattered incidents of violence, and European monitors declared the vote valid. The inauguration of the three presidents and the new parliament was seen by some as a first step toward integrating Bosnia's ethnic groups and forcing a cooperation that could eventually lead to a functional unified government. But the elections sparked intense controversy; some prominent U.S. newspapers and politicians urged that the vote be delayed since conditions precluded a free and fair election. Evidence of intimidation and fraud was widespread. Even more disturbing, the people of Bosnia rejected moderate leadership and elected avowed nationalists: embittered Bosnian President Alija Izetbegovic, Karadzic's confederate Momcilo Krajisnik, and Croat Kresimir Zubak. Krajisnik boycotted the opening of the new Bosnian parliament, reportedly to avoid pledging allegiance to a unified Bosnia.

Richard Holbrooke viewed the latest developments with some pessimism.[54] The United States was doing what it could, according to Holbrooke (who had been nominated for the 1996 Nobel Peace Prize). Now it was up to the Balkan leaders to find their own way to a lasting peace. Former team member Roberts Owen agrees. "It's possible that the Dayton plan as written won't work," he admits. "We may wind up with three different independent parts of Bosnia—Muslim, Croat, and Serb. But the main thing is the war is over, and if that holds, if peace remains with us, I think it was worth the effort."

# CHAPTER FOURTEEN

# Leading Negotiations

Richard Holbrooke brought Serbs, Croats, and Muslims to the table in Dayton using military force to alter their perceptions of the alternatives to agreement, mediation to facilitate the process, and promises of aid to enhance the attractiveness of an agreement. Although eager to help the warring parties reach a settlement, Holbrooke also represented the partisan interests of the United States and could reward and punish the disputants. He was simultaneously negotiator, mediator, and arbitrator. He also served as a bridge between the external negotiations—in the Balkans and with European allies—and internal negotiations within the United States. In all of these roles, Holbrooke exercised the extraordinary leadership abilities characteristic of breakthrough negotiators.

That negotiators must be leaders is a central premise of this book. But the leadership of negotiators is different in character from that of decision makers. Negotiators lead from the middle, not from the top. They may have some independent authority to coerce or to make binding commitments, but their primary source of power is credibility with their constituencies and their counterparts. As one negotiator put it, "You have to have the total confidence of the people who hired you. They have to feel that you are their creature, that they have complete trust in you, and that you have their authority to conduct that negotiation." The negotiator's credibility, in turn, is founded on a personal track record, mastery of substance and process, ability to build solid working relationships, and a personality suited to coping with the ambiguities and vagaries of negotiation.

In this chapter, we explore the leadership challenges facing breakthrough negotiators when they intervene in disputes and represent diverse and possibly internally divided constituencies. To assess leadership in negotiation, we have to disentangle individual qualities from the situational challenges facing the negotiators. The need for leadership arises in the interaction between the person and the situation. If the circumstances do not demand hard choices, leadership is unnecessary. If the people who make decisions lack leadership capabilities, good choices will not be made.

We begin by taking a fresh look at the range of intervention roles and representational roles played by the protagonists of our case histories. The choices that Robert Gallucci and Jimmy Carter faced in the North Korean crisis differed strikingly, for example, because they played very different roles—negotiator and mediator, respectively. Both roles present colliding sets of situational pressures. By identifying the characteristic dilemmas inherent in particular roles, we can infer the presence or absence of leadership from individuals' choices as they seek to manage these tensions.

## ROLES PLAYED BY INTERVENORS

Our point of departure is the three intervention roles of mediator, negotiator, and arbitrator.[1] In Chapter Eight, we defined the pure versions of these roles and their sources of power:

*Mediator.* The pure mediator is an impartial, mutually acceptable third party whose goal is to help the parties resolve their dispute. The mediator is not biased toward any of the parties or toward achieving or preventing a settlement to advance personal interests. Although mediators lack the power to coerce or bargain, they can use facilitative power to influence disputants. A mediator must gain entry to the dispute by being accepted by the contending parties.

*Negotiator.* The pure negotiator has well-recognized partisan interests in the outcome of the dispute, either in getting a settlement (substantive interests) or in seeing one of the disputants gain a favorable settlement (relationship or coalitional interests). Negotiators lack coercive power to impose terms on the disputants, but they may use bargaining power to buy entry into the dispute and advance self-interest.

*Arbitrator.* The pure arbitrator is an impartial third party with the coercive power to impose terms of settlement on the disputants. The arbitrator is not biased toward either of the parties in conflict and subordinates personal desires to some set of rules or values. Nor does the pure arbitrator have a personal stake in the outcome sufficient to bargain with the disputants.

Intervenors in complex negotiations typically play a mixture of these roles. Holbrooke went to the Balkans to help end the conflict, but he was by no means an impartial mediator. Although he represented the interests of the United States, he was far from a conventional negotiator. Willing to wield a stick to impose outcomes on the contending parties, he acted as a sort of arbitrator.

Other intervenors in the cases in this book likewise played hybrid roles. Jimmy Carter was much closer to being a pure mediator than Holbrooke, but he too exerted some coercive influence over the parties. Robert Gallucci was virtually a pure negotiator, but sometimes even he acted as a comediator, helping to bridge the distance between the two sides. James Baker and George Bush worked to arbitrate the dispute between Iraq and Kuwait but were strongly interested in the outcome. These hybrid roles are illustrated schematically in the intervention role grid in Figure 14.1.

Leadership in negotiation is largely about constructing these roles. This means shaping your external counterpart's perceptions of your role in the service of creating and claiming value for your side. How can you convince the other side that you are more than a mere messenger for your principals?

Holbrooke worked hard, for example, to create the impression that he wielded substantial control over such sticks as NATO bombing and such carrots as economic aid. To the extent that he convinced Milosevic and the others, Holbrooke moved in the direction of being a mediator with muscle, increasing his influence. Nimble manipulation of others' expectations and perceptions is fundamental to leading from the middle.

Representatives are also called on to play different roles in different arenas. Holbrooke operated differently in his interactions with the Balkan presidents than he did within the Clinton administration or within his negotiating team. He was a powerful emissary of the United States in his international dealings, a senior-level officer of the State Department in consultations within the Clinton administration, and the principal decision maker within his own negotiating team. Similarly, George Bush acted as an arbitrator in the dispute between Iraq and Kuwait and as a negotiator in his efforts to gain domestic and international support to confront Iraq.

## DILEMMAS CONFRONTING INTERVENORS

When intervening in conflicts, negotiators face foreseeable dilemmas concerning the goals they will pursue, the role they will play, the interests they will advance, and the means they will use to do so. Some of these dilemmas confront all intervenors, regardless of the roles they play. Others are unique to those

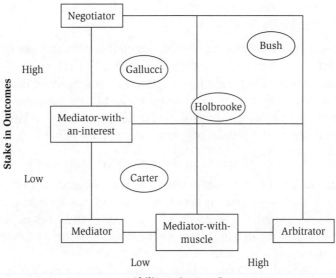

**Figure 14.1.**  Comparing Intervention Roles.

with an interest in the outcome or coercive power. In seeking to bring the parties to the table in Bosnia, Holbrooke successfully managed all of these tensions.

## Narrow Versus Broad Goals

Intervenors like Holbrooke may concentrate narrowly on the presenting problem—the positions and issues that are the crux of the immediate conflict—or they may direct the disputants' attention to the systemic root causes (underlying interests, patterns of interactions, and history of grievances) in the hope of reaching a long-term resolution. By focusing on the former, the intervenor may be able to suppress a current eruption of a bitter conflict, such as the war in Bosnia. But failure to address underlying root causes may simply set the stage for future flare-ups.

Deciding which way to go is therefore not a straightforward choice, as mediation scholar Leonard Riskin notes, because it involves unavoidable trade-offs:

> A narrow problem-definition can increase the chances of resolution and reduce the time needed for the mediation. . . . In addition, a narrow focus can avoid a danger inherent in broader approaches—that personal relations or other "extraneous issues" might exacerbate the conflict and make it more difficult to settle. On the other hand, in some cases the narrow approach can increase the chance of impasse because it allows little room for creative option generation or other means of addressing underlying interests which, if unsatisfied, could block agreement. Also, a narrow approach to mediation might preclude the parties

from addressing other long-term mutual interests that could lead to long-lasting, mutually-beneficial arrangements.[2]

Working incrementally, even if it builds confidence and sets the stage for agreement on broader issues, may ignore deeper causes and result in unsustainable agreements. But premature efforts to tackle root-cause issues can open up old wounds, weaken constituent support, and cause the process to stall or break down. Holbrooke faced this basic tension, and it also arose in efforts to end the conflicts on the Korean peninsula and in the Middle East.

## Facilitation Versus Activism

Simply facilitating the disputants' efforts to communicate is one option. The intervenor can act as a conduit between parties unable to communicate productively on their own. In the process, as we saw in the work of Terje Larsen, the intervenor may be able to soften the rhetoric, allow the parties to vent, and progressively promote a dialogue.

The opposite end of the spectrum is actively critiquing the parties' positions and seeking to craft agreements.[3] Intervenors who limit themselves to facilitation may forgo opportunities to help disputants move beyond entrenched positions. The activist approach, however, can be risky. In disputes characterized by a sharp imbalance in power, such as the one in Bosnia, a mediator's efforts to develop options predictably lead to accusations of bias. If the intervenor begins to make independent judgments about the parties' positions or seeks to nudge the parties in particular directions, the risk of being labeled as biased rises dramatically. So do the related risks that the parties will fail to take full ownership of the resulting agreements or get too far ahead of their constituencies and lose credibility.

Throughout his intervention in Bosnia, Holbrooke took a highly activist approach. He went far beyond simply facilitating communication between the parties (although his intensive shuttle certainly served this purpose); he actively challenged the parties on their positions. But he did so evenhandedly, exerting pressure on all of the combatants. Holbrooke also put prodigious effort into helping them confront their alternatives to agreement. Thus, Holbrooke successfully walked the tightrope. It helped, of course, that the parties had no choice but to deal with him.

## Own Interests Versus Best Interests

Intervenors with an interest in the outcome experience an additional tension: To what extent should they try to advance their own interests, including possible bias in favor of one of the disputants, versus the best interests of the contending parties? (This formulation assumes, of course, that the intervenor wants to see the dispute settled and is not a spoiler in disguise.) The interested intervenor is seeking both to resolve the dispute and advance self-interest. The resulting tension arises because these two sets of interests are not always compatible.

Holbrooke confronted this tension head-on in Bosnia. He, like many other Americans, was sympathetic to the plight of the dispossessed Bosnian Muslims, who had suffered greatly. On the other hand, he had to deal with the realities of the situation, including the likelihood that some of the villains in this drama would walk away with significant gains (at least in the short run). In the end, Holbrooke had to subordinate his preference for a just outcome to the more urgent imperative of achieving a settlement that stopped the bloodshed.

## Short Term Versus Long Term

Intervenors like Holbrooke who wield coercive power may experience yet another tension: coercing the disputants to shut down the current conflict may work against a longer-term resolution by reducing the costs to the parties of continuing contention, and hence sowing the seeds for future eruptions. This tension arises for the following reasons:

- Coercive power can be used to control disputants' behavior but not to change their attitudes.
- There are usually limits on an intervenor's staying power or the ability and willingness to police the terms of settlement.
- There are limits on the intervenor's ability to observe and control the actions of the disputants.

The use of power can temporarily suppress a dispute but may in the process prolong it. Rather than facing their problems and negotiating solutions, disputants who come to expect coercive intervention whenever conflict erupts may provoke each other in the hope that the intervenor will do damage to the other side.

Holbrooke came down squarely on the side of achieving short-term gains by stopping the fighting in Bosnia. But his efforts left many longer-term issues, such as Kosovo, unaddressed. In fact, it could be argued that the settlement crafted at Dayton, with its strong focus on the short-run goal of stopping the fighting and containing the conflict, sowed the seeds of the subsequent war in Kosovo. But it may simply not have been possible to address the longer-term issues in the region at the time. The same tension is evident, of course, in the continuing agony of relations between Israel and the Palestinians.

## Ends Versus Means

Finally, intervenors with coercive power face the age-old question of ends versus means. By announcing a breakthrough on CNN, for example, Jimmy Carter moved the dispute between the United States and North Korea toward resolution. But Carter's decision to box in the Clinton administration raises questions about his rights and responsibilities as an intervenor. Similarly, George Bush won support in the UN Security Council and in Congress for the use of "all necessary means" to eject Iraq from Kuwait. But by running roughshod over the deliberative processes of both bodies, the Bush administration set unfortunate precedents and mobilized opponents determined to prevent a recurrence and hence to constrain the flexibility of future U.S. administrations.

Holbrooke confronted the means-ends question in its purest form: When should an intervenor allow loss of life and destruction of property in order to get a resolution to a conflict? When is it defensible to use military force to achieve political objectives? Is the resulting loss of lives justified by the ends that are achieved? Holbrooke clearly believed that the ends in this case justified the means, as did the Bush administration in the Gulf conflict.

Intervenors who operate in the middle of the grid as mediators-with-an-interest-*and*-muscle must manage all of these tensions. As we have seen, Richard Holbrooke had to balance U.S. interests, his own interests, and the interests of the disputants. He had to end the violence in the short run and take steps toward a sustainable settlement. He had to choose between facilitation and activism. And in using NATO bombing to pressure the Bosnian Serbs, pressuring Izetbegovic to stop the Muslim advances, and doing business with indicted war criminals, Holbrooke made hard choices between ends and means that negotiators who are leaders have to make. At the same time, Holbrooke was acting as a representative of his government and not as a principal decision maker. This role presented another set of leadership challenges that awaits any negotiator who has to coordinate external negotiations and internal deliberations.

## ROLES PLAYED BY REPRESENTATIVES

In most significant negotiations, the negotiators at the table, such as Baker, Gallucci, and Holbrooke, represent the interests of others who are absent from the table.[4] The latter could be principals with decision-making power, or constituencies who expect the representative to lead them, or a hybrid of the two.[5] The internal interests being represented could be monolithic or riven with factions. And the representative could operate as a pure agent or pursue personal interests alongside the principals' interests. Regardless, the representative functions as the bridge between internal decision making and external negotiations, orchestrating the interacting facets of negotiating activity. Negotiators are like Janus, the Roman god of beginnings, who had two faces, one looking ahead and the other looking back. The obligation to face in both directions and to coordinate negotiation and decision making requires representatives to play multiple roles, which typically shift as the process evolves. As one of the Oslo negotiators expressed it, "At the negotiating table you have to convince the other party that your concessions are very, very painful. Then you have to go to your own public and tell them that the concessions are meaningless. So that contradiction is real, and is very difficult to manage."

One dimension on which representation roles vary is the extent to which representatives have their own legitimate interests in the outcomes of the negotiation. At one extreme, the representative is a mere agent; at the other end, the representative is a key decision maker (a principal). In between, the representative operates as a partner to the principals, representing both their interests and legitimate independent interests. As Fred Iklé put it in *How Nations Negotiate:*

> The diplomat who faces his opponent over the green baize sometimes acts only as a messenger. His powers may be so restricted that he can merely deliver prepared statements, outline positions as prescribed by his government and receive communications from the opponent. At the other extreme is the negotiator who can take all decisions by himself; that is, while in face-to-face contact with the opponent, he can accept new proposals from the other side, develop counter-proposals on the spot, and conclude agreements or break off negotiations at his own discretion. Negotiators with such wide powers appear only at summit meetings. . . . And even "at the summit" the chiefs of government from democratic countries are usually limited in the decisions they can take by themselves.[6]

Holbrooke was operating close to the middle of this spectrum. He represented the United States but had career interests in the outcome of the negotiations and in how history viewed his contribution. He certainly did not want to be viewed as a mere agent, although his actions were strongly shaped by the interests of his principals.

There is also striking variation in the degree to which representatives influence constituents' perceptions of their interests and alternatives. At one extreme, the representative acts as a messenger and does not try to influence the principals' thinking at all. At the other pole, the representative wields sufficient influence to act as a visionary internal leader, aggressively and charismatically shaping internal perceptions in line with external realities. In between, the representative functions more or less as a persuasive educator.

All of the negotiators whose work we have looked at operated in the middle of this spectrum. Holbrooke was highly skilled at molding domestic public opinion and at shaping the perceptions of his principals to support initiatives like the bombing of the Bosnian Serbs. Baker and Gallucci were as active in internal debates as they were in external negotiations. As Robert Gallucci expressed it, "Good negotiators are much more than messengers, because even if you put them on a very tight leash, they are going to come back and say, 'If we go here, we might get something.' It's very tough to stop you from exploring. At least I found it was very tough for them to stop me from exploring."

The third dimension on which representation varies is the degree to which representatives must manage internal differences in interests. If internal interests are monolithic, the representative can simply act as an agent of those interests (possibly while representing personal interests and seeking to transform internal perceptions). At the other extreme, the internal interests are so fractious that the representative must actively build an internal coalition and hence choose sides. In between the two extremes, the representative acts as an internal mediator, crafting consensus positions.

All of the negotiators we have described worked to build internal consensus. When necessary, they organized internal coalitions to push for what they believed to be the right course of action. Consider, for example, Holbrooke's efforts to create and sustain support for bombing and Gallucci's work to build a coalition in support of agreement with North Korea.

The range of possible variations in representational roles is depicted three-dimensionally in Figure 14.2. The horizontal axis illustrates the extent to which representatives have their own legitimate interests in the negotiation. The vertical axis depicts the degree to which the representative can (and is willing to) work internally to shape constituents' perceived interests to create value. The diagonal axis illustrates the extent to which the representative must manage internal differences in interests.

In Bosnia, Holbrooke was operating in the middle of the grid. He represented the United States but had personal career interests in the outcome. He educated his principals about what it would take to make peace in Bosnia and to build supportive internal coalitions, and on specific issues like resumption of NATO bombing and the site of peace talks he acted as an internal advocate for what he considered the best interests of the United States. In the face of divergent interests, he convinced his principals to resume bombing and risk the resulting strains within the alliance and with Russia.

Like Holbrooke, most representatives find that they have to shift from role to role within the same arena as the process evolves. The sequence of such shifts makes a decisive difference. A shift from mediator to coalition builder, for instance, can occur when the representative concludes that internal consensus is impossible and that less-than-unanimous agreement is more desirable than no agreement. Once a representative has chosen to side with a particular internal coalition, however, it is impossible to return to being a neutral mediator. It may be relatively easy for an intervenor with coercive power to begin by trying to mediate an agreement and then moving to arbitrate if necessary. A shift in the reverse direction is more difficult: having exercised coercive power, the intervenor may find it hard to convince the parties that she can act as a mediator.

## DILEMMAS CONFRONTING REPRESENTATIVES

Like intervenors, representatives face inescapable tensions if they exercise leadership by adopting roles other than that of mere agent. A move to function as more than an agent on any of these dimensions will present the representative with characteristic dilemmas to confront and manage.

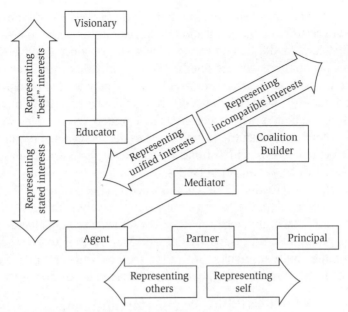

**Figure 14.2.** The Representational Role Grid.

## Creating Value Versus Claiming Value

Every negotiation calls for negotiators to be effective at both creating and claiming value. This tension between integrative and distributive opportunities is heightened when the negotiator represents others. A representative who moves from the role of classic agent to that of partner (horizontally, on Figure 14.2) can create or claim value in ways that serve personal interests or those of partners who are not at the table. This is because the relationship between representatives and those they represent can often involve mixed motives. Representatives may also control the flow of information to the disadvantage of those they represent, giving rise to a classic principal-agent problem.

But strong egocentric representatives like Holbrooke also experience the mirror image of this problem: they are constrained by distrust on the part of those they represent. Their superior grasp of what is going on at the table can paradoxically become a problem: they cannot convey every nuance of what happens at the table to those they represent, and the more intense the at-the-table efforts are to create value, the greater the likelihood is of generating doubt in constituents. Ironically, by virtue of knowing more, the representative is trusted less.

## Transformation Versus Ratification

A representative who moves toward functioning internally as an educator and even a visionary (vertically, on Figure 14.2) encounters another dilemma. A representative who is perceived by the other side as unable to reshape constituents' interests and positions can plausibly portray these needs as rigid and can use the need to secure internal ratification of agreements as a tool in external negotiations. Holbrooke did this when he feigned lack of control over NATO bombing in his negotiations with the Serbs. The catch is that mismatches between stated constituent interests and external realities may lead to no agreement, or a suboptimal agreement, when reshaping would have created joint value.

But a representative who is perceived by counterparts as able to modify the different interests of constituents will come under increasing pressure to do so. The representative is thus in a stronger position to create value, but less able to claim value by using ratification tactics.

Constraints on creating value are most acute for the traditional agent. Representatives who adopt the role of educator may be able, like Holbrooke, selectively to portray their influence over their constituents as limited and contingent. To the degree that a representative moves even further toward becoming a visionary, the ability to invoke ratification requirements credibly declines but may be counterbalanced by the ability to make credible commitments that stick.

## Flexibility Versus Commitment

The task of reconciling the divergent interests of constituents illustrates the adage that an agreement between two disputants requires three agreements: one between the parties and one each within the parties. The representative's dilemma is that an internal consensus imposes rigidity on external negotiations, but internal disagreement creates vulnerability to being divided and conquered. A representative who does not push for early internal consensus will have flexibility in external negotiations but will face more internal disagreement on returning with a proposed settlement. Conversely, a representative who pushes for early consensus will have less flexibility in external bargaining but an easier time ratifying a proposed settlement.

This dilemma becomes more acute if the representative moves toward functioning as an internal mediator (diagonally, on Figure 14.2). A representative who has to reconcile diverse internal interests may want to maximize flexibility by learning about external realities before pressing for internal consensus. But such a representative risks looking unprepared or weak in external negotiations. By extension, a partisan coalition builder may not want internal consensus at all, preferring to build a partisan internal coalition to maximize external flexibility. The risk is that a broader consensus would have facilitated subsequent implementation of the agreement.

Holbrooke successfully managed the tension between external flexibility and internal commitment by consulting his principals frequently on goals but retaining control of tactical decisions. Holbrooke said, "They gave me parameters but left the details to us." He vetted key decisions at the highest levels but left lower-level officials somewhat in the dark about what he was doing. This created some discomfort among his principals, but, having secured the necessary commitment to goals at the highest level, Holbrooke had the flexibility to make decisions on the spot and respond quickly to changing circumstances.

## THE NEGOTIATOR AS LEADER

Did Holbrooke exercise leadership in these negotiations? The unequivocal answer is yes. The fighting stopped, and many lives were saved as a direct result of his actions and hard choices. (See "Update of the Cases" at the end of book.) The plausible-alternative test is pertinent here: responsible criticism of someone else's decisions, in a situation requiring hard choices, calls for spelling out the outcome you would have preferred and how you would have achieved it. When we apply this test, it is difficult to find much fault with Holbrooke's actions. Although the outcome was imperfect, and perhaps even offensive to one's sense of justice and fair play, there are no obvious plausible alternatives that would have created more value.

More impressive, perhaps, are the multiple ways that Holbrooke was able to lead from the middle. He played a broad range of roles brilliantly—as both an intervenor and a representative—in the Bosnia negotiations. In the process, Holbrooke successfully blazed a trail through most of the built-in dilemmas that intervenors and representatives classically face. His capacity to orchestrate multiple levels of negotiation, build coalitions, and coordinate the use of force and diplomacy exemplify the leadership skills of the breakthrough negotiator.

# CONCLUSION

*Becoming a Breakthrough Negotiator*

How best can you continue to develop your negotiating ability? To help you answer that question and to bring our discussion of breakthrough negotiation to a close, we offer some guidelines here.

Research on the development of expertise suggests that experts manage complexity better than novices do and that they are able to do so because of superior abilities at pattern recognition, mental simulation, parallel management, and reflection-in-action.

*Pattern recognition* is the ability to see patterns, such as potential coalitional alignments, in complex and unstructured negotiating situations. Like expert chess players, skilled negotiators filter out irrelevant clutter; they see configurations that represent threats and opportunities. *Mental simulation* is the ability to generate promising courses of action rapidly and then project them forward in time imaginatively. This skill enables experienced negotiators to develop provisional action sequences, anticipate reactions and contingencies, and then refine or discard plans as necessary.[1] *Parallel management* is the ability to keep track of the substance of negotiations while simultaneously shaping the evolution of the process. In *Education for Judgment*, Roland Christensen describes this "dual competency" as a central component of expertise of all kinds.[2] *Reflection-in-action* is the ability to "go to the balcony" in the midst of tense and difficult proceedings, as negotiation theorist William Ury so aptly put it, for perspective on what is happening and why, and to adjust strategies accordingly.[3]

The best way to develop your capacities as a negotiator is to experience a range of negotiations, both real and simulated, and then to take the time to reflect actively on them and absorb their lessons. Gary Klein, a leading authority on the development of expertise, put it this way:

> The part of intuition that involves pattern matching and recognition of familiar and typical cases can be trained. If you want people to size up situations quickly and accurately, you need to expand their experience base. One way is to arrange for a person to receive more difficult cases. . . . Another approach is to develop a training program, perhaps with exercises and realistic scenarios, so the person has a chance to size up numerous situations very quickly. A good simulation can sometimes provide more training value than direct experience.[4]

Structured on-the-job training (possibly including formal mentorship) and formal study is the ideal combination. Formal study is important because negotiations come in such a range of types and magnitudes that it can be difficult to generalize well from real-world work experience. Negotiators who learn from experience alone are likely to develop characteristic styles that work well in some situations and not in others, without fully understanding why.

We hope that the conceptual framework we have presented in this book will help you begin to organize and internalize your experience. Success will foster your intuition and heighten your situational awareness, capacities that will equip you to develop workable options under time pressure, the true hallmark of expertise.

# SUGGESTED READINGS

## ON NEGOTIATION

Allison, G. *Essence of Decision: Explaining the Cuban Missile Crisis.* New York: Little, Brown, 1971.

Bazerman, M., and Neale, M. *Negotiating Rationally.* New York: Free Press, 1992.

Cialdini, R. B. *Influence: The Psychology of Persuasion.* New York: Morrow, 1984.

Fisher, R., Ury, W., and Patton, B. *Getting to Yes: Negotiating Agreement Without Giving In.* (2nd ed.) New York: Penguin, 1991.

Iklé, F. C. *How Nations Negotiate.* Millwood, N.Y.: Kraus, 1964.

Jowett, G. S., and O'Donnell, V. *Propaganda and Persuasion.* Thousand Oaks, Calif.: Sage, 1992.

Lax, D. A., and Sebenius, J. K. *The Manager as Negotiator.* New York: Free Press, 1986.

Neustadt, R. E., and May, E. R. *Thinking in Time: The Uses of History for Decision-Makers.* New York: Free Press, 1986.

Raiffa, H. *The Art and Science of Negotiation.* Cambridge, Mass.: Harvard University Press, 1982.

Salacuse, J. W. *Making Global Deals: Negotiating in the International Marketplace.* Boston: Houghton Mifflin, 1991.

Schein, E. H. *Organizational Culture and Leadership.* (2nd ed.) San Francisco: Jossey-Bass, 1992.

Ury, W. *Getting Past No: Negotiating Your Way from Confrontation to Cooperation.* New York: Bantam Books, 1991.

Walton, R., and McKersie, R. *A Behavioral Theory of Labor Negotiations.* Ithaca, N.Y.: ILR Press, 1965.

Walton, R., McKersie, R., and J. Cutcher-Gershenfeld. *Strategic Negotiations: A Theory of Change in Labor-Management Relations.* Boston: Harvard Business School Press, 1994.

Zartman, I. W., and Berman, M. *The Practical Negotiator.* New Haven, Conn.: Yale University Press, 1982.

Zimbardo, P., and Lieppe, M. *The Psychology of Attitude Change and Social Influence.* New York: McGraw-Hill, 1991.

# ON DISPUTE RESOLUTION

Arrow, K., Mnookin, R., Ross, L., Tversky, A., and Wilson, R. *Barriers to Conflict Resolution.* New York: Norton, 1995.

Fisher, R., Kopelman, E., and Schneider, A. K. *Beyond Machiavelli: Tools for Coping with Conflict.* Cambridge, Mass.: Harvard University Press, 1994.

Janus, I. *Groupthink: Psychological Studies of Policy Decisions and Fiascoes.* Boston: Houghton Mifflin, 1982.

Moore, C. W. *The Mediation Process.* (2nd ed.) San Francisco: Jossey-Bass, 1996.

Robinson, R. J. "Errors in Social Judgment: Implications for Negotiation and Conflict Resolution. Part 1: Biased Assimilation of Information." Case 897–103. Boston: Harvard Business School Publishing, 1997.

Robinson, R. J. "Errors in Social Judgment: Implications for Negotiation and Conflict Resolution. Part 2: Partisan Perceptions." Case 897–104. Boston: Harvard Business School Publishing, 1997.

Rubin, J. Z., Pruitt, D. G., and Kim, S. H. *Social Conflict: Escalation, Stalemate and Settlement.* (2nd ed.) New York: McGraw-Hill, 1994.

Touval, S., and Zartman, I. W. (eds.). *International Mediation in Theory and Practice.* Boulder, Colo.: Westview Press, 1985.

# ON DEVELOPING EXPERTISE

Christensen, C. R., Garvin, D., and Sweet, A. (eds.). *Education for Judgment: The Artistry of Discussion Leadership.* Boston: Harvard Business School Press, 1991.

Goffman, I. *Frame Analysis: An Essay on the Organization of Experience.* Cambridge, Mass.: Harvard University Press, 1974.

Klein, G. *Sources of Power: How People Make Decisions.* Cambridge, Mass.: MIT Press, 1998.

Schön, D. *The Reflective Practitioner: How Professionals Think in Action.* New York: Basic Books, 1983.

# UPDATE OF THE CASES

The negotiations we have chronicled unquestionably achieved break-throughs, but the conflicts they addressed are still very much with us today. Even highly successful negotiations between disputants are points on a continuum, not the end of the story. It may therefore be enlightening to trace the evolution of these conflicts since the events described in the cases. The following pages offer detailed chronologies of each conflict, in the same order in which they appear in the body of the book.

## UPDATE ON NORTH KOREA, 1994–2000

Since the signing of the Agreed Framework in October 1994, North Korea has suffered devastating floods, followed by famine and a severe economic downturn. These conditions have complicated implementation of the framework. Between North Korea and the United States, tension has alternated with small intermittent bursts of progress.

*January 1995*

- First fuel oil transfers from the United States to North Korea begin.
- The United States slightly lowers trade barriers to North Korea.

*February 1995*

- Problems arise over the details of the framework agreement: the United States wants South Korea to supply the light-water reactors to North Korea. Pyongyang rejects this plan.

- North Korea asks for more humanitarian aid.

*March 1995*

- The United States, South Korea, and Japan establish a consortium to implement the agreement with North Korea.

- Talks with North Korea stall over South Korean involvement.

*May 1995*

- North Korea reports food shortages.

*June 1995*

- A tentative deal is arrived at: the light-water reactors will not be labeled as originating in South Korea.

*September 1995*

- Floods devastate North Korea. Its government requests worldwide assistance.

*December 1995*

- A $4.5 billion agreement is signed on construction of light-water reactors.

- Widespread famine increases economic stress in North Korea.

*February 1996*

- The United States grants $2 million in humanitarian aid to North Korea over the objections of allies.

*June 1996*

- The United States grants $6 million more in aid to North Korea to prevent a flood of refugees into South Korea.

- Congress threatens to cut funding for the North Korean framework agreement.

*September 1996*

- A North Korean submarine is grounded in South Korean waters. Its presence there is seen as an aggressive move.

*December 1996*

- The United States, South Korea, and North Korea agree to preliminary discussions of negotiations to formally end the Korean War.

*Spring 1997*

- Severe famine continues in North Korea.
- Discussions continue on four-way (United States, North Korea, South Korea, and China) peace talks to end the Korean War.

*July 1997*

- The United States doubles food aid to North Korea.

*October 1997*

- Kim Jong Il officially takes control in North Korea.

*January 1998*

- The UN World Food Programme appeals for over $400 million in emergency assistance for North Korea.

*April 1998*

- South Korea and North Korea announce plans to resume bilateral talks on economic aid and other issues.

*June 1998*

- Another North Korean submarine is discovered in South Korean waters. Its entire crew is dead. The submarine sinks while being towed to shore.

*August 1998*

- A large underground facility is detected in North Korea.
- North Korea fires a ballistic missile into the Sea of Japan. Japan suspends food aid to North Korea. North Korea claims it launched a satellite that failed to reach orbit.

*September 1998*

- Another round of U.S.–North Korean talks is held. Progress is reported, but no agreement is reached on access to the underground facility.
- The United States admits that the suspected North Korean missile was indeed a failed satellite.

*October 1998*

- A new round of four-party talks is held in Geneva.

*November 1998*

- A U.S. inspection team visiting North Korea demands to visit the underground facility. North Korean officials denounce the demand as an insult and demand monetary compensation if the inspectors find no nuclear installation.

- The United States threatens to suspend the framework agreement unless inspections are allowed.

- Clinton visits South Korea. He and President Kim Dae Jung warn North Korea to clear up suspicions about the underground facility.

- North Korea continues to deny the existence of an underground nuclear site.

*December 1998*

- U.S. and North Korean negotiators hold talks on the suspect site. North Korea suggests food compensation instead of monetary compensation for permitting inspection of the site, but no deal is reached.

- South Korea's navy sinks a North Korean submarine off its southern coast. North Korea denies that the submarine was on a spy mission.

*January 1999*

- The United States and North Korea hold further talks on inspection of the suspect underground facility.

- Famine worsens in North Korea. Officials estimate 2 million deaths.

*March 1999*

- North Korea agrees to allow inspection of the suspect underground facility.

*April 1999*

- U.S. diplomatic efforts fail to convince North Korea to stop building and exporting missiles.

- North Korea, South Korea, China, and the United States begin a new round of talks.

*June 1999*

- North Korea and South Korea engage in a naval clash over their disputed sea border.

*July 1999*

- South Korea expresses alarm about potential long-range missile tests by North Korea.

- The United States warns North Korea that a missile firing would threaten the light-water reactor deal.

*August 1999*

- China test-fires a long-range missile, complicating efforts to prevent a similar North Korean test.
- North Korea agrees to talks with the United States about missile testing.

*September 1999*

- North Korea declares its sea border with South Korea invalid.
- North Korea agrees to freeze its missile-testing program.
- The Clinton administration announces plans to lift some trade sanctions on North Korea.

*April 2000*

- The two Koreas agree to a summit of their leaders in June.

*June 2000*

- North Korea's Kim Jong II and South Korea's President Kim Dae Jung begin a three-day summit in Pyongyang.

*July 2000*

- Russia's president, Vladimir Putin, visits North Korea. He asserts that North Korea will abandon its missile program if other nations provide it technology for space research.
- Putin presents a North Korean missile proposal at the G-8 summit.

*August 2000*

- Kim Jong II indicates that North Korea's missile offer was a joke.
- Some Korean families separated for fifty years by the war are reunited at a meeting sponsored by both governments.

*September 2000*

- In another sign of détente, South Korea repatriates sixty-three North Korean spies.
- The two Koreas march under a unified flag at the Sydney Olympics.

*October 2000*

- A high-level North Korean official meets with Clinton in Washington, D.C.

- South Korean president Kim Dae Jung receives the Nobel Peace Prize for his efforts to reduce tensions between North and South.

- U.S. Secretary of State Madeleine Albright visits North Korea and meets with Kim Jong II. Missile talks progress, but no agreement is reached.

*December 2000*

- The year ends with the possibility of a Clinton trip to North Korea fading until resolution can be reached in missile talks.

# UPDATE ON THE MIDDLE EAST PEACE PROCESS, 1994–2000

By the end of 2000, the Oslo Accord seemed like a distant memory. The peace process had limped along and then all but ended with incidents of violence by both sides. The year ended with continued violence and little hope of peace.

*February 1994*

- A militant Jewish settler massacres thirty-nine Palestinians praying at the main mosque in Hebron.

*May 1994*

- Israel and the PLO reach agreement on initial implementation of the Oslo Accords, including an Israeli military withdrawal from 60 percent of the Gaza Strip (excluding Jewish settlements and their environs) and the West Bank town of Jericho.

*July 1994*

- Arafat returns to Gaza after nearly twelve years in Tunis to serve as head of the new Palestinian self-rule authority.

*October 1994*

- An Israel-Jordan peace treaty is signed. Israel agrees to respect Jordan's special role as custodian of Muslim holy shrines in Jerusalem.

*September 1995*

- Arafat and Rabin sign an agreement, known as Oslo II, to expand Palestinian self-rule in the West Bank and Gaza and to allow Palestinian elections.

*November 1995*

- Israeli prime minister Yitzhak Rabin is assassinated by an orthodox Jewish student who opposes Israeli withdrawals from the West Bank. Shimon Peres becomes prime minister.

- Israelis pull out troops and give Palestinians limited autonomy in six cities on the West Bank as part of the Oslo Accords.

*January 1996*

- In their first elections since the formation of Israel, Palestinians elect Arafat president of the Palestinian Authority.

*February–March 1996*

- A series of suicide bomb attacks by Hamas kills fifty-seven Israelis.

*April 1996*

- Israel begins a seventeen-day bombardment of Lebanon. Lebanese guerrillas fire rockets at populated areas of northern Israel. Israel shells a UN base at Qana, killing about one hundred of eight hundred civilians sheltering there.

*May 1996*

- In Israeli parliamentary and prime ministerial elections, Shimon Peres loses to Benjamin Netanyahu, who campaigned against the Rabin-Peres peace program under the motto "Peace with Security."

*August 1996*

- The Israeli government begins to lift a four-year freeze on building new Jewish settlements in the West Bank and Gaza Strip.

*September 1996*

- Israel opens an archaeological site near Muslim shrines in Jerusalem. Violent protests claim the lives of sixty-one Arabs and fifteen Israeli soldiers.

*January 1997*

- Israel cedes 80 percent of Hebron to Palestinian rule but holds onto the remainder, where several hundred Jewish settlers live among twenty thousand Palestinians.

*March 1997*

- Israel defies world opinion by breaking ground on a settlement to complete a ring of similar Jewish settlements around occupied Palestinian East Jerusalem.

*September 1997*

- Israeli agents posing as Canadian tourists bungle an attempted assassination of a Hamas military leader in Jordan, leading to a crisis in relations between Israel and both Jordan and Canada. Jordan forces Israel to atone by releasing the Hamas spiritual leader Sheikh Ahmad Yassin.

*October 1998*

- Negotiations are completed on the Wye River Memorandum outlining further Israeli withdrawals from the West Bank in response to U.S. pressure to end eighteen months of stagnation on the Israeli-Palestinian peace track.

- The Wye agreement establishes a timetable: upon the Palestinians' fulfillment of each in a series of commitments, Israel agrees to transfer a specified percentage of land to the Palestinians within the context of the "further redeployments" as stated in previous agreements.

*January 1999*

- The Israeli Knesset votes to hold elections in May when the Netanyahu coalition collapses in disarray over implementation of the Wye deal. Israel suspends the Wye timetable.

*February 1999*

- King Hussein of Jordan dies. It was he who spearheaded movement toward normalization of relations between Israel and the Arab states.

*May 1999*

- Labor Party leader Ehud Barak decisively defeats Netanyahu and pledges to be a prime minister for all Israelis.

*September 1999*

- Israel and the Palestinians sign a revised deal, based on the stalled Wye River accord, aimed at reviving the Middle East peace process.

*November 1999*

- Final-status talks resume between Israel and the Palestinians.

*December 1999*

- The Palestinians withdraw from final-status talks to protest the construction of new Israeli settlements in the West Bank. Barak responds by announcing a freeze on the construction of eighteen hundred more houses in Jewish settlements around Jerusalem.

- Barak meets Syria's foreign minister, Farouk al-Shara, in Washington for high-level talks. Negotiations resume in the new year but are suspended in January without explanation. The breakdown triggers a new round of violence in Lebanon.

*February 2000*

- A summit between Barak and Arafat breaks down over disagreement about an Israeli withdrawal from the West Bank specified by the revised Wye accord.
- Final-status negotiations between Israel and the Palestinians deadlock.

*March 2000*

- Israel hands over 6.1 percent of the West Bank to the Palestinians, the final step in a transfer originally agreed to at Wye River in 1998. Palestinian and Israeli negotiators meet in Washington to restart final-status talks.
- Presidents Clinton and Assad fail to break the deadlock on the Syrian-Israeli track.

*July 2000*

- A peace summit at Camp David produces no agreement despite two weeks of intensive negotiations involving Barak and Arafat. The negotiators cannot reconcile their competing claims to Jerusalem.

*September 2000*

- Ariel Sharon, leader of the right-wing Israeli opposition, visits the Temple Mount, sacred to both Jews and Muslims. Coinciding with the failure of the peace process, the visit sparks violence that leaves over three hundred dead by mid-December.

*October 2000*

- Arafat, Barak, and Secretary of State Madeleine K. Albright hold three-way talks in Paris. Arafat declines to sign an accord because of failure to agree on terms for an international inquiry into Israeli actions in response to Palestinian protests.
- The UN Security Council adopts a resolution condemning Israel's use of force against the Palestinians.
- The UN secretary-general, Kofi Annan, scrambles to get agreement on a cease-fire. Violence ebbs slightly.
- Clinton presides over a summit in Egypt that produces plans to end weeks of Palestinian-Israeli violence. The plan promptly unravels.

*November 2000*

- As momentum for a cease-fire builds, a car bomb in Jerusalem kills two Israelis, including the daughter of a prominent Israeli politician.
- Barak and Arafat agree to separate talks with Clinton. As Arafat heads to Washington, violence claims seven more lives.
- A missile fired by an Israeli army helicopter kills a senior militia commander in a targeted slaying.
- Arafat expresses support for an unarmed UN presence in the West Bank, Gaza, and Jerusalem.
- Barak meets with Clinton and calls for Arafat to make public statements to quell the violence.
- In retaliation for the bombing of an Israeli school bus in Gaza, Israeli helicopter gunships launch missiles at Palestinian Authority offices.
- Israeli soldiers fire on two cars in the Gaza Strip, killing four Palestinians whom the army describes as militants. Later, a car bomb explodes in the Israeli town of Hadera, leaving two Israelis dead.
- In a telephone call arranged by President Vladimir Putin, Barak and Arafat agree to resume limited cooperation on security issues.
- Israeli warplanes and helicopters attack southern Lebanon for the first time in six months after a roadside bomb kills an Israeli soldier.
- Facing overwhelming defeat in parliament, Barak agrees to hold new elections.

*December 2000*

- Violence grips the West Bank and Jerusalem, killing seven Palestinians and three Israelis.
- Israeli and Palestinian negotiators agree to talks to try to revive the peace process.

*Early 2001*

- Ariel Sharon decisively defeats Barak to become prime minister of Israel and seeks to form a national unity government.

# UPDATE ON IRAQ, 1991–2000

Operation Desert Storm caused significant damage to Iraq but left Saddam Hussein in power. A cease-fire, negotiated in March 1991, provided for UN inspections and monitoring of Iraqi weapons sites for weapons of mass destruction.

These provisions have generated constant conflict, as have Iraqi demands that sanctions be lifted.

*March 1991*

- A cease-fire is negotiated with Iraq.
- Iraq releases American civilian hostages and prisoners of war.
- Kuwaitis who fled abroad return home.
- The UN eases restrictions on imports of food and humanitarian aid to Iraq.

*April 1991*

- Brutal fighting continues between Kurdish rebels and Iraqi troops loyal to Saddam Hussein.
- U.S. troops establish a safety zone for Kurdish refugees in northern Iraq.

*July 1991*

- A UN inspections team is denied access to a suspected weapons-of-mass-destruction site by Iraq.
- U.S. and allied troops pull out of southern Iraq.

*August 1991*

- Iraq admits to germ warfare research.
- The standoff over arms inspections continues.

*September 1991*

- Iraq allows UN Special Commission (UNSCOM) inspectors access to its sites, then detains them for thirteen hours and seizes their data.
- After a three-day standoff, the inspectors are released with data.

*March 1992*

- The UN charges Iraq with violations of the cease-fire agreement.

*Spring–Summer 1992*

- Political controversy emerges in the United States over prewar U.S. aid to Iraq after its war with Iran.

*July 1992*

- Another standoff occurs over inspectors' access to weapons sites.
- After a three-week delay, Baghdad allows UN inspectors access to requested documents.

*August 1992*

- The United States and allies establish a no-fly zone over the southern third of Iraq.

*October 1992*

- UN inspectors in Iraq are threatened but are eventually allowed to continue their work.

*January 1993*

- Iraq deploys surface-to-air missiles within the no-fly zone.
- The United States demands removal of the surface-to-air missiles. Iraq backs down and removes them.
- Iraq bars a plane carrying weapons inspectors from landing in Baghdad.
- The United States undertakes limited air strikes. Bush orders three attacks in six days during his last week in office.
- Clinton takes office.
- U.S. fighter planes attack an antiaircraft battery.

*May 1993*

- The Clinton administration uncovers an Iraqi plot to assassinate former president Bush during a visit to Kuwait.

*June 1993*

- The United States fires two dozen missiles at the headquarters of the Iraqi Intelligence Service in retaliation for the Bush assassination plot.

*July 1993*

- Iraq blocks installation of UN surveillance cameras at its missile-testing sites.
- UN inspectors leave Iraq after being prevented from sealing two missile-testing sites.
- The UN and Iraq continue talks to resolve inspection issues.
- Iraq agrees to long-term international monitoring of its weapons systems.

*September 1994*

- The United States faces international pressure to support lifting of sanctions on Iraq.

*October 1994*

- Iraq masses troops on the Kuwaiti border.
- The United States sends ground troops back to Kuwait.
- The initiative to lift sanctions on Iraq dissolves.
- After two weeks, Iraq pulls back its troops.

*November 1994*

- Iraq acknowledges the sovereignty of Kuwait.

*March 1995*

- The United States blocks efforts to lift the embargo on Iraqi oil.

*April 1995*

- The UN offers a partial easing of the embargo on Iraqi oil. Iraqi officials denounce the offer.

*July 1995*

- Iraq admits to production of biological weapons of mass destruction.

*August 1995*

- Two top-level Iraqi officials (both members of Hussein's family) defect to Jordan.
- Iraq gives the UN documentation of large-scale efforts to build nuclear weapons.

*February 1996*

- One Iraqi defector returns to Baghdad and is executed.

*March 1996*

- Iraq bars a UN inspection team seeking military records. An eleven-hour standoff ends with admission of the inspectors.

*May 1996*

- Iraq accepts the terms of a UN oil-for-food plan.

*September 1996*

- Iraqi troops enter the protected Kurdish zone in northern Iraq. In retaliation, the United States fires cruise missiles at an Iraqi air defense installation.

- The United States receives less international support than in earlier confrontations.
- Iraqis launch a missile attack on U.S. aircraft patrolling the no-fly zone.
- The United States sends more troops to the Gulf.
- Iraq agrees not to target U.S. aircraft.

*Fall 1996*

- Ethnic fighting continues in northern Iraq.
- The oil-for-food deal is delayed by disagreements over distribution.

*November 1996*

- The long-delayed oil-for-food deal proceeds.

*Spring 1997*

- The possible use of chemical weapons by Iraq during the Gulf War is disclosed.

*October 1997*

- Iraq threatens to expel the U.S. members of a multinational UN inspections team.

*November 1997*

- The UN Security Council tells the inspection team to ignore the Iraqi demand for expulsion of its American members.
- Iraq refuses entry to three American arms inspectors and subsequently expels six others.
- Russia negotiates with Iraq. The two nations reach agreement to allow the expelled inspectors to return.
- Iraq declares certain inspection sites off-limits, including the so-called presidential sites.

*December 1997*

- The Security Council extends the oil-for-food deal.
- Iraq shuts down its oil pipeline to protest the slow delivery of food and medical supplies.
- Chief UN arms inspector Richard Butler visits Iraq and reports little hope of gaining access to presidential sites.
- Iraqi oil exports resume after some food and supplies are received.

*January 1998*

- The United States calls for a probe of reported mass executions of political prisoners in Iraq.
- Iraq complains of too many Americans on the new UN inspection team and threatens to block their entry.
- In response, the United States and Britain send carriers to the Gulf. Both countries try to build an alliance to use force against Iraq.

*February 1998*

- The United States sends more troops to the Gulf while a diplomatic solution to the dispute over inspections is being sought.
- The United States threatens possible air strikes if inspections are not allowed.
- UN Secretary General Kofi Annan visits Baghdad to try to end the standoff over inspections. Annan announces that an agreement has been reached.
- The United States supports the deal but retains the right to attack if Iraq does not honor the agreement.

*March 1998*

- UN weapons inspections resume. The team is led by the U.S. inspector previously denied entry into Iraq.

*April 1998*

- No signs of nuclear or chemical weapons are found in Iraqi palaces.
- Iraq asks the UN to lift sanctions. The UN votes to continue sanctions.

*May 1998*

- The United States cuts its forces in the Gulf.
- The UN approves continuation of the oil-for-food plan.

*June 1998*

- UN chief weapons inspector Richard Butler shows the Security Council proof of Iraqi concealment of weapons of mass destruction. Iraq denies the charges.
- Iraq and the UN agree to a two-month timetable to resolve outstanding inspection questions.
- UN inspectors find traces of nerve gas on a destroyed missile at a weapons facility near Baghdad.

*August 1998*

- Hussein announces that Iraq will no longer cooperate with UN inspectors, but will allow existing monitoring cameras and sensors to stay in place.

- The United States threatens to use force if Iraq does not fully comply.

- The American leader of the UN weapons inspection team resigns in anger over lack of strong action against Iraq.

*September 1998*

- The inspections standoff continues.

*October 1998*

- Iraq announces suspension of all cooperation with UNSCOM, including monitoring functions.

*November 1998*

- Despite the announced suspension, the UN team is allowed to check its surveillance equipment at weapons sites.

- The United States seeks international support for military action against Iraq.

- The UN Security Council votes to condemn Iraq for its refusal to permit inspections.

- UN inspectors leave Iraq. U.S. forces are ready to strike.

- Iraq backs down and agrees to allow weapons inspections to resume. U.S. forces are within minutes of striking.

- Weapons inspectors return to Iraq and resume work. A dispute arises over access to critical documents.

*December 1998*

- UN inspectors carry out surprise inspections at multiple sites. They are denied access to Baath Party headquarters.

- UN inspectors leave Iraq and report that Iraq failed to cooperate fully.

- The United States and the United Kingdom launch a military strike, Operation Desert Fox, bombing Baghdad and military targets for four nights. International reaction is mixed. Heavy casualties are reported in Iraq.

- Iraq fires at U.S. planes patrolling the no-fly zone, and U.S. jets bombard an Iraqi missile site in response.

- Iraq vows to continue to defy the no-fly zone.

*January 1999*

- Iraq stops issuing visas to UN aid workers.

- It is revealed that the United States used a UN agency to spy on Hussein.

- U.S. warplanes bomb surface-to-air missile installations in southern Iraq. A misfire of a U.S. missile causes civilian casualties.

*February and March 1999*

- U.S. and British planes repeatedly bomb air defense sites in northern Iraq, citing violations of the no-fly zone.

- Iraq threatens to launch missiles at neighboring countries.

*April 1999*

- U.S. air strikes resume after a two-week break. Air strikes on radar and command-and-control centers become an almost daily occurrence.

*September 1999*

- A U.S.-British proposal to send weapons inspectors back to Iraq fails in the Security Council.

*December 1999*

- The UN oil-for-food plan is extended for six months.

- The UN Security Council is deeply divided over suspension of sanctions and sending weapons inspectors back to Iraq.

- The Security Council creates a new inspection agency to complete destruction of Iraqi weapons of mass destruction. The plan includes suspension of sanctions if Iraq cooperates with inspectors. Iraq rejects the plan.

*January 2000*

- The UN proceeds with the plan to create a new agency. An agreement is reached for Hans Blix to chair the new agency.

*June 2000*

- The Security Council undertakes an assessment of the impact of ten years of economic sanctions on the population of Iraq.

*August 2000*

- A new UN inspection team prepares to go to Iraq. Iraq indicates the team will be denied entry. The UN team avoids confrontation by delaying an attempt at inspection.

*September 2000*

- Defying sanctions, a French plane carrying physicians and other passengers on a humanitarian mission lands in Baghdad.

*October–December 2000*

- Soaring oil prices increase Iraq's negotiating power.
- Resumption of international flights to Iraq, a successful international trade fair in Baghdad, and renewed diplomatic ties all suggest that the trade embargo is on the verge of collapse.

# UPDATE ON BOSNIA, 1995–2000

Peace has not come easily to Bosnia since the Dayton accords, but the country has gradually begun to reestablish a sense of normalcy. NATO peacekeeping troops remain in place, and ethnic battles have erupted in other republics of the former Yugoslavia, but Bosnians have successfully held democratic elections and have significantly rebuilt since the end of the war. The War Crimes Tribunal has arrested, tried, and convicted a number of war criminals, and its work continues.

*December 1995*

- NATO troops start arriving in Bosnia.
- A peace treaty is formally signed in Paris.
- The UN hands over peacekeeping duties to NATO.

*February 1996*

- Balkan leaders meet and reaffirm their commitment to the Dayton accords.

*Spring 1996*

- The War Crimes Tribunal convenes in the Hague.
- Violations of the peace accords cause delays in implementation.

*Summer 1996*

- Tension builds over indicted war criminals still in office in Bosnia. Holbrooke returns to Bosnia to negotiate their removal.

*July 1996*

- Radovan Karadzic resigns as president of the self-declared Bosnian Serb Republic but is not arrested as an indicted war criminal.

- The UN uncovers evidence of a massacre of civilians in Srebrenica.

*August 1996*

- The first shipment of U.S. arms arrives as part of a plan to equip and train Croats and Muslims.

*September 1996*

- Bosnia's first national elections are held with little violence. A three-person copresidency (one Muslim, one Serb, one Croat) takes office.

*October 1996*

- The United States extends its troop commitment.
- The UN lifts economic sanctions on Bosnia.

*December 1996*

- The multiethnic presidency agrees to a six-member Council of Ministers consisting of two Muslims, two Serbs, and two Croats.

*Spring 1997*

- Ethnic skirmishes continue.
- Some convictions are handed down by the War Crimes Tribunal.

*July 1997*

- Palvsic, the Bosnian Serb president, dissolves parliament, defying Karadzic, who continues to wield power behind the scenes.
- A power struggle continues between Palvsic and hard-liners loyal to Karadzic.

*September 1997*

- The first municipal elections since 1990 are held in Bosnia.
- Another mass grave is found in Bihac.
- NATO troops thwart a plan by hard-line Serbs to oust Palvsic violently.

*November 1997*

- Parliamentary elections are held in Bosnia. The Bosnian Serb hard-liners lose their majority.

*December 1997*

- Clinton announces that U.S. troops will stay in Bosnia indefinitely.

*January 1998*

- The Bosnian Serb parliament elects a moderate prime minister. The hard-liners are losing ground.

*February 1998*

- Bosnia sends a team to the Winter Olympics.

*March 1998*

- Air travel resumes between Bosnia and the rest of Yugoslavia.

*Spring 1998*

- Conflict erupts in Kosovo, a semiautonomous region that is the seat of the Serbian church, but with a 90 percent ethnic Albanian majority.
- Serb forces attack ethnic Albanian towns defended by a separatist group, the Kosovo Liberation Army (KLA).

*May 1998*

- Serbia begins talks with Albanians regarding Kosovo.

*Summer 1998*

- Fighting continues in Kosovo.
- The KLA is severely weakened.

*September 1998*

- The UN Security Council calls for a cease-fire in Kosovo. Alarm is expressed about the safety of civilians who have fled to the mountains as winter approaches.
- National elections are held in Serbia. A Serb hard-liner is elected copresident, but many moderates win at other levels, including parliament.
- A Kosovo cease-fire is negotiated.

*November 1998*

- A senior Bosnian Serb general is arrested and charged with genocide in the massacre at Srebrenica.
- Skirmishes continue in Kosovo.

*December 1998*

- Karadzic is still at large.
- Sentiment grows within the U.S. government for the removal of Milosevic.

- The cease-fire in Kosovo is threatened by increased violence.
- A fragile truce is reestablished at Christmas.

*January 1999*
- The United States reduces its troop contingent in Bosnia.

*March 1999*
- An international arbitration panel designates a thirty-square-mile area of northern Bosnia as neutral and under international supervision, instead of granting it to the Bosnian Serb Republic. Bosnian Serbs react angrily.
- Reports continue of brutal violence against ethnic Albanians in Kosovo by Yugoslav troops.
- American jets shoot down two Yugoslav MiGs that cross into airspace over Bosnia.

*March–June 1999*
- In response to violence in Kosovo, NATO planes conduct seventy-eight days of air strikes against Yugoslavia.

*June 1999*
- Yugoslav and NATO generals sign a pact providing for an end to NATO bombing, withdrawal of Yugoslav troops from Kosovo, return of ethnic Albanian refugees to Kosovo, and deployment of forty thousand NATO-led international peacekeepers.

*July 1999*
- NATO cuts its Bosnia force by half in order to focus on Kosovo.

*November 1999*
- The UN admits partial responsibility for the July 1995 massacre in Srebrenica.

*April 2000*
- Tens of thousands of Serbs in Belgrade protest, calling for Milosevic's resignation.

*July 2000*
- Milosevic rewrites the constitution so he can run for reelection. He is opposed by a coalition of opposition groups lead by Vojislav Kostunica.

*September 2000*

- Serbs vote in unprecedented numbers.

- Kostunica declares victory.

- The state election commission announces election returns: 48 percent for Kostunica and 40 percent for Milosevic. A runoff is scheduled.

- Scattered strikes break out across Serbia, adding pressure on Milosevic to give up power.

*October 2000*

- Anti-Milosevic protests sweep across Serbia.

- Milosevic appears to lose the support of Serbian police.

- The UN denies Milosevic an immunity deal if he steps down.

- Hundreds of thousands seize control of parliament, the state-run media, and other key institutions.

- Russia officially abandons Milosevic.

- Commanders of the army side with Kostunica.

- The constitutional court declares Kostunica victorious.

- Milosevic surrenders power and concedes the presidency to Kostunica.

- The Serb parliament dissolves itself to pave the way for a transitional government. Milosevic's allies still jockey for power in government agencies.

- Kostunica's and Milosevic's allies agree to share power until new parliamentary elections in December.

*December 2000*

- Kostunica supporters in the Democratic Opposition of Serbia win 64 percent of the parliamentary vote; Milosevic's Socialist Party receives 14 percent. The year ends with Kostunica firmly in power and Milosevic's fate up in the air.

# NOTES

## Preface

1. The term *thick description* was coined by anthropologist Clifford Geertz. See C. Geertz, *The Interpretation of Cultures: Selected Essays* (Centerport, N.Y.: Fontana Press, 1993).

## Introduction

1. This distinction is developed in J. Sebenius, "Introduction to Negotiation Analysis: Structure, People, and Context," Harvard Business School Note 896–034 (1996).

2. H. Kissinger, *White House Years* (New York: Little, Brown, 1979), p. 62.

3. "U.N. Chief Tries Again to Get Iraq to Allow Arms Searches," *New York Times*, Aug. 10, 1998.

4. Roger Fisher argued that every negotiator has a dual role as partisan advocate and as comediator. See R. Fisher, "Negotiating Inside Out: What Are the Best Ways to Relate Internal Negotiations with External Ones?" in *Negotiation Theory and Practice*, ed. J. W. Breslin and J. Z. Rubin (Cambridge, Mass.: PON Books, 1991).

5. This model bridges the structure-process gap in the study of negotiation. It accounts for both the impact of structure on process and the impact of process on structure. An earlier version of this model is presented in M. Watkins, *Shaping the Structure of Negotiations*, Program on Negotiation Monograph M98–1 (Cambridge,

Mass.: PON Books, 1998). Walton, McKersie, and Cutcher-Gershenfeld developed a related framework, analyzing negotiation in terms of forces shaping negotiators' choices and an interaction system consisting of strategies, processes, and structures. See R. Walton, R. McKersie, and J. Cutcher-Gershenfeld, *Strategic Negotiations: A Theory of Change in Labor-Management Relations* (Boston: Harvard Business School Press, 1994). Sebenius analyzed negotiation in terms of structure, people, and context, as well as barriers and opportunities for creating and claiming value. See J. Sebenius, "Introduction to Negotiation Analysis: Structure, People, and Context," Harvard Business School Note 896–034 (1996).

# Chapter One

1. S. Coll and D. B. Ottaway, "New Threats Create Doubt in US Policy," *Washington Post,* Apr. 13, 1995.

2. General Robert Riscassi interview (Nov. 28, 1994). Unless otherwise noted, all Riscassi quotes are taken from this interview.

3. Just a few months earlier, Secretary of State Dean Acheson had declared that the United States considered Korea "outside the defense perimeter of U.S. interests," leading some observers to hold the United States partly culpable for the invasion.

4. The long, frustrating talks gave rise to a kind of mythology about Communist negotiating tactics, characterized in the West as devious, manipulative, exploitative of concessions, and geared toward propaganda rather than results. See, for example, Admiral C. Turner Joy, *How Communists Negotiate* (New York: Macmillan, 1955).

5. The U.S. government rarely wavered from its neither-confirm-nor-deny policy on the presence of U.S. nuclear weapons in South Korea, but it was widely believed to have had such weapons there since 1958.

6. Bruce Cumings interview (Nov. 22, 1994). Unless otherwise noted, all Cumings quotes are taken from this interview.

7. The phased reduction, part of the Defense Department's East Asia Strategy Initiative realignment, was halted after 7,000 troops had been withdrawn, leaving U.S. forces in South Korea at about 37,000.

8. Selig Harrison interview (Dec. 14, 1994). Unless otherwise noted, all Harrison quotes are taken from this interview.

9. NPT members, other than the five nuclear-power signatories (China, England, France, Russia, and the United States), were barred from possessing nuclear weapons, but received aid to develop nuclear energy for peaceful purposes.

10. Robert Manning interview (Dec. 20, 1994). Unless otherwise noted, all Manning quotes are taken from this interview.

11. Air-launched nuclear weapons were added to the pot the following month.

12. North Korea denounced the annual Team Spirit war games as a rehearsal for a U.S. nuclear attack, and each year responded with its own military buildup and display of saber rattling.

13. "The Koreas; Look, No Bomb," *Economist,* Jan. 4, 1992.

14. General Brent Scowcroft interview with writer (Jan. 4, 1995).

15. Arnold Kanter interview (Jan. 6, 1995). Unless otherwise noted, all Kanter quotes are taken from this interview.

16. M. Reiss, *Bridled Ambition: Why Countries Constrain Their Nuclear Capabilities* (Washington, D.C.: Woodrow Wilson Center Press, 1995), p. 293.

17. Richard Solomon interview (Jan. 23, 1995). Unless otherwise noted, all Solomon quotes are taken from this interview.

18. Robert Carlin interview (Jan. 5, 1995). Unless otherwise noted, all Carlin quotes are taken from this interview.

19. The IAEA had never before requested a special inspection of an undeclared site, and had only recently asserted its authority to perform such inspections in the wake of its negative experiences in Iraq.

20. William Clark interview (Dec. 15, 1994). Unless otherwise noted, all Clark quotes are taken from this interview.

21. Kent Wiedemann interview (Jan. 5, 1995). Unless otherwise noted, all Wiedemann quotes are taken from this interview.

22. Norman Wulf interview (Jan. 6, 1995). Unless otherwise noted, all Wulf quotes are taken from this interview.

23. Robert Suettinger interview (Jan. 4, 1995). Unless otherwise noted, all Suettinger quotes are taken from this interview.

24. A visiting Southeast Asian ambassador, asked for his country's reaction to a DPRK nuclear bomb, replied, "We think that would lead to Japan possessing nuclear weapons. And if Japan possesses nuclear weapons, we must."

## Chapter Two

1. For an early effort to characterize the structure of negotiations, see Chapter One of H. Raiffa, *The Art and Science of Negotiation* (Cambridge, Mass.: Harvard University Press, 1982). For a more developed framework, see J. Sebenius, "Negotiation Analysis: A Characterization and Review." *Management Science* 38 (1992): 18–38.

2. See D. Lax and J. Sebenius, "Thinking Coalitionally," in *Negotiation Analysis,* ed. P. Young (Ann Arbor: University of Michigan Press, 1991).

3. F. C. Iklé, *How Nations Negotiate* (Millwood, N.Y.: Kraus, 1964), pp. 222–233.

4. Fisher and Ury made the crucial distinction between positions and interests. See R. Fisher, W. Ury, and B. Patton, *Getting to Yes: Negotiating Agreement Without Giving In,* 2nd ed. (New York: Penguin Books, 1991).

5. Iklé (1964), Op. Cit., p. 2: "To begin with, two elements must normally be present for negotiation to take place: there must be both common interests and issues on conflict. Without common interests there is nothing to negotiate for, without conflicting interests there is nothing to negotiate about. . . . One should perhaps distinguish between two kinds of common interests: a substantive common interest

in a single arrangement or object, and a complementary interest in an exchange of different objects. In the substantive common interest, the parties want to share the same object or benefit from the same arrangement, which, however, they can bring about only by joining together. When parties are interested in an exchange, they want different things. These they cannot obtain by themselves but only can grant to each other."

6. For approaches to assessing interests, see Chapter Three of Fisher, Ury, and Patton (1991), Op. Cit., and Chapter Four of D. Lax and J. Sebenius, *The Manager as Negotiator* (New York: Free Press, 1986). Fisher, Ury, and Patton note that negotiators have interests in both substance and relationships. "Every negotiator wants an agreement that satisfies his substantive interests. That is why one negotiates. Beyond that, a negotiator also has an interest in his relationship with the other side" (p. 19).

7. People tend to have a strong psychological need for consistency. See Chapter Three of R. B. Cialdini, *Influence: The Psychology of Persuasion* (New York: Morrow, 1993). See also P. Zimbardo and M. Leippe, *The Psychology of Attitude Change and Social Influence* (New York: McGraw-Hill,1991).

8. For a discussion of side effects that can flow from negotiations, see Chapter Four of Iklé (1964), Op. Cit.

9. See Lax and Sebenius (1991), Op. Cit.

10. See Chapter 6 of Fisher, Ury, and Patton (1991), Op. Cit.

11. For a discussion of the relationships among BATNAs, ZOPAs, and reservation prices, see Chapter Four of Raiffa (1982), Op. Cit.

12. Walton and McKersie termed this "the bargaining range." See R. Walton and R. McKersie, *A Behavioral Theory of Labor Negotiations* (Ithaca, N.Y.: ILR Press, 1965). Raiffa (1982), Op. Cit., called it "the Zone of Agreement." Lax and Sebenius (1986), Op. Cit., called it "the Zone of Possible Agreement."

13. Lax and Sebenius define power as the ability to shape perceptions of the zone of possible agreement. See Chapter Nine of Lax and Sebenius (1986), Op. Cit. They note that "analyzing power in and of itself has often proved to be a sterile exercise. However, directly focusing on factors that can change perceptions of the bargaining set and the ways that such changes influence outcomes seems a more fruitful approach for both theory and practice" (p. 257).

14. Walton and McKersie (1965), Op. Cit., made the important distinction between distributive and integrative bargaining in Chapters Two through Five. They also noted that negotiators may engage in negotiations involving a mix of distributive and integrative bargaining, which they termed "mixed motive" (see Chapter Five). Lax and Sebenius (1986), Op. Cit., reconceptualized the distinction between distributive and integrative bargaining. Rather than discrete types of bargaining, they view value claiming and value creating as processes that go on in parallel in most negotiations. "Negotiators should focus on the dynamic aspects of negotiation, the process of creating and claiming value" (p. 254). "Value creating and value claim-

ing are linked parts of negotiation. Both processes are present. No matter how much creative problem-solving enlarges the pie, it still must be divided; value that has been created must be claimed" (p. 33).

15. For a discussion of approaches to claiming value, see Chapter Six of Lax and Sebenius (1986), Op. Cit.

16. Walton and McKersie (1965), Op. Cit., noted that negotiations may involve a mix of distributive and integrative bargaining, which they termed "mixed motive." See Chapter Five.

17. Raiffa (1982), Op. Cit., Chapter Ten, develops the idea of the efficient frontier in the context of two-party, many-issue negotiations. "The efficient frontier—sometimes called the Pareto Optimal Frontier after economist Vilfredo Pareto—is defined as the locus of achievable joint evaluations from which no joint gains are possible" (p. 139).

18. These ideas are developed in M. Watkins and S. Passow, "Analyzing Linked Systems of Negotiations," *Negotiation Journal* 12 (1996).

19. J. A. Baker, *The Politics of Diplomacy: Revolution, War, and Peace* (New York: Putnam, 1995), p. 134.

20. These ideas are developed in M. Watkins, "Building Momentum in Negotiations: Time-Related Costs and Action-Forcing Events," *Negotiation Journal* 14 (1998): 241–256.

# Chapter Three

1. Gary Samore interview (Jan. 5, 1995). Unless otherwise noted, all Samore quotes are taken from this interview.

2. Robert Gallucci interview (Jan. 19, 1995). Unless otherwise noted, all Gallucci quotes are taken from this interview.

3. Thomas Hubbard interview (Feb. 14, 1995). Unless otherwise noted, all Hubbard quotes are taken from this interview.

4. Korea Desk officers trying to arrange the talks could not figure out how to notify their North Korean counterparts, given longstanding U.S. policy forbidding direct communication with the DPRK. After reading speculation about talks in the press, the North broke the logjam by calling first.

5. Just days before the talks started, the North had raised the stakes by test-firing a nuclear-capable missile, the Rodong 1, with a range that included most of Japan.

6. The IAEA had conducted some limited inspections in May.

7. Thomas Flanagan interview (Jan. 6, 1995). Unless otherwise noted, all Flanagan quotes are taken from this interview.

8. The DPRK's mood may have been soured by Clinton's recent visit to Seoul, during which he had declared that if the North built and used nuclear bombs, it would "be the end of their country as they know it."

9. Although the request appeared far-fetched, North Korea had wanted LWRs since the mid-1980s, when the Soviet Union had pledged four such reactors as an incentive to join the NPT—a promise the Soviet Union had failed to fulfill.

10. Jon Wolfsthal interview (Nov. 30, 1994). Unless otherwise noted, all Wolfsthal quotes are taken from this interview.

11. Even the State Department got into the act. Spokesman Mike McCurry declared on November 8 that it was "a matter of days" before the continuity of safeguards was lost.

12. According to one State Department insider, no one in the administration wanted to cross the Joint Chiefs, whom Clinton had alienated with his early stand on allowing gays in the military.

13. Although Washington had sought Beijing's help from the start, China may have been in no mood to cooperate. Relations between the two capitals had been strained over China's most-favored-nation trading status, which the president had threatened to revoke for human-rights abuses.

14. The IAEA had by this time accepted a more limited inspection regime to help defuse the conflict. For more details, see Chapter Six of M. Reiss, *Bridled Ambition: Why Countries Constrain Their Nuclear Capabilities* (Washington, D.C.: Woodrow Wilson Center Press, 1995). According to one official, the decision to include Team Spirit was reached just hours before the agreement. "You wouldn't believe the frustration," he says. "You could not get a cohesive focus on this issue."

15. D. Sanger, "North Korea, on Long Leash, Runs Circles Around Its Foes," *New York Times,* Mar. 20. 1994.

16. On the day the United States extended most-favored-nation status to China, James Lilley, attending a meeting with Japanese, Chinese, and South Korean representatives, announced, "The black crepe goes up in Pyongyang today."

17. The care taken to downplay the buildup reflected both fear of intensifying North Korea's sense of being under siege and sensitivity toward the South, whose long years under repressive military rule had left it leery of armed intervention.

18. ". . . Nor Time to Waste on Korea," *Washington Post,* June 9, 1994.

19. "Korea: Time for Action," *Washington Post,* June 15, 1994.

# Chapter Four

1. The focus on barriers to agreement builds on Kenneth Arrow, Robert Mnookin, Lee Ross, Amos Tversky, and Robert Wilson, eds., *Barriers to Conflict Resolution* (New York: Norton, 1995), a very important cross-disciplinary examination of the reasons that conflicts persist.

2. The introductory chapter of Arrow et al. (1995), Ibid., posits three broad classes of barriers: tactical and strategic, psychological, and institutional, organizational, or structural barriers. See also R. Mnookin, "Why Negotiations Fail: An Exploration

of Barriers to the Resolution of Conflict," *NIDR Forum* (Summer–Fall 1993): 21–31. Sebenius proposes structural barriers as a distinct category. See J. Sebenius, "Introduction to Negotiation Analysis: Structure, People, and Context," Harvard Business School Note 896–034 (1996). We believe that cultural barriers are a distinct category. Note that these various types of barriers can complicate any negotiation, not just those involving conflicts.

3. These dimensions of negotiation structure are developed in M. Watkins, "Negotiation Analysis: A Synthesis," Harvard Business School Note 800–316 (2000). See also J. Sebenius, "Dealing with Blocking Coalitions and Related Barriers to Agreement," in Arrow et al. (1995).

4. See Chapters One and Six of Arrow et al. (1995), Op. Cit.

5. See Chapter Three of R. Fisher, R. Kopelman, and A. K. Schneider, *Beyond Machiavelli: Tools for Coping with Conflict* (Cambridge, Mass.: Harvard University Press, 1994).

6. See Chapters Five and Six of D. Lax and J. Sebenius, *The Manager as Negotiator* (New York: Free Press, 1986).

7. Luce and Raiffa attribute the formulation of the prisoner's dilemma game to A. W. Tucker. See R. D. Luce and H. Raiffa, *Games and Decisions* (New York: Dover, 1957), p. 94. The literature on one-shot and repeated prisoner's dilemma games is vast.

8. See R. Axelrod, *The Evolution of Cooperation* (New York: Basic Books, 1984).

9. See Chapter Thirteen of H. Raiffa, *The Art and Science of Negotiation* (Cambridge, Mass.: Harvard University Press, 1982), and Chapter Thirteen of Lax and Sebenius (1986), Op. Cit.

10. For an overview, see Chapter One of Arrow et al. (1995), Op. Cit. They include in this category equity and justice seeking, biases in assimilation and construal, reactive devaluation of compromises and concessions, loss aversion, judgmental overconfidence, and dissonance reduction and avoidance. More in-depth explorations of psychological barriers are presented in Robert J. Robinson, "Errors in Social Judgment: Implications for Negotiation and Conflict Resolution, Parts 1 and 2," Harvard Business School Notes 897–103 and 897–104 (1997), and L. Ross and A. Ward, "Psychological Barriers to Dispute Resolution," *Advances in Experimental Social Psychology* 27 (1995): 255–304. See also R. B. Cialdini, *Influence: The Psychology of Persuasion* (New York: Morrow, 1993), and P. Zimbardo and M. Leippe, *The Psychology of Attitude Change and Social Influence* (New York: McGraw-Hill, 1991).

11. For more on mental models, see P. N. Johnson-Laid, *Mental Models* (Cambridge, Mass.: Harvard University Press, 1983), and I. Goffman, *Frame Analysis: An Essay on the Organization of Experience* (Cambridge, Mass.: Harvard University Press, 1974).

12. Robinson (1997), Op. Cit., Parts 1 and 2.

13. For a discussion of these and other cognitive biases, see M. Bazerman and M. Neale, *Negotiating Rationally* (New York: Free Press, 1992).

14. See Chapter Eight of Bazerman and Neale (1992), Ibid.

15. See D. Kahneman and A. Tversky, "Conflict Resolution: A Cognitive Perspective," in Arrow et al. (1995), Op. Cit. For a good summary of "nonrational" biases in decision making, see Chapter Three, "Cognitive Limitations and Consumer Behavior," of R. H. Frank, *Microeconomics and Human Behavior* (New York: McGraw-Hill, 1994).

16. Ross and Ward provide this explanation of intermediate steps: "In order to reach a long-term resolution that is satisfactory to both parties, one or even both parties may be obliged to take a step backward—that is, to accept, at least temporarily, changes in the status quo that leave it poorer, weaker, or more vulnerable than before." See L. Ross and A. Ward, "Psychological Barriers to Dispute Resolution," *Advances in Experimental Social Psychology* 27 (1995): 255–304.

17. Robinson (1997), Op. Cit., Part 2.

18. J. Z. Rubin, D. G. Pruitt, and S. H. Kim, *Social Conflict: Escalation, Stalemate, and Settlement* (New York: McGraw-Hill, 1994). Residues are defined as "persistent structural change—in an individual, group, or community—which is due to past escalation and encourages further escalation" (p. 99).

19. See, for example, C. T. Joy, *How Communists Negotiate* (New York: Macmillan, 1955).

20. Rubin, Pruitt, and Kim (1994), Op. Cit., in Chapters Six and Seven, provide an overview of these concepts and others related to escalation of conflict.

21. R. J. Robinson, D. Keltner, A. Ward, and L. Ross, "Actual Versus Assumed Differences in Construal: 'Naive Realism' in Inter-group Perception and Conflict," *Journal of Personality and Social Psychology* 68 (1995): 404–417. The authors call this "naive realism," by which they mean lack of awareness of one's own subjectivity in making predictions about oneself and others. As Arrow et al. (1995), Op. Cit., note, "Disputants are bound to have differing recollections and interpretations of the past—of causes and effects, promises and betrayals, conciliatory initiatives and rebuffs. They are also bound to have differing interpretations or construals . . . of the content of any proposals designed to end that dispute" (p. 13).

22. Robinson (1997), Op. Cit., Part 2, notes that partisans "exaggerate their own group's extremism, suggesting that they view themselves as 'lone moderates' within their conflict. The lone moderate pattern suggests that people tend to dissociate themselves from partisan groups, perceive ideological extremism with some disdain, and assume that they alone are models of rational, principled judgment" (p. 5).

23. Ross and Ward (1995), Op. Cit., define reactive devaluation in the context of conflict resolution as "the fact that the very act of offering a particular proposal or concession may diminish its apparent value or attractiveness in the eyes of the recipient" (p. 270).

24. A related problem is that disputants may be overly confident about their chances of prevailing in a conflict. For example, both plaintiffs and defendants in legal dis-

putes tend to be overly optimistic about their chances of winning at trial and therefore discount the value of out-of-court settlements. Similarly, the United States and North Korea each believed that it would ultimately prevail (albeit at a high cost) if war came. Such overconfidence diminishes the likelihood of negotiating a settlement. See Kahneman and Tversky (1995), Op. Cit. The findings on legal cases are discussed in this chapter.

25. Irving Janus defines groupthink as "a mode of thinking that people engage in when they are deeply involved in a cohesive in-group, when the members' strivings for unanimity override their motivation to realistically appraise alternative courses of action. Groupthink refers to a deterioration of mental efficiency, reality testing, and moral judgment that results from in-group pressures." See I. Janus, *Groupthink: Psychological Studies of Policy Decisions and Fiascoes* (Boston: Houghton Mifflin, 1982), p. 9.

26. R. Fisher and L. Bolling, "Facilitated Joint Brainstorming," CMG Update (Cambridge, Mass.: Conflict Management Group, 1995).

27. Janus (1982), Op. Cit.

28. L. Babcock and G. Loewenstein, "Explaining Bargaining Impasse: The Role of Self-Serving Biases," *Journal of Economic Perspectives* 11 (1997): 109–126.

29. For an extensive discussion of bureaucratic politics and its impact on decision making, see G. Allison, *Essence of Decision: Explaining the Cuban Missile Crisis* (Boston: Little, Brown, 1971). See also F. Iklé, *How Nations Negotiate* (Millwood, N.Y.: Kraus, 1964).

30. As an example, consider the impact on efforts to make peace in the Middle East of Palestinian suicide bombings in Jerusalem on July 30, 1997. The bombings brought predictable crackdowns on the Palestinians, including the collective punishment associated with closing the border between Israel and Gaza and the West Bank. The Netanyahu government demanded that Arafat round up extremists. If Arafat had complied, he would have been viewed internally as doing the Israelis' bidding. When he did not comply, he was seen as promoting terrorism. In either case, the bombers succeeded in undermining the process and strengthening the right wing in Israel.

31. The principal-agent problem is discussed in Chapter One of Arrow et al. (1995), Op. Cit. See also J. Pratt and R. Zeckhauser, eds., *Principals and Agents: The Structure of Business* (Boston: Harvard Business School Press, 1985).

32. R. T. Moran and W. G. Stripp, *Dynamics of Successful International Business Negotiations* (Houston: Gulf, 1991), describe a culture's tendency toward ethnocentrism as a need for a "we" identity in order to successfully navigate within the culture. However, this "we" attitude creates a gulf between differing cultures. In an attempt to establish superiority by proving other cultures inferior, most societies resort to ethnic name calling and attribution of vices and shortcomings to the "inferior" society.

33. W. G. Sumner, *Folkways: A Study of the Sociological Importance of Usages,*

*Manners, Customs, Mores and Morals* (Boston: Ginn, 1906). Related concepts are in-groups and out-groups and the relative partisan perceptions of each. Also see R. A. LeVine and D. T. Campbell, *Ethnocentrism* (New York: Wiley, 1972).

34. S. E. Weiss, "Negotiating with Romans—Part 1," *Sloan Management Review* 35 (1994): 52.

35. E. H. Schein, *Organizational Culture and Leadership,* 2nd ed. (San Francisco: Jossey-Bass, 1992), refers to levels in this context as "the degree to which the cultural phenomenon is visible to the observer . . .[which can] range from the very tangible overt manifestations that one can see and feel to the deeply embedded, unconscious basic assumptions . . . [which is] the essence of culture" (p. 16).

36. H. R. Markus and S. Kitayama, "Culture and the Self: Implications for Cognition, Emotion, and Motivation," *Psychological Review* 98 (April 1991): 224–253.

37. See Moran and Stripp (1991), Op. Cit.

38. J. Salacuse, "Making Deals in Strange Places: A Beginner's Guide to International Business Negotiations," in *Negotiation Theory and Practice,* ed. J. W. Breslin and J. Z. Rubin (Cambridge, Mass.: PON Books, 1991), pp. 251–259.

39. Robert Gallucci interview (May 11, 1998).

# Chapter Five

1. Billy Graham had met with Kim Il Sung on a mission of personal diplomacy in April 1992.

2. Gallucci notes, "We wouldn't even negotiate with them again at the under-secretary-of-state level, and they get a visit from a former president of the United States."

3. Richard Christenson interview (Feb. 15, 1995). Unless otherwise noted, all Christenson quotes are taken from this interview.

4. The idea of freezing the North's nuclear program in exchange for LWRs had already been suggested the previous week during an unofficial visit to Pyongyang by Selig Harrison.

5. Daniel Poneman interview (Aug. 8, 1995). Unless otherwise noted, all Poneman quotes are taken from this interview.

6. Some in the Clinton administration were angered when Carter openly complained about the more demanding U.S. position over telephone lines subject to North Korean eavesdropping.

7. Speaking at the U.S. ambassador's house in Seoul on June 18, Carter declared that sanctions would be "a personal insult to their so-called Great Leader by branding him as a liar and criminal. This is something, in my opinion, which would be impossible for them to accept."

8. Daniel Poneman, describing the DPRK reply, says, "We essentially got verbatim back from the North Koreans what we had asked for. When that came in, we really thought we had nailed something."

9. Mitchell Reiss interview (Dec. 2, 1994). Unless otherwise noted, all Reiss quotes are taken from this interview.

# Chapter Six

1. For a further discussion of reframing, see Chapter Three of W. Ury, *Getting Past No: Negotiating Your Way from Confrontation to Cooperation* (New York: Bantam Books, 1991).

2. For further discussion of intervenor's power, see C. W. Moore, *The Mediation Process* (San Francisco: Jossey-Bass, 1996); J. Bercovitch and J. Z. Rubin, *Mediation in International Relations: Multiple Approaches to Conflict Resolution* (New York: Macmillan, 1992); R. Fisher, W. Ury, and B. Patton, *Getting to Yes,* 2nd ed. (New York: Penguin Books, 1991); and M. Watkins and K. Winters, "Intervenors with Interests and Power," *Negotiation Journal* 13 (1997): 119–142.

3. Zartman and Touval developed the idea that international disputes become ripe for settlement and proposed that mediators play three principal roles in dispute resolution: communicator, formulator, and manipulator. Conflicts become ripe for settlement when disputants reach a "hurting stalemate" and come to perceive negotiated settlement as preferable to continued contention. See I. W. Zartman and S. Touval, "International Mediation: Conflict Resolution and Power Politics," *Journal of Social Issues* 41 (1985): 27–45.

4. Kissinger provided such an opportunity in Middle East negotiations in the 1970s. As Stein notes, "The circular structure of payment was essential to promoting agreement among the parties: Egypt improved the image of the United States in the Arab world, especially among the oil-producing states; the United States gave Israel large amounts of military and financial aid; and Israel supplied Egypt with territory. Indeed a bilateral exchange between Egypt and Israel would not have succeeded, since each did not want what the other could supply." J. G. Stein, "Structures, Strategies, and Tactics of Mediation: Kissinger and Carter in the Middle East," *Negotiation Journal* 1 (1985): 334.

5. For a discussion, see J. R. Idaszak and P. Carnevale, "Third Party Power: Some Negative Effects of Positive Incentives," *Journal of Applied Social Psychology* 19 (May 1989): 449–466.

6. For example, it cost the U.S.-led coalition $61 billion to win the Gulf War.

7. This was the case in the aftermath of both the Gulf War and the signing of the Dayton agreements.

8. Fisher argues that every negotiator has a dual role as partisan advocate and as comediator. A negotiator may understandably have a bias in favor of his own side. In fact, a diplomat may correctly perceive his mandate as zealous advocacy of his nation's interests. But arguing in favor of one set of interests is less than half his job. Two diplomats negotiating on behalf of their respective countries also have the joint task of efficiently producing a workable agreement that reconciles the interests of the two governments in a manner acceptable to both. Although each

negotiator's task can thus be seen as that of a comediator, the normal relationship between internal and external negotiations does not make it possible for two negotiators to use the tools and techniques that a skilled mediator might employ. See R. Fisher, "Negotiating Inside Out: What Are the Best Ways to Relate Internal Negotiations with External Ones?" in *Negotiation Theory and Practice*, ed. J. W. Breslin and J. Z. Rubin (Cambridge, Mass.: PON Books, 1991).

9. J. A. Baker, *The Politics of Diplomacy: Revolution, War, and Peace* (New York: Putnam, 1995), p. 135.

10. For more insight into this relationship, see U. Savir, *The Process* (New York: Random House, 1998).

11. Bill Keller, "South Africa Pact: Unlikely Partners," *New York Times*, Nov. 19, 1993.

12. F. Iklé, *How Nations Negotiate* (Millwood, N.Y.: Kraus, 1964), pp. 134–135.

# Chapter Seven

1. "US Won't Condition North Korea Nuclear Agreement on Special Inspections," *Washington Post*, Sept. 10, 1994.

2. Kim Il Sung's death, and the uncertain status and health of his son and chosen successor, Kim Jong Il, only strengthened predictions of an imminent collapse.

# Chapter Eight

1. W. Ury, *Getting Past No: Negotiating Your Way from Confrontation to Cooperation* (New York: Bantam Books, 1991), p. 16.

2. R. H. Mnookin, S. R. Peppet, and A. S. Tulumello, "The Tension Between Empathy and Assertiveness," *Negotiation Journal* 12 (1996): 217–213.

3. R. Fisher, W. Ury, and B. Patton, *Getting to Yes: Negotiating Agreement Without Giving In*, 2nd ed. (New York: Penguin Books, 1991).

4. D. Lax and J. Sebenius, "Thinking Coalitionally," in *Negotiation Analysis*, ed. P. Young (Ann Arbor: University of Michigan Press, 1991), Chapter Three.

5. For further discussion of the use of force in diplomacy, see G. A. Craig and A. L. George, *Force and Statecraft: Diplomatic Problems of Our Time* (New York: Oxford University Press, 1995).

6. Zartman and Berman termed these stages the *diagnostic phase*, the *formula phase*, and the *detail phase*. See I. W. Zartman and M. Berman, *The Practical Negotiator* (New Haven, Conn.: Yale University Press, 1982).

7. See Lax and Sebenius (1991), Op. Cit., pp. 218–226, for a detailed discussion of potential impacts of adding and subtracting issues. Also see M. Watkins and S. Passow, "Analyzing Linked Systems of Negotiations," *Negotiation Journal* 12 (1996).

8. For a discussion, see Watkins and Passow (1996), Op. Cit.

9. The term "unbundling" is attributable to Lax and Sebenius (1986), Op. Cit. For a more detailed discussion of unbundling, see Chapter Five: "Where different interests are bundled into a negotiation, a good strategy can be to unbundle and seek creative ways to dovetail them" (p. 94).

10. For a detailed discussion of differences as a potential source of joint gains, see Chapter Five of J. Sebenius, *Negotiating the Law of the Sea* (Cambridge, Mass.: Harvard University Press, 1984), and Chapter Five of Lax and Sebenius (1986), Op. Cit.

11. In practice, of course, the processes of creating the pie and dividing the pie cannot be so neatly separated. The negotiators' efforts to agree on a formula will influence their ability to take positions during detailed bargaining.

12. See Chapter Two of Ury (1991), Op. Cit.

13. According to H. Raiffa, *The Art and Science of Negotiation* (Cambridge, Mass.: Harvard University Press, 1982), "Once two offers are on the table ($s_1$ and $b_1$), the best prediction of the final contract is the midpoint ($s_1 + b_1$)/2—provided that the midpoint falls within the zone of agreement" (p. 48).

14. For a detailed discussion of reciprocity, see Chapter Two of R. B. Cialdini, *Influence: The Psychology of Persuasion* (New York: Morrow, 1993).

15. For further discussions of anchoring, see Lax and Sebenius (1986), Op. Cit., pp. 134–135, and M. H. Bazerman and M. A. Neale, *Negotiating Rationally* (New York: Free Press, 1992), Chapter Four.

16. See Chapter One of R. Fisher, W. Ury, and B. Patton, *Getting to Yes,* 2nd ed. (New York: Penguin Books, 1991).

17. Raiffa (1982), Op. Cit., p. 128.

18. For further discussion of patterns of concessions, see Raiffa (1982), Ibid., pp. 84–85, and Lax and Sebenius (1986), Op. Cit., Chapter Six.

19. Lax and Sebenius (1986), Op. Cit., p. 136.

20. For a discussion of commitment tactics, see Chapter Two of T. C. Schelling, *The Strategy of Conflict* (Cambridge, Mass.: Harvard University Press, 1960).

21. For further discussions of "commitment tactics," see Fisher and Ury (1981), Op. Cit., Chapter Seven; Lax and Sebenius (1986), Op. Cit., Chapter Six; and Schelling (1960), Chapter Two.

22. See Chapter Eight of Fisher, Ury, and Patton (1991), Op. Cit.

23. A. D. Wilhelm, *The Chinese at the Negotiating Table: Style and Characteristics* (Washington, D.C.: National Defense University Press, 1994), p. 24.

24. Chapter Five of Fisher, Ury, and Patton (1991), Op. Cit.

25. See, for example, D. G. Pruitt and J. L. Drews, "The Effect of Time Pressure, Time Elapsed, and the Opponent's Concession Rate on Behavior in Negotiation," *Journal of Experimental Social Psychology* 5 (1969): 43–60; G. A. Yukl, "The Effects of Situational Variables and Opponent Concessions on a Bargainer's Perception, Aspiration, and Concessions," *Journal of Personality and Social Psychology* 29

(1974): 227-236; D. L. Smith, D. G. Pruitt, and P. J. Carnevale, "Matching and Mismatching: The Effect of Own Limit, Other's Toughness, and Time Pressure on Concession Rate in Negotiation," *Journal of Personality and Social Psychology* 42 (1982): 876–883; and A. E. Roth, J. K. Murnighan, and F. Schoumaker, "The Deadline Effect in Bargaining: Some Experimental Evidence," *American Economic Review* 78 (September 1988): 806–823.

26. Raiffa (1982), Op. Cit., p. 16.

27. D. G. Pruitt and P. J. Carnevale, *Negotiation in Social Conflict* (Pacific Grove, Calif.: Brooks/Cole, 1993), p. 59.

28. For a discussion, see Raiffa (1982), Op. Cit., pp. 80–85.

29. Walter Hoge, "Can-Do American's Patience Paid Off with an Ulster Pact," *New York Times*, Apr. 12, 1998.

30. D. Lax and J. Sebenius, "Thinking Coalitionally: Party Arithmetic, Process Opportunism and Strategic Sequencing," in *Negotiation Analysis*, ed. P. Young (Ann Arbor: University of Michigan Press, 1991).

31. J. Sebenius, "Sequencing to Build Coalitions: With Whom Should I Talk First?" in *Wise Choices: Decisions, Games, and Negotiations*, ed. R. Zeckhauser, R. Keeney, and J. Sebenius (Boston: Harvard Business School Press, 1996).

32. Huthwaite, *Behavior of Successful Negotiators* (Purcellville, Va.: Huthwaite, 1994). The authors note that "skilled negotiators tended to plan around each individual issue in a way which was independent of any sequence. They would consider issue C, for example, as if issues A, B, and D didn't exist. Compared with the average negotiators, they were careful not to draw sequence links between a series of issues. The clear advantage of issue planning over sequence planning is flexibility" (pp. 8–9).

## Chapter Nine

1. The struggle for Palestine had begun decades earlier, but took on new urgency with the creation of the state of Israel.

2. Hanan Ashrawi, *This Side of Peace* (New York: Simon & Schuster, 1995), p. 58.

3. Ahron Bregman and Jihan El-Tahri, *The Fifty Years War, Israel and the Arabs* (London: Penguin Books, BBC Books, 1998), p. 189.

4. Government representatives on official business were exempt from this prohibition.

5. Shimon Peres interview (Mar. 30, 1998). Unless otherwise noted, all Peres quotes are taken from this interview.

6. Yossi Beilin, *Touching Peace* (Tel Aviv: Yediot Aharanot, 1997), p. 24. From a manuscript translation by Philip Simpson, provided by Yossi Beilin's office, Tel Aviv.

7. The minister Ezer Weizmann said the meeting with Nabil Ramawalli, the PLO representative in Geneva, was a chance encounter in a hotel. Beilin (1997), Ibid., p. 52. Weizmann would later become president of Israel.

8. The approach to the PLO for the purpose of seeking missing soldiers was jointly approved by Shamir, Peres, and Rabin—the "prime ministers' club" within the national unity government. Details on these negotiations come from the Peres Center for Peace seminar, Tel Aviv, March 20, 1998.

9. Politicians are never off duty: Peres showed Beilin a note from Shamir approving the discussions with the PLO during the bat mitzvah of Uri Savir's daughter Maia.

10. For more details on these talks, see Mahmoud Abbas (Abu Mazen), *Through Secret Channels* (Reading, U.K.: Garnet, 1995), pp. 39–43.

11. Arafat dispelled lingering doubts over the PLO's intentions when he confirmed at a press conference in Stockholm on December 7, 1988, that the PLO "accepted the existence of Israel as a state in the region." In an address to the UN General Assembly in Geneva the following week, Arafat (responding to internal PLO criticism) qualified that acceptance. But U.S. pressure and the promise of reestablished U.S.-PLO relations led Arafat the same night to explicitly affirm Israel's right to exist.

12. Yair Hirschfeld interview (Mar. 31, 1998). Unless otherwise noted, all Hirschfeld quotes are taken from this interview.

13. Beilin (1997), Op. Cit., p. 36.

14. Hassan was a PLO political adviser, Hourani was a member of the executive committee of the PLO, and Safiyeh was the PLO representative in Holland.

15. In May the national unity government had even prohibited Israeli ambassadors from obtaining information about third parties' talks with the PLO.

16. In December 1990, Beilin pushed the envelope again, suggesting publicly that Israeli forces should withdraw from Gaza to permit the establishment of a Palestinian state. He drew heated criticism not only from Likud but also from fellow Labor Party members.

17. Beilin (1997), Op. Cit., p. 56.

18. Anders Sandvik, *A Joint Nordic Centre for Peace in Jerusalem* (Oslo: Courage, 1993), p. 23.

19. Ironically, these were the same conditions that Likud's Shamir had rejected in the 1987 Peres-Hussein initiative.

20. Any Palestinian with an East Jerusalem residence permit was also ineligible.

21. Ashrawi (1995), Op. Cit., p. 244.

22. Abbas (1995), Op. Cit., p. 38.

23. Hirschfeld and Beilin had cofounded the Economic Cooperation Foundation (ECF) in 1991 to promote economic development in the West Bank and Gaza.

24. Beilin (1997), Op. Cit., p. 78.

25. Uri Savir, *The Process* (New York: Random House, 1998), p. 25.

26. Eitan Haber interview (Mar. 30, 1998). Unless otherwise noted, all Haber quotes are taken from this interview.

27. Beilin (1997), Op. Cit., p. 91.

28. Norway expended more than $1 billion annually in foreign aid; it contributed $100 per capita to multilateral organizations, ten times more than U.S. per-capita expenditures.

29. Jan Egeland interview (Mar. 23, 1995). Unless otherwise noted, all Egeland quotes are taken from this interview.

30. Beilin (1997), Op. Cit., p. 92.

31. Beilin (1997), Ibid., p. 93.

32. Ashrawi (1995), Op. Cit., p. 212.

33. Work had not yet begun on six thousand or so units to which the "freeze" applied.

34. Uri Savir interview (Mar. 30, 1998). Unless otherwise noted, all Savir quotes are taken from this interview. At age forty, Savir became the Foreign Ministry's youngest ever director general in 1993.

35. Accounts vary on who first suggested Gaza Plus and when. Peres says he has trouble remembering dates. Beilin supports the view that Peres proposed it in this meeting with Mubarak. See Beilin (1997), Op. Cit., p. 113.

36. According to Uri Savir, during the Peres Center for Peace seminar, March 20, 1998.

37. Avi Gil interview (Mar. 30, 1998). Unless otherwise noted, all Gil quotes are taken from this interview.

38. From the Peres Center seminar.

39. Terje Roed-Larsen interview (June 24, 1995). Unless otherwise noted, subsequent quotes attributed to Larsen are drawn from this interview.

40. Ron Pundak interview (June 25, 1995). Unless otherwise noted, all Pundak quotes are taken from this interview.

41. The approach was to hold informal talks that produced creative ideas, take the ideas to Beilin who molded and modified them, and then take the revised proposals to Peres who could implement them politically.

42. Ahmed Qurei (Abu Ala) interview (Apr. 3, 1998). Unless otherwise noted, all Abu Ala quotes are taken from this interview.

43. Beilin had also approached Britain about sponsoring a back channel. Britain was encouraging but responded so officially that Beilin feared it would be difficult to keep a negotiations channel secret.

44. Abbas (1995), Op. Cit., p. 113.

45. Abbas (1995), Ibid., p. 103.

46. Pundak recalls that because he and Hirschfeld both held dual nationality, there had also been some discussion of meeting the PLO on its own turf in Tunis. Nothing came of this.

47. From the Peres Center seminar.

48. Pundak provided this citation at the Peres Center seminar.

49. Abbas (1995), Op. Cit., p. 50.

50. Beilin (1997), Op. Cit., p. 103.

51. The legislation did not, however, change the ground rules for the Washington talks. PLO members and Palestinian residents of East Jerusalem were still barred from the official negotiations.

52. Abbas (1995), Op. Cit., p. 121.

53. Abbas (1995), Ibid., p. 127.

54. Pundak at the Peres Center seminar said that Abu Ala always gave Abu Mazen the credit for "selling" Oslo to Arafat.

55. Beilin (1997), Op. Cit., p. 106.

56. From the Peres Center seminar.

57. From the Peres Center seminar.

58. From the Peres Center seminar.

59. From the Peres Center seminar.

60. Details from Beilin (1997), Op. Cit., pp. 114–115.

61. Beilin is referring to the August 1990 document eclipsed and later outdated by Iraq's invasion of Kuwait.

62. From the Peres Center seminar; also the following quote from Pundak and Peres's response.

63. Beilin (1997), Op. Cit., p. 122.

64. Abbas (1995), Op. Cit., p. 71.

65. From the Peres Center seminar.

66. There is, in fact, continuing ambiguity over whether Peres was really the author of this proposal. Uri Savir gives Arafat credit for the concept. Peres and Beilin say Peres conceived it. Abu Ala says it does not matter who thought of it first; what is important is that it became a workable proposition.

67. Beilin (1997), Op. Cit., p. 134.

68. Abbas (1995), Op. Cit., pp. 202–203.

69. Beilin (1997), Op. Cit., p. 135.

70. Beilin (1997), Ibid., p. 137.

71. From the Peres Center seminar.

72. Shimon Peres, *Battling for Peace* (New York: Random House, 1995), p. 285.

73. David Mokovsky, *Making Peace with the PLO* (Boulder, Colo.: Westview Press, 1995), p. 66. From an interview Mokovsky held with Rabin on Oct. 4, 1993.

## Chapter Ten

1. K. Lewin, *Field Theory in Social Science.* (New York: Harper, 1951), p. 173.

2. C. Tilly, *European Revolutions, 1492–1992* (Cambridge, Mass.: Blackwell, 1993), p. 13.

3. Similar efforts were undertaken by moderates in the PLO. Most important, Mohammed Abbas, director of the PLO's Department for National and International Relations and a trusted lieutenant of Yasser Arafat, established contact with Peres and Rabin through the Egyptians after the 1992 elections. Abbas had begun studying Israeli politics in the early 1970s, a risky project in that many in the PLO were vehemently, and sometimes violently, opposed to any contact with Israelis.

## Chapter Eleven

1. For an examination of the U.S.-Iraqi relationship before the invasion of Kuwait, see "Prelude to War: US Policy Toward Iraq 1988–1990," Kennedy School of Government, Harvard University, case C16-94-1245.0 (1994).

2. Lawrence Freedman and Efraim Karsh, *The Gulf Conflict, 1990–1991: Diplomacy and War in the New World Order* (Princeton, N.J.: Princeton University Press, 1993), p. 51.

3. In September, the United States was charged with unwittingly contributing to Saddam's decision to invade when Iraq released a transcript of the meeting that showed Glaspie's remarks to be highly conciliatory. Among the most controversial quotes from the transcript was Glaspie's statement that the United States did not have an "opinion on Arab-Arab conflicts, such as your border dispute with Kuwait." The ambassador immediately protested the transcript as a distortion of the actual discussion. For a more detailed account of this meeting, see "Twisting in the Wind? Ambassador Glaspie and the Persian Gulf Crisis," Parts A, B, and Sequel, Kennedy School of Government, Harvard University, cases C16-91-1056.0, C16-91-1057.0, and C16-92-1057.1 (1991).

4. Thomas Pickering interview (May 17, 1994). Unless otherwise noted, all Pickering quotes are taken from this interview.

5. General Brent Scowcroft interview (May 24, 1994). Unless otherwise noted, all Scowcroft quotes are taken from this interview.

6. Dennis Ross interview (July 7, 1994). Unless otherwise noted, all Ross quotes are taken from this interview.

7. P. Salinger and E. Laurent, *Secret Dossier: The Hidden Agenda Behind the Gulf War* (New York: Penguin Books, 1991), p. 102.

8. Salinger and Laurent (1991), Ibid., pp. 96–97.

9. Salinger and Laurent (1991), Ibid., pp. 104–105.

10. Kuwait's appeal to the United States for help after the invasion was accompanied by a second entreaty not to disclose any U.S. troops sent to aid in Kuwait's liberation, a request the United States firmly rejected.

11. Richard Cheney interview (June 29, 1994). Unless otherwise noted, all Cheney quotes are taken from this interview.

12. Richard Clarke interview (June 13, 1994). Unless otherwise noted, all Clarke quotes are taken from this interview.

13. "Aggressors, Go Home," *Economist*, Aug. 11, 1990.

14. Richard Haass interview (June 13, 1994). Unless otherwise noted, all Haass quotes are taken from this interview.

15. Hussein released Arab and Third World citizens as part of his campaign to present Iraq as a crusader against Western imperialism.

16. The value of UN action was driven home when Turkey's president, Turgut Ozal, agreed to close the Iraqi pipeline through Turkey within hours of the vote.

17. John Bolton interview (Dec. 3, 1994). Unless otherwise indicated, all Bolton quotes are taken from this interview.

18. Freedman and Karsh (1993), Op. Cit., p. 145.

19. Robert Kimmitt interview (June 1, 1994). Unless otherwise noted, all Kimmitt quotes are taken from this interview.

20. Enrique Penalosa interview (July 14, 1994). Unless otherwise noted, all Penalosa quotes are taken from this interview.

21. Elaine Sciolino and Eric Pace, "How US Got UN Backing for Use of Force in Gulf," *New York Times*, Aug. 30, 1990.

22. Mickey Edwards interview (July 11, 1994). Unless otherwise noted, all Edwards quotes are taken from this interview.

23. Both Japan and Germany, whose initial response to the Gulf conflict was sluggish at best, ultimately came through as major donors. Japan's nearly $10 billion donation made it the largest donor outside the Gulf, and Germany managed to contribute $6.5 billion despite the financial demands of its own reunification.

24. Juan Camilo Rodriguez Gomez, *Leadership and Autonomy: Colombia in the United Nations Security Council, 1989–1990* (Bogotá, Colombia: School of Finance and International Relations Externado de Colombia University, Center for Research and Special Projects, 1993), p. 54.

25. "The Peace Party Gathers Strength," *Economist*, Dec. 1, 1990.

26. M. L. Sifry and C. Cerf, eds., *The Gulf War Reader: History, Documents, Opinions* (New York: Times Books, 1991), pp. 236–237.

27. Internal Iraqi documents uncovered later suggested that Iraq may have been only eighteen to twenty-four months away from having a bomb. "So what Bush had done largely for propaganda turned out to have some truth," one official remarked.

28. *International Herald Tribune*, Oct. 26, 1990.

29. Philip Zelikow interview (May 2, 1994). Unless otherwise noted, all Zelikow quotes are taken from this interview.

30. Freedman and Karsh (1993), Op. Cit., p. 233.

31. Yemen's vote was costly: the United States immediately cancelled its aid to the Arab nation—worth $70 million—and encouraged other allies to do the same.

32. "Counting on New Friends," *US News & World Report*, Dec. 10, 1990.

33. Sifry and Cerf (1991), Op. Cit., pp. 265–266.

34. Sifry and Cerf (1991), Ibid., p. 258.

35. Freedman and Karsh (1993), Op. Cit., p. 292.

36. Lawrence Eagleburger interview (May 24, 1994). Unless otherwise noted, all Eagleburger quotes are taken from this interview.

37. "Triumph Without Victory," *US News & World Report,* 1992, p. 208.

# Chapter Twelve

1. Owen Harries, "A Primer for Polemicists," *Commentary* 78 (September 1984): 57.

2. D. Krackhardt and J. R. Hanson, "Informal Networks: The Company Behind the Chart," *Harvard Business Review* (July–Aug. 1993).

3. In such campaigns, persuasive information is targeted at opinion leaders, those who are recognized as sources of advice about "right" behavior and attitudes, and those who act as validators of new information. Opinion leaders are important because the process of opinion formation in mass audiences is a multistep flow, involving the gradual diffusion and acceptance or rejection of persuasive information. In this process, people are influenced directly by exposure to persuasive messages and indirectly in discussions with others in the target audience. In their studies of the 1940 presidential election, Lazarfeld and others made the early observation that people were influenced both directly by exposure to information and indirectly by people who passed along information or whom they consulted for clues about "right thinking." The result was the multistep flow model of opinion formation. See P. Lazarfeld, L. Bereson, and H. Gaudet, *The People's Choice: How the Voter Makes Up his Mind in a Presidential Campaign* (New York: Duell, Sloan, & Pearce, 1948). See also Chapter Eight of M. A. Milburn, *Persuasion and Politics: The Social Psychology of Public Opinion* (Pacific Grove, Calif.: Brooks/Cole, 1991).

4. See M. H. Bazerman, A. E. Tenebrunsel, and K. Wade-Benzoni, "Negotiating with Yourself and Losing: Making Decisions with Competing Internal Preferences," *Academy of Management Review* 23 (1998): 225–241.

5. G. S. Jowett and V. O'Donnell, *Propaganda and Persuasion* (Newbury Park, Calif.: Sage, 1992), p. 32.

6. For a classic treatment of agenda setting in government, see J. W. Kingdon, *Agendas, Alternatives, and Public Policies,* 2nd ed. (White Plains, N.Y.: Longman, 1995).

7. Harries (1984), Op. Cit.

8. The use of analogy to persuade is explored in detail in R. E. Neustadt and E. R. May, *Thinking in Time: The Uses of History for Decision-Makers* (New York: Free Press, 1986).

9. For a good summary of "nonrational" biases in decision making, see Chapter Eight, "Cognitive Limitations and Consumer Behavior," of R. H. Frank, *Microeco-*

*nomics and Human Behavior* (New York: McGraw-Hill. 1994). For a more extensive treatment, see M. Bazerman, *Judgment in Managerial Decision Making*, 4th ed. (New York: Wiley, 1998).

10. At least as far back as Aristotle, persuaders have been advised to inoculate their audiences against the arguments they expect their opponents to make. See *Rhetoric*, Book One, Chapter Two, of *The Complete Works of Aristotle*, vol. 2, ed. Jonathan Barnes (Princeton, N.J.: Princeton University Press, 1984).

11. For a discussion of threats and commitments, see Chapter Two of T. C. Schelling, *The Strategy of Conflict* (Cambridge, Mass.: Harvard University Press, 1960).

12. See R. Putnam, "Diplomacy and Domestic Politics: The Logic of Two Level Games," *International Organizations* 42 (1988): 427–460. See also Chapter Seventeen of D. Lax and J. Sebenius, *The Manager as Negotiator* (New York: Free Press, 1986).

13. R. B. Cialdini, *Influence: The Psychology of Persuasion* (New York: Morrow, 1993), p. 57.

14. See Chapter Two of Cialdini (1993), Ibid.

15. Cialdini (1993), Ibid., p. 19.

16. Jowett and O'Donnell note that "source credibility is one of the contributing factors that seems to influence change. People have a tendency to look up to authority figures for knowledge and direction. Expert opinion is effective in establishing the legitimacy of change and is tied to information control. Once a source is accepted on one issue, another issue may be established as well on the basis of prior acceptance of the source." G. S. Jowett and V. O'Donnell, *Propaganda and Persuasion*, 2nd ed. (Thousand Oaks, Calif.: Sage, 1992), p. 222.

17. Lax and Sebenius termed these "patterns of deference." See D. Lax and J. Sebenius, "Thinking Coalitionally," in *Negotiation Analysis*, ed. P. Young (Ann Arbor: University of Michigan Press, 1991). See also Krackhardt and Hanson (1993), Op. Cit., and Chapter Six in Cialdini (1993), Op. Cit.

# Chapter Thirteen

1. Serb leader Slobodan Milosevic was known to ignite nationalist sentiments by recounting the defeat of the medieval Serb army by Muslim Turks in the late 1300s.

2. Yugoslavia's six republics were Slovenia, Croatia, Serbia, Bosnia-Herzegovina, Macedonia, and Montenegro.

3. For a more detailed account of this meeting and other events leading to the breakup of Yugoslavia, see L. Silber and A. Little, *Yugoslavia: Death of a Nation* (New York: TV Books, 1995 and 1996).

4. Tudjman, for example, revived use of the red-and-white checkerboard emblem that had been the symbol of the Nazi-backed fascist Ustase regime in Croatia during World War II.

5. The Bosnian Serbs declared their intent to make Sarajevo their capital and set up headquarters in nearby Pale.

6. Bosnian Serb forces were backed by Bosnian Serb members of the Federal Army, who secretly stayed behind when the army departed following Bosnia's independence.

7. The EC soon dropped sanctions against all republics except Serbia and its close ally Montenegro, but the arms embargo continued to affect all of the former Yugoslavia.

8. The international arms embargo imposed on the entire former Yugoslavia was having a disproportionate impact on the besieged Muslims, who had gone into the war poorly equipped. They were also landlocked, with hostile neighbors on all sides.

9. Given that there was no peace to enforce, UNPROFOR's mission was unclear from the start. Peacekeepers primarily helped escort refugees to safety and delivered humanitarian aid.

10. The United States supported the safe-areas resolution despite concern about the size of the UN force as "a way of trying to draw a line in the sand," says an official at the U.S. Mission to the UN. "We hoped that doing so would give the international community a stake in defending some Bosnian territory from onslaught by the Serbs."

11. Lord Owen held the United States largely responsible for the failure of the plan, claiming that Christopher's alternative lift-and-strike initiative, coupled with an overt lack of U.S. support, derailed the effort. Many U.S. officials assert, however, that enforcing the many miles of cantonal boundaries would have proved unworkable.

12. The Serbs attributed the bomb to the Muslims. That the Muslim government was killing its own people to arouse international attention was a frequent Serb claim. Most U.S. officials discount such assertions, though a few believe the Muslims may have shelled their own city in a desperate bid to win support. Yasushi Akashi, the senior UN envoy to the former Yugoslavia, ordered an investigation at Karadzic's request. The results were inconclusive, but some UN officials remained convinced that Bosnians were responsible for the bomb.

13. Alexander Vershbow interview (Apr. 29, 1996). Unless otherwise noted, all Vershbow quotes are taken from this interview.

14. The Federation provided UNPROFOR what may have been its most useful role; with the agreement in place but tensions high between Muslims and Croats, UN troops worked skillfully to reduce conflict and mediate disputes.

15. Disclosure in spring 1996 of the Clinton administration's tacit support for the secret arms pipeline triggered a congressional investigation.

16. Even before the marketplace attack, the foreign ministers of France and Britain had complained to Secretary Christopher that it was time for the United States to take a larger role in negotiations.

17. Some observers have theorized that frequently voiced fears for the safety of the peacekeepers spurred the Serbs to harass them. In any event, the Bosnian Serbs quickly learned the impact of threatening or attacking peacekeepers.

18. Unlike his predecessor, Sir Michael Rose, Lieutenant General Smith was known to advocate use of force in Bosnia.

19. Ivo Daalder interview (Apr. 29, 1996). Unless otherwise noted, all Daalder quotes are taken from this interview.

20. Many faulted the Dutch peacekeepers not only for failing to protect the Muslims but also for giving credibility to Serb claims that they were treating people humanely. On July 24, the UN's chief human rights monitor in the former Yugoslavia quit in protest over the Srebrenica slaughter.

21. Walter Slocombe interview (May 1, 1996). Unless otherwise noted, all Slocombe quotes are taken from this interview.

22. NATO extended this ultimatum to Sarajevo and the other safe areas a few weeks later.

23. Even before Srebrenica fell, Slocombe had advocated brokering a deal that would give the Muslims control of Sarajevo in exchange for the enclave, which he claims had become more of a refugee camp than a community.

24. Clinton vetoed the bill on August 11, but Congress did not attempt an override because of ongoing diplomatic efforts.

25. According to Vershbow, the Europeans were pleased that the United States had modified its pro-Muslim line: "We were no longer seen by them as so close to the Muslims that we weren't prepared to push for an end."

26. Richard Holbrooke interviews (June 5 and July 1, 1996). Unless otherwise noted, all Holbrooke quotes are taken from these interviews.

27. Lieut. Gen. Wesley Clark interview (May 2, 1996). Unless otherwise noted, all Clark quotes are taken from this interview.

28. Christopher Hill interview (Apr. 30, 1996). Unless otherwise noted, all Hill quotes are taken from this interview.

29. One official at the U.S. Mission to the UN, who describes the two Bosnian Serb leaders as "unstable," says it was typical of them to panic under pressure: "That's a real fault of the UN negotiators, and especially those who had their fingers on the trigger, not to realize that earlier."

30. U.S. Ambassador to the UN Madeleine Albright had been trying to promote the usefulness of the tribunal as a political tool, but Holbrooke was the first to make it part of his negotiating tactics.

31. Downplaying the Patriarch Paper was classic Holbrooke, team members say. "He always painted a more negative picture than what was the reality," one negotiator recalls. "Holbrooke never put himself in a position of having to backpedal from appearing to deliver more than he could actually deliver."

32. Some news reports claimed that the Pentagon was considering a proposal that the

Bosnian Serbs merely silence their artillery but be allowed to keep them in place.

33. Roberts Owen interview (May 1, 1996). Unless otherwise noted, all Owen quotes are taken from this interview.

34. The political and constitutional negotiations were often spontaneous and opportunistic, but Clark stresses that the military component was carefully planned. Even before the team first met Milosevic, U.S. officials were trying to specify what a NATO implementation force would do in the event of a peace agreement. Clark made periodic trips to NATO and key European capitals to further refine the plan and keep the alliance on board.

35. The Americans usually turned down alcohol, spurring Milosevic to call them "the juice men" for their beverage of choice.

36. E. Sciolino, "Conflict in the Balkans: What Price Peace?" *New York Times,* Sept. 9, 1995.

37. One U.S. negotiator recalls an incident at the eventual peace talks when a cooling system emitted a boom and Momcilo Krajisnik, a Bosnian Serb leader known for his toughness, winced, then said in halting English, "NATO." "For Krajisnik to be flinching with air conditioning units going on," says the negotiator, "told me that there was a significant personal psychological impact."

38. Milosevic pressed for sanctions relief throughout the shuttle, but Holbrooke wanted to save that incentive for an eventual peace conference. "I kept saying, 'Well, that isn't my authority, that's Washington's,'" Holbrooke says, "but I was playing a game."

39. E. Sciolino, "US Envoy Highlights Fine Print on Bosnia," *New York Times,* Sept. 13, 1995.

40. One team member recalls thinking, "I'm glad I'm the junior partner in this deal. The negotiating consequences of that kind of meeting were absolutely unclear to me."

41. Owen and some other team members shook the hands of the Bosnian Serb leaders. "We didn't like it," Owen says, "but we did." Holbrooke maneuvered so that he did not have to.

42. The Bosnian government may not have been pleased, but a team member recalls "a very touching moment" a few days later when a group of Sarajevans on the street recognized Holbrooke and began applauding.

43. After a year and a half, the Federation was still an alliance more in name than in practice. Federation towns remained divided into Muslim and Croat sections.

44. The Balkan leaders were undoubtedly aware, however, that Clinton administration officials foresaw an infusion of $1 billion in regional aid over three years in the event of a settlement, perhaps $500 million of that sum slated for Bosnia.

45. One top Pentagon official remarks: "The Bosnians periodically fantasized that they had a military option. Whenever they tried it, they got their butts handed to them."

46. Two reporters, Joe Klein and Roger Cohen, were allowed in briefly under tight guidelines.

47. Holbrooke and Christopher argued for suspension of sanctions at the start of the peace talks "as an incentive for success," Holbrooke says, but NSC officials refused, insisting that there should be no relief until a comprehensive settlement.

48. The nature of the Serb–Bosnian Serb relationship continued to elude observers. Some U.S. officials believed Milosevic to be estranged from Karadzic and Mladic, as he insisted; others considered this an exaggeration, if not a lie. "I'm inclined to believe that Milosevic and all these guys are in cahoots, lock, stock, and barrel," declared one team member.

49. It had already been decided that Clinton would not attend, largely because the negotiation might fail. If the talks succeeded, Clinton would attend the signing ceremony.

50. Not that the political issues were easy. One negotiator complains that Bosnian Foreign Minister Muhamed Sacirbey was particularly contrary, continually insisting on new wording that often made no sense and that the other sides would not accept. "We would rush off and draft something that looked like his language but that meant something different, and try to persuade him that he could live with our version."

51. E. Sciolino, R. Cohen, and S. Engelberg, "In US Eyes, 'Good' Muslims and 'Bad' Serbs Did a Switch," *New York Times,* Nov. 23, 1995.

52. Largely as a result of military successes, the Bosnian Croats still ended up with 21 percent of Bosnia, 4 percent more than they had been offered under the Contact Group plan. "The Bosnians kept saying to us, 'You've got to get the Croatians back down to 17 percent,'" says Holbrooke, "and we said, 'That's not our business. These percentages are between the two of you.'"

53. Bosnian Foreign Minister Sacirbey told journalists that the negotiations were about to end, news that the press quickly disseminated.

54. Holbrooke had resigned from the State Department in early 1996 to return to Wall Street. He subsequently became U.S. Ambassador to the UN.

# Chapter Fourteen

1. This section draws on work done jointly with Kim Winters. See M. Watkins and K. Winters, "Intervenors with Interests and Power," *Negotiation Journal* 13 (1997): 2.

2. L. L. Riskin, "Understanding Mediators' Orientations, Strategies, and Techniques: A Grid for the Perplexed," *Harvard Negotiation Law Review* 1 (1996): 43.

3. Once again, notes Riskin (1996), Ibid., pp. 44–45, this is a difficult decision: "The evaluative mediator, by providing assessments, predictions, or direction, removes some of the decision-making burden from the parties. . . . In some cases, this makes it easier for the parties to reach an agreement. Evaluations by the mediator can give a participant a better understanding of his 'Best Alternative to a Negotiated Agreement' (BATNA), a feeling of vindication or an enhanced ability to deal with his constituency. . . . Yet in some situations, an assessment, prediction or recommendation can make it more difficult for the parties to reach agreement by

impairing a party's faith in the mediator's neutrality or restricting a party's flexibility. . . . Moreover these evaluative techniques decrease the extent of the parties' participation, and thereby may lower the participants' satisfaction with both the process and the outcome."

4. This section draws on work done jointly with Joel Cutcher-Gershenfeld. See J. Cutcher-Gershenfeld and M. Watkins, "Toward a Theory of Representation in Negotiation," in *Negotiating on Behalf of Others*, ed. R. H. Mnookin and L. E. Susskind (Thousand Oaks, Calif.: Sage, 1999).

5. For a wide-ranging exploration of issues in representation, see Mnookin and Susskind (1999), Op. Cit.

6. F. Iklé, *How Nations Negotiate* (Millwood, N.Y.: Kraus, 1964), p. 123.

# Conclusion

1. The role of pattern recognition and mental simulation in making expert judgment possible is developed in detail in G. Klein, *Sources of Power: How People Make Decisions* (Cambridge, Mass.: MIT Press, 1998).

2. See R. C. Christensen, "Premises and Practices of Discussion Teaching," in *Education for Judgment: The Artistry of Discussion Leadership,* ed. C. R. Christensen, D. Garvin, and A. Sweet (Boston: Harvard Business School Press, 1991).

3. The idea of reflection-in-action as a hallmark of expertise is developed in detail in D. Schön, *The Reflective Practitioner: How Professionals Think in Action* (New York: Basic Books, 1983).

4. Klein (1998), Op. Cit., p. 42.

# THE AUTHORS

**Michael Watkins** is an associate professor of business administration at Harvard Business School, where he teaches courses on negotiation and corporate diplomacy. He has also taught at Harvard's Kennedy School of Government. He is the coauthor of *Right from the Start: Taking Charge in a New Leadership Role* and *Winning the Influence Game: What Every Business Leader Should Know About Government.*

**Susan Rosegrant** is a case writer at the John F. Kennedy School of Government at Harvard University. She is the coauthor of *Route 128: Lessons from Boston's High-Tech Community* and was formerly a reporter for *Business Week* and the Associated Press.

# INDEX

**A**

Abu Ala (Ahmed Suleiman Qurei), 149, 150, 151, 152, 153, 154, 155, 157, 158, 159, 160, 163

Abu Mazen (Mahmoud Abbas), 145, 148, 151, 154, 157

Achieving side effects, 23

Action-forcing events: described, 35–36; mediator facilitation of, 91; spoilers and, 126; structuring of, 125–126

Active listening, 115

Agenda. *See* Issue agenda

Agreed Basic Principles (Bosnia War), 247–249, 254–255

Agreed Framework. *See* U.S.–North Korean Agreed Framework

Ala, A., 97

Albright, M., 53

AMAN (Israel), 155

Amirav, M., 141

Amr Moussa, Foreign Minister, 148

Analogy technique, 221

Analysis of changing balance of forces, 214*f*

Arab coalition (Persian Gulf War): assembling of, 185–188; private support of U.S. bombing plan by, 201; response to Bush's "extra mile" offer, 203–204; "tin-cup trips" made to, 194–195; UN authorization of force support by, 201–203

Arab League, 186, 188

Arafat, Y., 134, 136, 141, 148, 149, 151, 162, 163, 173

Arafat-Rabin correspondence (1993), 162–163

Arbitrators: described, 89–90; intervention grid role by, 94, 95*f*; role played by, 267–268

*The Art and Science of Negotiation* (Raiffa), 121, 123–124

Article 51 (UN Charter), 192, 201

Asfour, H., 142, 152

Ashrawi, H., 138, 144, 147, 149

Aspin, L., 40, 203

Assessing: negotiation effectiveness, 127–129, 128*t*; outcomes, 129–130

Away-from-the-table actions: applying pressure through, 124–125; building coalitions, 116–117; learning from, 114–115; orchestrating, 115–117; time costs of NATO bombing, 124

Aziz, T., 203, 204, 206–207

**B**

Baath Party (Iraq), 179

Back channel route, 134

Baker, J., 33, 97, 182, 185, 192, 194, 198, 199, 201, 202, 203, 205, 206–207, 220, 268, 273

Baker-Aziz session (1990), 206–207

Bandar Ibn Sultan, Prince, 187, 225

Barak, E., 138

Bargaining power, 92

BATNA (best alternative to negotiated agreement): assessing counterparts', 26–27f; building your, 26; defining walkaway position and, 27–28; described, 26; impact of coalitions on, 28; impact of Gulf War on, 143–144; impact of negotiation linkages on, 33; orchestrating actions to create, 115–117; Palestinians' changing perception of, 136; shaping perceptions of, 103; time cost of, 124; weakening counterpart, 116

Bay of Pigs invasion, 68

Bazerman, M., 65

Beilin, Y., 141, 142, 143, 145, 146, 147, 149, 150, 152, 154, 155, 156, 160, 174

Beliefs about future, 118

Berger, S., 40

Berlin Wall (1989), 8

Blix, H., 11, 44, 45, 46, 47–48, 49, 52

Blocking coalitions, 20

Bolton, J., 190, 191

Bosnia: regional map of, 230f; uneasy peace following war in, 264–265

Bosnia War: approach to setting principles for peace in, 98; background leading to, 229, 231–232; cease-fire called in, 255–256; challenges of negotiating end to, 228–229, 231–232, 256–261; Contact Group formed to address, 237, 240, 242, 253; Dayton Accord agreement ending, 261–264; failure of international response to, 232–237; historic background of, 229; international recognition of, 232; Muslim-Croat conflict during, 232, 252–253; Muslim-Croat Federation of, 236, 252, 253, 254, 265; patterns of NATO and Bosnian Serbs during, 237–241; rejection of "lift-and-strike" plan for, 234; uneasy peace following end of, 264–265

Bosnia War negotiations: Agreed Basic Principles agreement during, 247–249; building momentum of, 244–247; on cease-fire arrangements, 255–256; challenges and accomplishments of, 228–229, 231–232, 256–261; Contact Group role in, 237, 240, 242, 253; on Dayton Accord talks, 261–264; decision to begin NATO bombings, 243–244; Holbrooke led, 241–242; hunting lodge meeting during, 249–251; impact of NATO bombings on, 245–246, 249–251, 252; impact of the Patriarch Paper on, 243–244; on implementing Agreed Basic Principles, 254–255; preparing for peace talks, 258–261; renewed efforts for Western led, 240–241

Bosnian Muslims, 236, 252, 253, 254, 259, 265

Bosnian Serbs: foreign ministers' meeting and, 247; hostages taken by, 238; international response to, 239–241; NATO bombings pressure on, 249–251, 252; the Patriarch Paper establishing spokesperson for, 243–244; patterns of actions by, 237–241

Brady, N., 194

Breakthrough approach: four major elements of, 131–132; getting to the table as key to, 164; negotiator qualities required for successful, 279–280. *See also* Negotiators

Bridging parties, 225–228

"Broad and thorough" approach, 45–47

Building coalitions: carrots and sticks tools for, 215–216, 218; importance of, 211; mapping the landscape for, 211–212; mobilizing compatible interests for, 214–215; transforming balance of forces through, 212–213, 212–218, 214f, 216t–217t; of winning coalitions, 20, 213–215, 218–229. *See also* Coalitions

Building momentum: assessing effectiveness for, 127–129; assessing outcomes and, 129–130; channeling flow of, 37f; confidence-building measure for, 99, 176; defining, 1; designed by comediations, 98–100; during Oslo Accords, 175–176; during Persian Gulf crisis, 228–229; phased agreements for, 98, 176, 177; secret diplomacy for, 99–100, 175, 177; sequence to, 126–127; by shaping time cost perception, 36; strategies for, 109–126

Building momentum strategies: channel the flow, 123–126; finding formula for the deal, 117–118; laying foundation as, 119–123; orchestrating actions at/away from table, 115–117; organize to learn, 112–115; seven-element process for, 109–110; shaping the structure, 110–112, 111t

Bush administration: concerns over North Korean nuclear program by, 7–9; courting of Congress (1990) by, 207–209; diplomacy approach used with Iraq by, 179; economic embargo against Iraq supported by, 197; "Gang of Eight" created to respond to Iraq, 182–184, 189, 195; hands-off policy regarding Bosnia by, 233; internal politics barrier of, 70; last proposals for Persian Gulf peace by, 209; organizational strengths of, 72; parrying pressure on Iraq to negotiate, 195–197; public pressure on, 198–200; push for UN authorization of force by, 201–203; response to Kuwait administration by, 182–184;

sequencing to build momentum by, 228; Soviet support during Persian Gulf crisis, 184–185, 190, 191, 195, 228; "tin-cup trips" made by, 194–195; winning coalitions built by, 213–229. *See also* United States

Bush, G., 10, 39, 90, 93, 94, 178, 182, 185, 186, 187, 189, 192, 203–204, 268, 271, 272

Bush "telephone diplomacy," 189

**C**

Camp David agreement (1978), 135, 140

Carlin, R., 12, 13, 14, 40, 42, 46, 48, 50, 101, 102, 103–104

Carnegie Endowment for International Peace, 8, 106

Carnevale, P., 124

"Carrots, Sticks, and Question Marks: Negotiating the North Korean Nuclear Crisis" (Rosegrant and Watkins), 3

Carrots and sticks tools, 215, 216, 218

Carter, J., 73, 81–86, 87–88, 89, 90, 95, 96, 101, 135, 175, 183, 267, 271

Carter mediation, 81–86, 87–88, 89, 96, 101, 121

Ceaucescu, N., 8

Channel factors: described, 167; in PLO and Israeli conflict, 172–176

Channel the flow, 123–126

Cheney, R., 182, 183, 188, 189, 201, 208

China: insistence on non-interference in internal affairs by, 122; MFN status renewal for, 53, 312nn.14, 17; Persian Gulf interests of, 217t, 218; response to Persian Gulf crisis by, 193

Chirac, J., 238

Christensen, R., 279

Christenson, R., 83

Christopher, W., 40, 51, 52, 55, 156, 158, 163, 233–234, 235, 262, 263

CIA (Central Intelligence Agency), 47

Circular payoffs, 92

Claiming value negotiation, 29, 275

Clark, W., 13, 241, 242, 243

Clarke, R., 188, 195, 197, 199, 201, 204, 205, 244, 245, 248, 251, 257

Clinton administration: broad and thorough approach taken by, 45–47; calls for international economic sanctions, 53; Carter's intervention on behalf of, 81–86, 87–88, 89, 96, 101, 121; comprehensive package approach announced by, 46; criticism of Agreed Framework by, 106–108; internal politics barrier of, 70–71; organizational weaknesses of,

72; policies toward Bosnia War by, 233–234, 236; renewed Bosnia negotiations by, 239–242; tensions between Carter and, 85–86; unwilling to set adverse precedents, 33–34. *See also* United States

Clinton, B., 3, 13, 47, 48, 53, 55, 71, 81, 84, 85, 232, 238, 256, 263

CNN (Cable News Network), 82–83, 89, 125

Coalitions: away-from-the-table actions building, 116–117; blocking, 20; competitive linkage to break, 112; effect on BATNAs by, 28; winning, 20, 213–215, 218–229. *See also* Arab coalition (Persian Gulf War); Building coalitions

Coercive power, 92–93

Cold War equilibrium, 165, 166f

Collectivist culture, 76t

Colombia, 217t

Comediations: designing momentum-building processes, 98–100; initiatives by, 95–97; Middle East negotiations by, 142–143, 172–173; productive working relationships and, 97–98

Commitment tactic, 223

Commitment tactics, 122

Communication enhancement/shaping, 91

Complementary interests, 22

Comprehensive package approach, 46

Concessions: mediator facilitation of, 91; planning pattern of, 121

Concurrent linkages, 34–35

Confidence-building measures, 99

Confidence-building mechanisms, 176

Conflict: equilibrium and change in sustained, 164–168; leadership roles in managing, 172–175; managing, 1, 87–100

Conflicting interests, 22

Contact Group, 237, 240, 242, 253

Contingent commitments, 112

Continuity-of-safeguards inspections (IAEA), 44–45

Creating value negotiation: described, 29; dilemma of claiming vs., 275; mediator facilitation of, 91

Creekmore, M., 83

Critiquing position function, 91

Croatia, 90, 229, 231, 232, 236, 239

Crowe, W. J., Jr., 199

Cuba, 193, 202, 203

Cultural barriers: described, 57, 73–74; diagnosing, 77; overcoming, 79

Cultural diagnostic questions, 77

Cultural self-awareness, 79

Cultural sophistication, 79

Cultural standards, 79
Cultural stereotyping, 78
Culture: analyzing levels of, 74, 75*f*; cautions regarding, 78–79; collectivist and individualistic, 76*t*; probing underlying assumptions of, 74–75, 77
Cumings, B., 8, 106, 108
Currently perceived choice analysis, 61*f*

**D**
Daalde, I., 238, 240, 242, 251, 260
Dayton Accord, 261–264
Demonstrating competence, 23
Desert Shield, 188–190
DIA (Defense Intelligence Agency), 47
Diagnosing the structure: of action-forcing events, 35–36; of alternatives, 26–28; defining, 1; of goals/interests, 22–25, 24*t*; of issue agenda, 20–22; linkages of negotiations, 33–35; of U.S.–Korean negotiation parties, 17–20, 19*f*; of ZOPA (zone of possible agreement), 28–33
Distributive negotiations, 29–31, 30*f*, 310n.14
DMZ (demilitarized zone), 4, 7
DPRK (Democratic People's Republic of Korea). *See* North Korea

**E**
Eagleburger, L., 183, 208
Eastern European region, 230*f*
Ecuador-Peru border dispute (1995), 69
*Education for Judgment* (Christensen), 279
Edwards, M., 194, 198–199, 200, 202
Efficient frontier, 32–33
Egeland, J., 146, 147, 153
Egypt, 134, 195, 216*t*
Eliminating alternative options technique, 218–220
Emotional buffer function, 91
End-game effect, 62
Enhancing relationships, 23
Ethiopia, 217*t*
EU (European Community): Contact Group of, 237, 240, 242, 253; failure to negotiate Bosnian peace by, 235; recognition of Bosnia by, 232; rejection of "lift-and-strike" plan by, 234
Evaluative mediator, 331n.3
Experts, 225

**F**
Facilitation vs. activism goal, 270
Facilitatives power, 90–91
Facilitators, 175
Fahd, King, 187–188, 225

Fatah (Palestine National Liberation Movement), 136
Fisher, R., 22, 26, 95, 115
Fitzwater, M., 210
Flanagan, T., 14, 42, 50, 54–55, 81, 96, 101, 103, 107, 108
Flexibility vs. commitment dilemma, 276–277
Fog of negotiation, 118
Formula for the deal, 117–118
Framing, 220–222
France: Hussein's "peace plan" and, 196–197; Persian Gulf interests of, 216*t*, 219; Persian Gulf military support by, 205; proposal for Persian Gulf peace by, 209
Frasure, R. C., 238, 241, 242

**G**
Gallucci, R., 39, 40, 41, 42, 43, 45, 46, 50, 51, 52, 53, 54, 55, 64, 78, 82, 84, 85, 86, 96, 101, 102, 103, 106, 107, 108, 114, 115, 128, 267, 268, 273, 274
"Gang of Eight," 182–184, 189, 195
Gates, R., 182, 188, 195, 208–209
"Gaza Plus Jericho" proposal, 159, 173
Gaza Strip: map of, 137*f*; Oslo DOP regarding, 156; as Oslo negotiation issue, 153; Peres' idea of self-rule for, 140–141, 153; proposed visit by Arafat to, 148–149; sealed off after killings (1993), 158; suggested Israeli withdrawal from, 321n.16
Germany, 217*t*, 325n.23
*Getting Past No* (Ury), 112
"Getting to Dayton: Negotiating an End to the War in Bosnia" (Rosegrant and Watkins), 228
*Getting to Yes* (Fisher and Ury), 22
Gil, A., 148, 161
Glaspie, A., 180, 324n.3
Goal transformation perception, 67
Goals. *See* Interest/goals
Gorbachev, M., 184, 195, 202, 224
Gore, A., 55, 82
"Graduality" concept, 154–155
Graham, B., 82
Greece, 245–246
Gregg, Ambassador, 55
Groupthink, 68–69*t*, 315n.25
Guardians, 173
"The Gulf Crisis: Building a Coalition for War" (Rosegrant and Watkins), 178
Gulf War. *See* Persian Gulf War

**H**
Haass, R., 189, 191, 201, 204, 209–210
Haber, E., 146

Hague International War Crimes Tribunal, 234, 240

Hamas (Islamic Resistance Movement), 138, 149, 151, 152, 168, 169*f*

Harries, W., 212

Harris, M., 235

Harrison, S., 8, 106

Hierarchies of authority, 225

Hill & Knowlton, Inc., 200

Hill, C., 242, 244, 246, 248, 257, 259

Hirschfeld, Y., 142, 143, 145, 147, 149, 150, 151, 152, 154, 156, 157, 159, 160, 161, 173, 174

Holbrooke, R., 92, 95, 98, 228, 229, 232, 237, 240, 241–242, 243, 244, 245, 246, 248, 250–251, 252, 253, 254, 255–257, 258, 260, 262, 263, 265, 266, 268, 269, 270, 271, 272, 273, 274, 276, 277

Holst, J. J., 160, 162, 163

Hostage taking, 64, 99

*How Nations Negotiate* (Iklé), 21, 273

Hubbard, T., 39–40, 41, 45, 47, 48, 50, 51

Hussein, King, 136, 139–140, 185, 186, 187

Hussein, S. *See* Saddam Hussein

Hussein-Peres proposal, 139–140, 150

Husseini, F., 138, 141, 147, 156

**I**

IAEA (Atomic Energy Agency) [UN]: conflict between North Korea and, 13, 14, 15; described, 9; negotiations on continuity-of-safeguards inspections by, 44–45; negotiations over inspections by, 42–44; push for U.S.–North Korean talks by, 38–39; refused permission to monitor defueling, 52; response to Agreed Framework by, 106–107; Super Tuesday and disruption of, 48–49

Identifying barriers to agreement: cultural, 57, 73–79; defining, 1; guidelines for diagnosing five key barriers, 56–57; institutional, 57, 70–73; mutually reinforcing nature of barriers, 79–80; psychological, 57, 64–70; strategic, 56–57, 60–64; structural, 56, 57–60, 58*t*

IFOR, 264

Iklé, F., 21, 100, 273

Incrementalism, 63, 99

Individualistic culture, 76*t*

Informational asymmetries, 28–29

Inoculating against challenges, 222

Insecure agreements, 62–63

Institutional barriers: changes in Middle East, 170; defining, 57, 70; internal politics as, 70–72; organizational weaknesses and, 72; overcoming, 73; principal-agent problems as, 72–73; two-level negotiations as, 70, 71*f*

Integrative negotiations, 31, 32*f*, 310n.14

Interest/goals: analysis of U.S. and North Korean, 24*t*; assessing representatives', 23, 24; building coalitions through compatible, 214–215; facilitation vs. activism, 270; factor in process of, 23; getting underneath positions to, 22–23; of intervenors, 90; mediators with both power and, 95; narrow vs. broad, 269–270; own vs. best, 270–271; of Persian coalition key players, 216*t*–217*t*; predicting coalitional alignments to pursue, 25; sharing perceptions of, 103

Internal politics: as barrier to negotiation, 70–72; vicious cycle produced by, 73*f*

International disputes: breakthrough tasks for, 1; mediator roles in, 317n.3

Intervenors: dilemmas confronting, 268–272; interests of, 90; intervention role grid and, 93–94, 95*f*; mixed mediation roles by, 94–95; roles played by, 267–268; sources of power, 90–93; types of, 89–90

Intervention game, 87–88

Intervention role comparison, 269*f*

Intervention role grid, 93–94, 95*f*

Intervention strategies, 89

*Intifadah* (1987), 138, 139, 168, 170

Iranian Revolution (1979), 179

Iraq: Bush's "extra mile" offer to, 203–204; combination of economic sanctions/diplomacy tried with, 197–198; Hussein's "peace plan" offer, 196–197; Kuwait invasion by, 102, 178–180; nuclear bomb program of, 44, 47; oil pipeline shut down by Saudi Arabia, 188; UN authorization of force against, 201–203. *See also* Kuwait invasion (1989); Persian Gulf negotiations (1989/1990)

Iraqi economic embargo, 197

Israel: channel factors of, 172–176; creating Oslo channel between PLO and, 149–151; "Gaza Plus Jericho" proposal by, 159; guardians within, 173; historic conflict between PLO and, 133–135, 136, 138; Hussein-Peres proposed agreement in, 139–140; Iraq's "peace plan" proposal regarding occupied territories of, 196; lack of official recognition of PLO by, 136, 138; "Law of Association" (1986) of, 149; map of, 137*f*; Oslo Declaration of Principles (DOP) agreement with PLO, 98, 154–156, 158–160, 163, 173, 176; peace agreement between Egypt (1978) and, 134; Persian Gulf interests of, 217*t*; perspective on Palestinian problem by, 138–139; PLO overture toward, 141–142, 321n.11; pros/cons of unofficial representatives for, 155–156; response to *intifadah* by,

138, 139, 168, 170; secret contacts between PLO and, 142–143; secret diplomacy taken by, 175; shifting balance of forces impact on, 168–171t; suggested withdrawal from Gaza Strip by, 321n.16. *See also* Middle East relations; Oslo Accords (1993)

Israeli Labor Party: contacts between PLO and, 140–141; election victory (1992) of, 146, 147, 150, 170, 171t; negotiation positions of, 147–148; Palestinian policy by, 139

Israeli Likud Party: contacts between PLO and, 141; Palestinian policy by, 139

Issue agenda: continuous negotiation over, 20–21; identifying full set of, 21; linking of, 221; sequencing of, 21–22, 127; shaping for debate, 220–221; U.S. defined, 40

Issue architecture, 21

Ivory Coast, 217t

Izetbegovic, A., 228, 231–232, 233, 235, 246, 253, 255, 256, 259, 262, 263, 265


**J**

Janis, I., 68

Janvier, B., 238

Japan: Korean occupation by, 6; Persian Gulf interests of, 217t, 325n.23; regarding proposed sanctions, 54

Johnson, L., 208

Joint Declaration (U.S.–North Korea), 41–42, 98

Jowett, G. S., 215

*juche* concept, 6


**K**

Kang Sok Ju, 41, 43, 46, 85, 103

Kanter, A., 11, 12, 54, 70, 97, 101, 114

Karadzic, R., 232, 238, 251, 259, 264, 265

Kennedy, J. F., 68

Kerrick, D., 255, 257

Khomeini, Ayatollah Rubollah, 179

Kim Il Sung, 3, 4, 6–7, 13, 54, 83, 89, 101

Kim Young Sam, 13, 42, 46

Kimmitt, R., 192

Klein, G., 280

Korean peninsula: history of subjugation of, 4, 6–7; map of, 5f; post–W.W. II division of, 6; U.S. agenda on nonnuclear, 40. *See also* North Korea; South Korea

Krajisnik, M., 265

el-Kurd, M., 152

Kurtzer, D., 158

Kuwait, 216t

Kuwait invasion (1989): background leading to, 179–180, 182; Glaspie's remarks and, 180, 324n.3; immediate response of U.S. to, 178, 182–184; public support/propaganda tactics following, 199–200; UN security council response to, 190–193; U.S. pressure on Iraq to negotiate over, 195–197. *See also* Persian Gulf negotiations (1989/1990); Persian Gulf War (1990)


**L**

Lake, A., 40, 46, 84, 240, 241

Larsen, T., 146, 149, 152, 157

"Law of Association" (1986) [Israel], 149

Laying foundation: assessing walkaway positions, 119–120; crafting plausible supporting rationales, 121–122; described, 119; by judicious opening position, 120; planning pattern of concessions, 121; putting it all together, 122–123

League of Arab Nations, 186, 188. *See also* Arab coalition (Persian Gulf War)

Learning: at and away from negotiation table, 114–115; at the negotiation table, 115; establishing goals of, 113–114; organizing for, 112–115; three key levels of, 113

Legitimizing sponsors, 174–175

Lewin, K., 164

Linked negotiations: building winning coalitions using, 221; described, 33–35, 34f; forcing action using, 36; internal decision making and external, 59f; sequencing moves between, 127; shaping structure by using/breaking, 110–112, 111f

Lone moderate phenomenon, 67, 314n.22

Lord, W., 39, 51

*Los Angeles Times* poll (1989), 199

Loss aversion, 65–66t

Luck, G., 46–47, 48, 55, 83

Lundberg, K., 133

LWRs (light-water reactors), 43, 83, 99, 104–105


**M**

Macedonia, 245–246

Madrid Conference (1991), 143–144, 175, 177

Managing conflict: comediation initiatives for, 95–100; defining, 1, 87; intervention game for, 87–88; intervention strategies for, 89; leadership roles in, 172–175; types of intervenors used for, 89–95

Manning, R., 9, 39, 47, 107

Maps: Bosnia and surrounding region, 230f; Korean peninsula, 5f; Middle East region, 137f; Persian Gulf region, 181f

Marcos, F., 241

McCain, J., 49

Mediators: evaluative, 331n.3; with interests and muscle, 95; intervention grid role by, 93–94, 95f; roles played by, 267, 317n.4; secret channel created by Middle East, 145; time limits set by, 125–126

Mental management, 279

Mental models, 64–65

MFN (most-favored-nation) status, 53, 312nn.14, 17

Middle East region, 137f

Middle East relations: changing institutional forces of, 170; changing strategic forces in, 168–169t; channel factors of, 172–176; Hussein-Peres proposal and, 139–140, 150; impact of Gulf War on Madrid Conference on, 143–144, 175, 177; informal representation building momentum/overcoming barriers in, 147–148; Israeli "Law of Association" barrier to, 149–150; Oslo Accords and shifting balance of, 168–171t; perceptions of Israel political parties on, 138–139; roles played by Rabin and Peres in, 146. *See also* Oslo Accords (1993)

Middle East strategic forces, 168–169t

Midpoint rule, 120

Milosevic, S., 229, 231, 232, 233, 239, 242, 243, 244, 245, 246, 247, 249, 250, 256, 260, 261

Minimizing transaction costs, 23

Mitchell, G., 125, 126

Mitterrand, F., 196

Mixed mediation roles, 94–95

Mladic, R., 243, 251, 259, 264

Mubarak, H., 159, 173, 185, 186–187, 188

Muslim-Croat Federation, 236, 252, 253, 254, 265, 357

Mutual deterrence, 63, 99

**N**

Naive realism perception, 67, 68f

National Intelligence Council, 47

NATO: early attempts to protect Bosnian Muslims by, 234–235; first offensive operation in Bosnia by, 235; IFOR peacekeeping in Bosnia by, 264; new stance on Serb aggression by, 239; pattern of Bosnian War responses by, 237–241; threatens air strikes against Bosnian Serbs, 234–235

NATO bombings: balance of forces altered by, 167; decision to begin, 243–244; impact on negotiations by, 245–246, 249–251, 252; time

costs of continued, 124, 125. *See also* Bosnia War negotiations

Neale, M., 65

*Negotiating Rationally* (Bazerman and Neale), 65

"Negotiation dance," 121

Negotiation parties: analyzing internal decision making by, 18–19; assessing the, 18; decisions regarding structure of, 17–18; identifying winning/blocking coalitions in, 20; linked system of U.S.–Korean, 19f; mapping the, 18; productive working relationships between, 97–98; sequencing interactions with other, 126–127

Negotiations: assessing effectiveness of, 127–129, 128t; distributive, 29–31, 30f, 310n.14; finding the formula for the deal during, 117–118; integrative, 31, 32f, 306n.14; linkages of, 33–35, 34f, 59f; shaping structure of, 110–112, 111f; two elements necessary for, 309n.5; two-level, 70, 71f

Negotiators: abilities required of breakthrough, 279–280; arbitrator type of, 89–90, 94, 95f, 267–268; comediation type of, 95–100, 142–143, 172–173; dual roles played by, 317n.8; intervenor grid role by, 94, 95f; intervenor types of, 89–95f, 267–272; mediator type of, 93–94, 95f, 125–126, 145, 317n.3, 331n.3; representative type, 272–277, 275f; role played by, 267; training/development of, 280; unique leadership of, 266–267

Negotiator's dilemma, 60–62, 61t

*New York Times*, 49, 260

*New York Times* poll (1989), 199

Nonaligned Caucus (UN Security Council), 191

North Korea: Bush administration on nuclear program of, 7–9; Carter's visit to, 82–84; conflict between IAEA and, 13, 14, 15; creation of, 6; declining political/economic status of, 8; Kim Il Sung's leadership of, 6–7; new overtures to U.S. by, 8–9; thawing relationship between U.S. and, 9–11; U.S. push for sanctions against, 53–54; U.S. view of, 7; withdrawal from NPT, 9, 10, 126. *See also* U.S.–North Korean negotiations

North Korean nuclear program: Bush administration assessment of, 8; conflict with IAEA over, 13, 14, 15; continuity-of-safeguards inspections of, 44–45; 5-MW reactor built during, 7; IAEA refused permission to monitor defueling, 52; negotiations over IAEA inspection of, 42–44; shut down of 5-MW reactor announced by, 50; U.S.–North Korean agreement over, 104–105

North-South Declaration on a Non-Nuclear Korean Peninsula (1991), 10

Northern Ireland peace process, 125–126

Norway: facilitators role taken by leaders of, 175; legitimizing sponsor role by, 174–175. *See also* Oslo channel

NPT (Non-Proliferation Treaty): North Korea suspends withdrawal from, 41; North Korean withdrawal from, 9, 10, 126; renewal (1995) of, 13; UN resolution urging North Korea to stay in, 38

Nunn, S., 198

O

O'Donnell, V., 215

OPEC countries, 62

Opening position, 120

Opinion leaders, 326n.3

Organize to learn strategy: at/away from negotiation table, 114–115; described, 112–113; establishing learning goals for, 113–114; identifying levels of learning for, 113

Oslo Accords (1993): building momentum during, 175–176; creating the channel leading to, 149–151; development of ZOPA during, 148–149; events leading to, 151–152; fatal flaws of, 176–177; first meeting of, 152–153; "Gaza Plus Jericho" proposal and, 159, 173; Gaza Strip issue of, 153; Hirschfeld's "graduality" concept and, 154–155; historical background of, 133–139; internal deliberations by parties of, 154–155; leadership role during, 172–175; Norway selected as location of, 146–147; official turn of, 161–162; outcome of, 134; PLO acceptance of Israel leading to, 141–142; progress behind the scenes during, 156–158; psychological barriers overcome during, 69; Rabin-Arafat correspondence during, 162–163; reaching agreement during, 162–163; reaching a draft agreement during, 155–156; resumption of Washington talks and, 158–160, 176; role of Norwegians during, 153; secret contacts leading to, 140–141, 142–143; shifting balance of Middle East forces and, 168–171t; tentative contacts on location of, 145; third meeting during, 158–159. *See also* Middle East relations

Oslo channel: concerns over legitimacy of, 157; continued progress through, 156–158; creating the, 149–151; internal party deliberations and, 154–155; leading to talks, 151–152, 173; U.S. attitude toward, 158–159

"The Oslo Channel: Getting to the Negotiating Table" (Lundberg), 133

Oslo Declaration of Principles (DOP), 98, 154–156, 158–160, 163, 173, 176

Outside guarantors, 64, 99

Outside party intervenor, 90

Overconfidence, 65

Owen, Lord D., 235

Owen, R., 242, 247, 249, 251, 254, 257, 259, 261

P

Palestinian National Charter (1968), 136

Palestinian people: "graduality" concept and self-rule by, 154–155; *intifadah* revolt (1987) by, 138, 139, 168, 170; Israeli perspectives on, 138–139; Madrid Conference representation of, 143–144, 175; "mini-Marshall Plan" proposed for, 153, 154; Oslo negotiation goals of, 154; salvation through Israel for, 151. *See also* Israel; Middle East relations; Oslo Accords (1993)

Parallel management, 279

Partisan perceptions: goal transformation, 67; naive realism, 67, 68f; psychological barrier of, 66; reactive devaluation, 67–68

"The Patriarch Paper," 243–244

Patriot missiles (South Korea), 51

Pattern recognition, 279

Peacekeeping hostages, 238

Penalosa, E., 193, 196

Peres, S., 139, 140, 142, 143, 147, 148–149, 155, 156, 157, 159, 161, 163, 173

Peres-Hussein proposal, 139–140, 150

Perez de Cuellar, UN Secretary General, 192, 209

Perry, W., 3, 50, 55, 82, 96, 103

Persian Gulf negotiations (1989/1990): Baker-Aziz session during, 206–207; Bush's "extra mile" offer during, 203–204; economic embargo to push, 197; emerging U.S. bombing plans during, 200–201; "Gang of Eight" created to contact, 182–184, 189, 195; Hussein's "peace plan" during, 196–197; last proposals for peace during, 209; parrying pressure on Iraq during, 195–197; "tin-cup trips" made during, 194–195; transforming balance of forces through coalitions in, 212–218, 214f, 216t–217t; UN authorization of force during, 201–203; war as preferred alternative to, 203–205

Persian Gulf region map, 181f

Persian Gulf War (1990): assembling of Arab

coalition during, 185–188; Bush coalition during, 116–117; coercive power employed during, 93; efforts to build domestic U.S. support for, 207–209; events leading to, 179–181, 182; exposure of IAEA limits during, 9; impact on Middle East BATNAs by, 143–144; map of area, 181*f*; outcome and casualties of, 210; unwieldy military alliance during, 205–206. *See also* Kuwait invasion (1989)
Phased agreements, 98, 176, 177
Pickering, T., 191, 193, 196, 228
Plausible alternative test, 129–130
Plausible rationales, 121–122
Playing up threats, 221–222
PLO (Palestine Liberation Organization): channel factor of, 172–176; creating Oslo channel between Israel and, 149–151; efforts taken by moderates in, 324n.3; guardians within, 173; historic conflict between Israel and, 133–135, 136, 138; internal pressures to cooperate in Oslo meeting, 151–152; *intifadah* orchestrated by, 138, 139, 168, 170; Madrid peace conference position of, 143–144, 175, 177; origins and development of, 136; Oslo Declaration between Israel and, 98; Oslo DOP approval by, 163; Oslo negotiations representing, 152–153; overture to Israel by, 141–142, 321n.11; secret contacts between Israel and, 142–143; shifting balance of forces impact on, 168–171*t*
*The Politics of Diplomacy* (Baker), 33
Poneman, D., 14, 84, 86
Powell, C., 184, 204
Power: bargaining, 92; coercive, 92–93; ends vs. means dilemma of, 271–272; facilitative, 90–92; mediators with both interests and, 95; of reciprocity, 224–225; short term vs. long term exercise of, 271; sources of intervenor, 90–93
Preserving reputation, 23
Principal-agent problems, 72–73
Prisoner's dilemma, 60–62*t*, 65
Problem of intermediate steps, 65
Progressive entanglement process, 223–224
*Propaganda and Persuasion* (Jowett and O'Donnell), 215
Pruitt, D., 124
Psychological barriers: changing Middle East, 170–171*t*; defining, 57, 64; groupthink as, 68–69*t*, 315n.25; loss aversion as, 65–66*t*; overcoming, 69–70; overconfidence as, 65;

partisan perceptions as, 66–68; rigid mental models of, 64–65
Pundak, R., 154, 156, 158, 159, 160, 161, 173, 174
Punishment mentality, 66

**Q**
Quayle, D., 182, 208
Quinones, K., 14, 45

**R**
Rabin, Y., 134, 139, 143, 145, 146, 147, 148, 150, 152, 155, 156, 158, 159, 162, 172, 173
Rabin-Arafat correspondence (1993), 162–163
Raiffa, H., 121, 123, 124
Rapid Reaction Force, 239
Reactive devaluation perception, 67–68
Reagan, R., 179
Reciprocity power, 224–225
Reflection-in-action ability, 279
Reiss, M., 86
Remaining consistent, 23
Representational role grid, 275*f*
Representatives: dilemmas confronting, 274–277; roles played by, 272–274
Resolution 242 (UN), 135, 141, 142, 170, 171*t*
Resolution 338 (UN), 141, 142, 170, 171*t*
Resolution 660 (UN), 204
Resolution 665 (UH), 193
Resolution 678 (UN), 203
Riscassi, R., 4
Risk attitudes, 118
Riskin, L., 269–270
Robinson, R., 67
Robson, J., 197
Roed-Larsen, T., 145, 175
Roh Tae Woo, 10
ROK (Republic of Korea). *See* South Korea
Rose, Sir M., 236
Rosegrant, S., 3, 178, 228
Ross, D., 184, 185
Ross, L., 65
Rule of reciprocity, 224–225
Rumaila oilfield, 180

**S**
Saddam Hussein, 94, 178, 179–180, 183, 185, 195–197, 202, 204–205, 209
Safiyeh, A., 142
Samore, G., 14, 38, 41, 44, 45
Saudi Arabia: coalition building using relationships with, 228; contributions during Persian Gulf War by, 205; Desert Shield deployment

to, 188–190; Iraqi oil pipeline shut down by, 188; Kuwait invasion as threat to, 187–188; Persian Gulf interests of, 216t

Saving face, 91

Savir, U., 97, 146, 151, 153, 161

Schelling, T., 122

Schwarzkopf, N., 184, 188, 205

Scowcroft, B., 10, 39, 54, 82, 107, 182, 183, 187, 192, 193, 204, 206, 208

Secret diplomacy, 99–100, 175, 177

Selective perception, 67

Selective perception process, 64

Self-fulfilling prophecies, 67

Seoul Olympics (1988), 7

Sequencing to build momentum, 126–127, 228

Sequential linkages, 33–34

Serbian Communist Party, 229

Serbian Orthodox Patriarch, 243

Shamir, Y., 139, 140, 141, 145

Shared interests, 22

Shared uncertainties, 29

Sharon, A., 145

Shevardnadze, E., 184, 185, 202, 224

Shimon, P., 146

Silajdzic, H., 254

Singer, Y., 161

Six-Day War (1967), 136, 140

Slocomge, 256, 258

Slovenia, 231

Social influence, 222–228

Solomon, R., 13

Source credibility, 327n.16

South Korea: Agreed Framework role by, 104; creation of, 6; exchange of envoys recondition dropped by, 50; impact of possible North Korean collapse on, 107; Patriot missiles arrive in, 51; rising political/economic status of, 8

South Korean airline bombing (1988), 7

Soviet Union: collapse (1991) of, 8, 143, 169t, 171t; debate over Desert Storm military support by, 206; Hussein's "peace plan" and, 196–197; Persian Gulf interests of, 216t; pressure on Iraq by, 209; progressive entanglement of, 224; regarding proposed sanctions, 53; response to UN Article 51 by, 202; role during Persian Gulf crisis, 184–185, 190, 191, 195; sequencing to gain support of, 228

Spoiler action-forcing events, 126

Stambolic, I., 229

Sticks and carrots tools, 215–216

Strategic barriers: changes in Middle East, 169; described, 56–57, 60; impact of structure on, 63; insecure agreements as, 62–63; negotiator's dilemma as, 60–62, 61t; overcoming, 63–64

Structural barriers: defining, 56; identifying and overcoming, 57–60, 58t

Structure: of action-forcing events, 125–126; building momentum by shaping the, 110–112, 111t; diagnosing the, 1, 20–36; impact on strategic barriers, 63

Structure-process gap, 307n.5

Subcultures, 78–79

Suettinger, R., 15, 47

Sumner, W. G., 73

Sununu, J., 182

"Super Tuesday," 48–49

Supportable position, 119

Sustained conflicts: channel factors of, 167; Cold War equilibrium of, 165, 166f; driving and restraining forces of, 165–167; dynamics of, 164–165, 166f; shifting balance of forces in PLO-Israeli, 167–168

Syria, 195, 206, 215, 217t

T

Tarasenko, S., 185

Team Spirit military war games: cancellation of 1992, 10; debated as bargaining tool, 46–47; planned resumption of, 13, 49, 51; South Koreans on reinstatement of, 12

Terrorist attacks, 126, 315n.30

Thatcher, M., 183, 192

Tilly, C., 167

Time costs: action-forcing events and, 35–36; building momentum by shaping, 36; of continued NATO bombing, 124; of delayed BATNAs, 124; differences in sensitivity to, 118; shaping perceptions of, 123–125

"Tin-cup trips," 194–195

Tito, Marshal, 229

Transformation vs. ratification dilemma, 275–276

Trust: confidence-building mechanisms in absence of, 99, 176; techniques fostering cooperation in absence of, 63–64

Tudjman, F., 231, 239, 246, 253, 259, 262

Turkey, 195, 205, 217t

Two-level negotiations, 70, 71f

U

UAE (United Arab Emirates), 180

UN Charter (Article 51), 192, 201

UN partition plan, 135

UN Protection Force in Bosnia (UNPROFOR), 234, 236, 238

UN Resolution 242, 135, 141, 142, 170, 171*t*

UN Resolution 338, 141, 142, 170, 171*t*

UN Resolution 660, 204

UN Resolution 665, 193

UN Resolution 678, 203

UN Security Council: authorizing force against Iraq, 201–203; embargo against former Yugoslavia (1991) by, 233; Hague Tribunal established by, 234, 240; Nonaligned Caucus of, 191; response to Kuwait invasion by, 190–193

United Kingdom: Persian Gulf interests of, 216*t*, 219; Persian Gulf military support by, 205; support during Persian Gulf crisis by, 183, 192

United Nations: conflict between North Korea and, 13, 14, 15; resolution urging North Korea to stay in NPT, 38; response to Kuwait invasion by, 190–193; South Korea's admitted to, 8

United States: Camp David agreement (1978) negotiated by, 135, 140; concerns over North Korean nuclear program by, 7–9; military build-up in South Korea by, 54, 55; North Korean overtures to, 8–9; perception of North Korea by, 6; Persian Gulf interest of, 216*t*; push for sanctions by, 53–54; reappraisal of negotiating strategies/policy by, 49–51; recognition of Bosnia by, 232; response to Kuwait administration by, 178, 182–184; role in Oslo DOP agreement by, 98, 154–156; thawing relationship between North Korea and, 9–11. *See also* Bush administration; Clinton administration

Unofficial representatives, 173–174

Ury, W., 22, 26, 112, 115, 279

U.S. negotiating team (North Korea crisis): achieving unity of purpose, 51–52; conflict within, 47–48; issue agenda of, 40; mental models used by, 64–65; reappraisal of negotiating strategies/policy by, 49–51; resumes talks after Carter's visit, 84–85; unprepared response by, 14–15

U.S.–North Korean Agreed Framework: assessing outcome of, 129–130; compromise over LWRs as part of, 104–105; controversy over, 106–108; six key provisions of, 104–105; third round of talks leading to, 101–104

U.S.–North Korean Joint Declaration (1993), 41–42, 98

U.S.–North Korean negotiations: agreement reached during, 101–108; analysis of interests/goals of, 22–25, 24*t*; assessing effectiveness of, 127–129, 128*t*; assessing outcome of, 129–130; BATNAs of, 26–27*f*; breakdown of, 3–4; Carter mediation during, 81–86, 87–88, 89, 96, 101, 121; continuity-of-safeguards impasse in, 44–45; deadlock and deterioration of, 12–13; deteriorating situation of, 52–53; diagnosing structure of negotiation parties in, 17–20, 19*f*; distributive and integrative, 29–31, 30*f*, 32*f*; domestic complication affecting, 54–55; escalating deterioration of, 48–49; first meeting Joint Declaration of, 41–42, 98; first meeting of, 11–12; hardened postures during, 13–14; historic background leading to, 4, 6–7; impact of threatened UN sanctions on, 15–16; informational asymmetries in, 28–29; international pressure for starting, 38–40; issue agenda of, 20–22; linkages of, 34–35; partisan perceptions barrier to, 66–68; second meeting on IAEA inspections, 42–44; South Korean attempted sabotage of, 12; structural barriers to, 57–60; thawing relationship leading to, 9–10; U.S. broad and thorough approach to, 45–47; winning/blocking coalitions of, 20

U.S.–North Vietnamese negotiations, 123–124

USS *Eisenhower*, 188

**V**

Vance, C., 235

Verification regimes, 63, 99

Vershbow, A., 236, 238, 239

**W**

Walkaway positions, 27–28, 119–120

*Wall Street Journal*, 206

Ward, A., 65

Washington talks (1993), 158–160, 176

Watkins, M. D., 3, 133, 178, 228

Webster, W., 200

Weiss, S., 74

Wiedemann, K., 13, 14, 46, 53, 82, 84, 102, 103

Winning coalitions: eliminating options for building, 218–220; framing for building, 220–222; identifying, 20; interests in Persian Gulf, 216*t*–217*t*; outcomes of using, 229; using social influence to build, 222–228; techniques for building, 213–215, 218

Witnessing agreements, 91

Wolfsthal, J., 44

Woolsey, J., 40

Working Group on Refugees, 149
Working relationships, 97–98
Wright-Patterson Air Force Base, 259–260
Wulf, N., 14

**Y**
*Yedioth Aharanot* (newspaper), 148
Yemen, 193, 202, 203
Yugoslavian breakup, 229

**Z**
Zaire, 217*t*
Zelikow, P., 200
ZOPA (zone of possible agreement): assessing informational asymmetries for, 28–29; developed during Oslo negotiations, 148–149; seeking more efficient agreements, 31–33; types of negotiation and, 29–31, 30*f*, 32*f*
Zubak, K., 265

## DATE DUE

| | | | |
|---|---|---|---|
| | | | |
| | | | |
| | | | |
| | | | |
| | | | |
| | | | |
| | | | |
| | | | |
| | | | |
| | | | |
| | | | |
| | | | |
| | | | |
| | | | |
| | | | |
| | | | |

HIGHSMITH #45115